Foreign Investment in the Energy Sector

Nijhoff International Investment Law Series

VOLUME 2

The titles published in this series are listed at *brill.com/iils*

Foreign Investment in the Energy Sector

Balancing Private and Public Interests

Edited by

Eric De Brabandere and Tarcisio Gazzini

BRILL
NIJHOFF

LEIDEN | BOSTON

Library of Congress Cataloging-in-Publication Data

Foreign investment in the energy sector : balancing private and public interests / edited by Eric De Brabandere and Tarcisio Gazzini.
pages cm. — (Nijhoff international investment law series)
Includes index.
ISBN 978-90-04-24470-2 (hardback : alk. paper) — ISBN 978-90-04-24471-9 (e-book) 1. Energy industries—Law and legislation. 2. Investments, Foreign—Law and legislation 3. Energy industries—Capital investments. 4. Energy Charter Treaty (1994) 5. Energy policy—International cooperation. 6. Arbitration and award, International. I. Brabandere, Eric de, editor of compilation. II. Gazzini, Tarcisio, editor of compilation.

K3981.F67 2014
332.67'3—dc23

2014013176

This publication has been typeset in the multilingual 'Brill' typeface. With over 5,100 characters covering Latin, IPA, Greek, and Cyrillic, this typeface is especially suitable for use in the humanities.
For more information, please see brill.com/brill-typeface.

ISSN 2351-9542
ISBN 978 90 04 24470 2 (hardback)
ISBN 978 90 04 24471 9 (e-book)

This book is printed on acid-free paper.

Contents

Preface

The economic importance of foreign investment in the energy sector cannot be overestimated. In legal terms, foreign investment in the energy sector raises complex and controversial questions due to the interplay between private and public interests and rights. This book addresses this interplay.

The first and second parts discuss the specificity of foreign investment in the energy sector, both in substantive and procedural terms. The third part examines certain critical areas related to the economic activities of multinationals in the energy sector: safety and labour standards, the protection of the environment, the rights of indigenous peoples, and the protection of public health. The contributions to this volume have been finalized between September and December 2013, and do not therefore take into account subsequent developments.

This book groups contributions presented at the 2nd Leiden University – VU University Amsterdam Expert Seminar on Contemporary Perspectives on International Investment Law, organized jointly by the editors of this book. Our thanks go to both the contributors to the seminars and this volume, and the participants for their questions and comments.

We would like to thank the Netherlands Organization for Scientific Research (NWO) for the financial support in the organization of the expert seminar, through a three-year VENI research grant accorded to Dr. Eric De Brabandere. We would also like to thank Ms. Nivedita S. and Ms. Hilde Roskam at Leiden University for research and editorial assistance.

List of Main Abbreviations

ACHPR	African Charter on Human and Peoples Rights
AIPN	Association of International Petroleum Negotiators
MCHR	American Convention of Human Rights
BIT	bilateral investment treaty
CSR	corporate social responsibility
DCF	discounted cash flow
ECD	export customs duty
ECHR	European Court of Human Rights
ECT	Energy Charter Treaty
EEC	European Energy Charter
EIA	environmental impact assessment
EU	European Union
FDI	foreign direct investment
FET	fair and equitable treatment
FTA	Free Trade Agreement
GAL	global administrative law
GATT	General Agreement on Tariffs and Trade
GDP	gross domestic product
GPDF	Governmental Power Developments Fund
ICC	International Chamber of Commerce
ICCPR	International Covenant on Civil and Political Rights
ICESCR	International Covenant on Economic, Social and Cultural Rights
ICJ	International Court of Justice
ICMM	International Council on Mining and Metals
ICSID	International Centre for Settlement of Investment Disputes
IEA	International Energy Agency
IFC	International Finance Corporation
IIA	international investment agreement
IIL	international investment law
ICJ	International Court of Justice
ILC	International Law Commission
ILO	International Labour Organisation
IMF	International Monetary Fund
ISDS	investor-State dispute settlement
IPFSD	Investment Policy Framework for Sustainable Development
ISO	independent system operator
ITO	independent transmission operator

LNG	liquefied natural gas
MFN	most-favored-nation
MRPT	mineral resource production tax
MIGA	Multilateral Investment Guarantee Agency
MTPA	mandatory third party access
NAFTA	North American Free Trade Agreement
NPV	net present value
OECD	Organization for Economic Co-operation and Development
OPEX	operating expenditures
OTLA	Office of Trade and Labor Affairs
PAF	Petroleum Advisory Forum
PCA	Permanent Court of Arbitration
PEEREA	Protocol on Energy Efficiency and Related Environmental Aspects
REIO	regional economic integration organisation
PSA	production-sharing agreement
ROR	rate of return
RROR	reasonable rate of return
SCC	Stockholm Chamber of Commerce
SWF	sovereign wealth fund
TENI	Fuel and Energy Independent Institute, Moscow, Russia (Топливно-Энергетический Независимый Институт)
TNC	transnational company
UNCITRAL	United Nations Commission on International Trade Law
UNDRIP	United Nations Declarations on the Rights of Indigenous Peoples
UNECE	United Nations Economic Commission for Europe
VAT	value added tax
VCLT	Vienna Convention on the Law of Treaties
VIC	vertically integrated company
VMSB	duty for reproduction of mineral-resource base ("geology tax")
WB	World Bank
WHL	World Heritage List
WPT	windfall profit tax
WTO	World Trade Organization

List of Cases

Investment Arbitration

International Centre for the Settlement of Investment Disputes

Other Investment Arbitration Cases

World Trade Organization

Inter-state Arbitration

Permanent Court of International Justice

International Court of Justice

Human Rights

African Commission on Human and Peoples' Rights

European Court of Human Rights

Human Rights Committee

Inter-American Court of Human Rights

European Court of Justice

Decisions of National Courts

Contributor Biographies

Mr. Graham Coop

is a partner with Volterra Fietta. He is qualified as a barrister and solicitor in New Zealand and as a solicitor in England and Wales. He advises and represents companies, governments and international organisations on international dispute resolution and public international law, with a particular focus on the energy, natural resources and infrastructure sectors. His work on contentious matters has focused on the Energy Charter Treaty, investment treaties, price revisions under long-term energy sale contracts, and maritime boundary delimitation. He has appeared as counsel, advocate and expert before a wide range of international courts and tribunals, including the International Court of Justice, ICSID, the PCA and the ICC.

Before joining Volterra Fietta, Graham served for seven years as General Counsel to the Energy Charter Secretariat.

Graham has written and edited a wide range of publications, including *Energy Dispute Resolution: Investment Protection, Transit and the Energy Charter Treaty*. Graham is an Honorary Associate of the Graduate School of Natural Resources Law, Policy & Management of the University of Dundee's Centre for Energy, Petroleum and Mineral Law and Policy. He is an honorary member of the Investment Treaty Forum of the British Institute of International and Comparative Law. He is a member of the Editorial Committee of the *International Energy Law Review* and of the *Journal of Energy & Natural Resources Law*. He has lectured at numerous universities around Europe and is listed in the Who's Who in Public International Law.

Dr. Eric De Brabandere

(LL.B. (Ghent), LL.M. (Ghent), LL.M. (Geneva), Ph.D. (Ghent), is Associate Professor of International Law at Leiden University's Grotius Centre for International Legal Studies. He is also a Member of the Brussels Bar, a Visiting Professor at the Catholic University of Lille (Faculté libre de droit), Editor-in-chief of the *Leiden Journal of International Law* and a member of the Board of Editors of the *Revue belge de droit international* and the *Journal of World Investment and Trade*. His areas of expertise are international dispute settlement, investment law and arbitration, and general international law.

Dr. Tarcisio Gazzini

is Associate Professor in International Law at VU University Amsterdam and Visiting Professor at the Graduate Institute of International and Development

Studies (Geneva). He has previously taught at the Universities of Padua and Glasgow. He is a member of the International Law Association committee on "the role of international law in sustainable natural resources management development" and of the editorial board of the *Leiden Journal of International Law*.

Dr. Joachim Karl

of German nationality, is Chief of the Policy Research Section in UNCTAD's Division on Investment and Enterprise. Before joining the UN in November 2005, he worked for seven years on international investment matters at the OECD and the Energy Charter Secretariat in Brussels. He started his professional career in the German Ministry of Economics in 1987, where he dealt with regional state aids, European Law issues and international investment agreements.

Mr. Karl holds a Ph.D. in international law from the University of Konstanz in Germany, and a Master of Public Administration degree from Harvard's J.F.Kennedy School of Government. He has written numerous articles on European law and international investment issues, and was a lecturer at the German Federal Academy of Public Administration.

Professor Dr. Andrey A. Konoplyanik

Ph.D. (1978) and Dr. of Science in International Energy Economics (1995), Professor in International Oil & Gas Business (2012), is an energy economist. His is specialized in energy economics, energy and investment legislation, and energy financing. He is Adviser to the Director General, Gazprom Export LLC (since 2013) and Professor at the Chair "International Oil & Gas Business" of the Russian State Gubkin Oil & Gas University (since 2008). A detailed professional biography of Dr. Prof. Konoplyanik, his publications, presentations and interviews is available at www.konoplyanik.ru.

Professor Federico Lenzerini

(Ph.D. International Law) is Professor of International Law and European Union Law at the University of Siena, Italy. He has been consultant to UNESCO and legal advisor of the Italian Ministry of Foreign Affairs at international negotiations concerning the protection of cultural heritage. He was a member of the Committee on Biotechnology of the International Law Association (ILA) and Rapporteur of the ILA Committee on the Rights of Indigenous Peoples, and is currently a Member of the ILA Committee on Cultural Heritage Law and the Rapporteur of the ILA Committee on Implementation of the Rights of Indigenous Peoples. He has been Visiting

Professor in a number of foreign universities, including the Tulane University Law School of New Orleans and the St. Thomas University School of Law of Miami.

Professor Makane Moïse Mbengue
is Associate Professor at the Faculty of Law of the University of Geneva, and a Visiting Professor at Sciences Po Paris (School of Law) and the Catholic University of Lille (Faculté libre de droit).

Dr. Yannick Radi
is Assistant Professor in International Law at the Grotius Centre for International Legal Studies of Leiden University and a Visiting Professor at the Catholic University of Lille (Faculté libre de droit). He regularly appears as a speaker and lecturer on various issues of international law and international investment law. He is a Senior Editor of the *Leiden Journal of International Law*.

Mr. Deepak Raju
LL.M. (Cambridge), is Consultant in International Trade & Investment Law, Clarus Law Associates, New Delhi.

Dr. Stephan W. Schill
(Dr. iur. (Frankfurt), LL.M. (NYU), LL.M. (Augsburg)) is Senior Research Fellow at the Max Planck Institute for Comparative Public Law and International Law in Heidelberg, Principal Investigator of the ERC-project on "Transnational Public-Private Arbitration as Global Regulatory Governance", and Lecturer at the Frankfurt University and in the joint LL.M. program of Heidelberg University and the Universidad de Chile. In the past, he clerked for The Honorable Charles N. Brower, 20 Essex Street, London, and Judge Abdul G. Koroma, International Court of Justice. He is admitted to the bar in Germany and New York and has acted as counsel before the European Court of Human Rights.

Professor Attila Tanzi
(Ph.D.) is Professor of International Law at the University of Bologna. A legal consultant to the Ministry for Foreign Affairs (Italy) since 1987 and to the Ministry for the Environment since 1999, he also advises international organisations on aspects of international law.

Counsel or arbitrator in various inter-State arbitrations, he has served several times as a member of the Italian delegation to the General Assembly of the United Nations and its subsidiary bodies.

He is Chairman of the Legal Board of the UNECE 1992 Convention on Protection and Use of Transboundary Watercourses and International Lakes (2004–2012), Chairman of the Compliance Committee of the UNECE 1999 London Protocol on Water and Health (2007–2010) and currently a member of the Implementation Committee of the above UNECE 1992 Convention. Moreover, he is a Member of the Permanent Court of Arbitration and Visiting Professor at Queen Mary, University of London.

He has held numerous academic positions and has published extensively in English, Spanish, French and Italian on State responsibility, foreign investment law, environmental law, the law of international organisations and jurisdictional immunities.

Dr. Valentina Vadi

is an Emile Noel Fellow at the Jean Monnet Center for International and Regional Economic Integration, New York University and a Reader (Associate Professor) in International Economic Law at Lancaster University, United Kingdom. Dr. Valentina Vadi was a Marie Curie postdoctoral fellow at Maastricht University in the Netherlands (2011–2013). Dr. Valentina Vadi's main areas of research are in international economic law as well as international cultural law. She has published more than sixty articles in these areas in top journals, including the *Stanford Journal of International Law*, the *European Journal of International Law*, the *Journal of International Economic Law* and others. Valentina Vadi is the author of *Public Health in International Investment Law and Arbitration* (Routledge, Abingdon 2012) and *Cultural Heritage in International Investment Law and Arbitration* (Cambridge University Press, Cambridge *forthcoming* 2014).

Introduction

Graham Coop

Investment in the energy sector accounts for a large portion of foreign investment worldwide. As a strategic sector, the energy sector is inescapably linked to politics. Regulation of investment in the energy sector, therefore, requires a constant balance between the public interest of the State and the private interest of the investor. This book addresses the relationship between foreign investment in the energy sector and public policy through the study of specific energy industries such as the hydroelectric industry, specific geographical regions such as the Russian Federation, and specific public interests such as the protection of the environment, indigenous peoples' rights, labour rights or public health. It also addresses a number of treaties applicable to the energy sector, such as the Energy Charter Treaty ("ECT"), and the relevant dispute settlement mechanisms.

In "FDI in the Energy Sector: Recent Trends and Policy Issues", Joachim Karl focuses on the role of foreign direct investment (FDI) in the energy sector. Indeed, FDI can play a crucial role in satisfying rising energy demands and improve energy efficiency. Since FDI in the energy sector has the potential to affect national sovereignty over natural resources and create significant risks in terms of sustainable development and inclusive growth, it is more prone to State interference than FDI in other sectors. But increased State intervention results in an increasing number of disputes between investors and host States. Foreign investors seek a clear, stable and predictable investment climate while host States need to preserve sufficient policy space to regulate investments in the energy sector in light of changing circumstances. Therefore, FDI in the energy sector requires a balance between public and private interest. This balance can be achieved through the design of an overall policy framework for FDI, both at the national and international level. It can also be achieved through investment contracts between the host country and foreign investors or public-private partnerships.

In "Multiple Investment Regimes in Russian Subsoil Resources: Work in Progress or Utopia?", Andrey Konoplyanik argues for the benefit of the creation of an investment-friendly climate with respect to the Russian subsoil. This chapter offers an overview of the historical development of the Russian subsoil legislation and of the oil tax reform of the early 2000s. It considers investment regimes in Russia in the subsoil sector including (i) a licensing regime with a unified tax regime for all projects and fields, implemented in

 | DOI 10.1163/9789004244719_002

1992 and widely criticised; (ii) a set of individual derogations to the licensing regime with differentiated tax regimes for individual projects, group of similar projects or specific fields; and (iii) a regime based on production sharing agreements with individualised tax regimes, which has become impractical with the Russian tax reform of early 2000s. Andrey Konoplyanik argues that the current licensing investment regime of subsoil use imposes an inflexible taxation system and is subject to State authorities' decisions, while individual exemptions are not the most effective way to improve the licensing regime. Investors seek diversity of choices in investment regimes in the Russian oil sector because they require rules adapted to the particular conditions of their project. Andrey Konoplyanik advocates the introduction of a menu of four competing investment regimes for subsoil use in Russia, three of which do already exist (standard and differentiated licensing regimes plus regime based on PSAs) but need to be improved towards higher investment friendliness, and a concession-based regime for which there is no legal basis in this country's subsoil use today—in order to improve the investment climate with respect to the Russian subsoil.

Attila Tanzi explains, in "International Law and Foreign Investment in Hydroelectric Industry: A Multidimensional Analysis", that because of its nature, foreign investment in hydroelectric energy touches upon four multidimensional areas of international law: (i) international investment law; (ii) the international law of human rights; (iii) international water law; and (iv) international and domestic regulation of civil liability issues. Hydroelectric power offers both economic, environmental and social advantages and disadvantages. Hydroelectric power is cheap, reliable and produces almost no pollution. However, it requires the construction of dams and power plants, which are expensive. It also creates risk of flood and the lower water quality downstream affects plants, animals and human life. Despite these difficulties, the hydroelectric sector has attracted a considerable flow of foreign investment. The relationship between the foreign investor engaged in hydropower projects and the host State may lead to disputes which will often be settled through international investment arbitration. Foreign investment in the hydroelectric sector may adversely affect human rights and indigenous rights. These issues can be addressed by international arbitration tribunals or by human rights courts. Because of the trans-boundary character of watercourses used to produce hydroelectric power, hydropower projects may also lead to inter-State disputes, leading to the application of international water law. Finally, the private operator may incur civil liability for harm caused by water-related activities.

In "Energy Charter Treaty: Achievements, Challenges and Perspectives", Tarcisio Gazzini gives an overview of the main achievements and challenges of the ECT, which he describes as "a complex, ambitious and unique multilateral treaty". He focuses on two pillars of the ECT: investment protection and transit. The effective provisions on protection of foreign investment and the binding mechanism for the settlement of investment disputes are the main achievements of the ECT. The main difficulties of the ECT relate to transit. A protocol on transit was supposed to be implemented to complete the basic principles on transit provided for in the ECT, but the negotiations have so far been unsuccessful. The conciliation procedure to settle transit disputes and the mechanism to fix interim transit tariffs provided for in the ECT have in practice failed to prevent or settle transit disputes. Another difficulty is the Russian decision not to ratify the ECT, since the ECT constitutes one of the cornerstones of the regulation of the energy sector in the Eurasian region. While the ECT offers an efficient multilateral framework to regulate a crucial sector in which private and public interest need to be balanced, its modernisation, this chapter argues, remains to be completed.

In "The Settlement of Investment Disputes in the Energy Sector", Eric De Brabandere focuses on the specificities of investment disputes between foreign investors and host States in the energy sector. Disputes may be settled through non-binding methods, such as negotiation or mediation, or binding methods, such as litigation or arbitration, the last of which is appreciated for its flexibility and neutrality. The ECT offers direct access to investment arbitration, giving a choice of arbitration fora to the investor, as well as investment protection in the energy sector. The ECT entitles foreign investors to bring a claim against the host State for alleged breaches of the ECT's investment promotion and protection provisions by the host State. These protections are similar to the protections offered by bilateral investment treaties ("BITs"), as both instruments aim at promoting international investment. A second level of protection can be offered by contracts between foreign investors and host States. An overlap between such contracts and international treaties creates a risk of parallel proceedings. As the ECT is a multilateral treaty, there is also a risk of parallel proceedings caused by the overlap between the ECT and BITs. Since the risk exists only where the cause of action, the facts and the parties are similar, and since the ICSID Convention restricts the risk of parallel proceedings, parallel proceedings have not caused problems in practice.

In "Energy, Environment and Foreign Investment", Makane Mbengue and Deepak Raju analyse the interaction between international investment law and international environmental law in the energy sector. The relationship highlights the dichotomy between the protection of environment in the public interest and the protection of investment in the private interest. Investors may strengthen environmental goals, but might also increase environmental harm. There are points of divergence between these disciplines, such as environmental regulations increasing the cost of operations of investors, and the non-discrimination provisions in international investment agreements ("IIAs") which may conflict with governmental measures aimed at protecting the environment. But there are also points of convergence, such as the promotion of foreign investment in clean technologies, the call for fair, transparent and equitable institutions or the minimum standards of environment protection under IIAs. While some IIAs refer to environmental protection in their preamble, these guarantees are not enforceable. Other provisions in the IIAs, such as non-discrimination, fair and equitable treatment and expropriation might either foster or hamper the protection of the environment, depending on the context. However, in the opinion of these contributors, the procedural aspects of investment arbitration in practice prevent tribunals from addressing environmental claims.

In "Foreign Investment in the Energy Sector and Indigenous Peoples' Rights", Federico Lenzerini addresses the need to balance conflicts between values held by foreign investors in the energy sector and national authorities, on one hand, and indigenous peoples, on the other. When energy projects are carried out on indigenous peoples' land, it is essential to preserve their rights, or at least to balance their rights with the interest pursued by States and foreign investors. Indigenous rights are protected by international regulations, such as the ILO Convention No. 169 concerning Indigenous and Tribal Peoples in Independent Countries and the United Nations Declarations on the Rights of Indigenous Peoples (UNDRIP). Human rights monitoring bodies also protect indigenous rights at the international and regional level. Securing these rights in the presence of investment projects also largely depends on the State. Out of the many disputes concerning alleged breaches of indigenous peoples' rights due to investment projects, only a limited number have reached the stage of investment arbitration. The other disputes are settled in national courts, through extrajudicial settlements, or are sometimes left unresolved when the communities are prevented from accessing justice.

In "The Tripartite Dimension of Conflicts of Interests: Workers, Foreign Investors and Host States in the Energy Sector", Yannick Radi focuses on the tripartite relationship between workers, the foreign investor and the host State in FDI operations in the energy sector in relation to labour standards. This relationship is characterised by different conflicts of interest which result in labour issues. It raises a conflict between the public interest of the host State and the private interest of the foreign investor, as well as a conflict of interest "within the box" of the public interest between the protection of workers' rights and other interests protected by the host State. Labour rights are guaranteed by human rights conventions and the instruments adopted by the International Labour Organisation. Labour provisions may also be found in IIAs which provide for specific clauses fostering labour standards or corporate social responsibility standards in investment projects.

In "Foreign Investment in the Energy Sector and Public Health", Valentina Vadi provides an overview of the challenges raised by foreign investment in the energy sector in relation to public health. This relationship is once again characterised by a conflict of interest between the private interests of foreign companies and the public policy objectives of the host State. Access to energy is vital for public health. However, the development of energy resources may negatively affect public health. When this relationship results in a dispute, public health claims may be raised before arbitral tribunals in the context of investment claims. While States should be autonomous in their regulation of public health matters, arbitrators should scrutinise State conduct and determine whether the adopted measures are appropriate, reasonable and were taken in good faith. It is crucial to find a balance between the scrutiny of arbitral tribunals and the State regulatory autonomy. According to this contributor, the ECT has a significant role to play in this regard.

In "Foreign Investment in the Energy Sector: Lessons for International Investment Law", Stephan Schill concludes on the relationship between general international investment law and international energy investment law. While international energy investment law is an integral part of general international investment law, investment in the energy sector also presents some specificities. The energy industry is durable and continuously exposed to political risks. It also represents an essential policy goal. Stephan Schill argues that international energy investment law offers an interesting case study for more general issues of international investment law and investment dispute settlement. He observes that above all, investment in the energy sector relates to questions of governance.

As I noted at the outset, the energy sector is vast, and can be approached in an almost infinite variety of ways. These essays present a unique complementarity among functional, interest-oriented and geographical viewpoints. Together they give a fascinating insight into a sector which employs a large proportion of the world's human and financial resources and which affects every one of us in our daily life. I thank the contributors and publisher for making this unique combination of viewpoints possible and I commend this collection to whoever wishes to gain an overview of the energy sector in its integrality.

PART 1

Specificity of Foreign Investment in the Energy Sector

CHAPTER 1

FDI in the Energy Sector: Recent Trends and Policy Issues

Joachim Karl

1 The Importance of FDI in the Energy Sector

Energy makes the world go round, and countries cannot get enough of it. To meet rising energy demands, particularly in emerging economies, it is crucial to increase investment in the energy sector and to replace existing facilities that have reached the end of their operational lifecycle. This paper explores the role of FDI in this context and identifies a number of current policy challenges.

The International Energy Agency (IEA) estimates that investments of at least US $26 trillion will be required in the energy sector until 2030.[1] Of this amount, 52 percent will have to be spent in the electricity sector, 24 percent in the oil sector, 21 percent in the natural gas sector and the remaining in coal and other biofuels (Figure 1.1).

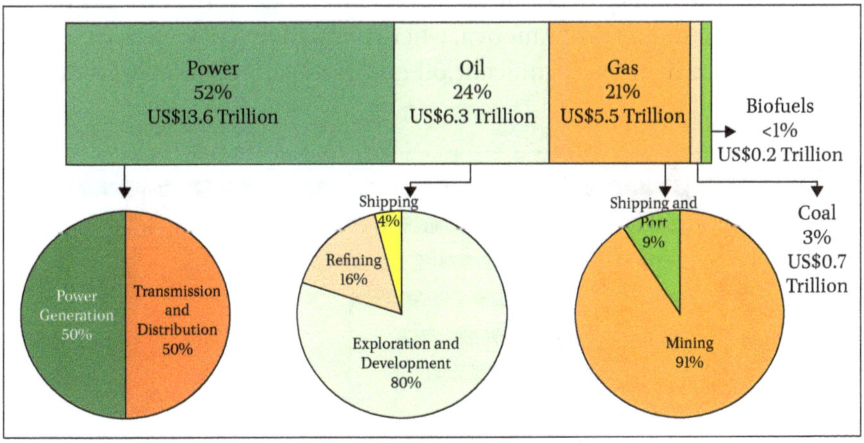

FIGURE 1.1 *Breakdown of investment requirements in energy sector*
SOURCE: IEA, WORLD ENERGY OUTLOOK 2008

---

* The views expressed by the author do not necessarily reflect those of UNCTAD.

1 International Energy Agency, *World Energy Outlook 2008*.

 | DOI 10.1163/9789004244719_003

Most of the aforementioned investments are needed just to maintain current energy supplies. As the degeneration rate of infrastructure increases, almost all of the required investments in the oil and gas sector are for upstream activities (an estimated US $8.4 trillion until 2030).

It is also important to note that energy investment, as a percentage of GDP is much higher in developing countries and countries in transition than in OECD countries. This means that a lack of investment in the former group has a stronger impact on GDP growth than in the developed world (Figure 1.2).

FDI can make a crucial contribution to meeting these urgent investment requirements. Some of the largest TNCs worldwide are active in the energy sector. Almost half of the "top-15 TNCs" are involved in extractive industries or the power sector (Table 1.1). A growing number of TNCs in these industries are based in developing and transition economies. In addition to these privately owned companies, there are numerous powerful state-owned enterprises that operate in the sector, such as Saudi Aramco, Qatar Petroleum, Sinopec (China), Gazprom (Russia) and Statoil (Norway).

Additionally, emerging economies – such as China – with fast rising demand for oil and gas but with limited domestic reserves have started to invest abroad in the oil and gas sector of resource-rich countries as one way to satisfy their energy needs. China National Offshore Oil Corporation has made several major investments in Africa, including its purchase of a 45 percent stake in Nigeria's "OML 130 deepwater" oil project worth US $2.27 billion, and a one-third stake in three of Tullow Oil plc's Exploration areas in Uganda worth US $1.47 billion. China is also active in Latin America, where it established a joint venture with Bridas Energy, which has significant oil and gas exploration and production

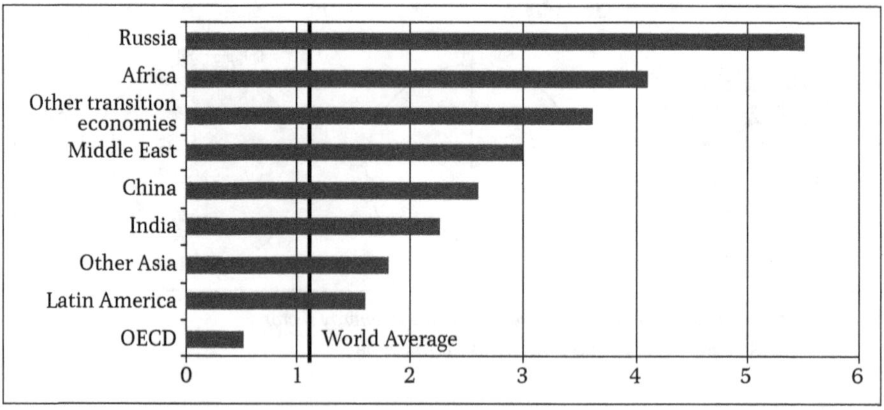

FIGURE 1.2 *Energy investment share in GDP 2001–2030*
SOURCE: IEA, WORLD ENERGY OUTLOOK 2003

TABLE 1.1 *The world's top 15 non-financial TNCs, ranked by foreign assets, 2011 (Millions of dollars)*

Ranking Foreign Assets	Corporation	Home Economy	Industry	Assets		Sales	
				Foreign	Total	Foreign	Total
1	**General Electric Co**	**United States**	**Electrical & electronic equipment**	502 612	717 242	77 480	147 300
2	**Royal Dutch Shell plc**	**Netherlands/United Kingdom**	**Petroleum expl./ref./distr.**	296 449	345 257	282 673	470 171
3	**BP plc**	**United Kingdom**	**Petroleum expl./ref./distr.**	263 577	293 068	308 437	386 463
4	**Exxon Mobil Corporation**	**United States**	**Petroleum expl./ref./distr.**	214 231	331 052	316 686	433 526
5	Toyota Motor Corporation	Japan	Motor vehicles	214 117	372 566	142 888	235 200
6	**Total SA**	**France**	**Petroleum expl./ref./distr.**	211 314	228 036	197 480	256 732
7	**GDF Suez**	**France**	**Utilities (Electricity, gas and water)**	194 422	296 650	82 731	126 040
8	Vodafone Group Plc	United Kingdom	Telecommunications	171 941	186 176	65 448	74 089
9	**Enel SpA**	**Italy**	**Electricity, gas and water**	153 665	236 037	66 817	110 528
10	Telefonica SA	Spain	Telecommunications	147 903	180 186	63 014	87 346
11	**Chevron Corporation**	**United States**	**Petroleum expl./ref./distr.**	139 816	209 474	139 344	236 286
12	**E.ON AG**	**Germany**	**Utilities (Electricity, gas and water)**	133 006	212 499	90 958	157 011
13	**Eni SpA**	**Italy**	**Petroleum expl./ref./distr.**	122 081	198 700	106 240	153 631
14	ArcelorMittal	Luxembourg	Metal and metal products	117 023	121 880	93 679	93 973
15	Nestlé SA	Switzerland	Food, beverages and tobacco	116 130	121 257	92 166	94 191

Source: UNCTAD, World Investment Report 2012

operations in Argentina, Bolivia and Chile. India established several energy cooperations with West Asian countries, such as Qatar and the UAE.[2]

The potential role of FDI for increasing energy supply – but also for reducing demand through improved energy efficiency and the transfer of relevant technologies – is particularly apparent in view of the high capital intensity of the energy industry and the huge amounts of investment required in the coming years and decades. Costs are likely to increase further as unexploited natural resources are often located in remote locations or deep waters. This is one of the reasons why supply has actually decreased lately in important producer countries. The exploration and exploitation of these resources also require high technological skills – a domain where FDI often excels. Furthermore, through their worldwide transportation and distribution channels, FDI plays an important role in respect of the marketing and distribution of energy.

Despite these urgent investment needs, the picture is not rosy for new FDI in the sector. UNCTAD estimates that cross-border greenfield investments in the energy sector totalled an approximate US $2.3 trillion in the period between 2003 and 2011. In 2011, foreign investment flows in the sector amounted to US $220 billion, which is significantly below their 2008 peak (Figure 1.3).

Although there is a continuous "appetite" to invest, FDI in the energy sector faces a number of significant impediments:[3]

1. There is a "cash overhang" in TNCs. Previous production over capacity resulted in unsustainable energy prices and dwindling profit margins. This made large energy groups cautious about making large-scale, long-term investments. There is also a trend to pay dividends to shareholders or consolidate ownership through a stock buy-back rather than investing profits into new projects.

---

2 The picture would not be complete without mentioning the growing role of sovereign wealth funds (SWFs) that are primarily financed through earnings from the energy sector. As a result, these SWFs have become important investors in their own right – although not necessarily in the energy sector. Their assets have grown rapidly to an estimated US$ 20 trillion in 2011. Oil-producing countries in the Middle East have the largest SWFs, including the Abu Dhabi Investment Authority, Saudi Arabia Monetary Authority Holdings, Kuwait Investment Authority and Qatar Investment Authority. Outside the region, Norway's Government Pension Fund and Russia's National Welfare Fund are the second and tenth largest in world, respectively. Although SWFs were established decades ago, it was until recently that they are making large-scale foreign investments.

3 Keppler, Jan Horts and Shulke, Christian, "Investing in the Energy Sector: An Issue of Governance", *European Governance and Geopolitics of Energy*, February 2009, at http://www.sefalliance.org/fileadmin/media/sefalliance/docs/Resources/Green_Economy/IFRI_Investing_in_Energy_KepplerFeb2009.pdf (accessed on 6 July 2013).

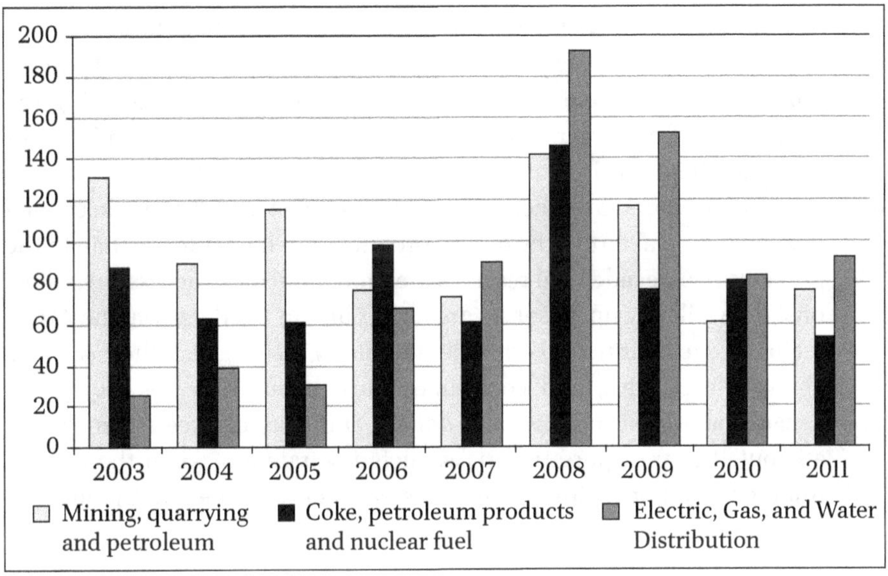

FIGURE 1.3 *Cross-border greenfield investments in the energy sector by year, 2003–2011 (billions of dollars)*
SOURCE: UNCTAD DATABASE

2. A new wave of resource nationalism among energy producing countries has affected the entry and expansion of TNCs. In recent years, as rents from exploiting natural resources have increased due to high energy prices, producer countries preferred to exploit resources by themselves. Access conditions in large energy exporting countries are becoming increasingly uncertain, including an unstable policy environment in a number of major energy producing countries.
3. Policymakers struggle on how to properly reflect and reconcile potentially conflicting issues such as environmental protection, national security and economic objectives when it comes to designing their overall energy strategies. This contributes to a climate of uncertainty among foreign investors. Inconsistent and unstable energy policies reduce investor confidence.
4. The lack of a global policy framework for energy investments makes TNCs hesitant to invest abroad in complex, long-term energy projects. Most countries opted for bilateral investment agreements; the Energy Charter Treaty (ECT) is confined to the Eurasian region, not including Norway and the Russian Federation as contracting parties. Moreover, international policy frameworks affecting the energy sector, such as the Rio+20 process, make slow progress.

5. Another significant factor is local resistance to new FDI in the energy sector. This "not in my backyard" phenomenon has made it very difficult for policymakers to implement energy investment projects, including the necessary infrastructure development. Examples are the building of refineries, high-tension lines, terminals or nuclear power plants.
6. Investment costs are increasing due to greater difficulty accessing resources. In real terms, the cost of production is higher today than in the previous two decades. Oil reserves are more difficult to access as shallow offshore wells dry up. Reserves are now found in the deep sea, the Arctic region or the continental oil shale. Technologies to extract these sources are very expensive, and companies must commit to the project for decades with cost in billions of dollars. Difficulty of access can also be attributed to transportation risks, such as pirate attacks in the Gulf of Aden or recent gas pipeline disputes between Ukraine and the Russian Federation.

2 FDI-related Policies in the Energy Sector

FDI in the energy sector is politically sensitive as it may affect national sovereignty over natural resources. The oil and gas industries – and to a lesser extent the power industry – are considered by many countries to be strategic sectors with a national security dimension. This is in particular the case when investments by state-owned enterprises are involved. It is also a socially sensitive sector, because energy supply as a basic good must remain affordable for the population. Investments in the energy sector can also have significant impact on human health, safety, the environment and human rights.

Not surprisingly, the energy sector is therefore more prone to State intervention than most other economic activities. In contrast to the general long-term policy trend in the treatment of FDI – which focuses on investment liberalisation and promotion – most policy measures related to investment in the energy sector nowadays fall into the category of regulations and restrictions (Figure 1.4).

2.1 *Policies Relating to the Establishment of FDI in the Energy Sector*

National policies regarding the establishment of foreign investors in the energy sector vary considerably. They range from the active promotion of FDI to outright prohibitions. In between is a whole spectrum of intermediate policies, including ownership ceilings, joint venture requirements or the existence of public monopolies, preventing all private investment in the sector.

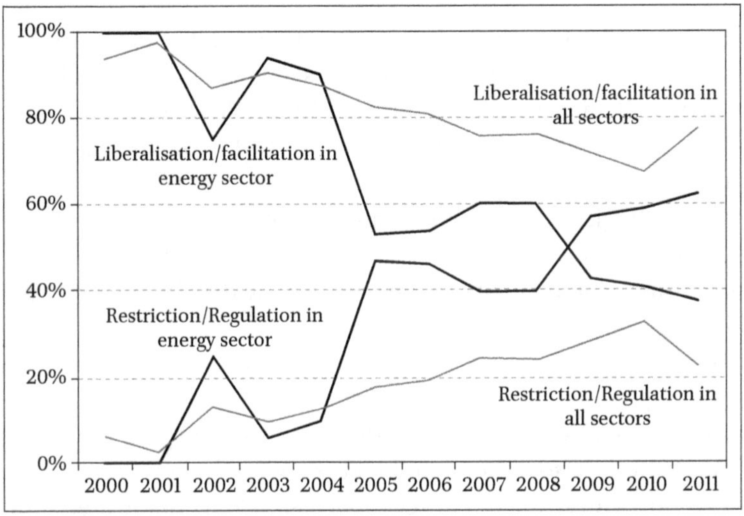

FIGURE 1.4 *Annual investment-related policy changes in the energy sector (2000–2011)*
SOURCE: UNCTAD DATABASE

FDI-related restrictions exist particularly in the oil and gas sector, while they are much less numerous for power generation.

Several major supplier countries allow FDI in the energy sector up to 100 percent foreign ownership (*e.g.* Kazakhstan, Nigeria, Norway, the Russian Federation and the United States). In addition, many countries actively promote FDI in the energy sector, for instance low-carbon FDI or outward FDI as a means to secure energy supply at home.

Other countries have embarked upon privatisation policies, especially transition economies. Some recent examples include the privatization of six regional power companies in the Ukraine,[4] and of the state-owned Albpetrol in Albania.[5] Developing countries have also been active – for example, the privatization of power plants in Kuwait,[6] or the termination of the monopoly of the state electricity company in Indonesia.[7] In some cases, governments do keep a share in the companies or retain a "golden share," as was for instance the case in Kuwait.

4 'Government adopted a decree on privatization of the fuel and energy complex enterprises', Government portal, 19 February 2013.

5 'The government seeks to privatise Albpetrol', *The Economist Intelligence Unit*, at http://www.eiu.com/ (accessed 23 October 2013).

6 'Kuwait MPs pass privatisation law, exclude energy production', France24, 12 May 2010.

7 Law No. 30/2009, Concerning Electricity.

At the other extreme are countries that prohibit private investment – domestic and foreign – in the oil and gas sector; thus maintaining a public monopoly (*e.g.* Qatar, Saudi Arabia and the United Arab Emirates). In between are policies that set certain capital ceilings for FDI in oil and gas (*e.g.* Algeria, Libya, and Venezuela). Some governments seek to retain a level of government control through joint venture requirements or mandatory production sharing agreements, for instance in Brazil and Mexico. Brazil recently included production-sharing arrangements as the basis for the development of its pre-salt oil fields.[8]

In case partial or complete foreign ownership is allowed, countries often have screening mechanisms in place, for instance with respect to national security or national economic benefits concerns.[9] They may also apply for power generation, as some intended mergers with foreign participation were blocked by host Governments in recent years.[10] Concerns related to national security may be particularly strong when the foreign investor is a state-owned enterprise. For example, Canada recently approved new guidelines for the screening of foreign investments by State-owned enterprises,[11] following the acquisition of Nexen by China National Offshore Oil Corporation. The government announced, in particular, that it would find the acquisition of control of a Canadian oil-sands business by a foreign SOE to be of net benefit to Canada on an exceptional basis only.[12]

In the case of Iran, while it allows full foreign equity in a company, it imposes a limit of foreign participation in the entire energy sector. Under its Foreign Investment Promotion and Protection Act, the foreign participation ratio shall not exceed 25 percent in each economic sector and 35 percent in each subsector.

2.2 *Treatment of Established Investors in the Energy Sector*

Given the huge importance of the energy sector for the domestic economy, it is not surprising that states interfere relatively frequently into the operations

8 Law No. 12.351, 22 December 2010.

9 For instance, in 2010 Canada blocked the acquisition of Potash Corporation by the Anglo-Australian mining company BHP as it did not pass the 'net benefit' test (Investment Canada Act and Canadian Ministry of Industry press releases, 3 and 14 November 2010).

10 This was the case, for instance, in France and Spain, where national governments recently opposed the takeover by foreign firms of their main national electricity companies.

11 Press release, Ministry of Industry, 7 December 2012, Investment Canada Act, Official Gazette, 12 January 2013.

12 Official Gazette, 12 January 2013.

of investors. Reasons are manifold and include, for instance, the wish to strengthen state control, substantial changes in the overall energy policy, climate change considerations and related environmental concerns, policy reactions to substantial price fluctuations in the energy markets or social protection.

Recent examples of such state interference relate to nationalisations and expropriations, the renegotiation of investment contracts, tax increases or exit from nuclear energy.

2.2.1 Expropriations and Nationalizations

Such measures were taken in recent years particularly in parts of Latin America. Some important examples are:

- In 2012, Argentina's National Congress enacted a law, which declared that the achievement of self-sufficiency in the provision of hydrocarbons (including exploration, exploitation, industrialization, transport and commercialization) is of national interest and a priority goal of Argentina. It also declared to be in the public interest and subject to expropriation the 51 percent of the share capital of YPF SA owned by Repsol YPF S.A. and the 51 percent of the share capital of Repsol YPF Gas S.A. owned by Repsol Butano S.A.[13]
- Similarly, the National Assembly of Venezuela passed a law in 2009 to nationalize the assets of certain domestic and foreign oil service companies.[14] At the same time, the government nationalized numerous companies, which provide services to the petroleum industry in Lake Maracaibo including ExxonMobil and ConocoPhillips.[15] It also seized the operations of the US oil company Helmerich and Payne in 2010. [16]
- Bolivia expropriated the Transportadora de Electricidad (TDE), owned by Spain's Red Eléctrica Española (REE). As the national power-grid company, it supplied 72 percent of the country's power.[17] It also introduced a decree

---

13 Law No. 26.741 (Official Gazette, 7 May 2012).

14 Organic Law for the Development of Petrochemical Activities (Official Gazette, 18 June 2009).

15 Bloomberg, "Venezuela Seizes 60 Oilfield Service Company Assets (Update 2)", (8 May 2009), at http://www.bloomberg.com/apps/news?pid=newsarchive&sid=an5G6qrs2JD8 (accessed 22 February 2013).

16 Latin America News Dispatch, "Venezuela Nationalizes 11 Oil Rigs Owned By U.S.-Based Helmerich & Payne" (25 June 2010), at http://latindispatch.com/2010/06/25/venezuela-nationalizes-11-oil-rigs-owned-by-u-s-based-helmerich-payne/ (accessed 22 February 2013).

17 Supreme Decree 1214/12.

providing for the transfer to the state-owned company Empresa Nacional de Electricidad (ENDE) of all the shares of the electricity distribution companies of La Paz (Electropaz) and Light and Power Corporation of Oruro (ELFEOSA), as well as of the management and investment service companies Business Bolivia SA (Cadeb) and Corporation Service Company (Edeser) – all of which were held by Iberbolivia Investment Corporation, belonging to Iberdrola of Spain.[18]

- Nigeria adopted the Oil and Gas Industry Development Act, which established the Nigerian Content Development Agency and sought to ensure that 70 percent of Nigeria's oil and gas production would be done locally by 2010. The Act directs that priority should be given to indigenous service companies.[19]

2.2.2 Increasing Taxes or Other Fees for Companies Operating in the Oil and Gas Sector

Recent examples of such policy measures are:

- Argentina approved legislation that mandates oil, gas and mining companies to exchange revenues in foreign currency from exports in the sectors in local financial institutions to local currency.[20]
- Ghana increased the corporate tax rate of mining companies from 25 percent to 35 percent; re-imposed a 10 percent windfall tax levy on mining companies, and introduced a uniform regime for capital allowances of 20 percent for five years for the mining sector including oil and gas industry.[21]
- Kazakhstan reintroduced an oil export duty for nearly all crude oil products in 2010. It also passed a law that requires prior approval from the government in any transaction involving assets in industries deemed as "strategic asset," which include trunk oil pipelines.[22]
- Uganda enacted a law that introduced taxation on income from the sale of oil exploration and production rights in the country.[23]

18 Press release, President of the Plurinational Legislative Assembly (29 December 2012).

19 Nigerian Oil & Gas Industry Content Development Act (23 April 2010).

20 Decree 1722/2011, Official Gazette (26 October 2011).

21 Ghana 2012 Budget.

22 Supreme Decree 1214/12.

23 Uganda, Income Tax (Amendment) Bill 2010.

2.2.3 Renegotiation of Investment Contracts

Some governments have demanded to renegotiate existing investment contracts with foreign investors in the energy sector to achieve a more favourable rent distribution. For instance, Ecuador passed a new law that compels private oil companies in the country to renegotiate new service contracts in order to replace production-sharing agreements with a flat rate per barrel of oil produced in 2010.[24]

2.2.4 Exit from Nuclear Energy

Some countries, such as Germany and Switzerland, recently decided to abandon nuclear energy, following the Fukushima nuclear meltdown in 2011. These policies affect established foreign investors in the nuclear industry and have already resulted in investment arbitration cases.[25]

2.3 *Investment Disputes in the Energy Sector on the Rise*

Not surprisingly, more state interventions in the energy sector has resulted in a significant increase in international investment disputes in recent years. This development is in line with an overall, cross-sectoral trend. On average, at least 10 new cases were filed per year in the energy sector since 2001 (Figure 1.5). Most of these disputes concern the oil and gas sector (44 percent), followed by power generation (29 percent) and energy transmission and distribution (25 percent). The most notable increase occurred in 2003 in the context of emergency measures taken by Argentina to fight financial crisis. In fact, almost half of all respondents in energy investment disputes are countries from Latin America and the Caribbean (Figure 1.7). Aside from Argentina, Ecuador and Venezuela were also heavily involved in investment disputes in the energy sector. Most of the claimant companies are from developed countries – more than 9 out of 10 claims.

---

24 Proyecto de Ley Reformatoria a la Ley de Hidrocarburos y a la Ley de Regimen Tributario Interno (24 June 2010).

25 Most recently, a case against Germany was brought by Swedish-owned Vattenfall to the International Center for Settlement of Investment Disputes for resolution. This is the second time Vattenfall brought the German government to an international arbitration. In 2009, it requested ICSID for arbitration of its investments to build a coal-fired power plant in Hamburg.

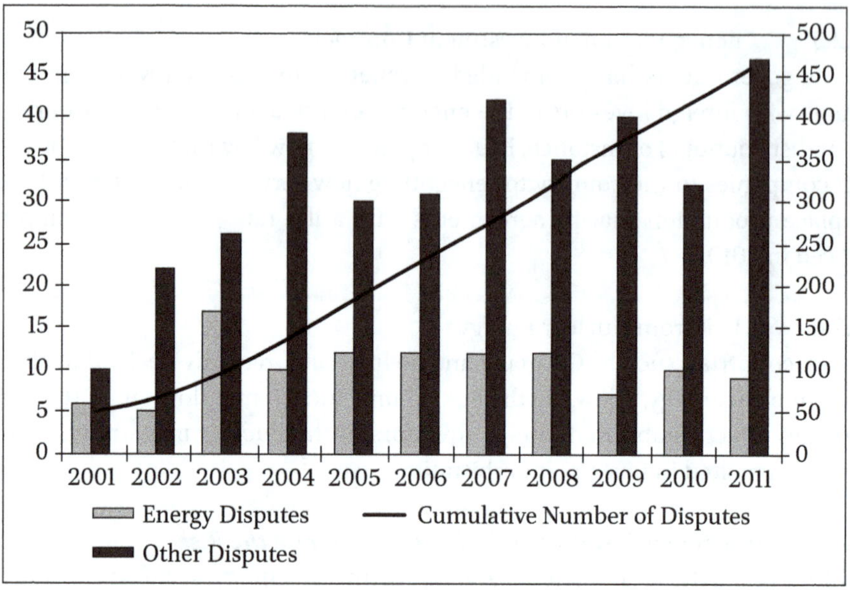

FIGURE 1.5 *Number of known energy-related investor-State disputes*
SOURCE: UNCTAD DATABASE

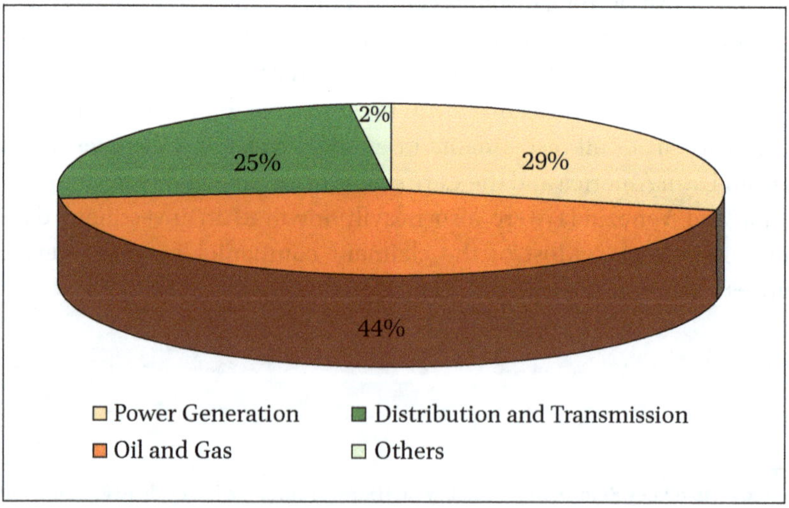

FIGURE 1.6 *Sectoral distribution of known energy-related investment disputes, 2001–2011*
SOURCE: UNCTAD DATABASE

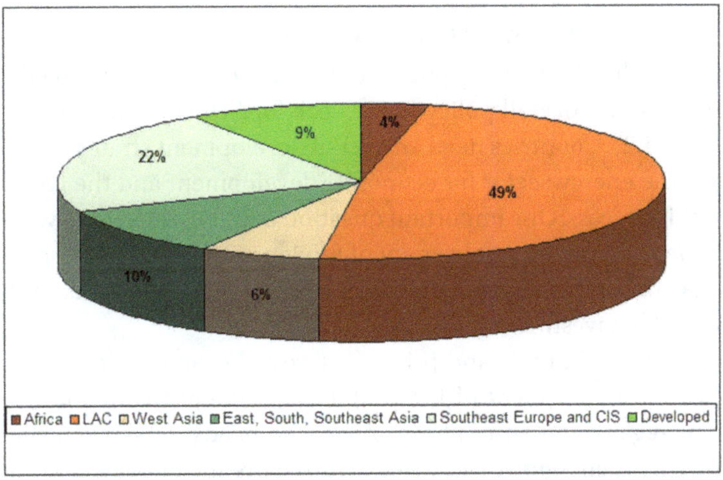

FIGURE 1.7 *Regional distribution of defendants in energy-related investment disputes, 2001–2011*
SOURCE: UNCTAD DATABASE

3 Reconciling Conflicting Interests of Host Countries and Foreign Investors in the Energy Sector

It follows from the above that more than in other industries, FDI in the energy sector is subject to conflicting interests. On one hand, foreign investors seek legal protection, clarity and stability for their long-term, highly capital-intensive and therefore risky investments. On the other hand, host countries are keen to preserve sufficient policy space for the regulation and possible control of this vital industry, including the right to intervene whenever they consider this necessary.

How to balance these potentially conflicting interests is part of the broader issue of how to design the overall policy framework for foreign investment in general, and for foreign investment in the energy sector in particular. Designing such a framework poses a number of important challenges both at the national and international level (see below). UNCTAD's recently published Investment Policy Framework for Sustainable Development (IPFSD) provides policymakers with detailed guidance in this process.[26] The remainder of this section is to a considerable extent based on the IPFSD, with a particular focus on its part dealing with the balancing of public and investor interests.

26 See http://investmentpolicyhub.unctad.org/Views/Public/IndexIPFSD.aspx (accessed 23 October 2013).

3.1 *Balancing Public and Private Interest in National Investment Policies*

At the national level, balancing public and private interests is a crucial element in the design of an overall policy framework for FDI, including in the energy sector (Table 1.2). Countries need an overall development strategy that defines the role of the energy sector for economic development and the contribution of FDI in this process. One important question in this context is, to what extent a country *depends* on the involvement of foreign investors to develop its energy sector? The higher this dependency, the stronger the need to attract FDI and to offer favourable investment conditions.

The balancing of public and private interests becomes relevant both with regard to the establishment of FDI and its subsequent treatment in the host country. As regards the entry phase, a decision needs to be taken whether to permit FDI in the energy sector, in what sub-sectors and under what conditions. This process may also imply choosing between alternative policy approaches. For instance, instead of imposing foreign ownership limits, host countries may

TABLE 1.2 *Balancing private and public interests in the energy sector – National investment policy challenges*

Integrating investment policy in development strategy	Defining the role of energy investment in the overall development process. Defining the role of private investment in the energy sector. Managing the revenue generated from oil and gas extraction, and the volatility of the energy market. Ensuring coherence with the host of policy areas geared towards overall development objectives.
Incorporating sustainable development objectives in investment policy	Maximizing positive and minimizing negative impacts of energy investment. Promoting energy efficiency. Fostering responsible investor behaviour.
Ensuring investment policy relevance and effectiveness	Building stronger institutions to implement energy investment policy. Measuring the sustainable development impact of energy investment.

Source: UNCTAD

wish to opt for less drastic approaches, such as a screening mechanism for inward FDI.

With regard to the treatment of energy investors in the post-establishment phase, it goes without saying that a clear, stable and predictable investment climate based on the rule of law is critical for satisfying basic investor interests. This includes non-discriminatory treatment, protection in case of nationalisation or expropriation, rights relating to capital transfers, the absence of political pressure, and access to neutral, independent domestic courts in case of an investment dispute.

Vice versa, countries need to safeguard the public interest by appropriate regulation of investments in the energy sector to minimize potential negative effects. Labour, social, safety and environmental laws in particular are essential to ensure that such FDI contributes to sustainable development and inclusive growth. It is critical to respect and enforce human rights, to avoid land grabs and the displacement of local communities. This implies that the latter, including indigenous people, are heard when new investments projects are planned or when there are problems with existing investments. There is also a need to strengthen corporate social responsibility of investors. The existence of an independent regulator helps to ensure competition and to avoid that energy supply becomes unaffordable for the poor.

Another important issue is how to manage and use the revenue generated from oil and gas extraction, and how to deal with the high volatility of oil and gas markets. Countries may seek to develop frameworks that are robust over different phases of the business cycle, such as some form of progressive taxation. Dealing with the issue of "changing circumstances" is also crucial in the investment contract between the foreign investor and the host country.

The promotion of energy efficiency is a further significant aspect of supporting sustainable development. Energy-saving production and distribution means can help to reduce energy consumption. However, attracting low-carbon FDI also poses new policy challenges for host countries. It implies creating an enabling policy framework for such investment, comprising both "traditional" elements of investment promotion and protection as well as specific policies for renewable energy, such as market creation mechanism and the establishment of emission standards (WIR 11).

Last, but not least, it is important that existing laws and regulations are enforced and that governments periodically review the success of their current policies.

Individual investment contracts between the host country and foreign investors, or public-private partnerships, can be particularly instrumental for balancing public and private interests in the energy sector. They can include contractual commitments of foreign investors to make certain development contributions (*e.g.* infrastructure development) in exchange for getting access to the energy sector. A crucial issue is the potential inclusion of a "stabilisation clause" in these contracts, prohibiting the host country to unilaterally amending the applicable rules and regulations for the investment after the contract has been concluded. Such clauses may unduly restrict domestic regulatory space. At a minimum, such clauses should remain valid only as long as there is no substantial change of circumstances ("clausula rebus sic stantibus").

Another critical issue for the energy investment contract is risk allocation. Key issues here are how specific risks (*e.g.* payment risks, price adjustments, frequent changes of law, exchange rate risks) can be minimized and which contracting party is in the best position to take on certain risks.

3.2 *Balancing Private and Public Interest in International Investment Policies*

Balancing private and public interests is also a key challenge for the design of an international policy framework for FDI, including investment in the energy sector (Table 1.3). The core instruments for achieving such a balance are international investment agreements (IIAs). They provide foreign investors with

TABLE 1.3 *Balancing private and public interests in the energy sector – international investment policy challenges*

Strengthening the development dimension of IIAs	Safeguarding policy space for sustainable development. Making investment promotion provisions more concrete and consistent with sustainable development objectives.
Balancing the rights and obligations of states and investors	Reflecting investor responsibilities in IIAs. Learning from and building on CSR principles.
Managing the systemic complexity of the IIA regime	Dealing with gaps, overlaps and inconsistencies in IIA coverage and content and resolving institutional and dispute settlement issues. Ensuring effective interaction and coherence with other public policies and systems.

Source: UNCTAD

basic guarantees concerning their treatment in the host country, including non-discrimination, protection in case of expropriation and the right to transfer capital and access to international arbitration in case of an investment dispute. A minority of IIAs provide foreign investors also with establishment rights, subject to certain exceptions and country-specific reservations. In addition to the more than 3,100 existing bilateral and regional investment treaties, the ECT, comprising more than 50 contracting parties from Eurasia, is of particular importance, although it does not include the major oil and gas producers Norway and the Russian Federation.

Since IIAs focus on the promotion and protection of FDI, thereby potentially shifting the balance of interests in favour of the investor, the domestic regulatory framework of host countries, within which foreign investors operate, needs to provide the necessary counterweight. To effectively play this role, it is crucial that IIAs do not unduly undermine national regulatory space through which governments can pursue sustainable development strategies and minimize negative impacts of investment in the energy sector.

To avoid the risk of an undue reduction of regulatory space for investments in the energy sector, countries may want to abstain from entering into specific international commitments at all. This is particularly an issue for the ECT, which lacks the membership of many major oil and gas producing countries.[27] The Russian Federation, which applied the Treaty at least provisionally in the past, reversed this decision in 2009. The ECT nowadays applies predominantly between European countries – a result that was not intended at the time of its conclusion.

Those countries that enter into IIAs have several options to secure sufficient regulatory space for FDI in the energy sector:

First, governments can conclude IIAs that only apply to the post-establishment phase, leaving host countries with freedom as regards their FDI entry policies. This approach may be favoured by countries where granting foreign companies access to the energy sector raises strong political sensitivities.

Second, if IIAs also cover the pre-establishment phase, contracting parties have the possibility to take sector-specific reservations. They can therefore deny or limit establishment rights to foreign investors in the energy sector.

Third, as regards post-establishment treatment, IIA negotiators can agree upon exception clauses allowing them to derogate from all or specific IIA obligations in certain circumstances. Examples are a threat to national security or public order. A crucial question in this respect is whether these exception

27 Prominent absentees include Norway, the Russian Federation, as well as all countries in the Middle East and Latin America.

clauses have a self-judging nature, i.e. whether they are subject to judicial review.

Fourth, IIA negotiators may wish to have a particular eye on a number of IIA provisions that are particularly susceptible of reducing host countries' regulatory space. Four provisions stand out: The so-called "respect clause," the fair and equitable treatment standard, the expropriation article and rules on investor-State dispute settlement (ISDS).

- The respect clause means that IIA contracting parties agree to honour any other commitment undertaken with regard to foreign investment. Such other commitments exist frequently in the energy sector in the form of individual investment contracts between the host country government and foreign investors. The respect clause has the effect of transforming the contractual obligation between the host country and the investor into an international obligation between the IIA contracting parties. It also makes the IIA dispute settlement mechanism applicable to such contracts, thereby overriding the original contractual arrangement as regards applicable dispute settlement mechanisms. Not every country wants to go so far. The ECT, for example, gives contracting parties the right to exclude the applicability of the ECT dispute settlement rules to individual investment contracts (Annex IA to the ECT).
- The fair and equitable treatment (FET) provision has received a broad and sometimes incoherent interpretation by recent arbitration tribunals, reaching far beyond the international minimum standard, which only prohibits arbitrary treatment of foreign investors. The arbitration practice, according to which the FET standard also proscribes, *inter alia*, to disappoint the legitimate expectations of foreign investors has triggered an avalanche of claims, making the FET provision the most frequently invoked treaty article in international investment disputes. It is particularly risky in the energy sector as policies in this area change relatively frequently and because there are no clear criteria as to when investor expectations are "legitimate" or not.
- The expropriation article usually applies to direct and indirect takings. The latter include regulatory takings that leave the property of the investor formally untouched, but have the effect of depriving it of all or a substantial part of its economic value. Once again, the relative intense regulatory activity in the energy sector results in a considerable risk for host countries of being confronted with allegations of an indirect expropriation.

– IIA provisions on ISDS provide foreign investors with access to international arbitration in case of an investment dispute. It is crucial from a host country perspective to clarify the preconditions for invoking the ISDS mechanism and possibly to limit access. More consideration should be given to alternative methods of dispute resolution, such as mediation and conciliation. The latter may be particularly promising for disputes in the energy sector, since both the investor and the host country are usually engaged in a long-term relationship that binding arbitration risks bringing to an end.

To conclude, safeguarding sufficient regulatory space in the energy sector requires careful drafting of key IIA provisions. This means clarifying to the extent possible the meaning and scope of the different clauses. The problem remains that thousands of IIAs already exist where these provisions are drafted in a relatively vague manner. To change this situation would require a renegotiation of IIAs – something countries are often reluctant to do because of the risk of opening up a pandora's box.

Another important element to strengthen the public interest in the investor-State relationship at the international level is to give more weight to the issue of investor responsibilities in the energy sector. In particular, IIAs could refer to commonly recognized international standards, such as the United Nations Guidelines on Business and Human Rights,[28] the UN Global Compact,[29] the ILO's Tripartite Declaration of Principles Concerning Multinational Enterprises and Social Policy,[30] the OECD Guidelines for Multinational Enterprises,[31] and the Extractive Industries Transparency Initiative aimed at ensuring transparency of payments from natural resources.[32] In addition, governments' support for private initiatives to strengthen corporate social responsibility is important.

28 Please see http://www.ohchr.org/en/NewsEvents/Pages/DisplayNews.aspx?NewsID=11164.

29 Please see http://www.unglobalcompact.org/AboutTheGC/index.html.

30 Please see http://www.ilo.org/empent/Publications/WCMS_094386/lang--en/index.htm.

31 Please see http://www.oecd.org/daf/inv/mne/.

32 Please see http://eiti.org/.

4 Concluding Remarks

FDI can make a vital contribution to satisfying increasing energy demands, but it can also create significant risks in terms of sustainable development and inclusive growth. In addition, there are concerns that FDI in this strategic industry could affect national security. These potential impacts have resulted in an ambivalent policy approach of many countries towards FDI in the energy sector, consisting both of elements of investment promotion and control/restriction.

Maximizing the benefits from FDI in the energy sector and minimizing associated risks requires a well-designed policy framework, both at the national and international level. What is needed is an overall strategy that defines the role of FDI for the sustainable development of the energy sector and translates this strategy into concrete, coherent and transparent policy action, both with regard to the establishment and the subsequent treatment of foreign investors.

Balancing the public and investor interests in respect of FDI in the energy sector is not an easy task. Some countries offered very favourable conditions to foreign investors in the past only to find out later that they did not secure a sufficient share in the profits or experienced other negative social or environmental consequences. The challenge is to offer investors reassuring investment conditions while at the same time allowing for necessary policy adaptations in light of changing circumstances that are not disruptive to the investor-State relationship.

It may help that increasingly countries have reciprocal interests related to upstream/downstream FDI in the energy sector. Energy-exporting countries that in the past were "only" hosts to FDI are nowadays becoming important outward investors to market their products or to improve domestic energy supply from the foreign base.

Enhancing the international energy dialogue, including on investment issues, can help to find the right balance between state and investor interests. The ECT plays an important role in this respect, especially if efforts to further increase the number of observer countries in the Energy Charter Process will show more success.

CHAPTER 2

Multiple Investment Regimes for Russian Subsoil Resources: Work in Progress or Utopia?

Andrey A. Konoplyanik

1 Introduction

This chapter presents the summary of academic views and results of some of my practical experience with regard to the creation of a friendly climate for Russian subsoil investors.[1] Over the past 20 years I have argued in favour of the creation of multiple Russian subsoil investment regimes based on the development of a legal *investment menu, i.e.* a set of investment regimes for subsoil use to be available within Russia for investors seeking to develop Russian oil and gas resources.[2] These regimes, to be established by law, should present to the investor/potential subsoil user different combinations of legal stability and tax advantages allowing the subsoil investor to select the most appropriate regime, from the investor's point of view, for various future investment projects based on the investor's evaluation of potential risks and rewards in developing a particular project.

I argue that the investment menu should consist of four major investment regimes with different combinations of legal and tax components:

(A) Current licensing regime, a legal reality since 1992 despite my rather critical attitude towards it;
(B) Licensing regime with exemptions for individual projects and groups of similar projects and specific geographical areas, which is the dominant strategy for improvement of the existing investment regime;
(C) Regime based on concessions, which is not legal in Russia at presently allowed and needs to be introduced into subsoil legislation; and
(D) Regime based on production-sharing agreements (PSA), which has existed in Russian legislation since 1996, but implementation of this

1 See my publications and presentations on these issues, all available at www.konoplyanik.ru.

2 Since Art. 6 of the Russian law "On Foreign Investments" (1991) established a national system for all investors and investments, I will not distinguish between foreign and domestic investors in my arguments and will refer to investors–subsoil users for the remainder of this chapter.

 | DOI 10.1163/9789004244719_004

regime has been artificially limited to situations made almost impractical by the Russian tax legislation reform of early 2000s and, in particular, by amendments to Chapter 26 of the Tax Code effective June 2003.

Regarding the legal component of the investment regime in subsoil, two regimes – (A) and (B) – have been developed within administrative law procedures while (D) was developed within the area of civil law which will also provide the framework for (C). Regarding the tax component of the investment regime of subsoil use, regime (A) presents (and regime (C) can present) a unified, single tax regime for all fields/projects, while (B) and (D) present differentiated/individualized tax regimes. The principal difference between (B) and (D) regimes, in respect of the tax regime, is that (B) has been developed as a centrally-determined (upside-down) set of individual exemptions to the tax treatment of individual projects, while (D) should be organized (based on existing but to-be-improved PSA law) as the regime that will provide opportunity for the resource owning host state and an investor-subsoil user to reach mutually beneficial and balanced sharing of resource rent based on negotiations on the specific PSA terms with sliding scales linked to financial and economic parameters of fields development. In the case of such improvement of the PSA regime and its non-restricted presence in the Russian legal system, no deviations from tax rules should be needed since this PSA model provides a mechanism for negotiation and achievement of bilateral agreement between the host state and an investor-subsoil user for optimal mineral rent-sharing.

This is a different approach compared to the single investment regime for subsoil use that has been dominant in Russia since the early 2000s. It is based on a licensing system with a flat-rate mineral resource production tax (MRPT) and an export customs duty (ECD), which was later supplemented by an open-listed number of individual exemptions from this basically unfriendly investment regime. These exemptions from the general rules are organized in the form of individual tax exemptions for individual projects, regions, and areas provided in a "handy" manner by government ordinances, which, inter alia, creates the risk that such decisions are arbitrary, under the table, discretionary, irregular, and, finally, corrupt.

Today's licensing investment regime for subsoil exploitation presents a very inflexible system of oil taxation (inflexible in regard to project economics, not with regard to world oil price fluctuations) and a legal system based on administrative law where the state always dominates over the investor. If the investor (regardless of whether it is a foreign investor or a Russian state or private company) seeks to realize a reasonable rate of return (RROR) within this inflexible and fiscal-oriented tax system, he has no choice except to approach authorities (now only federal) with requests for tax exemptions for his project.

In my opinion, the practice of providing individual exemptions within a basically unfriendly and inflexible investment regime is not the most effective way to encourage investment. Individual exemptions given by the state in a "handy" manner do not provide investment and legal stability for investors since they can be taken away at any moment in the same handy manner as they were given. A far better alternative would be to enact into law a flexible and adaptable investment regime where not only today's fiscal interests of the state are on the top of the agenda, but also the long-term investment aim of maximization of resource rent from project development and its fair sharing between the state and an investor. The latter means, in my view, that an investor receives RROR including adequate risk premium, which should be different for different fields/projects, and the state receives the remainder of the resource rent. This remaining portion will present the maximum possible government share of resource rent that will still leave for the investor adequate stimuli to develop the project based on his assessment of risks and rewards. And this aim can be best achieved when the state and the investor have multiple legal and tax models from which to structure an effective and balanced combination for any single project, *i.e.* when competition between the different investment regimes is available to an investor in the host state.

The argument in favour of multiple investment regimes in Russian subsoil is justified by the extensive geography of this country with major differences in geologic formations of its non-renewable energy resources. Such distinctions become more and more evident with further developments both onshore and offshore, which means that one single investment regime for subsoil use (especially the current inflexible purely fiscal-oriented licensing regime of flat-rated MRPT + ECD) cannot provide optimal (meaning investment-oriented) rent sharing for diverse capital-intensive and highly risky upstream projects. The optimal investment regime for an upstream investment project (*i.e.* balancing perceptions of risks and rewards both for the host resource-owning state and for the investor-potential subsoil user), within one area in Russia *e.g.*, in the center of such a "mature" area as Western Siberia with rather well developed infrastructure, might not be optimal for another project in a pioneer area such as onshore in Eastern Siberia with no infrastructure at all or in the Arctic offshore, where a totally different organization of oil and gas production should be developed.

I think the trend for Russian oil production to move into more remote provinces, with severe and diverse natural environments, calls for a shift in the institutional structure, including the transition of investment regimes for subsoil use from a single, basically non-investment friendly fiscal-oriented regime with individual exemptions to make projects profitable, to a system of different and competitive investment regimes providing an opportunity to an investor–potential subsoil user to choose an – in his view and for his specific project – optimal regime from the regulatory menu.

In the next section of this chapter I will briefly explain the trends and tendencies during the past 20 years in the development of investment regimes in Russian subsoil starting with the subsoil law adopted in 1992.[3] Article 12 of this law initially allowed a spectrum of investment regimes in the subsoil based on different types of petroleum arrangements: concessions, PSA's, and risk- and pure service contracts. Since then, a search for the most effective model of investment regime in the subsoil looked like a U-curve, at least in its most important tax component. The curve moved from an initial limited differentiation of oil taxation presented in the 1992 subsoil law to upwards to additional tax flexibility provided by a PSA law enacted in 1995,[4] then to total resignation of differentiation in taxation in 2003–2006 as a result of the Tax Code Chapter 26 amendments[5] and, returning to slow, step-by-step implementation of limited, non-systematic differentiation.

2 Implementation of Subsoil Resource Investment Regimes Worldwide

Let's start with some worldwide experience. Usually (at least in my country) when people begin to discuss, examine, and try to understand something new to them or non-traditional, (and the concept of multiple investment regimes sounds like non-traditional philosophy to quite a few people) they would like to find international and/or historical precedents. Such evidence provides a

3 Federal Law "On Subsoil," No. 2395-I (Feb. 21, 1992), restated as Federal Law "On Subsoil," No. 27-FZ (Mar. 3, 1995).

4 Federal Law "On Production Sharing Agreements," No. 225-FZ (Dec. 30, 1995).

5 The amendment of Tax Code Chapter 26, signed in June 2003, can be surprisingly called a "Putin-Khodorkovsky" law, since it was developed and sponsored primarily by Yukos company and its CEO M. Khodorkovsky in the early 2000s and was almost immediately signed by then-President V. Putin (А. Конопляник. «Ошибка президента. В чьих интересах в России фактически ликвидирован режим СРП?». (A. Konoplyanik. "The mistake of the President. In which interests the PSA regime is de facto liquidated in Russia?") *НефтьРоссии*, (*Oil of Russia*) 9 (2003) 62; 10 (2003) 47).

framework for discussion with no obligation to agree with a concept or accept a proposal for change.

To explore this further, the natural first question that arises is whether international experience provides evidence of functional multiple investment regimes. Are there some countries that have more than one investment regime for subsoil resource exploration and exploitation, *i.e.* more than one type of national petroleum investment arrangement offered to would-be investors? The answer to this question is presented in Table 2.1, based on data kindly presented to the author by Gordon Barrows, Vice President of the Association of International Petroleum Negotiations (AIPN) and the owner of Barrows Company, Inc. which, according to the quite broad spectrum of views within the professional community, including my own, provides one of the best – if not the best – collection of petroleum arrangements and legislation worldwide.

Data provided by Gordon Barrows shows that worldwide there are about 180 countries with existing petroleum legislation. About half of them are oil-producing countries. And there are 11–12 states that possess at least two types of petroleum arrangements, if the tax component of the petroleum investment regime is taken into consideration: 1) a "tax plus royalty" (which means licensing and/or concessions) and 2) PSA. This means that about 10% of oil producing countries offers more than one regime to would-be investors in domestic subsoil resources. This can be considered one precedent.

Moreover, our analysis shows that in the countries where the single investment regime is applied, there is a clear correlation between the state of

TABLE 2.1 *Comparative data on implementation of subsoil use tax/investment regimes worldwide, 2003 & 2009*

	2003		2009	
Number of States in analysis, incl.:	180		177	
Oil producing states, using:		91		104
– Tax + Royalty (T+R)	113	45	111	55
– PSA	54	34	55	38
– Both T+R & PSA	13	12	11	11

SOURCE: А. КОНОПЛЯНИК. СРЕДСТВО ОТ «ПРАВОВОГО ВАКУУМА». УРОВЕНЬ ЭКОНОМИЧЕСКОГО И ПРАВОВОГО РАЗВИТИЯ ГОСУДАРСТВА ОПРЕДЕЛЯЕТ ВЫБОР ИНВЕСТИЦИОННЫХ РЕЖИМОВ В НЕДРОПОЛЬЗОВАНИИ – «*НЕФТЬ РОССUU*», 2012, NO. 8 C. 20–24; NO. 9, C. 26–29; NO. 10, C. 16–23. BASED ON DATA, KINDLY PROVIDED TO AUTHOR BY GORDON BARROWS (BARROWS INC./AIPN).

development of the host state and the dominant investment regime. If the oil taxation component is used as a distinct parameter to compare the regimes, then both 'tax plus royalty' (concessions and/or licenses) and PSA regimes are characterized by bell-type distribution curves with upper extremes, where the peak for PSA is located in the zone for less economically developed states (lower per capita GDP) and the peak for "tax plus royalty" schemes, in the zone of more economically developed states.[6] This is because the PSA regime is, basically, more project-oriented than a licensing system, and is better adjusted to the risky legal environment associated with less economically developed states rather than the licensing regime, especially if the latter is constructed in a non-flexible manner like the current flat-rated MRPT-based regime in Russia.

3 Historical Development of Russian Subsoil Legislation (Including Variations with Respect to Petroleum Taxation)

My former colleague within the group of drafters of the PSA law in Russia in the mid-1990s, Dr. Elena Diachkova, in her recent book,[7] identified five major periods in development of subsoil legislation in post-Soviet Russia since 1991 up to the present, with the oil taxation component as a key element. This corresponds to my own vision that I have analyzed in detail at least through the mid-2000s.[8] The major characteristics of the periods according to Diachkova and Konoplyanik[9] are:

6 А. Конопляник. «Средство от «правового вакуума».Уровень экономического и правового развития государства определяет выбор инвестиционных режимов в недропользовании» (A. Konoplyanik. "The mean against the legal vacuum. The level of economic and legal development of the state predetermines selection of investment regimes in the subsoil"). *НефтьРоссии* (*Oil of Russia*), 8 (2012) 20, 9 (2012) 26, 10 (2012) 16.

7 Е. Дьячкова, Экономическое регулирование нефтегазовой отрасли в постсоветской России (Москва: Геоинформмарк, 2011). (E. Diachkova. Economic regulation of the oil and gas industry in the post-Soviet Russia. Moscow: Geoinformmark, 2011)

8 А. Конопляник, Реформы в нефтяной отрасли России (налоги, СРП, концессии) и их последствия для инвесторов (Москва: Олита, 2002) (A. Konoplyanik. Reforms in the oil industry of Russia (taxes, PSA, concessions) and its consequences for the investors. Moscow: Olita, 2002); A. Konoplyanik, Alternative Investment Regimes for Direct Foreign and Domestic Investments in Russian Subsoil *The Harriman Review Occasional Paper Jan 2013*, vol. 19 (1) (2013).

9 I will not discuss in this chapter the pre-1991 developments of subsoil legislation both in pre-Soviet Russia, as well as in the USSR. My vision on this is presented in: A. Konoplyanik and A. Kursky 'State Regulation and Mining Law Development in Contemporary Russia' –

First Period (1991–1996): Development of oil legislation and oil taxation system within the market-oriented economy was started under the authority of the then-Supreme Soviet of the Russian Federation (USSR). The World Bank was deeply involved in this with the University of Houston – winner of the corresponding World Bank grant – as a major consultant. A licensing system for subsoil use was introduced, developed mostly by the representatives of the geology industry. The law "On Subsoil" adopted in 1992, allowed implementation of multiple investment regimes with different taxation models (Art. 12). Payments for subsoil use (royalties) were introduced with differentiated levels. The law "On concessions and other petroleum agreements with foreign investors" (although the law "On foreign investments" introduced previously provided national treatment for these investors and their investments which means that concessionary law should also and equally have addressed both foreign and domestic investors based on national treatment of investors and their investments provided for by the foreign investments law) was first approved by the Supreme Soviet but then vetoed by the President of Russia in June 1993. A PSA regime was established first by a Presidential Decree effective December 1993 and the law "On PSA" was introduced and adopted by the State Duma in December 1995 and became effective in January 1996. The Law "On Concessions" in its second version – for foreign & domestic investors, based on the concept of national treatment – was incorporated in the same package with the PSA law (within the concept of multiple investment regimes for Russian subsoil use) but was not passed by the State Duma in the first reading in 1995 for political reasons. Tax legislation was not codified during this period.

Second Period (1997–2000): Tax Code was introduced and the "tax on incremental earnings" (windfall profit tax) was adopted in the first reading. A differentiated tax regime was *de facto* in place under the licensing system with differentiated royalty. The PSA regime was further developed by supporting documents correlating this tax with corresponding pieces of legislation.

Third Period (2001–June 2003): Period was characterized by transition from a differentiated tax regime back to a unified one. The reform in oil taxation undertaken in this period led to the substitution of royalty, VMSB (the tax for

---

in *International and Comparative Mineral Law & Policy: Trends and Prospects*, ed. E. Bastida, T. Wälde, T. and J. Warden-Fernández (The Hague: Kluwer Law International, 2005) 969; A. Konoplyanik and A. Kursky, 'State regulation and Mining Law Development in Russia from the 15th Century to 1991', *Journal of Energy and Natural Resources Law* May 2006, vol. 24 (2) pp. 73–106.

reproduction of mineral-resource base, or so-called geology tax) and excise tax with the flat-rated MRPT. The introduction of systemic oil customs export duty took place in this period. The PSA regime was still in existence.

Fourth Period (June 2003–2006): *De facto* cancellation of the PSA regime in Russia took place under the amended chapter 26 of the Tax Code. A single and unified tax regime was established. A law on infrastructure concessions was adopted in 2006, but excluded subsoil use.

Fifth Period (2007–present): Differentiation of MRPT-based tax regime started. Introduction of tax allowances of two types (regional and for individual projects) began to take place, which can be considered a slow start to deviation from a unified tax regime, though quite chaotic in nature and through a "handy" management.

Sixth Period (sometime in the hopefully near-future and onwards): Further differentiation of tax regimes for subsoil use (based on economically justified logic incorporated into the legal system), including, hopefully, multiple investment alternatives for subsoil resource developers.

Figure 2.1 illustrates the U-curve type evolution of investment regimes for subsoil use in Russia, taking into consideration the changing character of the tax component (from more to less and back again to more differentiation of oil tax regimes within licensing system).

Figure 2.2 presents my vision of the changing overall attractiveness of multiple Russian subsoil investment regimes, if both legal and tax components are taken into consideration within the evolving government system of Russian subsoil management. The unfortunate tendency, in my view, in the 20-year long development of the subsoil legislation in Russia, is that it has been dominated by a purely fiscal, instead of a balanced fiscal v. investment, approach.[10] This is one of the major reasons why the state's preferred alternative for managing Russian subsoil use always worsened the oil and gas investment climate.

Neither version of proposed subsoil concession law (for foreign investors only and for both domestic and foreign investors), drafted and approved through legislative procedures in 1991–1993 and 1994–1995, respectively, has succeeded in becoming law: the first one was vetoed by the President, the latter has not passed even the first reading in the State Duma (lower house of the Federal Assembly of Russia). These laws were intended to introduce into the

10 See my publications and presentations on this issue at www.konoplyanik.ru.

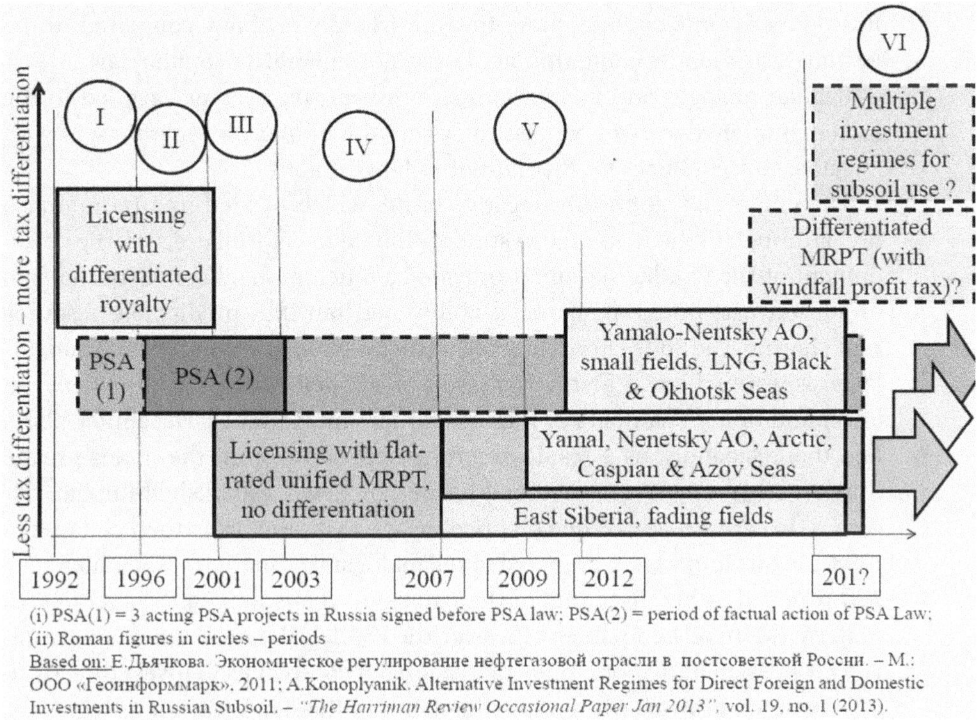

FIGURE 2.1 *Six periods in the evolution of a differentiated Russian oil tax regime*

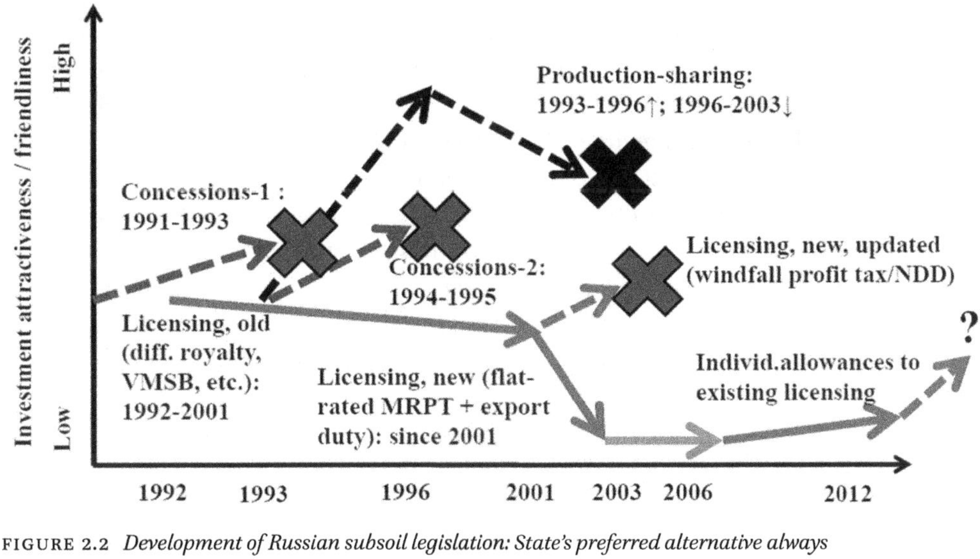

FIGURE 2.2 *Development of Russian subsoil legislation: State's preferred alternative always worsened oil and gas investment climate*

Russian economic climate, more investor-friendly civil law compared to the less investor-friendly contemporary Russia administrative (public) law.

Regular changes and adaptations of the licensing system have led to the incremental increase in tax pressure within the public law environment with negative consequences for Russian subsoil investment.

The major change in this negative trend, which has led to a (temporary) breakthrough in the Russian investment climate for subsoil use, was the development of the PSA legislation. It provided a much more effective mechanism of subsoil use aimed at financial ability and fair and predictable resource rent-sharing. The State Duma adopted its first version in autumn 1995. Then this law was watered down firstly, as a result of a conciliatory procedure between lower and upper chambers of Russian Parliament (October–December 1995), and then, secondly, as a result of strong opposition from the major private Russian oil companies, owned and headed by newly-established Russian oligarchs (in early 2000s). When oil prices began to recover from their collapse in 1998, the oil barons were prepared to sell major stakes in their VICs, which they had received at big discounts in the course of "loans for shares" auctions, to major Western oil companies. However, the PSA legislation created opportunities for Russian and, more importantly, foreign companies to invest directly in the upstream projects without buying shares of Russian VICs. On the contrary, Russian oligarchs would have liked to create for Western companies only one legitimate way to invest in Russian subsoil – by buying a package of minority shares of the new Russian VICs. By creating an alternative way for investing into Russian subsoil, PSA became a competitor for such plans of major Russian VICs, downgrading their selling price. This is why the efforts of fiscal agencies (Ministry of Finance, Tax and Customs Services) and major private Russian oil VICs (headed by Yukos and Sibneft companies) have collaborated in fighting against the PSA regime. Their successful joint efforts have, in fact, stopped practical implementation of PSA in Russia.[11]

The two options for the differentiation of the licensing regime were: 1) individual allowances to some areas (*e.g.* East Siberia) and for specific types of projects (*e.g.* fading fields) or 2) establishing a more systemic mechanism (*e.g.* windfall profit tax). The first avenue was chosen, which is less attractive for any investor who would prefer not to rely on individual exemptions from basically unfriendly investment regimes, especially if they are granted in a "handy" manner, but to rely, instead, on systemic mechanisms of tax differentiation introduced by law.

11 The detailed Russian PSA story is presented in my publications available at www.konoplyanik.ru.

Whereas today's regulation governing Russian subsoil investment was created mostly by oil taxation reform in the early 2000s, there is now a demand for rather radical improvement.

4 Oil Tax Reform of Early 2000s: Administrative Simplicity vs. Economic Efficiency

This reform has presented a turning point in movement from a differentiated to a single tax regime disregarding the particularities of specific upstream projects. The driver of this reform was an intended/expected maximization of tax receipts from oil fields development starting with the very first barrel of oil produced and simplification of tax administration. So the fiscal interests of the state and administrative interests of tax authorities were placed at the top of the agenda, rather than more general and more complex micro- and macroeconomic benefits of the host state, which should be interested in maximization of its resource rent generation and extraction through most effective development of its non-renewable energy resources. Thus, the host state should be interested, in my view, in maximization of not only direct tax revenues from the oil flow, but also in the sum-total of direct and indirect benefits and the multiplier effect of upstream project development.[12]

A good illustration of pure fiscal orientation of MRPT (a key innovation of the oil tax reform of early 2000s) is that it is a flat-rated tax, linked solely

---

12 The issue of the multiplier effect of oil fields development was examined in the works of late Prof. Alexander Arbatov, including his famous joint study with the Petroleum Advisory Forum in mid-1990s on the multiplier effect of six PSA projects (Russian Social and Economic Impact Evaluation for Large-Scale Oil and Gas Investments under Six Production-Sharing Agreements, ed. Alexander Arbatov (Moscow: KEPS-PAF, 1996)). I have evaluated the correlation between direct tax and indirect and multiplier effects in, for instance: А. Конопляник, Реформы в нефтяной отрасли России (налоги, СРП, концессии) и их последствия для инвесторов (Москва: «Олита», 2002) (A. Konoplyanik. Reforms in the oil industry of Russia (taxes, PSA, concessions) and its consequences for the investors. Moscow: Olita, 2002); А. Конопляник, «Анализ эффекта от реализации нефтегазовых проектов СРП в России для бюджетов разных уровней (к вопросу об оценке воздействия на социально-экономическое положение страны крупномасштабных инвестиций в реализуемые на условиях СРП нефтегазовые проекты)» (A. Konoplyanik. "Effect analysis of oil and gas PSA projects for the budgets of different levels (to the issue of evaluation of impact on socio-economic situation in the state of large-scale investments made into PSA-based oil and gas projects)"), *Нефтяное хозяйство* (*Oil Economy*), 10 (2000) 24.

to fluctuations in international oil prices and without considering whether a taxpaying domestic oil producer (subject to MRPT) supplied oil only to the domestic market or had obtained an export quota and exported its oil. So, the higher the international price, the higher the flat rate of this domestic tax, even if the company only supplied the domestic market (as small and medium non-integrated oil companies did).

According to my view, the philosophy of this reform aimed against multiplicity of investment regimes and in favour of the simple and single flat-rated oil taxation is still dominant among decision-making bodies. But why, in my view, is MRPT not good for the host state from the long-term economic perspective (though it is a simple, straightforward and effective pure fiscal instrument)? What are the negative consequences (major deficiencies) of this flat rate system? What does the state lose in this case? And who wins instead?

Let's distribute all the fields in the country through the X-axis from left to right by diminishing percentage of the mineral (resource) rent in the oil price. The biggest, the youngest (at the earlier stages of production) fields will be located to the left, the oldest, at the late and fading production stages, the most expensive fields will be located to the right. Flat-rated MRPT will cut off the fixed absolute value of rent from every field (see Figure 2.3-1). The crossover of two lines and perpendicular from this crossover point down to the X-axis will show the cut-off volume of reserves (to the right from this perpendicular) for which development will provide zero or negative value of resource rent – zero/negative rate of return (ROR). But since no company will develop any project without some reasonable positive ROR (potential to break even is not sufficient incentive), the number of the fields to be developed will be less (the cut-off vertical line will go further to the left). This tax model does, firstly, significantly diminish the number of fields to be developed (only the most profitable fields will be exploited). Secondly, the flat rate leaves the "lucky" companies that have received subsoil use rights for the most efficient fields with extra super-high ROR (with the highest portion of resource rent in the price and the abnormally higher portion of economic rent) which can be considered windfall profit and further taxed with reasonable ROR and not with extra super-high ROR (Figure 2.3-1).

Introduction of the MRPT flat rate (effective January 1, 2002) has put an end to the initial period of at least limited oil tax differentiation in Russia (1992–2001), which existed by virtue of a corridor of subsoil royalty payments (6–16%) and the PSA regime, though the latter at a very limited scale. Only three PSA projects were developed before the PSA law came into force and thus grandfathered them. PSA projects were strongly suppressed from the very beginning based on a number of perceptions, such as the claim that PSA is:

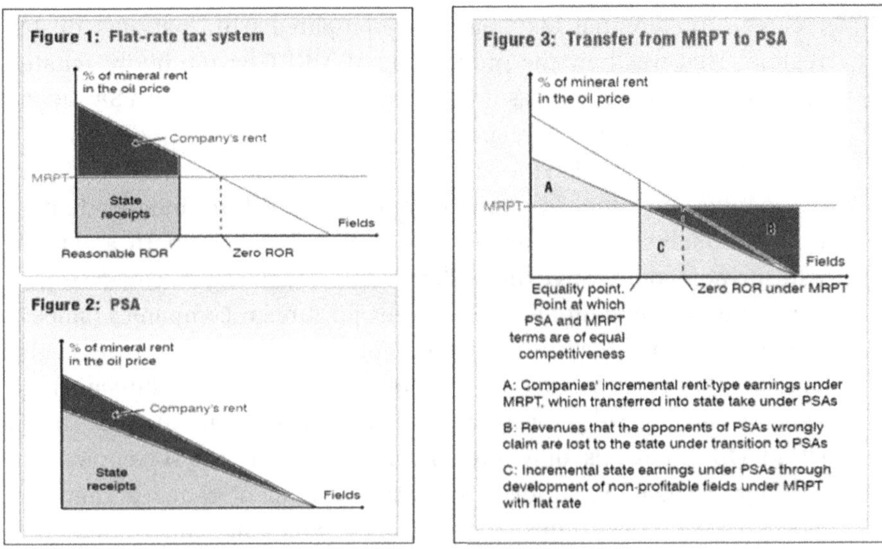

FIGURE 2.3 *Comparison of flat-rate MRPT with PSA system: Why host state is the loser under MRPT*
SOURCE: ANDREY KONOPLYANIK, 'A STRUGGLE FOR MINERAL RENT', "PETROLEUM ECONOMIST", AUGUST 2003, PP.23–24; АНДРЕЙ КОНОПЛЯНИК, 'УХУДШЕНИЕ ЭКОНОМИЧЕСКИХ УСЛОВИЙ ВОЗВРАЩАЕТ НА ПОВЕСТКУ ДНЯ ЗАКОНОДАТЕЛЕЙ ВОПРОС РЕАБИЛИТАЦИИ СРП', «НЕФТЬ И КАПИТАЛ», 2009, №3, С.18–23.

(i) is an attribute of colonialism and less (even the least) developed countries and we, the Russians, would not wish to be identified with such countries by using an instrument associated with them, and since PSAs are usually used in monarchies and autocracies, implementation in Russia might spoil the image of Russia as a democratic state;[13]

---

13 This issue was specifically addressed by my analysis of worldwide distribution of PSA and licensing/concessionary schemes ('tax + royalty' regimes in oil taxation) compared to state of economic development of the host states (measured in per capita GDP), which shows that: (i) distribution curves for both regimes have a bell-type character with upper peaks, (ii) the PSA peak refers to the states with lower per capita GDP level than "tax + royalty" schemes, and (iii) Russia has been slowly moving through the 2000s from the per capita GDP area well correlated with the peak of PSA in the early 2000s to the zone between two peaks nowadays. (А. Конопляник, «Средство от «правового вакуума». Уровень экономического и правового развития государства определяет выбор инвестиционных режимов в недропользовании» (A. Konoplyanik. "The mean against the legal vacuum. The level of economic and legal development of the state predetermines selection of investment regimes in the subsoil"), *Нефть России* (*Oil of Russia*), 8 (2012) 20, 9 (2012) 26, 10 (2012) 16).

(ii) creates a preferential tax treatment compared with 'national oil tax regime'. That was how the proponents of MRPT have proudly agitated against the PSA regime – as if it had a "foreign" nature. The PSA regime indeed does not have a "foreign" nature as claimed by its opponents since it does not favour foreign investors over domestic investors; it does "favor" competitive investors over non-competitive investors independent of their nationality since it provides a level-playing field for both, and those who are non-competitive thus will fail;

(iii) constitutes a preferential tax treatment for foreign companies (since it was first and foremost the foreign companies, who from the very beginning have been supporting the creation of a PSA regime in Russia – individually and on a collective basis through the Petroleum Advisory Forum (PAF). On top of this, only foreign companies were the stakeholders in the first successful PSA project in Russia "Sakhalin-2" known at that time as MMMMS (a consortium consisting of the companies MacDermott and Marathon (USA), Mitsui and Mitsubisi (Japan), and Royal-Dutch/Shell (UK/Netherlands)).

The PSA does not constitute a preferential tax regime for companies. Taxation is rent-based. PSAs will, overall, always yield greater revenue to the state than the licensing system. In projects that provide subsoil users with higher-than-average rents, PSAs can maximize state revenues by allowing case-by-case adjustments to taxation levels. In small projects, the burden of the flat tax rate will prevent companies from achieving an adequate rate of return (ROR) and fields will not be developed. State revenues in these cases will be zero. A PSA would enable the same project to go ahead, as it allows the state and the investor to compromise on economic terms of the project development scheme. The result is a reasonable ROR for companies and additional tax revenues for the state from the projects that alternatively would not be developed (Figure 2.3-2).

Figure 2.3-3 indicates the consequences for the state budget of transferring from the MRPT to the PSA system. The state would have received additional revenues, denoted by zones A and C. Under MRPT, it would not have received this revenue, as Zone A rents would have been retained by the companies (with the flat rate of tax capping state revenues). And Zone C rents would not have been generated in the MRPT case because, under this system, no company would have developed the fields, given the prospect of negative profitability.

The opponents of PSAs view the picture differently. They argue that if PSAs are used to develop fields to the right of the equality point, the state would face "lost revenues" (Zone B at Figure 2.3-3). This conclusion is based on a mathematical calculation of the virtual tax that would have been generated by the

MRPT's flat tax rate. Although this is higher than tax revenues under PSAs, the argument is invalid because no investor would develop a field with an unreasonably low or negative ROR. Therefore, PSA revenues in this Zone must be compared with zero revenues under the MRPT regime.

Secondly, they have kept quiet about the possibility of PSAs being employed in another part of the resource spectrum where the share of rent in the price exceeds the tax level (effective tax rate) under the MRPT by more than reasonable ROR (Zone A at Figure 2.3-3). In that zone, PSA arrangements would considerably increase the tax burden on companies. They would result in a larger state take at every budgetary level (federal, regional, local), while preserving investors' RORs at an acceptable level, in turn stimulating investment in exploration and production. This was precisely what Russian oil companies opposing PSAs have feared most: they would have to share revenues more fairly with the state (as well as facing more competition).

Nevertheless, the existence of such misconceptions does not mean that the licensing system should be dispensed with and PSAs introduced for all subsoil developments (even though Western companies lobbied for such proposals in the mid-1990s both individually and through PAF). The different categories of risks arising under PSAs and the licensing system make peaceful coexistence of both regimes possible. All other conditions being equal, PSAs are more effective from the standpoint of fair rent allocation. But negotiations on PSA terms are more time-consuming and delay field development, and, therefore, cash-flow.

5 Multiple Investment Regimes for Russian Subsoil (Author's Historical Proposal)

The core element of my historical proposal is to present investors with a legally adopted "menu" of subsoil investment regimes and thus create competition among different investment regimes for investors. This investment menu is project-based, not company-based. If investors have an opportunity to choose among investment regimes for subsoil development, they will vote with their money in favor of this or that regime. That will enable the host state to monitor at the everyday level the comparative attractiveness of the available investment regimes and, over time, improve the less attractive regimes so as to stimulate the inflow of resource investment capital. Meanwhile, as a result of comparative monitoring and analysis, the host state will manage to evaluate whether the comparative advantages of the most attractive regime are excessive within the given state of the market. This might help the host state support the optimal level of attractiveness and efficiency of its subsoil investment.

The evolving structure of investment regimes should correspond to the current state of economic development of this or that country as well as the market for a particular resource.

To make it simple, I have proposed to organize the system of investment regimes for Russian subsoil as a matrix consisting of four such regimes. Each regime presents a combination of two major parameters – the legal system and the tax system. The legal parameter consists of either (administrative) public law or civil law, while the tax system can be based on either a unified, general taxation or a differentiated (individualized) taxation. In case of disputes, as a general rule, the individual investor has no right to international arbitration. Within the civil law, according to my vision/proposal, the investor shall have such rights which are provided in international law, inter alia, by Article 26 of the Energy Charter Treaty (ECT).[14]

Based on my approach each investment regime differs from one another (see Figure 2.4):[15]

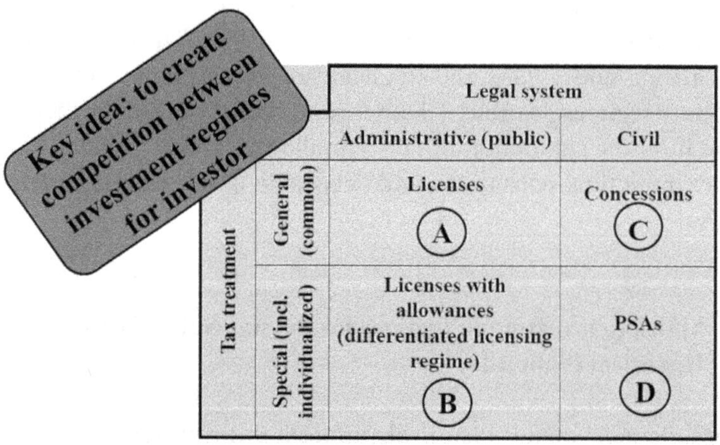

FIGURE 2.4 *Author's historical proposal: Possible composition of investment regimes for Russian subsoil use (investment menu/matrix within legal vs. taxation axes)*

14 The fact that Russia withdrew from the provisional application of the ECT in 2009 and has stated then that it does not intend to ratify the ECT, does not mean that this decision – which, from my view, has no visible justification behind it – should be considered as a final one, once and for all. ECT has brought into international law by its Art. 26 an innovation – direct application of the private/foreign investor to one of the international arbitration tribunals (ICSID, UNCITRAL, SCC) – which can be used in Russia as well, when Russian authorities reverse their decision regarding ratification.

15 First presented in this configuration in: А. Конопляник. «Договор концессии: возможное место и роль в инвестиционном законодательстве России» – в кн. *Нефтегаз, энергетика и законодательство, 2001–2002.* Информационно-правовое

(A) Licensing regime is based on administrative (public) law and treatment of upstream investment projects. According to administrative law the investor and the state are not equal partners in their agreement regarding subsoil development – an investor is always subordinate to the host state. All changes, even with best intentions, in the domestic law are usually applicable in full to the projects in question which creates legal and tax instability for project development. This is a major negative characteristic of the existing Russian subsoil investment regime;

(B) Licensing regime with allowances (differentiated licensing regime) is based on administrative (public) law and special (differentiated) tax treatment which is mostly being developed in the form of individual fixed exemptions for a limited period of time and for a particular project or group of projects or for an area;

(C) Concessionary regime is to be based on civil law and general (common) taxation. In this case, the tax burden can be fixed through stabilization clauses for the whole project life, thereby boosting the predictability of project economics. The investor would be further protected by an opportunity to use international arbitration in case the host state violates its contractual obligations, thereby creating stability of investment contracts terms and conditions;

(D) Regime of production-sharing agreements is based on civil law and individualized tax treatment. This is the most transparent and predictable and also the most economically attractive regime for the investor–subsoil user since it provides a flexible and adaptable mechanism of rent sharing over the life of the project.

Legal attractiveness of investment regimes for subsoil users differs for regimes based on administrative (public) law and on civil law in petroleum arrangements. The former does not provide adequate legal stability for an investor while the latter can provide incremental legal stability and adequate legal protection through the possibility to apply for international arbitration in case of dispute settlements between the host state and an investor–subsoil user.

Tax burden within the proposed "investment menu" of four regimes also differs. From my point of view, PSA provides optimal proportions of rent-

издание ТЭК России (ежегодник), (Москва: Нестор Экономик Паблишерз, 2001) 77. (A. Konoplyanik. "Concessionary agreement: possible place and role in the investment legislation of Russia". – in: *Oil & Gas, Energy, Legislation: 2001–2002*. Informative and legal publication of Russian fuel & energy complex (annual), (Moscow: Nestor Economic Publishers, 2001) 77).

sharing between the state and an investor for individual projects, given skilled and knowledgeable negotiators on both sides. All other regimes do not provide optimal tax allocation by definition since they provide proportions of rent-sharing that are determined in a centralised manner (unilaterally established by the host state) rather than a project-based mechanism. Within all regimes there is a trade-off between its simplicity/complexity, on the one hand, and its optimal/non-optimal economic character, on the other hand. So it is for the investor, in my view, to choose whether he would like to receive optimal proportions of rent-sharing through a rather lengthy and more costly negotiating process, or whether he will be ready to relinquish to the state part of his ROR in exchange for speeding up the administrative procedures regarding access to subsoil exploration and thus saving some costs upfront.

Current generalised and fiscal-oriented, flat-rated licensing regime in such a large and diverse country as Russia cannot provide anything else except non-optimal oil taxation. Such approach cannot – by definition – optimize resource rent sharing between the state and an investor. Partial differentiation of taxation within the licensing regime through the mechanism of individual exemptions softens its suboptimal character but does not provide stability, while the concessionary regime provides stability by fixing non-optimal tax parameters for the whole project life thus also diminishing the non-optimal character of general taxation (Figure 2.5).

Investment regime	Investment regime's characteristics during project life-time	
	Tax pressure	Legal stability
Licensing (A)	Non-optimal (high), established unilaterally	No
Licensing with allowances (special / differentiated tax regimes) (B)	Non-optimal (high / diminished), established unilaterally	No
Concessions (C)	Non-optimal (high), established unilaterally	Yes
PSA (D)	Optimal, negotiated	Yes

FIGURE 2.5 *Different investment regimes in subsoil use: Comparative legal and tax advantages/ disadvantages*

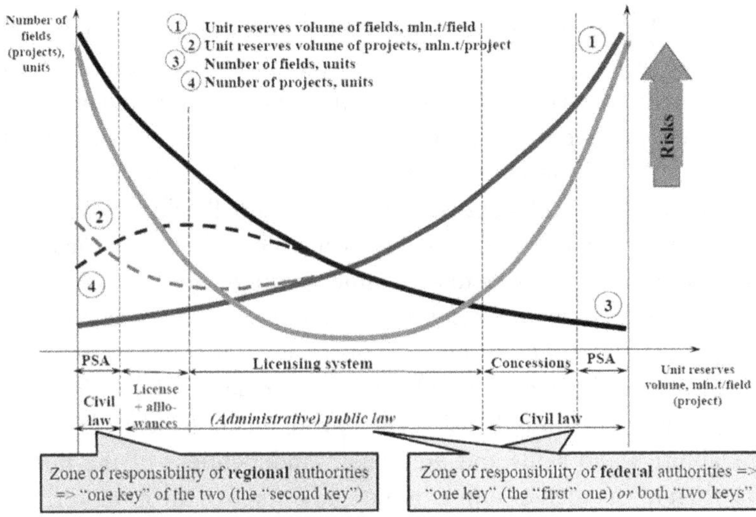

FIGURE 2.6 *Application zones proposed for different Russian subsoil investment regimes*

6 Proposed Application Zones for Different Investment Regimes in Subsoil Use in Russia

From my perspective, it is possible to justify preferential zoning with implementation of the proposed menu of investment regimes dependent on the scale of projects and economic attractiveness of their development measured by the portion of resource rent in the oil price (Figure 2.6). This can be argued based on the different type/origin and value of investment risks which are faced by the investor–subsoil users while developing different categories of fields/upstream projects.

Due to geologically-proven asymmetry of natural (including energy) resource concentration in the subsoil worldwide, there is a well-known correlation between the size of the discovered fields and their quantity: the larger the size (reserves/resources volume) of the individual field, the smaller their quantity (see Figure 2.6). Due to different geological characteristics of the fields and the natural conditions of the geographical areas of subsoil deposits, there is no direct correlation between the size of the field and the value of resource rent in the price (equal to the difference between the price and the cost) since the size of the field is an important but not the only factor influencing the level of the production costs. In principle this deviation does not change the inverse correlation between field size and quantity, which is mostly the result of economies of scale.

This is why I identify development of mega-fields and small-fields as most economically risky (in terms of the risk of possible no-return of CAPEX invested) and thus most dependent on stability, transparency and predictability of the regulatory environment in the host country.[16] In case of mega-fields this is explained by the highest capital value of the single upstream project, so by the absolute value of CAPEX at risk. In the case of small fields, the investor subsoil–user does not benefit from economies of scale; on contrary, the investor is under pressure of the opposite to economies of scale effect.

So the risk-curve of energy resources development has a U-curve character with lower extreme point and peaking in the area of small- and mega-fields (Figure 2.6). And if the investors–subsoil users can deal with commercial risks, including "below the ground" risks (geological, technological, which depend on their abilities and skills and are usually independent of the host state's actions), then in the area of non-commercial or "above the ground risks" they are fully dependent on the legal environment within the host state to determine profitability.

As we know, there is an economic limit for profitable development of any small field. This means that below some quantitative level of geologically known and technically recoverable reserves, development of a field becomes unprofitable since the value of oil/gas extracted and marketed would in no case justify the discounted amount of CAPEX and OPEX through the project life. Below this level, such reserves would not be considered as proven recoverable reserves. Bearing this in mind, it makes economic sense, in my opinion, to allow investors–subsoil users to unite a group of small fields located near each other into one single project to attain this profitability benchmark. Our calculations, based on the real group of small fields in Russia's Udmurtia Republic (when we have developed for the local authorities a justification of the different development options for the so-called "Udmurtia project" on its prelicensing stage: based on the individual development of the fields to be licensed, and on the same fields to be unified in the single project, arguing in favour of a corresponding amendment to Russia's subsoil legislation)[17] show that if the

---

16 А. Конопляник, Реформы в нефтяной отрасли России (налоги, СРП, концессии) и их последствия для инвесторов (Москва: Олита, 2002) (A. Konoplyanik. Reforms in the oil industry of Russia (taxes, PSA, concessions) and its consequences for the investors. Moscow: Olita, 2002).

17 Е. Дьячкова, А. Конопляник, «Соглашения о разделе продукции: удмуртский вариант» (E. Diachkova and A. Konoplyanik. "Production-sharing agreements: Udmurtia case"), *Нефть и капитал* (*Oil & Capital*), 12 (1995) 14; В. Грушин, А. Конопляник. «О подготовке и заключении СРП по мелким месторождениям» (V. Grushin and A. Konoplyanik. "On preparation and making PSA on small fields"). *Минеральные ресурсы России. Экономика и управление* (*Mineral resources of Russia. Economics and*

group of small fields would have been unified into one single upstream project, the value of peak CAPEX would have been diminished by 20%, zero DCF would have been reached in 8.5 and not in 12 years, and at the end of licensing period (after 20 years) cumulated positive DCF could have been almost three times higher than in the case of individual development of each individual field as a single project (Figure 2.7).

Moreover, in the case of small fields, even when they are united in a bigger, single upstream project, the duration of the period for passing through regulatory procedures does matter much more than in the case of mega-fields, consider the value of discounted cash-flows (where time does cost money). So from my perspective, it would be practical in my country to distinguish between regulatory authorities who review small projects and the ones that review all other projects. I consider it reasonable to transfer all authority for decision-taking regarding small fields/projects from the federal (as existing since 2004 and until today) to regional authorities, who are much better

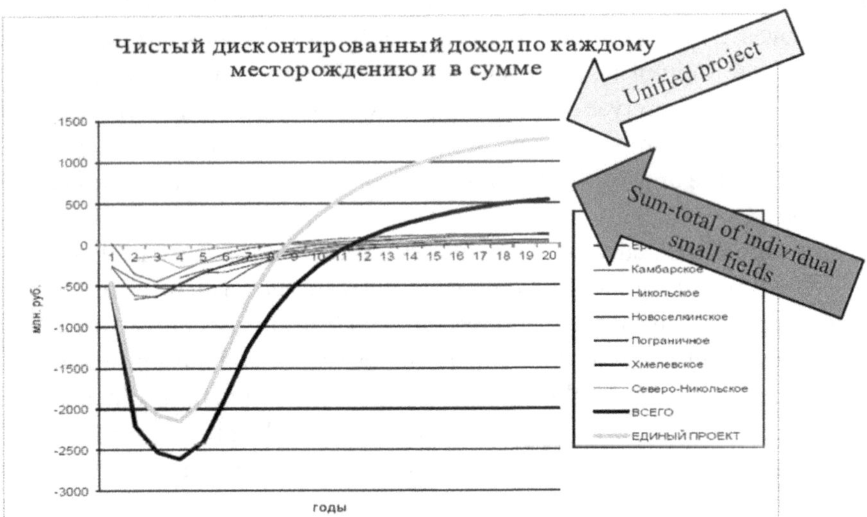

FIGURE 2.7 *Cumulated DCF/NPV of individual and combined field development (Udmurtia Project)*
SOURCE: В.ГРУШИН, А.КОНОПЛЯНИК, Н.ОКСЕНГОРН. О ПОРЯДКЕ ПЕРЕВОДА МЕЛКИХ МЕСТОРОЖДЕНИЙ УГЛЕВОДОРОДОВ НА РЕЖИМ СРП (В ПОРЯДКЕ ОБСУЖДЕНИЯ). – «НЕФТЯНОЕ ХОЗЯЙСТВО», ИЮНЬ 2002, №6, С.83–89.

Management), 1–2 (2002) 68; В. Грушин, А. Конопляник, Н. Оксенгорн. «О порядке перевода мелких месторождений углеводородов на режим СРП (в порядке обсуждения)» (V. Grushin, A. Konoplyanik and N. Oxengorn. "On the rules for transferring small fields to the PSA regime (in the order of discussion)"). *Нефтяное хозяйство* (*Oil Economy*), 6 (2002) 83.

placed to make decisions regarding a big number of small projects within their territories then civil servants in Moscow. The development of large numbers of small fields within many different Russian regions will have much more local (region-wide) indirect and multiplier effects compared to country-wide indirect and multiplier effects of the mega-fields. This is why I consider it to be quite natural that they can stay within the sphere of the regional authorities contrary to the current practice (Figure 2.6).

This will also enable regional authorities to be less dependent on transfers from the federal center and more economically independent in their judgments. From my view, this is to the benefit of the whole federal state. For me, a strong country means, primarily, strong territories and provinces, even though it is easier to control the territories with top-down power if they are dependent on donations/transfers from the central government.

The ability to join/unite few small fields in a single project, if allowed by the state within its licensing policy, would change the risk curve. (This approach is not the case yet in Russia despite a strong campaign in favor of permitting such unification in the late 1990s).[18] The number of such unified projects would be much lower than the number of corresponding small fields involved in unification, and the unit reserves value of unified projects will be much higher than the value of reserves of the individual fields involved (effect of artificially created economies of scale). This would also downgrade the left wing of the risk-curve in the area of the small fields after transition to unified projects in this area.

This type of risk-curve explains my vision of the distribution of the proposed investment regimes in the Russian subsoil based on an investor's preference. At the margins of the field's reserves (their resource rent) (Figure 2.6, at the left and right margins of the X-axis) an investor would most probably prefer the PSA regime which through its sliding scale of rent-sharing mechanism provides effective opportunity for both parties to reach optimal proportions of rent sharing.[19] PSA will be especially attractive for the mega-fields since this

18 Ibid.

19 I do not mean precisely the currently existing PSA regime in Russian legislation, radically being worsened since its adoption by the State Duma in December 1995 and finally almost killed by the Law on amendments to Chapter 26 of the Tax Code of 2003. This current version of PSA law and implementation procedure needs to be radically improved. Argumentation for this and other benefits of the PSA regime in general and in Russia in particular can be found at my numerous PSA-related publications and presentations at www.konoplyanik.ru, especially through the period since early 1990s till, mostly, through 2003. Also for PSA-related discussion in Russia see websites www.concessions.ru and www.yabloko.ru.

is a project-oriented, individualised regime which provides thorough (though lengthy) negotiations for balanced distribution of resource rent between host state and investor. So the time factor matters less in this case than the value at risk due to usually enormous CAPEX per project. The development of such fields will have a much greater country-wide indirect and multiplier effect, so it is natural that it can stay within the full authority of the federal government and its regulatory bodies.

The central zone at Figure 2.6 will possibly remain the dominant zone of the pure licensing regime. It is, generally speaking, the zone of medium to big fields. For such fields, especially if located within the area with well-developed infrastructure, the trade-off will be as follows: the investor might prefer to go through a standardized licensing process and procedures (permissions, etc.) which will enable time-saving in DCF terms by shortening the period between investment of capital and production/return on investment. On the other side of the equation will be some additional costs (hopefully, not to exceed the above-mentioned cost savings) due to unbalanced taxation within the current licensing system. Russian subsoil tax regime with flat-rated MRPT can in some cases lead to a higher or a lower portion of the government take in the price (see Figure 2.3).

The zone to the right from the central one, from the area of dominance of pure licensing regime (see Figure 2.6) is, generally, the zone from medium and big to very big and mega-fields. It will be, most probably, the zone of primary preference for concessionary regime.[20] This is explained, in my view, by the fact, that in this zone the fields/projects are generally larger than in the left part of the diapason, project life-cycles are longer, so investor's demand for transparency, stability, predictability of investment regime is stronger, the urge for opportunities for more effective dispute settlement procedures is higher. And the latter are better provided for by the instruments of civil law, like international arbitration. Bigger reserves per single project plus legal stability provide more opportunities to survive within non-optimal taxation.

20 In 1995 we presented a package to the State Duma, consisting of two proposed laws for subsoil investment regimes: 1) PSA and 2) concessions. This was based on Art. 12 of the law 'On the subsoil' (1992) which allowed multiple uses of different types of petroleum arrangements in Russia. The PSA law has passed the Duma and came into force (though much spoiled by the Upper chamber of Russian Parliament in the conciliatory procedure); the law on concessions was vetoed by the Duma (see: www.konoplyanik.ru). Since then the new law "On concessions" was adopted by the State Duma and came into force, implementation of this mechanism for Russian subsoil investment was rejected.

The zone to the left from the central one at Figure 2.6 is the zone from medium and big to small fields' diapason. For the investors in this zone time does matter much more. So, most probably, they would prefer to use the licensing regime with exemptions as a dominant route for developing their projects: rather than long negotiations for optimal rent-sharing they would prefer to take the non-optimal but shorter route to start production. A shorter time-period within administrative law procedures is preferable for this type of project than fine-tuning within a longer time frame under civil law.

This means that in the center of the diapason is the zone where administrative or public law would be located and at its margins would be the two zones of civil law.

7 Vicious Circle

If we create the development curve of Russian oil tax regimes, presented in paragraph 3, inside the matrix of investment regimes in the subsoil, presented at Figure 2.4, we'll come to the illustration presented at Figure 2.8. It shows that after 20 years of search for optimal investment regime in the Russian subsoil, the state has come to the starting point: attempts to introduce differentiation within the dominant (de facto solely existing) licensing regime by some

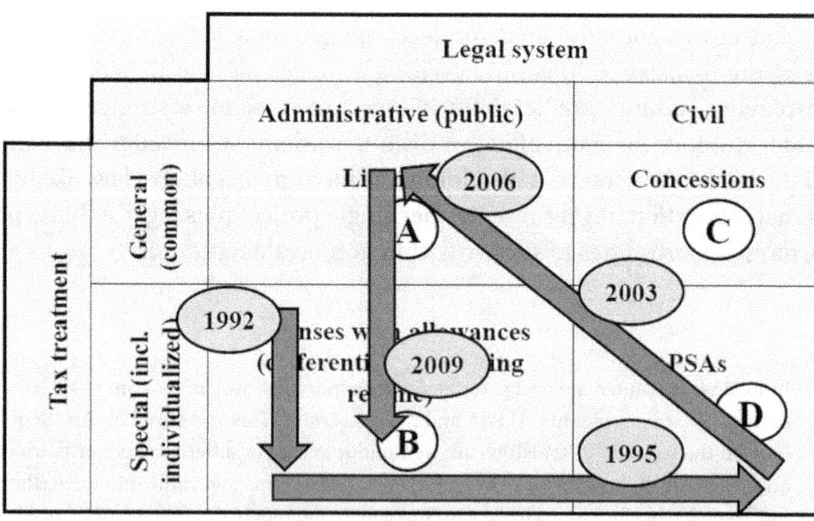

FIGURE 2.8 *Evolution of tax regimes in Russian subsoil: From systemic though limited differentiation (1990's) through withdrawal of differentiation (2000's), to chaotic and "handy" differentiation (2010's)*

groups of tax allowances within purely fiscal oriented oil taxation. Figure 2.8 shows that evolution of tax regimes in Russian subsoil has made sort of a circle: starting from systemic though limited differentiation in the 1990s, it has passed through resignation of differentiation in the 2000s and the search for differentiation in oil taxation in the 2010s has been taking place in a chaotic and handy, *e.g.* non-systemic manner. However, the lack of systematic mechanism can be considered as a system in action.

Dominant methods of providing differentiation in oil taxation differ between the early 1990s period and the present time. When subsoil legislation was in the early stage of development, limited differentiation was introduced through the royalty values established by law, while presently, such allowances have been presented through downgrades of MRPT and deductions from, up to full cancellation of, export duties, sometimes together with allowances in other taxes. Such deviation from a basically unfriendly investment climate creates a situation where the only way forward for a capital-intensive upstream project is the avenue of individual tax allowances. Thus, deviations or exemptions from subsoil licensing rules established in the early 2000s under the new oil tax system, became the dominant way forward with such projects, *i.e.* exceptions to the rules became the rule.[21] But any exception from the general

21 I would like to underline that this is not only a phenomenon for Russia, where deviation from the rule becomes the rule. In the EU, both its Second and Third energy packages establish the market rules which, while considered to be favourable for trade, have definitely discouraged investments, inclusive of such rules as unbundling of vertically integrated companies (VIC), mandatory third party access (MTPA), etc. The clever EU legislators envisaged this problem (lack of investment stimuli for long-term capital-intensive investment projects, especially in infrastructure developments such as pipelines, LNG import terminals, etc.) and established special clauses in the legislation providing for derogations from general EU rules for individual projects on a case by case basis. Thus legal procedures for such individual derogations were established by law (for instance in gas, it is Art. 21–22 of the Second and Art. 35–36 of the Third EU Gas Directives). Thus the way for obtaining derogations in the EU is established by law which is a better option compared to lack of legal procedure for obtaining derogations that we face today in Russia where it still need to be done in a handy manner. Though the best option is to improve investment climate (nondependent, whether in Russia or in the EU) in such a way, so there will be no more need in derogations from the legally established flexible and adaptable procedures. For more details on EU, see, for instance: A. Konoplyanik, Russia and the Third EU Energy Package: Regulatory Changes for Internal EU Energy Markets in Gas and Possible Consequences for Suppliers (Including Non-EU Suppliers) and Consumers, *International Energy Law Review*, 8 (2011) 24; А. Конопляник, «Уменьшить риски и неопределенности Третьего Энергопакета ЕС» (A. Konoplyanik. To reduce risks and uncertainties of the Third EU Energy Package), *Нефтегазовая Вертикаль* (*Oil*

rules, if not established by law, means a manipulative way of achieving an extra-legal advantage. This is a most risky and potentially corrupt way of doing business and it is not welcomed by reputable companies.

I think it is possible to mention at least some of the key names – proponents of this or that type of petroleum arrangement, that have influenced the 'see-saw' process of development of subsoil investment regimes in Russia depicted in Figure 2.8. This list reflects purely and solely my vision of the particular names and their roles. I will try to link them to the corresponding matrix of investment regimes.

Key proponents of the upper left quadrant in the matrix (licensing regime) have been: the Ministry of Finance (drafters headed by Deputy Minister S. Shatalov), former Yukos oil company and its former CEO M. Khodorkovsky (sponsor and promoter in the State Duma in late 1990s–early 2000s), President V. Putin (post-2000), and Minister of Economy G. Gref (post-2000).

Key proponents of the lower-left quadrant (licensing regime with differentiation) have been M. Gazeev and N. Volynskaya from the Fuel and Energy Independent Institute (TENI) in Moscow – key drafters of different concepts of differentiation through the whole period, and at the very initial stage the World Bank and its winner-consultant Houston University with the team headed by J. Hardi III, Ministry of Energy, Ministry of Natural Resources. This is currently a preferential government's approach to improve the Russian subsoil investment climate.

Key proponents of the upper-right quadrant (concessions in the subsoil) have been myself (as a leader) and my other colleague-drafters of the second version of concessions law, the "Yabloko" political party which initiated the idea of redrafting of the first concessions law in 1994, Ministry of Energy, and Ministry of Economy (in the 1990s, during pre-Gref times).

Key proponents of the lower-right quadrant (PSA regime) have been myself (as a leader) and my other colleague drafters of the PSA law,[22] Yukos (in pre-Khodorkovsky time) and other Russian oil companies in the mid/late-1990s, Petroleum Advisory Forum (PAF), Yabloko political party,[23] E. Gaidar

---

& Gas Vertical), 7 (2012) 79; A. Konoplyanik, 'Reducing risks and uncertainty of EU Third Energy Package', *Energy Dialogue. Review of International Energy Policy and Security*, 3 (2012) 12.

22 Both groups of my colleague – drafters include the same key people (M. Subbotin, I. Amirov, A. Averkin, E. Diachkova, V. Grushin L. Linnik, and S. Sosna) since we prepared the two laws – on concessions and on PSA – in a package within (and then developed in practice) the concept of multiple investment regimes in Russian subsoil.

23 And especially two of its major deputies in the State Duma – A. Melnikov and A. Mikhailov.

(especially in the 1990s, first in his government capacity and afterwards in the State Duma), President V. Putin (at least just immediately after his inauguration in 2000),[24] Ministry of Energy, Ministry of Natural Resources, and Ministry of Economy (in the 1990s, during pre-Gref times).

The composition of these groups of opponents and proponents of various models of oil taxation, and their comparative administrative powers explains the configuration of the current investment regime.

8 Which Way Forward

There are two possible ways of further development.

First – the Government will continue to stay within the so called "national investment regime" and so called "national tax system" – the terms proposed and promoted by former Yukos CEO M. Khodorkovsky (licensing regime based on public law, MRPT with flat rate and customs export duty). Necessity to advance oil and gas exploration and production to the remote areas such as Arctic offshore, Eastern Siberia, etc. will stimulate the government to provide in a "handy" manner individual exemptions from existing unified restrictive rules in order to make corresponding projects profitable and attract foreign investors – mostly major oil companies possessing advanced technologies and managerial skills (see Figure 2.9, Option 1). Second – to implement the concept of "multiple investment regimes" advocated in this paper (which is my preferred and long-argued option) (see Figure 2.9, Option 2).

The most recent statements of high-ranking Russian government officials have demonstrated their understanding that changes are inevitable. However, there is no consolidated view in the Russian government on this issue. On the one hand, the Ministry of Energy has recently proposed again (this time by the new Minister A. Novak, whose immediate previous position was deputy Minister of Finance) an introduction in the oil industry of the "windfall profit tax" or the "tax on financial results." According to the Minister, the fiscal pressure on the oil industry in Russia is one of the highest compared to other oil producing states. It is not the financial result, which is taxed and levied, but the absolute value of the gross revenue of the company. This helps to ease tax administration and tax collection, but this does not consider project

24 See, for instance, his presentation at the First International PSA-2000 conference in Yuzhno-Sakhalinsk at 1–2 September 2000 (see: *Нефтегазовая Вертикаль*, специальный выпуск «СРП-2000», 10 (2000) (*Oil & Gas Vertical*, Special Issue "PSA-2000", 10 (2000))).

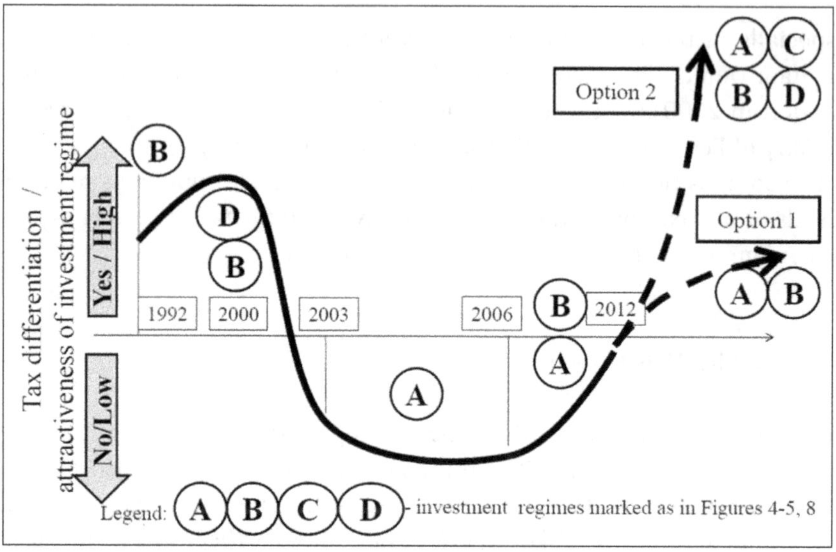

FIGURE 2.9 *Evolution of differentiation in tax treatment in Russian investment regimes for subsoil use: At the cross road*

economics and hinders inflow of investment in Russian oil. This also makes non-profitable both new oil production and continuation of development of existing fields. If nothing is changed this would lead to a decline in oil production in Russia.

But Deputy Prime Minister A. Dvorkovich considers that the new approach should be first tested on a few fields since he is not confident in the advantages of windfall profit taxation compared to the active oil tax regime with different concessions (temporary deviations) from its common rules. Among those, the following can be mentioned: individual concessions in flat-rated MRPT for some limited period of time at the project start-up to zero downgraded MRPT value, temporary downgrading of customs export duty up to full cancellation, nullified rates of some other taxes – such as property tax and VAT.

But recently long-standing Deputy Minister of Finance S. Shatalov (responsible for oil taxation all throughout his period in office for almost two decades) has stated that the idea of windfall profit tax (WPT) has lost its momentum.

In the recent years during the debate on differentiation of oil taxation, several alternatives were examined:

- Stay with MRPT, diminish export customs duty and introduce WPT,
- Cancel export customs duty and stay with MRPT and introduce WPT;
- Introduce WPT only for early stages of offshore fields development; and
- Other configurations of oil taxation system based on MRPT.

This discussion of alternatives makes it clear to me that there is a demand for differentiation of oil taxation and for diversity of choices for the investors so the rules are best adapted to particular project conditions. But there is no consensus in the decision-making circles on this.

In my view, the optimal way to radically improve the Russian subsoil investment climate would be to implement the concept of "multiple investment regimes" advocated in this paper (see Figure 2.9, "option 2").

How can these regimes be simultaneously implemented in Russia? My vision is presented in Figure 2.10 and outlined below.

First, the law "On PSA" should be revitalized (at least returned to its initial version).

Secondly, either the law "On concessions in the subsoil" should be specifically developed as separate from the existing law "On concessions" (which aims mostly for infrastructure concessions) or the existing law should be expanded to include subsoil use. Before making a choice, we need to determine whether the rules in the current concessions law are applicable and effective for the purpose of creating multiple subsoil investment regimes.

Thirdly, there is a regular bidding procedure for access to subsoil rights introduced by the law "On the Subsoil." This existing mechanism should be slightly adapted by giving investors the opportunity to choose between all available regimes in the bidding procedure. The state should prepare model

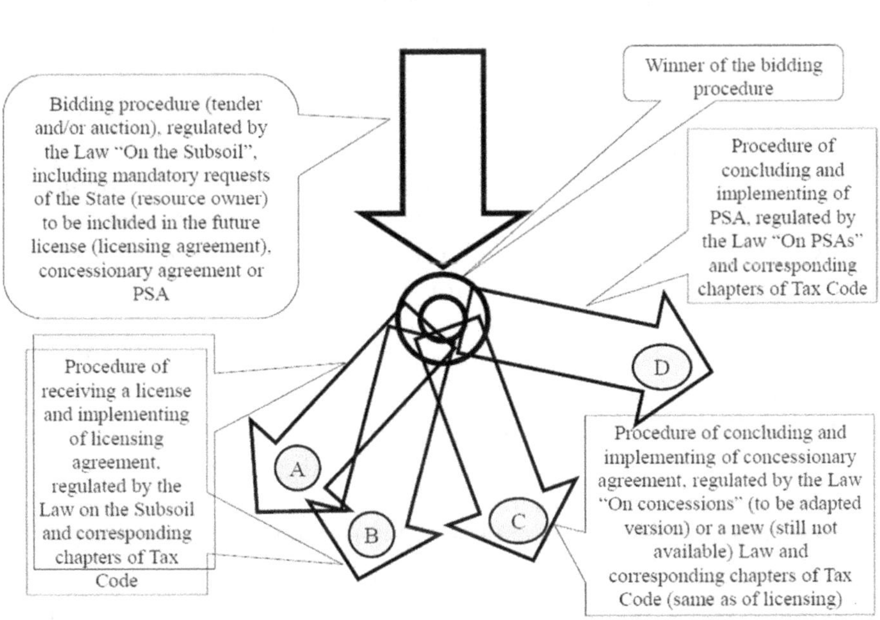

FIGURE 2.10 *Equal and competitive investment regimes in Russian subsoil use (historical proposal of author)*

licensing, PSA, and concession agreements and make these available to the potential bidders in advance. The open element in them (bidding criteria) should be the discounted value of rent collection by the state throughout the project life (contrary to today's practice with auctions where just initial financial payment matters). Today only the *de facto* financial capabilities of the bidders matter, not their technical capacities and skills which, in my view, is best demonstrated not by the sum of initial payment, but by an accumulated value of reserves extraction through the project life and corresponding mineral rent collection. Initial financial payment thus has nothing to do with the accumulated DCF for the state throughout the project life.

Rights for subsoil use are granted in Russia for 20 years (production) and a further 5 years (exploration). An investor applying for subsoil use should indicate in his bidding proposal not only this value of accumulated DCF for the host state through project life (the bigger will win) but also the type of investment regime of subsoil use under which he would like to develop this project. The rule should be that after the investor is granted rights for exploration and exploitation, he cannot change his choice of regime under which he has won the bid.

A winner indicating in his bidding proposal his willingness to operate under licensing system, will receive his license and licensing agreement and his future operations will be governed by the law "On the subsoil" including the tax system attributable to the licensing regime and governed by corresponding Chapters of the Tax Code. If his fields are located in the area where allowances to licensing regimes are applicable, investors working at these particular projects under the licensing regime may receive such specific area allowances (see Figure 2.10).

By the same token, a winning investor indicating in his bid his willingness to operate under a PSA regime will receive his PSA and future operations will be governed by the law "On PSA" and corresponding chapters of the Tax Code, including a system of rent collection characteristic of the PSA regime (see Figure 2.10).

The same procedure would be operative under the potential new law "On concessions in the subsoil."

Most probably, development of resources in complicated and remote areas (such as the Arctic offshore, for which Figure 2.11 is an illustration) will be organized in the form of consortia formed between Russian companies and major Western oil companies with available technologies, managerial skills, access to financial resource with lower cost of raising capital due to the high credit ratings these companies can provide compared to Russian companies

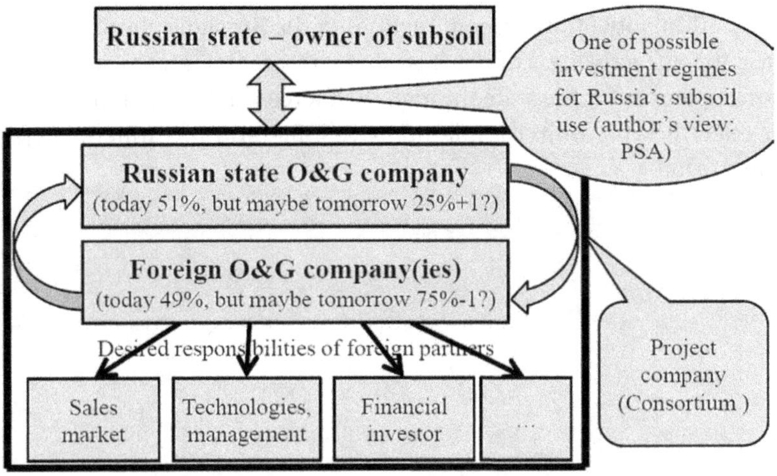

FIGURE 2.11 *Possible organizational structure of consortia for Russian Arctic offshore oil and gas development (within author's concept of multiple investment regimes for subsoil use)*

can provide, and other factors. In the case of Russian offshore development, Russian state companies, Rosneft and Gazprom, are by law the only companies which can be granted a license for subsoil use in offshore areas. Recent agreements on strategic alliances for development of Russian offshore resources, including the Arctic, between Rosneft and ExxonMobil, ENI, Statoil, and BP supports this expectation.

Agreements on subsoil use between the host state–resource owner (Russia) and consortia should be one of the arrangements offered in the "investment menu" and the competitive process should be organized based on the procedure presented in Figure 2.10. Consortia would be structured according to the specific competencies of its members and relative importance of various competencies for this or that particular project.

In my view, the current Russian legislation which demands majority control of Russian state companies–license holders in the consortia (no less than 50% plus one stock) leaving to foreign or non-Russian companies only minority participation, can be updated in the future by leaving with the state-controlled companies an ownership interest (25% plus one stock) which will be sufficient to block any decisions that the host state will consider as incompatible with the state's interests in regard to a particular project development. Besides, this will diminish the "financial burden" on the state-controlled companies in any such project by two-fold.

Such multiplicity of investment regimes in the Russian subsoil will strongly increase the attractiveness of the Russian investment climate with all its positive consequences for the state through the increased direct, indirect and multiplier effect flowing from capital-intensive long-term investment projects in Russian subsoil.

CHAPTER 3

International Law and Foreign Investment in Hydroelectric Industry: A Multidimensional Analysis

Attila Tanzi[1]

1 Introduction: A Multidimensional Analysis

Hydroelectric power stations account for about 20% of the world's electric energy. Nonetheless, one would argue that the international legal analysis applicable to foreign investment in the hydroelectric power industry would largely apply on par with foreign investment in the energy industry in general. Still, some specifics characterize this sector depending on the logistics of the investment, its transboundary relevance, or the country-specific economic regulatory framework.

Basically, hydroelectric energy partakes of the general division of the energy economic process into three sections, separately or cumulatively relevant, *i.e.*, electricity generation, transmission and distribution. Some characteristics particular to hydroelectric power may pertain to the fact that the hydrological nature of the generation process combines the actual building of the power plant with the construction of a dam which may have environmental and social impacts unknown to other energy related investment. The interpretation and application of the international rules pertinent to investment in the field have to take into consideration the specific regulatory setting of the host country. In this respect, the regulatory concerns pertaining to investment in hydroelectric energy apply on par with investment in electric energy proper. In many countries, particularly in the past, electric power companies used to own the whole infrastructure from generating stations to transmission and distribution infrastructure. For this reason, electric power has been viewed for a long time as a natural monopoly.[2] Market reform of the energy sector, especially through

1 The author is grateful to Dr. Federica Cristani and Dr. Cristina Contartese for their invaluable help and assistance in the bibliographical research.

2 International Energy Agency (IEA), *Security of Supply in Electricity Markets: Evidence and Policy Issues* (Paris: OECD Publishing, 2002), 9–10.

 | DOI 10.1163/9789004244719_005

the '90s,[3] has allowed private electric companies to be involved in one or more of such processes without having to own the entire infrastructure.

Economic, environmental and social cost-benefits considerations[4] provide the basic context for the international legal analysis that will be made below. On the one hand, hydroelectric energy offers a significant number of economic and even environmental advantages that are legally relevant:

- Namely, once the dam is built, the energy production process is not very expensive and produces little, or no pollution, while minimizing dependence on fossil fuels;
- The energy production process is generally more reliable than wind, solar or wave power;
- Electricity can be generated constantly;
- Water can be kept in store above the dam to cope with peaks in demand – hence, representing a significant potential for the export market – while hydroelectric power stations can quickly increase to full power;
- Many dams may also be used for flood control or irrigation, allowing for the costs of building and maintenance of the dam to be shared between several economic actors.

---

3 See, generally, R.W. Bacon and J. Besant-Jones, "Global Electric Power Reform, Privatization and Liberalization of the Electric Power Industry in Developing Countries", 26 *Annual Review Energy & the Environment* (2001), 331–359. See also World Bank, "Private Sector Development in the Electric Power Sector: a Joint OED/OEG/OEU Review of the World Bank Group's Assistance in the 1990s", *Report* No. 26427 (2003), 2, at http://documents.worldbank.org/curated/en/2003/07/2485412/private-sector-development-electric-power-sector (accessed 24 October 2013); J. Lampietti (ed.), "Power's Promise: Electricity Reforms in Eastern Europe and Central Asia", *World Bank Working Paper No 40* (2004). From an international investment law perspective, see, for all, P.D. Cameron, *International Energy Investment Law* (Oxford: Oxford University Press, 2010), particularly at 20 ff.

4 See, amongst others, N.K. Dubash (ed.), *Power Politics: Equity and Environment in Electricity Reform* (Washington: World Resources Institute, 2002), 10 and 21; D. Touche Tohmatsu, "Sustainable Power Sector Reform in Emerging Markets: Financial Issues and Options", *Joint World Bank/USAID Policy Paper* (18 June 2004) at http://www.energytoolbox.org (accessed 24 October 2013); D.G. Victor and T.C. Heller (eds.), *Political Economy of Power Sector Reform: the Experience of Five Major Developing Countries* (Cambridge: Cambridge University Press, 2007). See also on a case-study basis, R. Kozulj and N. di Sbroiavacca, "Assessment of Energy Sector Reforms: Case-Studies from Latin America", *Energy for Sustainable Development* 8 (2004), 74; R.V. Lindo, "Hydroelectric Power Production in Costa Rica and the Threat of Environmental Disaster Through CAFTA", *Boston College International & Comparative Law Review* 29 (2006), 297.

On the other hand, the major factor accounting for the economic, environmental and social disadvantages of hydropower lies in the fact that, usually, hydroelectric power plants need dams. The latter are very expensive to build, while large ones flood large areas upstream resulting in the reduction of land for agriculture and pasture and, often, also in the displacement of people, sometimes adversely affecting pieces of cultural heritage. Water quality and quantity downstream is usually also significantly affected by dams through the adverse effect on plant, animal and human life. Furthermore, most of the advantages of hydroelectric power referred to above may be curbed by the potential effects of climate change, with special regard to drought. From the legal standpoint of the present contribution, the above may involve measures taken by the Public Administration of host States that may have a significant bearing on foreign investors in the field and, therefore, on the application of international investment law. Likewise, the above factual scenario may have a significant transboundary impact, hence, triggering the relevance of international water law. Despite extraordinary economic, infrastructural, engineering, legal and administrative difficulties and complexities, investment in the hydroelectric energy sector has nonetheless attracted a considerable flow of foreign capital.[5]

Given the multifaceted relevance of foreign investment in this field for the purpose of international law, the following legal analysis will address the multidimensional character of the relevant international regulatory framework, emphasizing the different actors involved in the different legal relationships stemming therefrom. Accordingly, the analysis will be four-fold.

The first and most evident applicable international legal dimension to be addressed will be that of international investment law deriving from international investment treaties (IITs), bilateral investment treaties (BITs) and free trade agreements (FTAs) or the Energy Charter Treaty (ECT).[6]

As a matter of course, given its subjective scope of application, this part of the analysis will refer to the relationship between the host State and the

5 See Cameron above note 3, 20. However, as emphasized by Erik Woodhouse, based on World Bank data (World Bank Public Participation in Infrastructure Database at http://ppi.worldbank.org), "[f]rom a high of $46 billion in 1996, private infrastructure investment in emerging economies dwindled to $15 billion by 2003, and is only recently beginning to show signs of recovery" (E. Woodhouse, "The Obsolescing Bargain Redux? Foreign Investment in the Electric Power Sector in Developing Countries", *International Law and Politics* 38 (2005–2006), 122).

6 Energy Charter Treaty, signed at Lisbon, 17 December 1994, 2080 *U.N.T.S* (2002), 95–630.

foreign investors engaging in the construction and, or, operation of the dams and plants, hence in the production and/or in the distribution of electricity.

The primary dispute settlement context will accordingly be that of international investment arbitration. The second international legal perspective of the present analysis will be that of the body of international law of human rights, both in combination with international investment law as interpreted and applied by investment arbitration tribunals[7] and as a self-contained body of law as interpreted and applied by the human rights courts.[8] The third body of international law relevant to the present study, even though its relevance may appear less obvious, will be that of international water law.[9] Here, the basic principles of State responsibility as well as those of State liability in a transboundary context[10] will be considered. Even though they pertain to inter-State relations they may, nonetheless, affect private investment related to the construction and operation of dams and hydropower plants. Indeed, as it will be illustrated below, the position of private foreign investors may be significantly affected by the interpretation and application of the relevant international rules by the States involved, or by inter-State adjudication. The fourth and last legal dimension to be addressed by the present study will be that of the internalization of the legal accountability for the transboundary harm caused by private operators in terms. To that end, consideration will be given to the international and domestic regulation of civil liability issues, with spe-

---

7 See, generally, C. Reiner and C. Schreuer, "Human Rights and International Investment Arbitration", in P.M. Dupuy, E.U. Petersmann and F. Francioni (eds.), *Human Rights in International Investment Law and Arbitration* (Oxford: Oxford University Press, 2009). See also below note 38.

8 See R. Teitel and R.L. Howse, "Cross-Judging: Tribunalization in a Fragmented but Interconnected Global Order", 41 *NYU Journal of International Law and Politics* (2009), 959 ff. and C. Tomuschat, "The European Court of Human Rights and Investment Protection", in C. Binder, U. Kriebaum, A. Reinisch and S. Wittich (eds.), *International Investment Law for the 21st Century: Essays in Honour of Christoph Schreuer* (Oxford: Oxford University Press, 2009), 654 ff. In the latter contribution, the Author, in addressing the investor's options for submitting their claims to human rights bodies, reaches the conclusion that only the European Court of Human Rights may offer effective remedies.

9 See, generally, S.C. McCaffrey, *The Law of International Watercourses* (Oxford: Oxford University Press, 2°ed., 2007), A. Tanzi and M. Arcari, *The UN Convention of 1997 on International Watercourses. A Framework for Sharing* (London-The Hague-Boston: Kluwer Law International, 2001) and A. Tanzi, "Furthering International Water Law or Making a New Body of Law on Transboundary Aquifers? An Introduction", *International Community Law Review* 13 (2011), 193–208.

10 A. Tanzi, "Liability for Lawful Acts", in R. Wolfrüm (ed.), *Max Planck Encyclopaedia of Public International Law* (Oxford: Oxford University Press, 2012).

cial regard to the determination of the applicable law and of the competent national courts.[11]

A few concluding remarks will follow, highlighting the entanglement between the different legal dimensions involved in the present analysis.

2 On International Investment Law and Hydroelectric Industry

2.1 *As Exemplary of the Operation of International Investment Law*

International investment law can be said to apply to hydroelectric industry within the general template of this body of law, obviously with some specificities as will be shown in due course. In line with the above general statement, it is telling how in his overview of the "Changing Dimensions of International Investment Law", Professor Vaughan Lowe referred precisely to disputes concerning the electricity industry in order to illustrate the conciliation and arbitration functions of the International Centre for Settlement of Investment Disputes (ICSID)[12] or the Multilateral Investment Guarantee Agency (MIGA)'s mediation role as being exemplary of the way they would apply to foreign investment disputes generally.[13]

Since the electricity sector pertains to the public utility sector, foreign investment comes into play upon privatization. One is to take into account different patterns of privatization as occurring particularly since the '90s, especially in Latin America and Eastern Europe.[14] Also, one is to consider with which fraction of the hydroelectric chain the foreign investment is concerned, from construction, or operation, of the dam or of the power plant to the transmission and distribution services. A case-specific approach will be required in the application of the fairly general international legal framework, also taking

---

11 See below note 141.

12 "There have been only a handful of [ICSID] conciliations, and the most recent, involving a French electricity company and the Government of Togo, ended in failure and the dispute was referred to arbitration" (V. Lowe, "Changing Dimensions of International Investment Law. Lectures delivered at the Chinese Academy of International Law in Xiamen, China, in September 2006", *Oxford Legal Studies Research Paper No. 4/2007* (March 2007), 30).

13 Referring to MIGA's role as a mediator when investment disputes arise, Professor Lowe emphasized by way of example how "[i]t did this in relation to a dispute arising from investments that it had guaranteed in the electricity industry in China in the 1990s; for example. MIGA intervened and brokered a settlement which preserved the long-term relationship between the parties" (Ibid., 32).

14 *Supra* notes 3 and 4.

into consideration, the domestic economic and regulatory settings pertaining to the sector in point.[15]

If one refers directly to specific case law bearing on foreign investment related to hydroelectricity industry – such as, the 2005 *Impregilo v. Pakistan*,[16] the 2009 *Cementownia "Nowa Huta" SA v. Turkey*[17] and *Europe Cement Investment and Trade SA v. Turkey*,[18] or the 2011 *Libananco v. Turkey*[19] awards on jurisdiction, which were declined in all such cases – traditionally general investment issues emerge. These issues include the nationality of the investor, the definition of investment, the consent to arbitration, and the relationship between State contracts and BITs violations, which appear to have been treated on par with the generality of foreign investment disputes.

2.2 *A Tentative Adjudication Policy Consideration Arising out of Recent Arbitration Case Law*

The relative dearth of investment case law on the merits in the area under consideration appears to show that the kind of investment disputes at issue, when they have not been disposed of by an award rejecting jurisdiction, or admissibility, over the claim,[20] largely tend to be terminated by out-of-court settlements. These are usually formalized by an order taking note of the discontinuance of the dispute issued by the Arbitration Tribunal originally seized pursuant to ICSID Arbitration Rule 44.[21]

---

15 See the exemplary domestic sceneries emerging from the studies referred to ibid. As a matter of fact, while privatization was expected to increase competition, energy production and distribution has often been in the hands of very few private investors providing them with little incentive to improve efficiency and distribution rates. This has been the root cause behind many foreign investment disputes eventually submitted to investment arbitration.

16 *Impregilo S.p.A. v. Islamic Republic of Pakistan*, ICSID Case No. ARB/03/3, Decision on Jurisdiction, 22 April 2005, 12 *ICSID Re*(2007), 245 ff.

17 *Cementownia "Nowa Huta" S.A. v. Republic of Turkey*, ICSID Case No. ARB(AF)/06/2, Award, 17 September 2009.

18 *Europe Cement Investment & Trade S.A. v. Republic of Turkey*, ICSID Case No. ARB(AF)/07/2, Award, 13 August 2009.

19 *Libananco Holdings Co. Limited v. Republic of Turkey*, ICSID Case No. ARB/06/8, Award, 2 September 2011.

20 *Zhinvali Development Ltd. v. Republic of Georgia*, ICSID Case No. ARB/00/1, Award, 24 June 2003, 10 *ICSID Reports* (2006), 3–113.

21 *Empresa Nacional de Electricidad S.A. v. Argentine Republic*, ICSID Case No. ARB/99/4, Order taking note of the discontinuance, 8 February 2001; *Impregilo S.p.A. v. Islamic Republic of Pakistan*, ICSID Case No. ARB/03/3, Decision on Jurisdiction, 22 April 2005, 12 *ICSID Re*(2007), 245 ff and Order of discontinuance of the proceeding, 25 September 2005.

An example of the above consideration may be found in the out-of-court settlement of the investment dispute concerning the assets involving hydroelectric facilities are *AbitibiBowater*.[22] There, the US Corporation, after claiming to have been expropriated of its assets in Canada in 2008 without compensation, withdrew its Notice of arbitration and Statement of Claim under North American Free Trade Agreement (NAFTA) Chapter 11 in August 2010,[23] seeking redress in the amount of US $500 million, upon settlement of US $130 million.[24] Indeed, the Canadian Province of Newfoundland, as a reaction to the Company's announcement to wind up a hailing business had adopted in 2008, the "Abitibi Act," which expropriated the majority of the company's provincial assets.[25] In part, such a legislative measure had cancelled water and hydroelectric contracts and agreements between the province and Abitibi, on-going legal proceedings Abitibi had against the province and blocked Abitibi's access to Newfoundland's courts.[26]

A tentative adjudication-policy consideration deriving from the above trend may lead one to find the reasons behind this trend in a host of features highly characteristic of the kind of investment under consideration, even though not exclusive of them. Namely, those consisting of the domestic economic, financial and regulatory setting of the investment sector in point which may differ on a case-by-case basis. Generally, one should point to the highly capital intensive nature of this kind of investment and to the wealth in number and complexity of the actors interacting with the foreign investor, mostly in the financial sector, that can be both private and institutional, domestic and foreign.

Indeed, practice shows that "ramification of investment in the hydropower sector is equity investment by the entrepreneurs with complementary debt financing from financial intermediaries [...]."[27] Long-term infrastructure investment of this kind usually involves private, domestic, commercial and national banks as well as foreign financial institutions, such as the World Bank.

One may think of "Governmental Power Developments Funds (GPDF)" supported by the World Bank. In some countries, the fact that governmental funds

---

22 *AbitibiBowater Inc., v. Government of Canada*, NAFTA (case pending).

23 North American Free Trade Agreement (US-Mexico-Canada), signed on 17 December 1992, 32 ILM 3 (1993), 605–799.

24 Press release of 24 August 2010, available at http://www.italaw.com (accessed 24 October 2013).

25 The Abitibi-Consolidated Rights and Assets Act, 16 December 2008, available at http://www.assembly.nl.ca (accessed 24 October 2013).

26 Ibid.

27 R.S. Shresta, "Investment in Hydropower Sector: Opportunity and Risk", *Hydro Nepal: Journal of Water, Energy and Environment* 1 (2007), 46 (internal footnotes omitted).

for energy are administered by commercial bank accounts for the complex promiscuity between the public and private components of the local financial regulatory settings. At the same time, the intervention by other governmental entities usually vested with an environmental competence is often appropriately required for the clearance of the loan by governmental entities.[28] Such settings widen the scope of the host State's public articulations over which due diligence burdens are spread that pertain to power projects, with special – though not exclusive – regard to hydroelectric projects.

Such a complex infrastructural, financial and institutional background, implying a wide involvement of the host State's public sector wholly, or partly, in foreign investment – often associated with funding by international financial institutions – may provide a deterrence for host States with respect to measures adversely affecting such measures.[29] It is arguable that, when such measures are taken nonetheless, the all-or-nothing scenario offered by international arbitration is one which is hardly regarded as desirable by the diversified host State and international guarantor or other participating States in the project. Such a picture emerges from the hydroelectric sector, with special relevance to the construction and operation of dams – but it is not unique and shares some of its features with the energy sector at large.

2.3 *The Structural Complexity of the Chain of Actors and of the Activities Involved in this Sector and the Definition of Investment*

The involvement in a given hydrological project of a high number of stakeholders referred to above, may take the form of direct participation in the foreign energy company. In fact, the above-mentioned complexities add to the situation which presents itself when foreign or local investors associate themselves with new affiliates or create subsidiary companies, usually linked to BITs or double taxation "shopping."

This certainly accounts for the fact that many cases pertaining to the sector under consideration involve, more often than not, the classic issue of whether

28 See ibid. with specific reference to Nepal as an exemplary case study.

29 As put it by Cameron, "These [energy] companies are [...] prone to involving other investors as stakeholders to deter host States from making adverse decisions. This participation by 'prominent victims' can take one or more of four main forms. It can involve the participation of international financial institution such as the World Bank or the European Bank for Reconstruction and Development (EBRD), either directly or as guarantor of commercial loans; political risk insurance such as the US OPIC; co-investment in the form of equity with an international financial institution; and involvement of commercial banks, which have a stake in financing host States around the world" (*supra* note 3 21, footnotes omitted).

the investor and the investment, qualify for the legal protection afforded by international investment law.[30] The problem under consideration encompasses both the issue of the subjective international character of the investor and the objective definition of investment under the international applicable law, which often represent two sides of the same coin.[31]

It is arguable that international investment law affords its protection to a fairly long string of direct and indirect foreign investors that may be involved in a hydroelectric power project. However, the cut-off point remains open for discussion. While foreign investment falling within the scope of the general ICSID system remains subject to the well-known problems of the definition of "investment" under Article 25 of the Washington Convention,[32] the scope of protection appears to be extremely wide when the investment falls under the reach of ECT. Indeed, Article 1, paragraphs 5 and 6, of the latter covers a very wide range of economic activities in the field of energy – from production to trading, and of assets related thereto, to intangible ones such as moveable property, property rights to returns and permits concerning energy-related activity. In particular, it should be noted that Article 1, paragraph 6, defines covered "investments" as investment associated with an "economic activity in the energy sector" which is further defined in paragraph 5 as an economic activity concerning the exploration, extraction, refining, production, storage, land transport, transmission, distribution, trade, marketing or sale of Energy Materials or Products. Such materials and products are defined in paragraph 4 as including the items listed in Annex EM. The latter refers to nuclear energy, coal, natural gas, petroleum and petroleum products, and "electrical energy."[33]

30 See generally, R. Dolzer and C. Schreuer, *Principles of International Investment Law* (Oxford: Oxford University Press, 2°ed. 2012), 44–78.

31 Exemplary of the relevance of the determination as to whether the investor falls within the subjective scope of the applicable investment regulation for the purposes of the assessment of the existence of an "investment" under the same investment law, see, amongst others, *SD Myers Inc. v. Canada*, NAFTA/UNCITRAL, First Partial Award, 13 November 2000 (particularly at paras. 226–231). See also *Pope & Talbot, Inc. v. Government of Canada*, NAFTA/UNCITRAL, Interim Award, 26 January 2000, para. 26. For a general comment, B. Legum, "Defining Investment and Investor: Who is Entitled to Claim", *Arbitration international* 22 (2006), 521–526.

32 See C. Schreuer, L. Malintoppi, A. Reinisch and A. Sinclair (eds.), *ICSID Convention. A Commentary* (Cambridge: Cambridge University Press, 2°ed., 2009), 71 ff and, more recently, S. Kang, "Definition of Investment under ICSID Convention: did we go beyond Salini?", in T.J. Weiler and I.A. Laird (eds.) *Investment Treaty Arbitration and International Law. Vol.* 5, (Huntington: JurisNet, 2012), 153–187.

33 See Article 1(4)(6) of the ECT.

As emphasized in *Plama Consortium vs. Bulgaria* (2005), the ECT provides "a covered investor an almost unprecedented remedy for its claims against a host State."[34] This is not an unlimited cover, as it did not prevent the decline of jurisdiction in *Libanaco*, or in the other applications of the "Uzan saga" which, as we shall see below, eventually ended before the European Court of Human Rights (ECHR) to no avail for the applicant investor.[35]

A similarly extensive approach, though in more synthetic terms, is to be found in most BITs, as well as in Article 1139 of the NAFTA.[36] It was on the basis of the latter provision that in *AbitibiBowater* the Tribunal entertained its jurisdiction before the out-of-court settlement referred to above with regard to the hydro-electric facilities, as well as to the rights stemming from a contract with the local Public Administration for electric power generation.[37]

The above extensive approach to the definition of investment, in combination with the structural complexity of the chain of actors and of the activities involved in this sector, increase the chances of cross-interests between foreign investors and local ones, private and institutional. One would make the case that when a dispute arises, this may be a significant factor for preferring, on a balance, an amicable settlement, despite the jurisdictional competence of investment tribunals.

---

34 *Plama Consortium Limited v. Republic of Bulgaria*, ICSID Case No. ARB/03/24, Decision on Jurisdiction, 8 February 2005, para. 141.

35 See below section 3.2.5.

36 For the relevant part, it reads as follows: "investment means: a) an enterprise; (b) an equity security of an enterprise; (c) a debt security of an enterprise (i) where the enterprise is an affiliate of the investor, or (ii) where the original maturity of the debt security is at least three years, but does not include a debt security, regardless of original maturity, of a State enterprise; (d) a loan to an enterprise (i) where the enterprise is an affiliate of the investor, or (ii) where the original maturity of the loan is at least three years, but does not include a loan, regardless of original maturity, to a State enterprise; (e) an interest in an enterprise that entitles the owner to share in income or profits of the enterprise; (f) an interest in an enterprise that entitles the owner to share in the assets of that enterprise on dissolution, other than a debt security or a loan excluded from subparagraph (c) or (d); (g) real estate or other property, tangible or intangible, acquired in the expectation or used for the purpose of economic benefit or other business purposes; and (h) interests arising from the commitment of capital or other resources in the territory of a Party to economic activity in such territory, such as under (i) contracts involving the presence of an investor's property in the territory of the Party, including turnkey or construction contracts, or concessions, or (ii) contracts where remuneration depends substantially on the production, revenues or profits of an enterprise [...]" (Article 1139 of the NAFTA).

37 *Supra* note 22.

3 On the Application of Human Rights Law to Hydro-Electric Industry and Its Potential Impact on Foreign Investment in this Area

Foreign investment in hydropower may easily become involved in the increasingly relevant legal problems pertaining to the interpretation and application of international investment law in connection with international human rights law.[38] This may occur in relation to the application of international investment law, or in isolation within a human rights regime. On the one hand, the operation of the hydroelectric utility is to meet the requirements provided for under a generally recognized human right to access to electricity, either as an autonomous human right, or insofar as ancillary to the right to life, and also in terms of the right to an adequate standard of living under Article 25 of the UN Universal Declaration of Human Rights and Article 11 of the UN Covenant on Economic Social and Cultural Rights.[39] On the other hand, in the various stages of the process leading to the construction and operation of a hydropower plant, including the related dams, it may occur that the entrepreneurial conduct infringes upon other human rights on par with other foreign

---

38 See, generally, *supra* note 7. See also P.M. Dupuy, F. Francioni and E.U. Petersmann (ed.), *Human Rights in International Investment Law and Arbitration* (Oxford: Oxford University Press, 2009), A.A. Faruque, "Mapping the Relationship Between Investment Protection and Human Rights", *The Journal of World Investment & Trade* 11 (2010), 539–560; C.A. Meckenstock, *Investment Protection and Human Rights Regulation: Two Aims in a Relationship of Solvable Tension* (Baden-Baden: Nomos, 2010), B. Simma, "Foreign Investment Arbitration: A Place for Human Rights?", *The International and Comparative Law Quarterly* 60 (2011), 573–597, S.L. Karamanian, "Human Rights Dimensions of International Law", in E. De Wet and J. Vidmar (eds.), *Hierarchy in International Law: The Place of Human Rights*, (Oxford: Oxford University Press, 2012), 4–6, A. Tanzi, "Trends in International Investment Arbitration and the Protection of Human Rights in the Public Services Sector", in N. Boschiero, T. Scovazzi, C. Pitea and C. Ragni (eds.) *International Courts and the Development of International Law. Essays in Honour of Tullio Treves*, (The Hague: Springer, 2013), 587 ff and *id.* "Public Interest Concerns in International Investment Arbitration in the Water Services Sector: Problems and Prospects for an Integrated Approach", in T. Treves, F. Seatzu and S. Trevisanut (eds.), *Foreign Investment, International Law and Common Concerns*, (Abingdon: Routledge, 2013), 308–324.

39 See, generally on the right to access to energy, A.J. Bradbrook and J.G. Gardam, "Placing the Access to Energy Services within a Human Rights Framework", *Human Rights Quarterly* 28 (2006), 389–415. See more specifically in relation to access to electricity, S. Tully, "The Human Right to Access to Electricity", *Electricity Journal* 19 (2006), 30–39 and *id.*, "Access to electricity as a human right", *Netherlands Quarterly of Human Rights* 24 (2006), 557–587. See also below note 60.

investment activities. As will be briefly shown below, one specific set of human rights that is often characteristically endangered by investment in hydroelectricity is the one pertaining to the basic human rights of indigenous populations, particularly in relation to their displacement due to the building of dams.

3.1 *On the Actual and Potential Impact of Human Rights Law on Investment Law Relevant to Investment in Hydroelectricity*

International investment arbitration has long neglected the relevance of human rights law for the purposes of the application of international investment law.[40] When the former body of law may have had an impact on the investment arbitration adjudication policy, this appears to have been the result of implicit reasoning.[41] Only recently, particularly with the *Suez*[42] and *Saur*[43] cases, the above trend appears to have been reversed, at least in principle.[44]

Indeed, the present author has hailed the *Suez* award as "a turning point in the case-law on the subject," insofar as the relationship between the two bodies of international law at issue has been explicitly addressed.[45] At the same time, some dissatisfaction has also been expressed by the present writer in relation to the fact that such an explicit statement of principle has not been fully applied in substance, particularly looking at the decision in *Saur* two years later.[46] The two decisions under consideration, with special regard to the latter, while considering the two bodies of law in point as mutually compatible, end up treating them as distinct, hence falling short of interpreting and applying a relationship of complementarity.[47]

Consequently, emphasis is placed on the host State as the subject who is to comply with both bodies of law at the same time: namely, with its investment

40 *Supra* note 38.

41 See A. Tanzi, "On Balancing Foreign Investment Interests with Public Interests in Recent Arbitration Case Law in the Public Utilities Sector", *The Law and Practice of International Courts and Tribunals* 11 (2012), 52 ff and *id.* "Public Interest Concerns in International Investment Arbitration in the Water Services Sector", in Treves, Seatzu, and Trevisanut, *supra* note 38, 308–324.

42 *Suez, Sociedad General de Aguas de Barcelona S.A. and Vivendi Universal S.A. v. Argentina Republic*, ICSID case ARB/03/19.

43 *SAUR International SA v. Republic of Argentina*, ICSID Case ARB/04/4.

44 See Tanzi, "On Balancing Foreign Investment Interests with Public Interests in Recent Arbitration Case Law in the Public Utilities Sector", *supra* note 41, 52.

45 Ibid., 55.

46 *SAUR International SA v. Republic of Argentina, supra* note 43, Decision on Jurisdiction and Liability, 6 June 2012, para. 331. See Tanzi, "Public Interest Concerns", *supra* note 41.

47 See below note 52.

obligations *vis-à-vis* the foreign investor and with human rights law *vis-à-vis* its population. There is no denying that host States are equally bound by both sets of obligations. While this is self-evident before an investment tribunal with respect to investment law, the same holds true with respect to human rights obligations before investment tribunals and human rights courts, alike.[48]

However, one may detect an increasing trend towards looking at the legal relationship between host States and foreign investors in more symmetrical terms.[49] While, obviously, it would remain primarily for arbitrators to assess the lawfulness of conduct undertaken *vis-à-vis* foreign investors by host States in their position as defendant – whereas the reverse would be exceptional –[50] it appears appropriate and in conformity with the rationale of the majority of BITs and investment related agreements to base such an assessment on the general principles of proportionality, reciprocity and good faith in more symmetrical terms than so far interpreted and applied in investment arbitration (*i.e.* also considering the conduct of foreign investors and the legitimate expectations of host States about it).

3.2 *A Symmetrical Interpretation and Application of the General Principle of Proportionality in Terms of Reciprocity and Good Faith*

Proportionality in investment arbitration has been basically applied so far to the relationship between the adverse effect on the foreign investment and the benefits for the public interest deriving from the regulatory measures complained of.[51] However, it is arguable that an appropriate application of the

48 *Supra* section 1.

49 See Simma, *supra* note 38, Tanzi, "Public Interest Concerns in International Investment Arbitration in the Water Services Sector", *supra* note 41 and the some jurisprudential indications slowly emerging to that effect, as well as the conventional and soft-law practice here referred to.

50 See, for the appropriateness of more host State claims, G. Laborde, "The Case for Host State Claims in Investment Arbitration", *Journal of International Dispute Settlement* 1 (2010), 97–122.

51 See the case law, especially in the gas supply cases of *S.D. Myers v. Canada*, NAFTA/UNCITRAL, First Partial Award, 13 November 2000, para. 281, *CME Czech Republic B.V. v. Czech Republic*, UNCITRAL, Partial Award, 13 September 2001, 9 *ICSID Reports* (2006) 121 ff, paras. 326, 330, *Técnicas Medioambientales Tecmed, S.A. v. United Mexican States*, ICSID Case No. ARB(AF)/00/2, Award, 29 May 2003, 19 *ICSID Rev. – FILJ* 1 (2004), 158 ff, para. 115, *CMS Gas Transmission Company v. Argentine Republic*, ICSID Case No. ARB/01/08, Award, 12 May 2005, 11 *ICSID Re*(2007), 237 ff, para. 260, *Methanex Corp. United States of America*, NAFTA, Final Award on Jurisdiction and Merits, 3 August 2005, 44 *International Legal Materials* 6 (2005), 1345 ff, Part IV, Chapter D, para. 7, *Saluka v.*

principle of proportionality should also encompass the relationship between the degree of compliance with the basic principles of due diligence on the part of the host State, on the one hand, and by the corporate actor, on the other. This approach to the principle of proportionality together with that of reciprocity is grounded on the articulation of the principle of good faith in relation to the ancillary principles of legitimate expectations and due diligence.

One could question the legal grounds for evaluating the conduct of a foreign private operator by the yardstick of the general principles of international law regulating the relationship between States and of human rights obligations. However, since foreign investors benefit from the rights stemming from an international treaty concluded by their State of nationality with the host State, the scope of the same rights is to be assessed on the basis of the rules of interpretation generally applicable to treaty interpretation. Therefore, the relevant BITs, not only will have to be interpreted and applied on the basis of Article 31.1 of the Vienna Convention on the Law of Treaties whereby a treaty must be interpreted "in the light of its object and purpose" – usually providing for the fostering of cooperation and the enhancement of economic prosperity or development of the contracting Parties – but also on the basis of Article 31.3.c, according to which the provisions of a treaty should be interpreted taking into account "any relevant rules of international law applicable in the relations between the parties," hence, also the general principles of international law. It may be noted in passing that the above interpretative approach fully conforms to the recent systemic approach put forward by the International Law

Czech Republic, UNCITRAL case, Partial Award, 17 March 2006, para. 262, *Azurix Corv. Argentina Republic*, ICSID Case No. ARB/01/12, Award, 14 July 2006, 43 *International Legal Materials* 2 (2004), 262 ff, para. 310, *LG&E Energy Corp./LG&E Capital Corp./LG&E International Inc. v. Argentine Republic*, ICSID Case No. ARB/02/1, Decision on Liability, 3 October 2006, 46 *International Legal Materials* 1 (2007), 40 ff, par. 189, *Continental Casualty Company v. Argentine Republic*, ICSID Case No. ARB/03/9, Award, 5 September 2008, par. 227 and *Glamis Gold Ltd. v. United States of America*, UNCITRAL, Award, 8 June 2009, 48 *International Legal Materials* (2009), 1038 ff, par. 356. See in general J. Krommendijk and J. Morijn, " 'Proportional' by What Measure(s)? Balancing Investor Interests and Human Rights by Way of Applying the Proportionality Principle in Investor-State Arbitration", in P.M. Dupuy, F. Francioni and E.U. Petersmann (eds.), *Human Rights in International Investment Law and Arbitration* (Oxford: Oxford University Press, 2009), 422–450 and B. Kingsbury and S. Schill, "Public Law Concepts to Balance Investors' Rights with State Regulatory Actions in the Public Interest – The Concept of Proportionality", in S. Schill (ed.) *International Investment Law and Comparative Public Law* (Oxford: Oxford University Press, 2010), 75.

Commission (ILC) in its work on the fragmentation of international law and endorsed by the UN General Assembly.[52]

Furthermore, since the assessment of the legitimate expectations of the foreign investor is often relevant in international investment arbitration in order to substantiate its rights,[53] the same should apply in order to limit its rights when its expectations are not legitimate or are based on negligence. In line with this reasoning, in *Biwater*, the Tribunal addressed the issue "whether the host State breached specific representations the investor reasonably relied on" and, recalling *Saluka*,[54] emphasized that "[t]he question is not what the investor would prefer to have happened, or even what the investor *subjectively* expected to happen, but what the investor was *objectively* entitled to expect."[55] To that end, the Tribunal stressed that "all relevant circumstances, including the governing municipal law, should be considered in determining what was objectively reasonable [including] the economic and other circumstances generally prevailing in Tanzania."[56] Among such circumstances, it appears appropriate to encompass the human rights obligations of the host State pertaining to the public utilities in which the foreign investor has engaged or would engage.[57]

3.2.1 Elements of Guidance for the Assessment of Compliance with Due Diligence by the Relevant Actors in Terms of Proportionality

When considering the equitable and proportionate regulatory criteria to be followed in the assessment of the reciprocal conduct of the foreign investor and the State, apart from the merely procedural context,[58] factual and legal imbalances are apparent and several. While from the domestic legal standpoint, at

52 See Report of the Study Group of the International Law Commission (ILC), "Fragmentation of International Law: Difficulties arising from the Diversification and Expansion of International Law" (UN Doc. A/CN.4/L.702), 18 July 2006, para. 8.

53 *Técnicas Medioambientales Tecmed, S.A. v. United Mexican States, supra* note 51, para. 154. See, amongst others, S. Fietta, "Expropriation and the Fair and Equitable Standard: The Developing Role of Investors' Expectations", 23 *Journal of International Arbitration* (2006), 375.

54 *Saluka v. Czech Republic, supra* note 48, para. 304.

55 *Biwater Gauff (Tanzania) Ltd. v. United Republic of Tanzania*, ICSID Case No. ARB/05/22, Award, 24 July 2008, para. 566.

56 Ibid.

57 *Supra* note 41.

58 See C. Schreuer, L. Malintoppi, A. Reinisch and A. Sinclair (eds), *Commentary to the ICSID Convention* (Cambridge: Cambridge University Press, 2° ed., 2009), 672–707 (comment on Article 44 – Rules of Procedure) and T. Waelde, "'Equality of Arms' in Investment Arbitration: Procedural Challenges", in K. Yannaca-Small (ed.), *Arbitration Under*

the stage of the performance of a concession contract, the foreign investor may appear to be at the mercy of the sovereign regulatory power of the host State. At the pre-contractual and contractual levels, the foreign investor may have a prevailing leverage over a host State when the latter, not being technically in a position to offer directly a given public service, such as electricity, fully relies on the availability of the foreign investor for that purpose.[59]

When public utilities, such as the provision of electricity, are operated by private operators the host State is under the due diligence obligation to take all the preventive, monitoring and enforcement measures concerning the private enterprise, which are necessary in order to ensure that the public service is provided in a sufficiently satisfactory way.[60] While from the standpoint of the foreign investor, knowledge of such due diligence obligations should be con-

---

International Investment Agreements: A Guide to the Key Issues, (Oxford: Oxford University Press, 2010), 161–188.

59 "States are often in a weaker situation, whereas the investors have the stronger hand. States are often under high pressure, due to ailing public finances or to international agencies favouring privatization. The investor, on the contrary, will understandably only agree to the contract if it appears profitable. The imbalance is even bigger where [...], as in some of the cases above, there is only one bidder" (P. Thielborger, "The Human Right to Water Versus Investor Rights: Double-Dilemma or Pseudo Conflict?", in P.M. Dupuy, F. Francioni and E.U. Petersmann (eds.), *Human Rights in International Investment Law and Arbitration* (Oxford: Oxford University Press, 2009), 503 ff).

60 The International Covenant on Civil and Political Rights (ICCPR) and International Covenant on Economic, Social and Cultural Rights (ICESCR) make no explicit recognition of a universal right to electricity. However, the issue of access to energy has consistently arisen in the interpretation and implementation of international human rights instruments. The Committee on Economic, Social and Cultural Rights has recognized, with respect to the right to adequate housing under Art. 11(1) of the ICESCR that "[a]ll beneficiaries of the right to adequate housing should have sustainable access to (...) energy" (General comment No. 4: The right to adequate housing (Art. 11(1) of the Covenant). Sixth session (1991)" (Document E/1992/23), reproduced in *Human Rights Instruments. Volume I. Compilation of General Comments and General Recommendations Adopted by Human Rights Treaty Bodies. Note by the Secretariat* (HRI/GEN/1/Rev.9 (Vol. I)), 27 May 2008, 12). Article 14 of the Convention on the Elimination of All Forms of Discrimination Against Women (CEDAW) explicitly recognizes rural women's rights to electricity as part of the right to adequate housing (Office of the United Nations High Commissioner for Human Rights, *The Right to Adequate Housing, Fact Sheet No. 21 (Rev. 1)* (2009), at http://www.ohchr.org). While Art. 36 of The Charter of Fundamental Rights of the European Union recognizes the access to services of general economic interest, the Court of Justice of the European Union has interpreted this provision so as to include among such services the provision of electricity (*Municipality of Almelo and Others v. Energiebedrijf IJsselmij NV*, Case C-393/92, *European Court Reports I-1277* (1994)). See L.A.

sidered as essential for an objective assessment of its legitimate expectations,[61] it is to be assumed that the principle of good faith, as a general principle of law, applies to the host State and the foreign investor alike. This should apply to their position as claimant and defendant and consequently, to the legal evaluation of their conduct prior to the arising of the dispute from the beginning of their relationship.

Practical guidance on the contents of the due diligence conduct to be followed by both States and foreign investors, particularly when providing essential public services, such as electricity provision, may be found in human rights treaties as well as in authoritative soft-law instruments. As to the former, suffice it to recall the 1966 International Covenant on Economic, Social and Cultural Rights (ICESCR)[62] and the Additional Protocol to the American Convention on Human Rights in the Area of Economic, Social and Cultural Rights (Protocol of San Salvador).[63] As to the latter, one may mention the General Comments of the Committee on Economic, Social and Cultural Rights (CESCR) established under the above Covenant[64] the UN Global Compact;[65] the Report of the Special Rapporteur, Hadji Guissé, on the guidelines for the realization of the right to drinking water supply and sanitation;[66] the Principles for Private Sector

Alives "Electric Energy Access in European Union Law: A Human Right?", 19 *Columbia Journal of European Law* 1 (2012), 4 ff. See also *supra* note 39.

61 See below notes 70–71.

62 Signed on 16 December 1966 (entered into force 1976) 6 *International Legal Materials* (1967), 360 ff. See, in particular, General Comment No 14, "The right to the highest attainable standard of health (Art. 12 of the ICESCR)", UN Doc. E/C.12/2000/4, 11 August 2000; General Comment No 15, "The right to water (Arts. 11 and 12 of the ICESCR)", UN Doc. E/C-12/2002/11, 20 January 2003 and General Comment No 16, "The equal right of men and women to the enjoyment of all economic, social and cultural rights (Art. 3 of the International Covenant on Economic, Social and Cultural Rights (ICESCR)", UN Doc E/C.12/2005/4, 11 August 2005.

63 Signed on 17 November 1988 (entered into force 1999), 28 *International Legal Materials* (1989), 161 ff.

64 See, in particular, General Comment No 14, "The right to the highest attainable standard of health (Art. 12 of the ICESCR)", UN Doc. E/C.12/2000/4, 11 August 2000; General Comment No 15, "The right to water (Arts. 11 and 12 of the ICESCR)", UN Doc. E/C-12/2002/11, 20 January 2003 and General Comment No16, "The equal right of men and women to the enjoyment of all economic, social and cultural rights (Art. 3 of the ICESCR)", UN Doc E/C.12/2005/4, 11 August 2005.

65 Announced by the then Secretary General Kofi Annan at the Economic Global Forum of Davos on 31 January 1999 and officially launched in New York on 26 July 2000, at http://www.unglobalcompact.org.

66 UN Doc. E/CN.4/Sub.2/2005/25, 11 July 2005.

Participation in Infrastructure of the *Organisation for Economic Cooperation and Development* (OECD)[67] – expressly referring to the OECD Guidelines for Multinational Enterprises, in order to complement its guideline function –[68] and the Report of the Special Representative of the Secretary-General, John Ruggie, on the issue of human rights and transnational corporations and other business enterprises, "Principles for responsible contracts: Integrating the management of human rights risks into State-investor contract negotiations: guidance for negotiators."[69]

As to the instruments adopted at the intergovernmental level, their internationally legally binding force for the States that have taken part in the process of their adoption may be derived through the international general principle of law of good faith.[70] As such, the latter may be applied as a source of international law on par with, if not above, any other international customary rule, let alone the fact that it has been appropriately considered as a constitutional principle of international law, as much as of any system of law.[71] When similar instruments are not of an intergovernmental nature, they may be taken as authoritative terms of reference by the private investor and the host State in their mutual relationship. Likewise, it will be for investment tribunals whether to consider such instruments as elements of guidance in the interpretation

67 OECD, *Principles for Private Sector Participation in Infrastructure* (2007), at http://www.oecd.org.

68 See the latest version (5th ed. 2011), at http://dx.doi.org/10.1787/9789264115415-en.

69 UN Doc. A/HRC/17/31, 21 March 2011. See the commentaries pertinent to the topic under consideration on previous versions of this Report by F. Marrella, "On the Changing Structure of International Investment Law: the Human Right to Water and ICSID Arbitration", *International Community Law Review* 12 (2010), 345.

70 As clearly illustrated by the late Professor Schachter, "[w]hen States enter into a non-legal commitment, they generally assume a political (or moral) obligation to carry it out in good faith. Other States concerned have reason to expect such compliance and to rely on it. What we must deduce from this is that the non-binding declarations that express political or moral commitments are governed by the general principle of good faith. Inasmuch as good faith is an accepted general principle of international law, it is appropriate to apply it to such commitments. There is no reason for distinguishing the legal meaning of 'good faith' from a supposed political meaning of that concept. Whether called legal or political, its meaning is essentially the same. A significant legal consequence of the 'good faith' principle is that a party which committed itself in good faith to a course of conduct or to recognition of a legal situation would be stopped from acting inconsistently with its commitment or position [...]" ("Non-Conventional Concerted Acts", in M. Bedjaoui (ed.), *International Law: Achievements and Prospects* (Paris: UNESCO, 1991), 267).

71 For a general overview on the principle of good faith, R. Kolb, *La bonne foi en droit International public*, (Paris: Presses Universitaires de France, 2000).

and application of the legal framework made up of the applicable investment treaty and the relevant internationally codified interpretative and substantive rules and principles.

Irrespective of whether the latter principles will be recognized in investment arbitration case law, foreign investors and host States alike are well advised to take such standards and principles into account at the pre-contractual and contractual stages in dealings pertaining to investment in public utilities and infrastructure, with special regard to those related to hydropower.

This will enhance the chances of dispute prevention, while fostering the legal positions of both the private and public actors involved as potential applicants or defendants.

3.2.2 In Relation to the Interpretation and Application of Human Rights Law as a Self-contained Regime before a Human Rights Judicial Body

The entanglement between investment and human rights may also lead to the triggering of judicial mechanisms of protection of the latter against host States, provided for by the human rights body of law, as a self-contained regime.[72] This applies with respect to the case in which the applicants against the host State are its residents, alleging to have suffered an infringement of a basic human right in relation to a foreign direct investment – in our case the construction, or operation, of a power-plant, or related infrastructure, with special regard to dams – as well as to the case of foreign investors claiming the infringement of their right to property.[73]

---

72 See B. Simma, "Self-contained Regimes", *Netherlands Yearbook of International Law* 16 (1985), 129–135 and B. Simma and D. Pulkowski, "Of Planets and the Universe: Self-contained Regimes in International Law", *European Journal of International Law* 17 (2006), 524–529.

73 See Art. I, Protocol I to the European Convention on Human Rights (signed on 4 November 1950, 213 *UNTS*, 222 ff) whereby "[e]very natural or legal person is entitled to the peaceful enjoyment of its possessions [...]", Art. 21 (1) of the American Convention of Human Rights (signed on 22 November 1969, 1144 *UNTS*, 123 ff) providing that "[e]very one has the right to the use and enjoyment of his property [...]". See on the right to property and its relation to the human rights body of law, A.R. Coban, *Protection Of Property Rights within the European Convention on Human Rights* (Aldershot: Ashgate-Surrey, 2004), 35 ff and T. Allen, "Compensation for Property under the European Convention on Human Rights", 28 *Michigan Journal of International Law* (2007), 287 ff? See in general on the relationship between the right to property and human rights, C.H. Schreuer and U. Kriebaum, "The Concept of Property in Human Rights Law and International Investment Law", in L. Wildhaber and S. Breitenmoser (eds.), *Human Rights, Democracy*

3.2.3 In Defence of the Alleged Local Victims of the Foreign Investment Against the Host State

As anticipated, investment in hydropower may adversely affect international human rights, precisely with respect to the right to access to electricity, either directly, or in relation to the right to an adequate standard of living.[74] A specific set of human rights that one may identify as highly likely to be affected by investment in hydropower, with special regard to the building of dams, is the one pertaining to indigenous rights.[75] The subject is particularly relevant in the Americas in relation to the protection of indigenous peoples often subject to displacement for the building of dams. Two recent cases, one of which is still pending, are exemplary of the point at issue.

3.2.4 Two Exemplary Cases on Indigenous Rights

In the *Four Ngoebe indigenous communities and their members v. The Republic of Panama (2010)* the Inter-American Commission on Human Rights in January 2010 submitted to the Inter-American Court of Human Rights, a request for provisional measures requiring the Government of Panama to adopt with respect to a given hydro-electric project "all measures necessary to [*inter alia*] [s]uspend the construction of works and other activities related to the concession granted."[76] It may be noted that, among the requested measures were those "intended to avoid immediate and irreparable damages resulting from the activities of third parties entering the community's territory or exploiting the existing natural resources."[77]

---

and the Rule of Law: Liber Amicorum Luzius Wildhaber (Zürich: Dike, 2007), 743–762 and Karamanian, *supra* note 38. On the so called "human right to investment", see J.E. Alvarez, *The Public International Law Regime Governing International Investment* (The Hague: Martinus Nijhoff, 2011), especially at 57–75.

74 See *supra* note 39.

75 See generally, on FDI and the rights of indigenous populations, G.K. Foster, "Foreign Investment and Indigenous Peoples: Options for Promoting Equilibrium between Economic Development and Indigenous Rights", *Michigan Journal of International Law* 33 (2012), 627–691. More specifically, in relation to the building of dams, with special regard to an Amazonian case that will be addressed below, see B.J. Cummings, "Dam the Rivers; Damn the People: Hydroelectric Development and Resistance in Amazonian Brazil", *GeoJournal* 35 (1995), 151–160.

76 Inter-American Court of Human Rights, *Request for Provisional Measures by the Inter-American Commission on Human Rights Regarding the Republic of Panama. Four Ngoebe Indigenous Communities and their Members*, Order, 28 May, 2010, para. 1.

77 Ibid.

Indeed, among the rights invoked with respect to which the construction of the plant and related infrastructure were alleged to be at variance, were the right to life, the right to freedom of movement of the members of the indigenous communities and their right to a special relationship with their ancestral territory, with special regard to the use and enjoyment of collective property and the natural resources therein. On the other hand, among the adverse impact complained of, one may mention flooding and deforestation of the communities' territory leading to displacement, relocation, and significant harm to the health of the members of the communities.

The Court eventually rejected the request stating that the Commission failed to "demonstrate *prima facie* the situation of extreme gravity and urgency of preventing irreparable damage."[78]

Considering that the Court was not ruling on the merits, it is arguable that, had the Court found that the three requirements of gravity, urgency and irreparable nature of the damage had been met, it could – at least in principle – have upheld the rights invoked, possibly even at the expense of the disputed investment. In any case, it is noteworthy that the Court felt the need to insert in its decision an *obiter dictum* which recalls and emphasizes as follows:

> [I]ts jurisprudence in the sense that while the American Convention does not prohibit *per se* the issuance of concessions for the exploration or exploitation of natural resources in indigenous or tribal territories, the legitimate restriction to the right of community property demands: i) conducting prior tests on the environmental and social impact; ii) conducting consultations with the affected communities regarding the development projects carried out in the traditionally occupied territories; and, when dealing with large-scale development or investment plans, obtain the free, informed and prior consent of the communities, according to their customs and traditions,[79] and iii) share the reasonable benefits with them.[80] In addition, a crucial factor to consider is whether the restriction implies a denial of traditions and customs in a way that endangers the subsistence of the group and its members.[81] The obligation to guarantee the effective participation of the members of the

78 Ibid., para. 12.

79 See Inter-American Court of Human Rights, *Case of the Saramaka People v. Surinam. Preliminary objections, Merits, Reparations, and Costs*, Judgment, 28 November 2007, Series C No. 172, para. 134.

80 Ibid.

81 Ibid., para. 128.

> communities or indigenous or tribal towns requires the State to accept and provide information, and implies constant communication between the parties. The consultations should be conducted in good faith, through culturally adequate procedures, and with the intention to achieve an agreement.[82]

In the *Indigenous Communities of the Xingu River Basin, Pará, Brazil (2011)*,[83] on April 1, 2011, the Inter-American Commission on Human Rights granted a host of precautionary measures in favour of the members of the indigenous communities of the Xingu River Basin in Pará, Brazil.[84] The request for precautionary measures had alleged that the life and physical integrity of the beneficiaries were jeopardized in relation to the potential impact of the construction of the Belo Monte hydroelectric power plant.[85] The Inter-American Commission on Human Rights requested the State of Brazil to immediately suspend the licensing process for the Belo Monte Hydroelectric Plant project and stop any construction work from moving forward until certain minimum conditions were met. Furthermore and in line with the above *obiter dictum* in the *Four Ngoebe indigenous communities* case, the Commission requested that Brazil: a) would conduct consultations with the affected indigenous communities beneficiaries of the precautionary measures in conformity with international law, that are, "free, informed, of good faith, culturally appropriate, and with the aim of reaching an agreement;"[86] b) in order for such consultations to be part of a duly informed consultation process, would afford beforehand the indigenous communities access to the project's Social and Environmental Impact Study "in an accessible format, including translation into the respective indigenous languages;"[87] c) would adopt measures to protect the life and physical integrity of the members of the indigenous peoples that found themselves in voluntary isolation and to prevent the spread of diseases among the beneficiaries indigenous communities, with special regard to those diseases that could be derived

---

82 Inter-American Court of Human Rights, *Request for Provisional Measures by the Inter-American Commission on Human Rights Regarding the Republic of Panama. Four Ngoebe Indigenous Communities and their Members*, Order, 28 May, 2010, para. 18.

83 Inter-American Commission on Human Rights, *Indigenous Communities of the Xingu River Basin, Pará, Brazil*, Reference No. PM 382/10, Precautionary Measures, 1 April 2011. See Cummings, above note 73.

84 Ibid.

85 Ibid.

86 Ibid.

87 Ibid.

from the massive influx of people into the region prompted by the construction of the power plant, as well as by water-related diseases such as malaria.[88]

On July 29, 2011 the Inter-American Commission on Human Rights reviewed the above precautionary measures further to the submission of additional information provided both by Brazil and the petitioners. Basically, it supplemented the above measures further requesting the Government of Brazil to ensure that the processes still pending in order to regularize the ancestral lands of the Xingu Basin indigenous peoples would be expeditiously finalized, and to adopt "effective measures to protect those ancestral lands against intrusion and occupation by non-indigenous people and against the exploitation or deterioration of their natural resources."[89]

It is arguable that disputes over hydroelectric projects are significantly enhancing the process defining the human rights, with special regard to indigenous rights, potentially adversely affected by investment in general and, consequently, by foreign investment in particular. At the same time, the extensive enunciations made in the above cases with a view to indicating the requirements for there to be compliance with indigenous rights may be taken to add to the criteria of guidance referred to above, to the assessment of the due diligence obligations pertaining to investment projects, particularly in the field under consideration.[90]

3.2.5 In Defence of Foreign Investors Against the Host State

The human rights body of law has traditionally been invoked also to uphold the interests of the (foreign) investor against the host State on different grounds.[91] This applies no less with respect to investment in the specific field under consideration.

Problems of legal compatibility between the construction of dams and basic human rights has also come to the fore before international human rights fora, such as the ECHR, upon application by the investor. To that end one may recall the case of *Gorraiz Lizarraga and Others v. Spain* of 2004 in which the Strasbourg Court – not called upon to rule directly on the right to property, but on Artsicle 6 and 8 – eventually found for the respondent State.[92]

88 Ibid.

89 Ibid.

90 *Supra* section 3.1.1.

91 *Supra* notes 38 and 73. On the adjudicatory remedial side of breaches of the right to property, *supra* note 8.

92 The case originated in an engineering project of February 1989 for the construction of a dam in Itoiz (Navarre province) which would result in the flooding of three nature

Similarly, one may refer to the *Kemal Uzan and others v. Turkey* of 2011 before the ECHR.[93] There, the ECHR found for the defendant State ruling that the $165 billion claim as compensation for the alleged expropriation of electricity interests was "manifestly ill-founded" and therefore inadmissible.[94] It may be noted in passing that the *ne bis in idem* argument, claimed by the Government of Turkey to the effect that the case was inadmissible as the same dispute had already been heard by ICSID tribunals,[95] was simply avoided by the Court who focused on other grounds of inadmissibility.

Most importantly, the Court addressed the merits of the claim holding that the unilateral termination of the concession and transfer to the State of the electricity infrastructure operated by the *Uzan Group* did not amount to a violation of the right to property of the claimant under Article 1 of Protocol 1 to the European Convention on Human Rights.[96] The alleged wrongfulness of the Turkish law to that effect was found to be precluded by the fact that it constituted a response to repeated breaches of contract by the applicants in combination with repeated warnings from the government.[97] The Court also noted *ad abundantiam* that the concession contract provided that no compensation

reserves and a number of small villages, including Itoiz, where the applicants live. See European Court of Human Rights, Fourth Section, *Case of Gorraiz Lizarraga and Others v. Spain*, Application no. 62543/00, Judgment, 27 April 2004, ECHR 2004-III, para. 1.

93 European Court of Human Rights, *Kemal Uzan and others v. Turkey*, Application No. 18240/03, Decision declaring the application inadmissible, 29 March 2011. See J. Hepburn, "European Human Rights Court Dismisses Claims Against Turkey in Uzan Electricity Dispute", *IA Reporter* (3 May 2011).

94 European Court of Human Rights, *Kemal Uzan and others v. Turkey*, *supra* note 93, paras. 121–122.

95 Ibid., par. 61 It may be recalled that on the two above referred 2009 ICSID awards, *Cementownia "Nowa Huta" SA v. Turkey* (*supra* note 17) and *Europe Cement Investment and Trade SA v. Turkey* (*supra* note 18), jurisdiction was denied over claims by Polish shareholders in the two Uzan electricity companies that were parties to the Governmental concession, Çukurova Elektrik AŞ (CEAS) and Kepez Eletrik TAŞ (Kepez). The claim also covered the same denial of jurisdiction in the above referred ICSID case *Libananco Holding Co Ltd v. Turkey* (in an annulment decision rendered on May 22, 2013, but not yet published, the Ad-hoc Committee has declined all requests made by Libananco. See L.E. Peterson, "Cypriot Firm, Libananco, Fails to Annul $15 Million Costs-Order in ICSID Case with Turkey" *IA Reporter* (23 May 2013), at http://www.iareporter.com).

96 European Court of Human Rights, *Kemal Uzan and others v. Turkey*, *supra* note 93, paras. 121–122.

97 Ibid., paras. 105, 109.

should be paid in case of termination for fault; thus, the claimants should not have expected any pay-out.[98]

It is noteworthy that, bearing precisely on the same kind of claims of expropriation that may be brought before investment arbitration tribunals, the Court did not feel bound to avoid passing judgment on breaches of contract as such, differently from ISCID Tribunals who tend to abstain from such evaluations, particularly since the 2007 *Siemens v. Argentina*[99] precedent as confirmed, amongst others in the *Suez v. Argentina* award of 2010 on liability.[100]

Eventually, the Court upheld the plaintiffs' arguments that the rights under the concession were "possessions" of the claimants and that Turkey's actions constituted an interference with such possessions.[101] However, it found for Turkey on the basis of the argument of fair balance between the claimants' rights and the public interest pursued as precluding the wrongfulness of the State measures.[102] In particular, the Court found that the termination of the concession and the seizure of the foreign investor's rights was a legitimate response to the Uzan group's repeated breaches of their contractual obligations, including the failure to make the necessary investment in order to produce and distribute sufficient electricity to satisfy the demand and failure to apply the agreed tariffs.[103]

Particularly in view of the entanglement between investment and human rights interests and legal evaluations, it is noteworthy that the ECHR also found that the public interest criterion was met by the Turkish Government since the measures complained of pursued the aim of improving the domestic electricity market though liberalization and competition in line with the pertinent World Bank and the International Monetary Fund (IMF) recommendation as well as with European Union (EU) law.[104]

98 Ibid., para. 109.

99 *Siemens A.G. v. Argentine Republic*, ICSID case ARB/02/8, Award, 6 February 2007, 14 *ICSID Reports* (2007), 18 ff, para. 248.

100 *Suez, Sociedad General de Aguas de Barcelona S.A. and Vivendi Universal S.A. v. Argentina Republic, supra* note 42, Decision on Liability, 30 July 2010.

101 European Court of Human Rights, *Kemal Uzan and others v. Turkey, supra* note 93, para. 86.

102 Ibid., para. 102.

103 Ibid., para. 109.

104 Ibid., para. 99.

4 The Inter-State Dimension of Hydropower Projects and the Relevance of International Water Law to Foreign Investment in this Sector

The transboundary relevance at the inter-State level of investment in the infrastructure related to hydroelectric energy is probably more significant than in other sectors of energy industry. This is due to the often transboundary character of the watercourses supplying water to the hydroelectric plants and to the often transboundary nature of the impact of the uses thereof.

The above consideration is corroborated by the fact that transboundary water disputes rank among the most egregious recent or pending inter-State disputes. While most such disputes pertain to projects pertaining to hydropower, international water law is certainly key to the prevention, management and settlement of water disputes.[105] Having regard to disputes that have reached the International Court of Justice (ICJ) or international arbitration tribunals, one may recall the *Gabčíkovo-Nagymaros* case between Hungary and Slovakia[106] and the *Kishenganga* dispute between India and Pakistan.[107] One

105 See A. Tanzi, "The UN Convention on International Watercourse As a Framework for the Avoidance and Settlement of Water Law Disputes", *Leiden Journal of International Law* 11 (1998), 441–472, *id.*, "Recent Trends in International Water Law Dispute Settlement", in *International Investments and Protection of the Environment: The Role of Dispute Resolution Mechanisms* (The Hague-London: Kluwer Law International, 2001), 133–174, *id.* C. Pitea, "The Role of Non-State Actors in International Water Disputes", in *Resolution of International Water Disputes* (The Hague: Kluwer Law International, 2003), 259–297 and A. Tanzi and E. Milano, "Article 33 of the UN Watercourse Convention: a Step Forward for Dispute Settlement", *Water International* 38 (2013), 166–179.

106 International Court of Justice, *Gabčikovo-Nagymaros Project (Hungary/Slovakia)*, Judgment, 25 September 1997, I.C.J. Reports (1997), 7 ff.

107 Permanent Court of Arbitration, *Indus Waters Kishenganga Arbitration (Pakistan/India)*, Order on the Interim Measures, 23 September 2011, and Partial Award, 18 February 2013. Since 2007 the Kishenganga Hydroelectric Power Project (KHEP) has been a cause of disagreement between India and Pakistan. After the failure of bilateral negotiations Pakistan has brought the dispute before an arbitration tribunal set up within the framework of the Permanent Court of Arbitration on the basis of the1960 Indus Water Treaty claiming that the construction of the Indian power project would significantly adversely affect it by causing a shortfall of about 21% of the river Neelum's inflow and impairing the expected usage of the Neelum Jhelum Hydropower Project (NJHP) under construction in Pakistani Kashmir. It is noteworthy for the purposes of the present paper that a Chinese consortium is working on the NJHP on the same river upon which India has started the KHEIn its *Order on Interim Measures* the Tribunal requested India to stop those permanent works on the KHEP on or above the Kishenganga-Neelum River that

may also refer to the significant on-going conflicts of interest in Central Asia on the matter at issue – an area particularly relevant to the scope of application of the ECT – directly, or indirectly.[108]

Where conflicts of interests, possibly even when they have evolved into a dispute, are managed through negotiation eventually leading to cooperation between the co-riparian States involved, this may articulate the complexity of the treaty and contractual relations pertaining to the infrastructural projects related to such forms of water cooperation. The latter usually also involve foreign private investors operating within the framework of bilateral, or sub-regional, inter-State cooperation. Exemplary of this scenario is the Indian-Nepalese cooperation on the Gandak River for the generation, transmission and distribution of hydropower. Such a cooperation relationship is carried out originally on the basis of the 1959 Agreement between the two Countries.[109] It provided for India to be in charge of the building and operation of the

---

could affect the full flow of the river to its natural channel. In its Partial Award, the Court of Arbitration unanimously decided that KHEP constitutes a Run-of-River Plant under the Treaty, and India may accordingly divert water from the Kishenganga/Neelum River for power generation by the KHEP in the manner envisaged. However, India has been placed under the obligation to maintain a minimum flow of water in the Kishenganga/ Neelum River which will be decided by the Tribunal in its final award, expected by the end of 2013, and to maintain a minimum level of water above the "Dead Storage Level" in the reservoirs of Run-of-River Plants located on the rivers allocated to Pakistan under the Treaty, except for unforeseen emergency and with respect to plants already in operation or under construction. For a summary of the case, see J. Ahmad, "The Court of Arbitration Issues Partial Award in Indus Waters Kishenganga Arbitration", *EJIL: Talk!* (12 June 2013), at http://www.ejiltalk.org/the-court-of-arbitration-issues-partial-award-in-indus-waters-kishenganga-arbitration (accessed 24 June 2013).

108 On water and conflict in Central Asia, see amongst others, D. Kemelovaand and G. Zhalkubaev, "Water, Conflict, and Regional Security in Central Asia Revisited", N.Y.U. Envtl L.J. 11 (2002–2003), 479 ff, Z. Karaev, "Water diplomacy in Central Asia", 9 *Middle East Review of International Affairs* 1 (2005), 63–69, B. Libert, "Water and Energy Crisis in Central Asia", *China and Eurasia Forum Quarterly* 6 (2008), 9–20, Y. Makhmedov, M. Madmusoev and S. Tavarov, *Water and Energy Disputes Between Tajikistan and Uzbekistan, and Their Negative Influence on Regional Co-operation* (2012), at http://www.nupi.no (accessed 24 October 2013) and E. S. Hurvitz, "Water Scarcity in Central Asia May Lead to Conflict", *The Human Rights Brief* (14 November 2012), at http://hrbrief.org (accessed 24 October 2013).

109 Agreement between the Government of Nepal and the Government of India on the Gandak River Irrigation and Power Project, signed at Kathmandu on 4 December 1959, see *Legislative Texts and Treaty Provisions concerning the Utilization of International Rivers for other Purposes than Navigation. Book 12*, in *United Nations Legislative Series* (New York: United Nations Publication, 1963), Treaty No. 96.

hydroelectric plant infrastructure and of the transmission of electricity to the Indian territory, and to allot a certain amount of energy to Nepal, while the latter would be in charge of the building and operating of the transmission installations and distribution of the electricity allotted to it. The Canadian-US water cooperation based on the 1961 Columbia River Treaty – negotiated and concluded precisely in view of the high hydropower potential of the River – reproduces a similar model.[110] Along the same lines, one may refer to the 1973 Agreement between Brazil, Paraguay (and Argentina) on the level of the River Parana in relation to the Itaipu dam which supplies water to one of the largest hydroelectric power plants in the world, whose construction has involved Italian and US Companies, amongst others.[111]

In order to appreciate the relevance of international water law for foreign private investors in waterworks related to the construction and/or operation of hydropower plants – foreign ones in our case – one may look at the Argentina v. Uruguay *Pulp Mills* case scenario, even though the disputed plants were not hydropower stations. In fact, the first pulp mill at the root of the dispute was planned by "Celulosas de M'Bopicuá S.A.," a company formed by the Spanish company ENCE (*Empresa Nacional de Celulosas de España*), while the second industrial project involved in the dispute was undertaken by "Botnia S.A." and "Botnia Fray Bentos S.A.," registered under Uruguayan law in 2003 by the Finnish company "Oy Metsä-Botnia AB."[112]

---

110 Treaty between the United States of America and Canada relating to co-operative development of the water resources of the Columbia River Basin, signed at Washington, 17 January 1961, see *Legislative Texts and Treaty Provisions concerning the Utilization of International Rivers for other Purposes than Navigation, supra* note 109, Treaty No. 65. Canada and the United States ratified the Columbia River Treaty in order to manage and coordinate flood control and optimize hydroelectric energy production in the Columbia River Basin. Canada built three storage dams, Hugh Keenleyside, Duncan and Mica, while the United States realized a fourth one, Libby. The agreement also foresees that in return for the storage of water, Canada is entitled to one half of the additional power generated at the American power plants on the Columbia River. For further information, see the Centre for Columbia River History and Columbia Basin Trust's web sites, respectively at http://www.ccrh.org and http://www.cbt.org/crt (accessed 24 October 2013).

111 The Itaipu dam supplies approximately 17.3% of the energy consumed in Brazil and 72.5% of consumption in Paraguay. It has 20 generator units and 14,000 MW of installed capacity, this latter is shared equally between the two countries. The party that does not use its share of the energy must sell it to the other party, while the buying party pays compensation for the additional benefits it receives from using the other's hydraulic resource entitlement. For further information, see the 'Itaipu Binacional's' web site, at http://www.itaipu.gov.br/en/energy/dam (accessed 24 October 2013).

112 The *Pulp Mills* case (International Court of Justice, *Pulp Mills on the River Uruguay* (*Argentina v. Uruguay*), Judgment, 20 April 2010, *ICJ Re*(2010), 14 ff) concerned two

The time frame of relevance of international water law for potential or actual foreign investors and their lawyers is both prior and contemporaneous to the actual realization of the given project. That is to say that international water law should be relevant at the international business planning stage, at the time of the negotiation of the concession contract concerning the construction of the waterworks related to a hydroelectric power plant, as well as of the actual operation of the plant.

The fact that host State authorities may be acting contrary to the international obligations protecting the legal interests of co-riparian States may produce significant economic harm and legal nuisance for the investor. On the one hand, this may occur with regard to breaches of international procedural obligations, such as those concerning notification and consultation of the "planned measures" and them being subject to an authorization regime under environmental impact assessment (EIA) procedure;[113] on the other, it may also occur with respect to the circumstance in which the host State would act at

---

pulp mills to be constructed, and later actually constructed, on the Uruguayan territory of the banks of the River Uruguay between Argentina and Uruguay. Argentina initiated proceedings before the ICJ against Uruguay alleging breaches of the 1975 Statute of the River Uruguay with special regard to alleged beaches of the obligation of notification and consultation, as well as of substantive obligations of environmental protection enshrined. See C.R. Payne, "Pulp Mills on the River Uruguay: The International Court of Justice Recognizes Environmental Impact Assessment as a Duty under International Law", *ASIL Insights* 14 (2010), at http://www.asil.org/insights100422.cfm (accessed 24 October 2013) and O. McIntyre, "The World Court's on-going contribution to international water law: The Pulp Mills Case between Argentina and Uruguay", *Water Alternatives* 4 (2011), 124–144.

113 In the *Pulp Mills* case, in particular, the ICJ underlined the importance of inter-State notification of new projects or activities, explaining that "... the environmental impact assessments which are necessary to reach a decision on any plan that is liable to cause significant transboundary harm to another State must be notified by the party concerned to the other party [...] to enable the notified party to participate in the process of ensuring that the assessment is complete, so that it can then consider the plan and its effects with a full knowledge of the facts [...]" (par. 119). Most importantly, the Court also found that "it may now be considered a requirement under general international law to undertake an environmental impact assessment where there is a risk that the proposed industrial activity may have a significant adverse impact in a transboundary context, in particular, on a shared resource. Moreover, due diligence, and the duty of vigilance and prevention which it implies, would not be considered to have been exercised, if a party planning works liable to affect the regime of the river or the quality of its waters did not undertake an environmental impact assessment on the potential effects of such works" (*Pulp Mills on the River Uruguay* (*Argentina v. Uruguay*), *supra* note 112, para. 204). On the procedural obligations in point, see O. McIntyre, "*The Proceduralization and Growing Maturity of International Water Law: Case Concerning Pulp Mills on the River Uruguay* (*Argentina v.*

variance with the substantive due-diligence obligations of equitable utilization and/or harm-prevention, mitigation or restoration.[114] Accordingly, foreign investors and their lawyers would be well advised to give close consideration to this kind of public international law matters in their decision making process about whether to invest in a given project and, if so, in structuring the deal. There, the regulatory framework relevant to the foreign investor –though indirectly – is customary international water law, as codified under the UNECE 1992 Helsinki Water Convention[115] and the UN 1997 New York Convention on international watercourses[116] and, possibly, as specified and adjusted to the specific relevant transboundary basin by the bilateral, or multilateral, watercourse agreements the host State may have entered into with its co-riparians.

In line with the above, it is noteworthy that, since the legal context in which public or private operators in this field are acting is ultimately public international law, particularly when the host State is party to a dispute settlement mechanism, domestic courts (apart from the civil liability aspect, which will be discussed below) may deny its jurisdiction, declaring such domestic jurisdiction subservient to the inter-State legal dimension.[117]

4.1 *Hydropower in International Water Law*

The relevance of hydroelectric power projects for the application and development of international water law is far from being a new phenomenon. On the

---

Uruguay)", Journal of Environmental Law 22 (2010), 475–497; Tanzi and Arcari, *supra* note 9, 179–222 and McCaffrey, *supra* note 9, 464–482.

114 On the general principles of equitable utilization and harm prevention to other riparian States, see Tanzi and Arcari, *supra* note 9, 93–178 and McCaffrey, *supra* note 9, 359–446.

115 UNECE Convention on the Protection and Use of Transboundary Watercourses and International Lakes (adopted 17 Mar 1992, entered into force 6 Oct 1996), 1936 *UNTS* 269 (UNECE Water Convention), at http://www.unece.org/env/water/text/text.html, and the Draft guide to implementing the Convention (ECE/MP.WAT/2009/L.2, 31 August 2009), at http://www.unece.org/fileadmin/DAM/env/documents/2009/Wat/mp_wat/ECE_mp.wat_2009_L2_%20E.pdf (accessed 24 October 2013). For an analysis of the UNECE role on water law, see A. Tanzi, "Regional Integration and the Protection of the Environment: The UN/ECE Process on Water Law as a Model for the Global Dimension", *Italian Yearbook of International Law* 10 (2000), 71–112.

116 See Tanzi and Arcari, *supra* note 9; F.R. Loures and A. Rieu-Clarke (ed.), *The UN Watercourses Convention in Force. Strengthening International Law for Transboundary Water Management* (London: Routledge, 2013).

117 An example in this direction was provided by the *Société énergie électrique du littoral méditérraneen v. Compagnia imprese elettriche liguri* (9 *Ann. Dig.* 120, (Italy, Court of Cassation (United Sections), 1939), at 121), where the Court declined the jurisdiction of the domestic courts given the prevailing inter-State relevance of the dispute.

contrary, one would argue that, ever since the main focus of this body of international law has gone beyond the mere regulation of competing navigational uses of international rivers, the construction and operation of waterworks related to hydroelectric power plants having a transboundary impact has been the primary "non-navigational use of international watercourses" addressed by international water law.

Later, with the increase in industrial development – particularly in the chemical and pharmaceutical sectors – the rationale of the international regulation of economic uses of transboundary watercourses has shifted from a purely economic one to one encompassing environmental and human rights concerns, adding water quality issues to water quantity allocation.

Nonetheless, hydropower related works and activities have remained a top priority within the scope of application of international water law. Considering that hydroelectric industry sensibly affects the water flow of watercourses, periodically, if not permanently, one is to consider that dams upstream may produce significant impact downstream, both in terms of water quantity and quality as one entangled issue. Indeed, a significant reduction in the water flow – even if periodical – inevitably affects its quality insofar as it diminishes a watercourse capacity to absorb pollutants.[118]

It is, therefore, apparent that the construction and operation of hydroelectric plants and of the related waterworks, especially dams, may easily produce conflicts of interest escalating into inter-State disputes between co-riparians inevitably affecting private investors, arguably also foreign ones. The settlement of such differences leading to cooperation would benefit all stakeholders, public and private alike, and *vice versa*. Consequently, investors and their lawyers are well advised to be knowledgeable about the relevant international legal standards in the field and the attitude towards them by the State of

118 See already G. Gaja, "River Pollution in International Law", in *Colloque of the Hague Academy of International Law on The Protection of the Environment and International Law* (1973), 366, 371 and 377 ff. More recently, Brunnée and Toope observed that "(...) the very distinction between water quantity and water quality that underlies much of the existing conflict analysis is of limited relevance to a model of environmental security aimed at protecting ecological balance and allowing for sustainable human development. Arguably, even under the traditional conflict framework, the explanatory power of the distinction is not compelling. Conflicts caused by water quantity problems and those caused by water quality degradation may not actually result in differing patterns of State behaviour, for, in both cases, access to usable water ultimately becomes constrained" (J. Brunnée and S. Toope, "Environmental Security and Freshwater Resources: A Case for International Ecosystem Law", *Yearbook of International Environmental Law* 5 (1994), 47).

investment and its co-riparians, before their investment becomes involved in a major inter-State dispute.

While at the time prior to the process of industrialization, competing uses between co-riparians would hardly lead to disputes, apart from disputes over navigation, after the inception of industrialization, waterworks involving alteration of the flow of a river, such as dams and dikes, would likely affect co-riparians by some sort of "deprivation" of water. Indeed, joint development projects, or at least coordinated through consultation, between the States concerned, have appeared as the best way forward on a case-by-case basis for all the actors involved, public and private alike.

As anticipated, the need to regulate hydroelectric power stations and their transboundary impact can be said to have been the pilot area in the process of the "international law of the non-navigational uses of international watercourses," the pivoting pillar of which is the principle of cooperation as supplemented by the principles of equitable utilization and no-harm, and *vice versa*. Indeed, emerging concerns in this field at the beginning of the last century would lead to a significant number of bilateral or sub-regional arrangements, possibly induced by a multilateral authoritative framework. To that end, one may note that already in 1913, after extensive negotiations, France and Switzerland entered into a bilateral treaty regulating the management of hydraulic power of the River Rhone.[119]

Most importantly, at the multilateral level, one may recall the 1923 Geneva Convention relating to the Development of Hydraulic Power Affecting More Than One State.[120] This Convention represents a milestone in the evolution of international water law pertaining to the non-navigational uses of international watercourses based on the principle of cooperation. It provides the first multilateral authoritative enunciation of *opinio juris* pertaining to

119 Convention between France and Switzerland for the development of the water power of the Rhone between the power-station planned at La Plaine and a point to be specified up-stream of the Pougny-Chancy bridge, signed at Berne on 4 October 1913, see *Legislative Texts and Treaty Provisions concerning the Utilization of International Rivers for other Purposes than Navigation, supra* note 109, Treaty No. 197.

120 Eleven States ratified the Convention or finally acceded thereto: Thailand; New Zealand (including the Mandated Territory of Western Samoa); British Empire (also for Southern Rhodesia, Newfoundland, British Guiana, British Honduras, Brunei, Federated Malay States, Gambia, Gold Coast, Hong Kong, Kenya, Unfederated Malay States, Nigeria, Northern Rhodesia, Nyasaland, Palestine, Sierra Leone, Tanganyika Territory, Uganda Protectorate); Denmark; Austria; Greece; Hungary; Free City of Danzig; Panama; Iraq; Egypt. See *Legislative Texts and Treaty Provisions concerning the Utilization of International Rivers for other Purposes than Navigation, supra* note 109, Second Part, Treaty No. 2.

the customary international water law process related to the non-navigational uses of watercourses. For the purposes of the present paper, one may single out that the negotiating Parties based the pursuit of "promoting international agreement for the purpose of facilitating the exploitation and increasing the yield of hydraulic power"[121] on the principles of consultation and cooperation under the two following specific circumstances:

> Article 3: If a Contracting State desires to carry out operations for the development of hydraulic power, partly on its own territory and partly on the territory of another Contracting State or involving alterations on the territory of another Contracting State, the States concerned shall enter into negotiations with a view to the conclusion of agreements which will allow such operations to be executed.
>
> Article 4: If a Contracting State desires to carry out operations for the development of hydraulic power which might cause serious prejudice to any other Contracting State, the States concerned shall enter into negotiations with a view to the conclusion of agreements which will allow such operations to be executed.

This remains a rather unique multilateral instrument in the area of transboundary watercourses also for it being specifically focused on hydroelectric power. It can be said to have been largely successful – irrespective of the number of formal ratifications obtained – insofar as it can be said to have promoted and served as an authoritative term of reference for the negotiation of a large quantity of water agreements bearing on hydroelectric power.[122] Its relevance

121 Preamble of the 1923 Geneva Convention.

122 One may mention, amongst others, the international agreements on the following transboundary watercourses: Douro (Spain and Portugal), Convention between Spain and Portugal to Regulate the Hydro-Electric Development of the International Section of the River Douro, signed at Lisbon on 11 August 1927 (see *Legislative Texts and Treaty Provisions concerning the Utilization of International Rivers for other Purposes than Navigation, supra* note 109, Treaty No. 248); Doubs (France and Switzerland), Convention between France and Switzerland respecting the Chatelot Falls Concession on the Doubs, signed at Paris on 19 November 1930 (see *Legislative Texts and Treaty Provisions concerning the Utilization of International Rivers for other Purposes than Navigation, supra* note 109, Treaty No. 199); Maritza-Ebros (Greece and Turkey), Agreement between Greece and Turkey Concerning the Control of Hydraulic Works on Both Banks of the River Maritza-Ebros, signed at Ankara on 20 June 1934 (see *Legislative Texts and Treaty Provisions concerning the Utilization of International Rivers for other Purposes than Navigation, supra* note 109, Treaty No. 220); Reno di Lei and Other Rivers Situated in the Averserrhein Basin (Italy

in more recent times is testified by its recognition by the International Law Association in the elaboration of its "Helsinki Rules" of 1966, which, in its turn, have played a major role as a term of reference in the exercise of the International Law Commission that eventually led to the adoption of the 1997 UN Convention on the Non-navigational Uses of International Watercourses.[123]

---

and Switzerland), Agreement between Italy and Switzerland on the Reno di Lei Hydraulic Power Concession, with Additional Protocol, signed at Rome on 18 June 1949 (see *Legislative Texts and Treaty Provisions concerning the Utilization of International Rivers for other Purposes than Navigation, supra* note 109, Treaty No. 231); Sûre (Germany (Federal Republic of) and Luxembourg), State Treaty between the Grand Duchy of Luxembourg and the Land Rhineland-Palatinate in the Federal Republic of Germany Concerning the Construction of a Hydroelectric Power Plant on the Sauer (Sûre) at Rosportj Ralingen, signed at Trier on 25 April 1950 (see *Legislative Texts and Treaty Provisions concerning the Utilization of International Rivers for other Purposes than Navigation, supra* note 109, Treaty No. 201); Lake Mont-Cenis (France and Italy), Provisional Agreement and Exchange of Notes between France and Italy Regarding the Operation of the Gran Scala Power Station, signed at Rome on 12 January 1955 (see *Legislative Texts and Treaty Provisions concerning the Utilization of International Rivers for other Purposes than Navigation, supra* note 109, Treaty No. 181); Spöl (Italy and Switzerland), Convention between the Swiss Confederation and the Italian Republic Concerning the Use of the Water Power of the Spöl, and an Additional Protocol, signed at Berne on 27 May 1957 (see *Legislative Texts and Treaty Provisions concerning the Utilization of International Rivers for other Purposes than Navigation, supra* note 109, Treaty No. 235); Paatsojoki (Norway and The USSR), Agreement between Norway and the Union of Soviet Socialist Republics on the Utilization of Water-Power on the Pasvik (Paatso) River, signed at Oslo on 18 December 1957 (see *Legislative Texts and Treaty Provisions concerning the Utilization of International Rivers for other Purposes than Navigation, supra* note 109, Treaty No. 239); Our (Germany (Federal Republic of) and Luxembourg), State Treaty between the Grand Duchy of Luxembourg and the Land Rhineland Palatinate in the Federal Republic of Germany Concerning the Construction of Hydro-Electric Power Installations on the Our, with Annexes, signed at Trier on 10 July 1958 (see *Legislative Texts and Treaty Provisions concerning the Utilization of International Rivers for other Purposes than Navigation, supra* note 109, Treaty No. 202); (Greece and Yugoslavia) Agreement between the Federal People's Republic of Yugoslavia and the Kingdom of Greece Concerning Hydro-Economic Questions and Annex concerning the Regulations of the Yugoslav-Greek Permanent Hydro economic Commission and Exchange of Letters, signed at Athens on 18 June 1959 (see *Legislative Texts and Treaty Provisions concerning the Utilization of International Rivers for other Purposes than Navigation, supra* note 109, Treaty No. 224).

123 The Helsinki Rules on the Uses of the Waters of International Rivers, adopted by the International Law Association at the fifty-second Conference, held at Helsinki on the 20 August 1966 (International Law Association, *Report of the Fifty-second Conference, held at Helsinki, 1966*, London, 1967, 484–532). See on this point Tanzi and Arcari, *supra* note 9, 1–37.

Without embarking on an overview of the basic principles of international water law, for the purposes of the present paper, suffice it to consider that waterworks projects related to hydropower, feature among the most representative case-studies concerning case-specific applications of the principle of equitable and reasonable utilization, possibly in combination with the due-diligence obligation of harm prevention, through the procedural principle of cooperation.[124]

When similar forms of transboundary cooperation may not be achieved, the situation falling most directly within the scope of the present paper – in case of the involvement of foreign investors in the construction and/or operation of a hydroelectric plant and its infrastructure – is the one likely to reproduce the above mentioned *Pulp Mills* case scenario: diplomatic protests from a neighbouring Country, blockades and other forms of social unrest against the host State, but eventually also against the economic activity, or the infrastructure related to the investment and the foreign company itself.[125] Here, from an international standpoint, usually, the economic and legal interests of the foreign investor are closely linked to those of the host State. However, in order for the foreign investor to legally protect its interests, directly with respect to the domestic administrative and constitutional framework and indirectly with respect to the international legal position of the host State, it is essential that the foreign investor makes sure that its pre-contractual and contractual relations with the host State conform to the international legal requirement of an authorization regime in the project at issue, including a proper environmental impact assessment.[126] It is also crucial for the investor to verify that the governmental authorities of the host State have duly observed, in their relations with their co-riparians, the international legal requirements pertaining to the project in point with respect to its potential transboundary impact, with special regard to its obligations of notification and, eventually, of consultation.[127] Otherwise, the non-commercial risks for the investor would depend on whether a dispute would, or not, arise with a co-riparian in relation to the

124 See, for all, the above referred Gandak River, Columbia River and Itaipu Dam case-studies, see notes 107–109. One may also refer to the example galore of transboundary water cooperation in the Pan-European region, under the umbrella of the UNECE 1992 Helsinki Water Convention, reported in the Draft guide to implementing the Convention, see note 113.

125 See *Pulp Mills on the River Uruguay* (*Argentina v. Uruguay*), *supra* note 112, paras. 25–47.

126 On the customary nature of the EIA obligation in respect of projects or activities potentially having transboundary effects, see the *Pulp Mills* case, *supra* note 113.

127 Ibid.

project involving the foreign investor and, in that case, on the settlement of that dispute.

Those are highly sensitive international legal problems which should be duly taken into account in the due-diligence role of the company lawyers and counsel at the preventive level in the phase of the business-plan making, or, at the negotiation stage of a concession contract, whereby the State should undertake some financial responsibility for the loss incurred from the non-commercial risks deriving from transboundary disputes over the project.

On this score, those that may be considered as "international financial or security incentives and diplomacy" promoting compliance with international environmental law, dispute prevention and settlement deserve special consideration.[128] Indeed, the assessments by international financial agencies on compliance with the environmental and social standards relevant to a given project of the kind at issue may bear significant authority on the diplomatic or judicial assessment of its legality next to operating as a condition for international funding.

As to the World Bank (WB) in relation to the transboundary dimension of a given hydropower project, one would refer to its Operational Policies on Projects on International Waterways of 2001 as revised in March 2012.[129] It may primarily be emphasized that, in the indication of the kind of projects falling within their scope of application, "hydroelectric projects" stand first on the list.[130] The assistance that the WB provides with a view to conducing agreement between the host States and its co-riparians on projects of the kind

128 On the dispute resolution mechanisms on water law, see A. Tanzi, "Recent Trends in International Water Law Dispute Settlement", in *International Investments and Protection of the Environment: The Role of Dispute Resolution Mechanisms* (The Hague-London: Kluwer Law International, 2001), 133–174; *id.* and E. Milano, "Article 33 of the UN Watercourse Convention: a step forward for dispute settlement", *Water International* 38 (2013), 166–179; A. Tanzi, "Regional Contributions to International Water Cooperation: The UNECE Contribution", in L. Boisson de Chazournes, C. Leb and M. Tignino (eds.), *International Law And Freshwater: The Multiple Challenges*, (Edward Elgar, Cheltenham, 2013), 155–178.

129 The Operational Policy on Projects on International Waterways is available on the World Bank's web site, at http://go.worldbank.org/NEYC01UF60 (accessed 24 October 2013).

130 Par. 2 reads as follows: "This policy applies to the following types of projects: (a) hydroelectric, irrigation, flood control, navigation, drainage, water and sewerage, industrial, and similar projects that involve the use or potential pollution of international waterways as described in para. 1 above; and (b) detailed design and engineering studies of projects under para. 2(a) above, including those to be carried out by the Bank as executing agency or in any other capacity".

under consideration is also noteworthy. It actually operates as a precondition for funding such projects.[131] One should add that, while the prior notification of the project to co-riparians is another preliminary requirement of legality and for funding in order to facilitate the meeting of such a requirement, the WB may represent the host State for the purposes of notification.[132]

Most importantly, when disagreement between co-riparians bears on a project of the kind at issue which has been submitted to the WB for a loan, the Bank Procedures on Projects on International Waterways of the same Operational Manual[133] vests the Bank with the power to trigger unilaterally a third party enquiry procedure. Rules 5 to 12 set out a rather articulated procedure to that end. For example, when a proposed project is objected to by a co-riparian, the competent departments draw up a Bank staff's assessment on the following issues: on the objections raised;[134] on "whether the proposed project will cause appreciable harm to the interests of the other riparians, or be appreciably harmed by other riparians' possible water use;"[135] whether it is appropriate to "urge the parties to resolve the issues through amicable means [...];"[136] and, especially, on "whether the objections are of such a nature that it is advisable to obtain an additional opinion from independent experts."[137] When the governing bodies, in consultation with the competent departments of the Bank, consider that an opinion of independent experts is necessary, the issue is referred to "one or more experts selected from a roster of ten names which is updated yearly by the Bank itself."[138] It is important to note that

131 Par. 3 reads as follows: "Projects on international waterways may affect relations between the Bank and its borrowers and between states (whether members of the Bank or not). The Bank recognizes that the cooperation and goodwill of riparians is essential for the efficient use and protection of the waterway. Therefore, it attaches great importance to riparians' making appropriate agreements or arrangements for these purposes for the entire waterway or any part thereof. The Bank stands ready to assist riparians in achieving this end. In cases where differences remain unresolved between the state proposing the project (beneficiary state) and the other riparians, prior to financing the project the Bank normally urges the beneficiary state to offer to negotiate in good faith with the other riparians to reach appropriate agreements or arrangements".

132 See paras. 4–6.

133 The Operational Manual is available on the World Bank's website, at http://go.worldbank.org/2G5SSZAET0.

134 See Rule 6, lett. (b).

135 See ibid., lett. (c).

136 Ibid., lett. (d).

137 Ibid., lett. (e).

138 See Rules 7–10. On the composition and maintenance of the roster, see Rule 12.

"the experts have no decision-making role in the project's processing. Their technical opinion is submitted for the Bank's purposes only, and does not in any way determine the rights and obligations of the riparians."[139]

Along the same lines and to the same end, one may also refer to the International Financial Corporation (IFC) and MIGA's environmental and social policies both for the domestic and transboundary dimension of the legal problems in hand.[140]

5 On Civil Liability Aspects for Harm Caused by Water-related Activities

Against the above inter-State legal scenario, one is to mention the general trend, or, rather, the diffused aspiration towards the internalization of liability for damage, mostly of a transboundary character, bearing on the position of the private operators from whose activity, damage is likely to occur, or has occurred, hence, possibly also with respect to hydropower related activity. Such a trend or aspiration is epitomized by Principle 13 of the Rio Declaration which reads as follows:

> States shall develop national law regarding liability and compensation for the victims of pollution and other environmental damage. States shall also co-operate in an expeditious and more determined manner to develop further international law regarding liability and compensation for adverse effects of environmental damage caused by activities within their jurisdiction or control to areas beyond their jurisdiction.

The internalization of liability involves a shift from an inter-State liability approach[141] under both national and international law to a civil liability under

---

139 See Rule 11.

140 See the IFC and MIGA's web sites, respectively at http://www.ifc.org/wps/wcm/connect/Topics_Ext_Content/IFC_External_Corporate_Site/IFC+Sustainability/Sustainability+Framework/Environmental%2C+Health%2C+and+Safety+Guidelines/ (accessed 24 October 2013) and http://www.miga.org/projects/index.cfm?stid=1822 (accessed 24 October 2013).

141 See in general on the issue of civil liability of private operators, A. Daniel, "Civil Liability Regime as a Complement to Multilateral Environmental Agreements: Sound International Policy or False Comfort?", *Review of European Community & International Environmental Law* 12 (2003), 225–241 and S. Cassotta, *Environmental Damage and Liability Problems in a Multilevel Context* (The Netherlands: Kluwer Law International, 2012). More in general, on

domestic law of the private operator whose activity has caused damage. In the case of the foreign nature of the harm caused by a private operator, or of the transboundary nature of the facts involved, this approach presents conflict of laws issues concerning the determination of the competent forum and of the applicable law for the assessment of the civil liability of the operator. One is to signal that serious attempts at the multilateral conventional level to develop – at least within the Pan-European context – a homogeneous private international law framework, possibly supplemented by compulsory insurance and compensation funds, have failed at the ratification level. This is the case of the 1993 Lugano Convention on Civil Liability for Damage Resulting from Activities Dangerous to the Environment[142] under the auspices of the Council of Europe and of the 2003 Protocol on Civil Liability and Compensation for Damage Caused by the Transboundary Effects of Industrial Accidents on Transboundary Waters to the UNECE 1992 Convention on the Protection and use of Transboundary Watercourses and International Lakes and to the 1992 Convention on the Transboundary Effects Of Industrial Accidents.[143]

Despite the above failures, one may note that at the level of individual domestic legislations, a rather scattered trend – though, certainly homogeneous within the EU, through the European Court of Justice case law, first, and, later, EU legislation[144] – towards affording the victims of transboundary harm the

---

the issue of liability for environmental damage, Sands, J. Peel, A. Fabri and R. MacKenzie (ed.), *Principles of International Environmental Law* (Cambridge, Cambridge University Press, 3°ed., 2012), 700 ff and of the concept of liability for lawful acts, Tanzi, *supra* note 10.

142 Signed at Lugano on 21 June 1993, *International Legal Materials* (1993), 1228 ff.

143 Signed on 21 May 2003, at http://treaties.un.org.

144 As to the applicable law, the German Courts in the 1961 River Possel case, admitted the so-called "favoritism principle", according to which the victim of a cross-border injury be entitled to choose between the law of the place where the harmful event occurred (*Handlungsort*) and the law of the place where the damage was suffered (*Erfolgsort*). This approach found confirmation in the EU Rome II Regulation (864/2007) (Regulation (EC) No 864/2007 of the European Parliament and of the Council of 11 July 2007 on the Law Applicable to Non-Contractual Obligations (Rome II), *O.J L 199* (31 July 2007), 40–49),whose Article 7 provides that that the law applicable to a non-contractual obligation arising out of environmental damage or damage sustained by persons or property as a result of such damage shall be the law determined pursuant to Article 4(1) of the Regulation, that is to say the law of the Country in which the damage has occurred, while Article 7 provides that the person seeking compensation may choose as the applicable law also the one of the Country where the event giving rise to damage has taken place. Similarly, as to the competent court, the choice is left to the applicant between the *forum* of the place (Country) where the defendant has its seat, or principal

free choice of the domestic competent court and, hence, of the applicable law between the judge and the applicable law of either the State where the damage was suffered or of the State where the activity was carried out which caused the harm.

6 Concluding Remarks

The above overview is primarily intended to focus on the four-tier multidimensional international legal relevance of foreign investment in hydropower rather than on each of the four sectors addressed. It will be for further academic research and practice in this area to delve into such specific sectors and promote the on-going processes in each of them, possibly taking into account and further exploring the interconnections highlighted above.

Indeed, the multidimensional characteristic of the international legal framework under consideration appears to apply both horizontally – *i.e.* between different bodies of international law bearing on the same kind of activities from different angles, with special regard to investment law and human rights law – and vertically, through the international law and domestic law dimensions.

Under both perspectives, the relationship between the different sets of rules under consideration is generally one of compatibility, in the sense that the application of the rules belonging to one would not preclude the application of those belonging to another one. Though, under the different bodies of law at issue, their respective competent courts and tribunals tend to give prevalence to the substantive rules of the legal framework under which they have been established. This certainly applies under the horizontal dimension in the fields of investment law and human rights law, despite some timidly emerging

---

place of business, and that of the place where the harmful event has actually occurred. The latter concept has been interpreted by the European Court of Justice as to include both the place where the activity took place which caused the harmful event, as well as the place where the damage was actually suffered. This was in the case of the *Mines de Potasse d'Alsace* (*Handelskwekerij G.J. BV v. Mines de Potasee d'Alsace SA*, Case 21/76, Judgment, 30 November 1976, *ECR* (1976), 1735 ff, paras. 18–25) where the Court was called to ascertain the meaning of Article 5(3) of the 1968 Brussels Convention (Convention on Jurisdiction and the Enforcement of Judgments in Civil and Commercial Matters, signed on 27 September 1968, 1262 *UNTS*, 153 ff), later reproduced in Article 5(3) of the EU Regulation 44/2001 (Council Regulation (EC) No 44/2001 of 22 December 2000 on Jurisdiction and the Recognition and Enforcement of Judgments in Civil and Commercial Matters, *OJ L 12* (16 January 2001), 1–23).

elements of cross-fertilization.[145] There, investment arbitration tribunals give prevalence to the rules on the protection of foreign investors with respect to the human rights affected by their economic activities, while the reverse tends to apply with respect to the case law of human rights courts. Here, some mitigation of the above general statement applies, let alone the fact that both the American and the European Conventions on the protection of human rights, amongst other human rights instruments, encompass the right to property, while in connection with the latter right some have argued the existence of a basic human right to investment.[146]

Still on the relationship between investment law and human rights law in connection with a situation in which both bodies of law are pertinent to a given case, the present paper has lamented the prevailing tendency in investment arbitration case law to announce in principle a relationship of mutual compatibility between the two bodies of law at hand without bringing this general statement to its logical consequences in terms of complementarity.[147] A concise reference has been made to clues that may assist arbitration tribunals to that end through the principles of good faith and due diligence in terms of reciprocity, hence, without necessarily introducing bias in favour of the host State, and possibly enhancing the dispute preventive function of the proposed regulatory framework.[148] On the latter point, useful guidance has emerged from the Inter-American Court of Human Rights with respect to cases involving indigenous populations, vulnerable to hydroelectric projects, particularly when involving the building of dams.[149]

As to the vertical perspective between the international and domestic rules relevant to the use of international watercourses for the purposes of hydropower, this paper has emphasized how "international water law for uses different from navigation" was originally developed precisely in order to regulate conflicts of uses of transboundary watercourses pertaining to the production of hydroelectricity.[150] Reference to most recent case law has illustrated

145 See, for example, the reference by the Arbitration Tribunal in *Azurix* (ICSID case ARB/01/12, Award, 14 July 2006, 14 *ICSID Reports* (2009), 367 ff), amongst others, to the *James* case decided by the ECHR (*James and al. v. United Kingdom*, Proceeding 8793/79, 21 February 1986) in order to substantiate the argument that State measures restricting the right of property are lawful if the harm caused to the investor is proportionate to the benefits derived from the pursuit of the general interest.

146 *Supra* note 73.

147 *Supra* text at notes 45 and 50.

148 *Supra* section 3.1.1.

149 *Supra* section 3.2.2.

150 *Supra* section 4.

how this issue has remained highly topical. The relevance of such a regulatory framework for the long string of potential private operators interested in hydropower projects – from the building of a dam to the operation of the power plant and electricity distribution – has been emphasized, despite its immediate inter-State scope of application. Such relevance has been highlighted with respect to the need for private operators to interact with officials of the State of investment on compliance issues with the relevant substantive and procedural obligations vis-à-vis co-riparians at the international level, as well as with those applicable at the domestic level, including a license regime providing for EIA, hence, corroborating the relevance of the legal framework under consideration in a vertical perspective.

Finally and still in a vertical perspective, the relevance has been concisely illustrated in the trend towards the internalization of liability for damage, mostly of a transboundary character caused by private operators, hence, likely to occur in hydropower activities related to transboundary watercourses. The vertical perspective here has been shown to apply in an international law-making prospect both ways: *i.e.*, top down and bottom up. On the one hand, the influence has been illustrated, which has been exercised at the international level by Principle 13 of the Rio Declaration to promote a shift from State responsibility, or liability, for harm – mostly, but not exclusively, of a transboundary character – to the internalization of liability precisely at the domestic civil liability level. It has been shown how that law-generative function of the Principle in point is far from having been brought to completion, since the attempts to elaborate in binding conventional terms, the Principle at issue, have failed so far. At the same time, it has been shown how – though in a rather scattered fashion, but more consistently at the regional level in Europe – domestic systems are providing emerging indications towards the adoption of common standards on the applicable law and the choice of the competent forum on the basis of which to bring a civil liability claim for transboundary harm. In the long term, a more widespread practice to the same effect might give rise to a generally agreeable international legal standard on the point at issue.

PART 2

The Energy Charter Treaty

CHAPTER 4

Energy Charter Treaty: Achievements, Challenges and Perspectives

Tarcisio Gazzini

1 Introduction

The Energy Charter Treaty (ECT) is a complex, ambitious and unique multilateral treaty intended to promote long-term cooperation in the energy field. It is based on complementarities and mutual benefits, as well as on the principles of sustainable development and sovereignty over energy resources.[1] Concluded on 17 December 1994 upon the political foundations set by the 1991 European Energy Charter (EEC), the ECT entered into force on 16 April 1998.

About 18 years have elapsed since the conclusion of the ECT and 47 States (plus the European Community/Union and Euratom) have ratified the treaty or accepted its provisional application under Article 45 of the treaty.[2] This is the equivalent of 1,081 bilateral investment treaties (BITs) between the State parties. Additionally, several States signatory of the EEC have been granted the status of observer to the ECT (including Canada, Pakistan, Morocco, Afghanistan and the United States), while other States enjoy observer status by invitation (including China, Iran, Nigeria, Saudi Arabia and Venezuela).[3]

---

1 Available at http://www.encharter.org/fileadmin/user_upload/document/EN.pdf. In literature, see, in particular: T.W. Wälde, *The Energy Charter Treaty. An East-West Gateway for Investment Trade* (The Hague: Kluwer, 1996); T.W. Wälde, 'Energy Charter Treaty-based Investment Arbitration', *JWI&T* 5 (2004), 373; C. Ribeiro (ed.), *Investment Arbitration and the Energy Charter Treaty* (Huntington: Juris Publishing, 2006); A. Konoplyanik and T.W. Wälde, 'Energy Charter Treaty and its Role in International Energy', *Journal Energy & Natural Resources Law* 24 (2006), 523; G. Coop and C. Ribeiro (eds.), *Investment Protection and The Energy Charter Treaty* (Huntington: Juris Publishing, 2008); G. Coop, *Energy Dispute Resolution: Investment Protection, Transit and the Energy Charter Treaty* (Huntington: Juris Publishing, 2011); Y. Selivanova, 'The Energy Charter and the International Energy Governance', *Eur. Yearbook of International Economic Law* 3 (2012), 307.

2 Currently, only Belarus applies provisionally the ECT.

3 The EEC is still open to signature. Montenegro has been the last State to sign it on 27 November 2012.

 | DOI 10.1163/9789004244719_006

Meanwhile, the landscape has changed significantly due to a number of events and developments, including the entry into force on 1 January 1995 of the Treaty establishing the World Trade Organization (WTO) and its related agreements,[4] the subsequent accession to the WTO amongst others by Ukraine and the Russian Federation, the enlargement of the EU, the progressive liberalization of the energy sector within the European Union (EU), the EU competence with regard to foreign investment under the Lisbon treaty,[5] the development of several important gas projects already functioning or under construction (including Nord Stream,[6] South Stream,[7] and Nabucco[8]) and the creation of the Energy Community.[9]

If one event needs to be singled out, however, this is the decision of the Russian government not to ratify the treaty, which was announced on

---

4 On the role of the WTO in regulating the energy sector, see G. Marceau, 'The WTO in the Emerging Energy Governance Debate', 106 *Proceedings American Society Int. Law* (2012) 385. See also Y. Selivanova (ed.), *Regulation of Energy in International Trade Law: WTO, NAFTA, and Energy Charter* (The Hague: Kluwer, 2011).

5 The treaty extends the common commercial policy to foreign direct investment (Article 207(1) TFEU) and pursues the progressive abolition of restriction on such investment (Article 206 TFEU). In literature, see in particular: M. Bungenberg, J. Griebel, S. Hindelang (eds.), "International Investment Law and EU Law", Special Issue of the *European Yearbook of International Economic Law* (2011); A. Dimopoulos, EU Foreign Investment Law (Oxford: Oxford University Press, 2011); F. Ortino and P. Eeckhout, "Towards an EU Policy on Foreign Direct Investment", in A. Biondi, P. Eeckhout, S. Ripley (eds.), *EU Law after Lisbon* (Oxford: Oxford University Press, 2012), 312.

6 Official website: http://www.nord-stream.com. The 1,224 twin offshore pipelines run from Vyborg, Russia to Lubmin near Greifswald, Germany. The pipelines were built and are operated by Nord Stream AG. They are both operative. Shareholders are OAO Gazprom (Russia, 51%), Wintershall Holding GmbH (Germany, 15,5%), E.ON Ruhrgas AG (Germany, 15,5%), N.V. Nederlandse Gasunie (Netherlands, 9%), and GDF Suez (France, 9%).

7 Official website: http://www.south-stream-offshore.com. The 930 kilometer offshore pipeline originates at the Russian Black Sea shore in the area of Anapa, crosses the Turkish Exclusive Economic Zone of the Black Sea and lands on the Bulgarian coast near Varna. Commercial operations are expected to start in 2015. Shareholders are OAO Gazprom (Russia, 50%), Eni S.p.A. (Italy, 20%), EDF (France, 1%), and Wintershall Holding GmbH (Germany, 15%).

8 Official website: http://www.nabucco-pipeline.com. The 1329 kilometer pipeline originates at the Turkish-Bulgarian border, traverses Bulgaria, Romania and Hungary, and ends at Baumgarten, in Austria. Shareholders are The Nabucco shareholders are: Bulgarian Energy Holding (Bulgaria), Botas (Turkey), FGSZ1 (Hungary), OMV (Austria), Transgaz (Romania).

9 Official website: http://www.energy-community.org. The organization has 10 parties (European Community, Albania, Bosnia-Herzegovina, Croatia, FRY Macedonia, Moldova, Montenegro, Serbia, Kosovo and Ukraine), 15 EU member States participants, and a few observers.

18 November 2009. The decision terminated the provisional application of the ECT to the Russian Federation – the main actor within the ECT constituency alongside the EU – and calls into question the energy relationship between the EU and the Russian Federation as well as the future of the ECT itself.[10]

This chapter aims at examining the main achievements and challenges of the ECT, taking into account that the ECT is the treaty expression of a process for the development of a stable and predictable legal framework of the energy sector as well as the creation of an international energy policy forum with a much broader mandate. From this perspective, the Energy Charter Conference (ECC) is charged *inter alia* of the periodic revision of the treaty (Article 34(7) ECT), whereas Articles 33 and 42 ECT expressly provide, respectively, for the conclusion of protocols and declarations, and for the adoption of amendments.

It also explores the perspectives ahead, with special attention to the role the Russian Federation may be expected to play with regard to foreign investment in the energy sector, to the reshaping of the energy-related relations between the EU and the Russian Federation and to the potential extension of the ECT constituency, especially to China, the Asian sub-continent and North Africa.

2 Preliminary Remarks on Some Specific Features of or Related to the ECT

This chapter deals essentially with two of the four pillars upon which the ECT has been built: foreign investment and transit. The other two pillars, namely trade and energy efficiency, are certainly related to the topic of this volume, but less central to it given its focus on balancing public and private rights in the field of foreign investment.

A couple of preliminary general considerations are in order, the first of which relates to trade. The ECT does not directly regulate trade issues. As between members that are also members of the WTO, WTO rules apply fully and exclusively.[11] Otherwise, the ECT adopts the so-called "WTO by reference" approach, whereby for the purpose of trade in energy materials and products, non-members of the WTO are treated as if they were members of the WTO and

10 For a political analysis of the implication of the Russian decision, see C. van Agt, "Tabula Russia. Escape from the Energy Charter Treaty", Clingendael International Energy Programme, Briefing Papers, September 2009, at http://www.clingendael.nl/publications/2009/20091001_ciep_paper_cvanagt_russia.pdf (accessed 25 October 2013).

11 Article 4 ECT.

WTO law – although with several important exceptions – is applied to their relationships with each other and with parties to both the ECT and the WTO.

The Trade Amendment to the ECT has subsequently extended the application by reference of WTO rules to trade in energy-related equipment.[12] It also includes a best endeavours tariff commitment for both energy materials and products and energy-related equipment, and establishes a mechanism to introduce a legally-binding stand-still on customs duties and charges for energy related import and export.

The importance of the trade-related provisions of the ECT, however, has significantly decreased in importance following the accession to the WTO of several parties to the ECT such as Kyrgyz Republic (1998), Georgia (2000), Armenia (2004), Ukraine (2008) and Tajikistan (2013), as well as the Russian Federation (2012), which had meanwhile terminated the provisional application of the ECT. As a result, only six parties to the ECT are still outside the WTO (Azerbaijan, Belarus, Bosnia and Herzegovina, Kazakhstan, Turkmenistan, and Uzbekistan).

The second consideration concerns the relationship between the EU and the Russian Federation in the energy sector. It would be incorrect to reduce the discussion on the ECT to such a relationship. At least for the time being, however, these two subjects remain by far the most important parties to the ECT process, and the future of the ECT hinges to a large extent on their capacity to conciliate their primary interests as, respectively, energy consumer and energy producer, keeping in mind that a stable and predictable legal framework in the energy sector is of vital importance for both of them.[13]

The third consideration is about the international market in the energy sector. It is worth recalling that Article 3 of the ECT, headed "International Market," reads: "The Contracting Parties shall work to promote access to international markets on commercial terms, and generally to develop an open and competitive market, for Energy Materials and Products."[14]

Within this general and qualified obligation, parties to the ECT may establish within their jurisdiction their own principles and schedules with a view of creating an internationally competitive market. Not surprisingly, the process

---

12 Entered into force on 21 January 2010.

13 On the importance of the energy sector for both parties, see, for instance, European Commission, EU – Russia Energy Relations, at http://ec.europa.eu/energy/international/russia/doc/20120329_pl_presentation_ep_eu_russia-clean.pdf (accessed 25 October 2013).

14 For similar commitments, see Article IV.1 of the Draft Convention on Ensuring International Security Energy proposed by the Russian Federation in December 2010.

of liberalization in the energy sector within the EU and the Russian Federation has developed at quite different paces and on the basis of often significantly different agendas and interests. The different approaches adopted by the EU and the Russian Federation to the international energy market have provoked tension between the two and cannot be ignored when discussing their energy relations and the future of the ECT. Mention should be made in this context to the progressive liberalization of the energy market on the European side and of the dual-price policy on the Russian side, not without noting that in both cases, the ultimate objective of both actions is the protection of domestic consumers.

With the adoption of the Third Energy Package, in particular, the European Union has reached a very high level of liberalization.[15] One of the cornerstones of the package – probably the most controversial one as far as the Russian Federation is concerned – is the introduction of an unbundling regime on transmission system operators imposing upon member States[16] the obligation to separate the network operations from production and supply activities of vertically integrated.

Three models are available to Member States. Under the so-called ownership unbundling, transmission undertakings are separated from supply, generation or production undertakings (ownership unbundling model). Two alternative models permit the company to maintain a vertically integrated structure but impose, respectively, the establishment of an independent system operator (ISO) or an independent transmission operator (ITO). Under the first option, the company keeps its network while renouncing to manage commercial and investment decisions. Under the second option, an autonomous operator must be equipped with all financial, technical, physical and human resources to perform all activities related to the transmission of electricity or gas.[17]

---

15 See, in particular, Directive 2009/73 (concerning common rules for the internal market in natural gas), 13 July 2009, OJ L211/94; Regulation 715/2009 (concerning the conditions for access to the natural gas transmission network), 13 July 2009, OJ L211/36. In literature, see A. Konoplyanik, "Russia and the Third EU Energy Package: Regulatory Changes for Internal EU Energy Markets in Gas and Possible Consequences for Suppliers (Including Non-EU Suppliers) and Consumers", *International Energy Law Review* 8 (2011), 24.

16 The same obligations are extended to the members of the Energy Community, see below Part 6.

17 For the specific requirement and conditions of each model, see Interpretative Note on Directive 2009/72/EC and Directive 2009/73/EC. The Unbundling Regime (non-legally binding), Brussels, 22 January 2010, 4, at http://ec.europa.eu/energy/gas_electricity/interpretative_notes/doc/implementation_notes/2010_01_21_the_unbundling_regime.pdf (accessed 25 October 2013).

According to the European Commission, the three models of unbundling models

> remove the incentive for vertically integrated undertakings to discriminate against competitors as regards access to the network, as regards access to commercially relevant information and as regards investments in the network. The three models should create incentives for the necessary investments and guarantee the access of new market entrants under a transparent and efficient regulatory regime.[18]

In addition to the requirements applicable to all companies regardless of their nationality, companies controlled by person(s) from third countries need to demonstrate that their activities will not put at risk the security of energy supply of the EU or its Members. Officially aimed at enhancing competition and consumer protection, the unbundling requirement is perceived by the Russian Federation as amounting to a trade distortive measure as well as a conduct discriminating and damaging Gazprom, which is traditionally a vertically integrated company.[19]

Still related to the unbundling requirement, mention must be made to the so-called contractual mismatch problem suppliers may face when the duration of long term supply and that of transport contracts do not correspond. The supplier could be exposed to the risk of being unable to honour the first contract and liability for the consequences non-compliance may entail. The problem can be overcome by granting suppliers a priority right over putative competitors with regard to the renewal of the transport contract (right to first refusal).[20]

The Russian Federation, in turn, adopts a dual pricing policy on natural gas, thus setting the domestic price at an affordable level and letting the export price to be fixed by the market. The question remains controversial and was hotly debated during the negotiations leading to the accession of the Russian Federation to the WTO. According to the Report of the Working Party, the

---

18 Interpretative Note, *supra* note 17, p. 4.

19 See A. Konoplyanik, "Why is Russia Opting Out of the Energy Charter?", *International Affairs. A Russian Journal of World Politics, Diplomacy and International Relations* 52 (2009), 84. On the recent strategy of Gazprom, see C. Locatelli, "Industrie gazière russe: le « modèle Gazprom » en question?", Cahier de recherche EDDEN n° 2/2013, April 2013, at http://halshs.archives-ouvertes.fr/docs/00/81/25/41/PDF/CL_CR2-2013-EDDEN.pdf (accessed 25 October 2013).

20 See A. Konoplyanik, "Gas Transit in Eurasia: Transit Issues between Russia and the European Union and the Role of the Energy Charter?", *Journal Energy & Natural Resources Law* 27 (2009), 445, especially pp. 479–482.

Russian Federation will continue to fix the price of domestically consumed natural gas and other goods and services as listed in tables 7 and 8.[21] The accession process was an opportunity for all parties to clarify the dual pricing issue and to find a mutually acceptable understanding as well as some guiding principles, including a commitment toward progressive liberalization as well as toward greater publicity and transparency of the price setting procedure.[22]

It cannot be ruled out that the consistency with WTO law of the two practices – unbundling regulations and dual pricing – could be challenged before WTO adjudicatory bodies, which after the Russian Federation's accession to the WTO and its termination of the provisional application of the ECT, seems the appropriate forum for these types of disputes. Both questions may nonetheless be expected to influence or to be linked to the negotiations on the future of the ECT or similar legal instruments.

A further complicating factor in the energy relations between the EU and Russia is the opening by the European Commission of an investigation against Gazprom for alleged abuse of its dominant market position in upstream gas supply in Central and Eastern European Member States.[23] This investigation

---

21 *Report of the Working Party on the Accession of the Russian Federation*, WT/ACC/RUS/70 WT/MIN(11)/2, 17 November 2011, paras 130 ff. Tables 7 and 8 contain, respectively, List of Goods and Services for Internal Consumption for which Prices are Regulated by the Government of the Russian Federation and Federal Executive Bodies, and List of Goods and Services for Internal Consumption for which Prices are Regulated by the Sub-Federal Executive Bodies. It has been reported that regulated gas prices have significantly increased recently, see J. Hendersen, "Domestic Gas Prices in Russia – Towards Export Netback?", Oxford Institute For Energy Studies, NG 57, November 2011, at http://www.oxfordenergy.org/wpcms/wp-content/uploads/2011/11/NG_57.pdf (accessed 25 October 2013).

22 The Russian Federation denies that dual pricing may amount to subsidies since the pricing system is not specific, but applies generally across Russian economy, *Report of the Working Party*, *supra* note 21, para. 124. Interestingly, Article IV.3(5) of the Draft Convention on Ensuring International Security Energy expressly admits the compatibility with WTO law of difference in pricing that are neither conditional on export nor specific. In literature, see in particular, Y. Selivanova, *Energy Dual Pricing in the WTO: Analysis and Prospects in the Context of Russia's Accession to the World Trade Organization* (London: Cameron May, 2008); V. Pogoretskyy, "The System of Energy Dual Pricing in Russia and Ukraine: The Consistency of the Energy Dual Pricing System with the WTO Agreement on Anti-dumping", *Global Trade and Customs Journal* 4 (2009), 313.

23 Case No. 39816: *Upstream gas supplies in Central and Eastern Europe*, Press release 4 September 2012, at http://europa.eu/rapid/press-release_IP-12-937_en.htm?locale=en. For a political analysis of the political implications of the case, see N. Sartori, "The European Commission vs. Gazprom: An Issue of Fair Competition or a Foreign Policy

is quite unique due to its economic magnitude and political implications, as confirmed by the importance attached by the Russian government to this case and in general to Russian investment in strategic sectors.[24]

3 Main Achievements of the Energy Charter Treaty

The history of the ECT is a largely successful one for several reasons. The conclusion of a multilateral treaty on the energy sector, including foreign investment, is in itself an achievement, especially since it required striking a delicate balance between the interests of energy-producing and energy-consuming countries, as well as the interests of States, private and State controlled companies and consumers.

This was possible thanks to the remarkable political momentum existing in the early 90s toward the creation of Eurasian legal framework in the energy sector, backed by the awareness of the enormous economic mutual advantages and the sharing amongst the contracting parties of the basic principles underpinning the EEC and subsequently the ECT.

The contracting parties to the ECT managed to agree on a comprehensive and quite sophisticated legal framework for the entire cycle of energy, from production to delivery. The holistic approach based on the four pillars must be emphasized. Whereas other attempts to conclude multilateral investment treaties have failed due to insurmountable divergences on key issues, including the definition of investment, safeguard clauses or the settlement of disputes,[25] the contracting parties of the ECT not only managed to agree on the legal protection of foreign investment – which remains the core of the treaty –

Quarrel?", International Affairs Institute Working Paper 13/03, January 2013, at http://www.iai.it/pdf/DocIAI/iaiwp1303.pdf (accessed 25 October 2013). See also A. Riley, "Commission v. Gazprom: The antitrust clash of the decade?", CEPS Policy Briefs (No. 285, 31 October 2012), at www.ceps.eu/ceps/dld/7433/pdf.

24 See, in particular, the reaction of the Russia Presidency, which took the form of the Executive order on measures protecting Russian interests in Russian legal entities' foreign economic activities, Moscow, 11 September 2012, at http://eng.news.kremlin.ru/news/4401 (accessed 25 October 2013).

25 See, in particular, OSCE, Multilateral Agreement on Investment Draft Consolidated Text and Commentary, 22 April 1998, respectively DAFFE/MAI(98)7/REVI and DAFFE/MAI(98)8/REVI; UNCTAD, *Lessons from the MAI, New York and Geneva*, 1999, UNCTAD/ITE/IIT/MISC. 22; P.T. Muchlinski, "The Rise and Fall of the Multilateral Agreement on Investment: Where Now?", *International Lawyer* 34 (2000), 1033.

but also completed it with rules on trade and transit as well as a protocol on energy efficiency.

The ECC and then the ECT created a permanent international policy forum from the beginning. The contracting parties considered regulating the energy sector as a continuing process due to the need to adapt the legal framework to the rapidly evolving energy landscape and the changing needs of the various stakeholders.

The substantive provisions on the protection of foreign investment contained in Part III of the ECT can be considered as the successful synthesis and elaboration of the typical provisions that are normally found in bilateral investment treaties, including fair and equitable treatment, protection and security, expropriation, national treatment and most favoured nation treatment.

Moreover, the ECT took quite an innovative stand with regard to the protection of the environment. In addition to the reference to multilateral environmental treaties in the preamble, which may be of great relevance with regard to both interpretation of the ECT and the law applicable to disputes brought before domestic courts or arbitral tribunals, the treaty consecrates a long provision on the protection of the environment and is complemented by the Protocol on Energy Efficiency and Related Environmental Aspects (PEEREA).[26]

Under Article 19 ECT, in particular, parties shall strive to minimize in an economically efficient manner the harmful environmental impacts of the activities in the energy sector, including through precautionary measures where appropriate, and taking into account the polluter-pays principle.[27] Although falling outside the scope of application of Articles 26 and 27, respectively on the settlement of disputes between foreign investors and State and between States, the importance of Article 19 must be stressed given the scarce attention normally paid to environmental issues in investment related treaties.[28]

An essential feature of the ECT is the mandatory mechanism for the settlement of disputes between foreign investors and State parties in relation to

26 The PEEREA entered into force as the ECT on 16 April 1998 and has the same parties.

27 See also Article 7 of the Draft Protocol on Transit.

28 For some sharp criticism on the attitude of negotiators of the draft Multilateral Agreement on Investment at the OECD, see the United Kingdom House of Commons, Trade and Industry Committee, *3rd Report*, 1998–99, at http://www.publications.parliament.uk/pa/cm199899/cmselect/cmtrdind/112/11201.htm, especially para. 52. The recent study by K. Gordon, J. Pohl, "Environmental Concerns in Investment Agreements: A Survey", OECD Working Papers on International Investment, No. 2011/1, May 2011, at http://www.oecd-ilibrary.org/finance-and-investment/environmental-concerns-in-international-investment-agreements_5kg9mq7scrjh-en (accessed 25 October 2013), reveals an increasingly attention for the protection of the environment in investment treaties.

alleged violations of the obligation contained in Part III (Investment promotion and protection).[29] Significantly, under Article 26, arbitration is available to foreign investors but not to the host State. This confirms the – so far – manifestly unbalanced nature of investment treaties in which foreign investors have no obligations susceptible of adjudication. Article 26 generously offers three *fora* for international arbitration, in addition or in alternative to domestic tribunals:[30] arbitration under the Convention of for the Settlement of Investment Disputes between States and National of another States (ICSID), arbitration under UNCITRAL rules or arbitral proceedings under the Arbitration Institute of the Stockholm Chamber of Commerce. Arbitral awards issued in application of Article 26 clarified a number of important issues related to the ECT including the definition of investment,[31] the functioning of denial of benefits clause[32] and the provisional application of the ECT.[33]

It is safe to maintain that the treaty at the normative level and the related arbitral awards at the jurisprudential level have contributed to the emergence and consolidation of the ECT *acquis* in the field of foreign investment. Any future arrangement or agreement related to, replacing or concurring with the ECT would naturally build upon and develop such *acquis*. Significantly, the Road Map for the Modernisation of the Energy Charter Process, agreed in 2010, clearly maintained that "the ECT's investment provisions should remain untouched in their fundamentals."[34]

---

29 See, for instance, *Plama Consortium Limited* v. *Bulgaria*, ICSID Case No. ARB/03/24, Jurisdiction, 8 February 2005, para. 141 *in fine*. In literature, see in particular, K. Hobér, "Investment Arbitration and the Energy Charter Treaty", *Journal of International Dispute Settlement* 1 (2010), 153; T. Roe and M. Happold, *Settlement of Disputes under the Energy Charter Treaty* (Cambridge: Cambridge University Press, 2011) and the chapter by Eric De Brabandere in this volume.

30 Article 26(3)(b) provides for an optional "fork-in-the-road" clause.

31 See, for example, *Petrobart Ltd. (Gibraltar) v. Kyrgyzstan*, SCC Case 126/2003, Award, 24 March 2005; *Limited Liability Company Amto v. Ukraine*, SCC Case No. 080/2005, Final Award, 26 March 2008.

32 See, for example, *Plama Consortium Ltd. (Cyprus) v. Bulgaria*, ICSID Case ARB/03/24, Award, 27 August 2008.

33 See, for example, *Yukos Universal Ltd. v. Russian Federation*, PCA Case AA 227, Interim Award on Jurisdiction and Admissibility, 30 November 2009; *Hulley Enterprises Ltd. v. The Russian Federation*, PCA Case No. AA 226, Interim Award on Jurisdiction and Admissibility, 30 November 2009; *Veteran Petroleum Ltd. v. The Russian Federation*, PCA Case No. AA 228, Interim Award on Jurisdiction and Admissibility, 30 November 2009. Hereinafter reference is made only to the first case.

34 At http://www.encharter.org/fileadmin/user_upload/document/Road_Map_ENG.pdf, p. 6 (accessed 25 October 2013).

4 Main Difficulties of the Energy Charter Treaty

The major problems in the history of the ECT relates to transit. They have caused controversy and some of them still continue to undermine the functioning of the treaty and call for its modernization.

From the outset, transit was perceived as part and parcel of the energy legal framework. To conclude the ECT rapidly, the contracting parties defined the basic principles on transit issues in Article 7, a rather long and complex, but far from clear and satisfactory provision.[35]

Article 7 contains no mandatory third party access to transit facilities.[36] Rather, it imposes upon the parties the obligation to take the necessary measures to *facilitate* transit of energy materials and products without distinction as to their origin, destination or ownership and to refrain from making any discrimination as to pricing or imposing any unreasonable delays, restrictions or charges. Contracting parties have also committed themselves not to interrupt or reduce existing transit flows, even in the event of a transit-related dispute.

It was almost immediately evident that Article 7 needed to be complemented by a protocol on transit, not only to improve the norms on transit and enhance the mechanism for the settlement of disputes, but also to permit the ratification of the ECT by the Russian Federation. Already in 2001, the Russian Duma clearly expressed that the conclusion of a protocol on transit was a pre-condition for the ratification of the ECT by the Russian Federation.[37]

Whereas it had been possible to reach an agreement on most transit issues, a couple of questions proved rather problematic and are still outstanding, including the scope of the obligations related to transport, the coordination of long term supply and transit contracts, the so-called Regional Economic Integration Organization (REIO) clause and the settlement of energy transit disputes.[38]

Article 7(3) deals with transport and is open to two plausible interpretations bearing important economic implications. Article 7(3) reads:

---

35 See Konoplyanik, *supra* note 20.

36 Final Act of the European Energy Charter Conference, Understandings, Section IV (1) (b) (i) Energy Charter Secretariat, *The Energy Charter Treaty. A Reader's Guide*, 25, at http://www.encharter.org/fileadmin/user_upload/Publications/ECT_Guide_ENG.pdf.

37 A. Konoplyanik, "Russia-EU, G-8, ECT and Transit Protocol", *Russian/CIS Energy & Mining Law Journal* 4 (2006), 9.

38 Negotiations on an ECT Transit Protocol began in 2000. In spite of the agreement reached on several key issues, negotiations were suspended in 2003. Following the submission by the EU of anew common position in October 2011, the ECC repealed the mandate for negotiations on November 2011.

> Each Contracting Party undertakes that its provisions relating to transport of Energy Materials and Products and the use of Energy Transport Facilities shall treat Energy Materials and Products in Transit in no less favourable a manner than its provisions treat such materials and products originating in or destined for its own Area, unless an existing international agreement provides otherwise.[39]

Depending on the inclusive or exclusive character of the conjunction "or", parties to the ECT have or do not have an obligation to apply to international transit the same transportation tariff they apply to domestic transport.[40] Divergent interpretations of Article 7(3) have sharply divided the EU and the Russian Federation, although it has been reported that a compromise had eventually been reached in the context of the (so far unsuccessful) negotiations to conclude a transit protocol.[41]

The controversy however has not been definitely settled yet. The ambiguity needs to be eliminated, not only in the context of the reshaping of the legal relationship between the Russian Federation and the other parties to the ECT, but also amongst the latter and eventually between them and any future new party.

Another major problem relates to the application of the ECT to regional economic integration organisations (REIO) – such as the EU – alongside their member States. According to the EU, transit obligations apply to the territory

---

39 G. Coop, "The Energy Charter Treaty. What Lies Ahead?", in Coop and Ribeiro, *supra* note 1, 325, in which the author pointed out that '[t]he fact that this ambiguity remained in the final ECT after three years of negotiations suggests that its being permitted to remain was a deliberate choice by the negotiating parties. On this basis, it would seem extremely difficult to predict how an arbitral tribunal would resolve the ambiguity'.

40 For a full discussion, see N. Nychay and D. Shemelin, "Interpretation of Article 7(3) of the Energy Charter Treaty", Graduate Institute of International and Development Studies, Trade and Investment Law Clinic Papers (2012), at http://graduateinstitute.ch/webdav/site/ctei/shared/CTEI/Law%20Clinic/memoranda2012/Law_Clinic%20NNDS%20ECT.pdf (accessed 25 October 2013).

41 See, A. Konoplyanik, "Regulating Energy Relations: *Acquis* or Energy Charter?", in K. Barysch (ed.), *Pipelines, Politics and Powers* (London: Center European Relations, 2008), 108. In this sense, see the understanding with respect to Draft Article 10 regarding ECT Article 7.3 included in the Final Act on the ECT Conference on the Energy Charter Protocol on Transit, Preliminary Draft, 22 January 2010, at http://www.encharter.org/fileadmin/user_upload/document/TTG_87_ENG.pdf (accessed 25 October 2013). The document clarifies that the understanding was brought forward by the Russian paper submitted to the Trade and Transit Group on 10 June 2008 based on the unofficial EU-Russian Federation expert meetings in 2005 and 2006.

of a REIO as a whole, rather than to both the territory of the REIO and the territory of its Members.

The argument of the EU is based on the assumption that the combination of the application of the national treatment to products in free circulation within the territory of the EU and the obligation to provide an overall standard at least equivalent to that resulting from the protocol would ensure other parties to the ECT an adequate protection in terms of transit.

The position was translated into the so-called "REIO clause" that was included in Article 20 of the Draft Energy Charter Protocol in the following terms:

> A Regional Economic Integration Organisation undertakes to ensure that its provisions treat Energy Materials and Products originating in another Contracting Party and in free circulation in its Area no less favourably than Energy Materials and Products originating in its constituent member-states. Furthermore, the rules of a Regional Economic Integration Organisation shall provide an overall standard at least equivalent to that resulting from the provisions of this Protocol.[42]

This provision was deemed unacceptable by the Russian Federation. For the Russian Federation, transit obligations are quite different if applicable to the territory of each members of the RIEO, or that of the RIEO as a whole.[43] In practical terms, Article 20 would ultimately reduce the relevance of the transit obligations contained in the ECT to transit through the territory of the EU, as in the case of transport to Russian enclaves, Switzerland or Turkey. From this perspective, the REIO can hardly be considered as not entirely satisfactory *inter alia* because the interpretation and concrete application of the expression "overall standard" and the notion of equivalence may be problematic.

42 Adopted on 31 October 2003 as Annex 1 of the Final Act of the Energy Charter Conference, available at http://www.encharter.org/fileadmin/user_upload/document/CC251.pdf (accessed 25 October 2013). Compare Article 20 of the draft protocol it with Article V.4 of the Convention on Ensuring International Security Energy, according to which, "If the Parties to the Convention are not only REIOs but also their Member States, the definition of Transit and corresponding Transit provisions of the Convention shall apply to the REIOs as well as to each of these States".

43 The position of the Russian Federation is clearly stated in Article V.4 (Transit through a REIO) of the Draft Convention on Energy Security, according to which "If the Parties to the Convention are not only REIOs but also their Member States, the definition of Transit and corresponding Transit provisions of the Convention shall apply to the REIOs as well as to each of these States".

From an international law perspective, it is certainly possible for the EU to take responsibility for international commitments of its members, as it has happened under the GATT Agreement.[44] However, such an arrangement cannot affect the full enjoyment by the concerned party or parties of the rights protected under the relevant treaty. Furthermore, it remains to be seen which kind of deference to European institutions, most importantly the European Court of Justice, would be appropriate in the context of transit disputes that may arise under the ECT.

Article 7 of the ECT establishes a conciliation procedure to settle transit disputes and set up a mechanism to fix interim transit tariffs for period of maximum 12 months. In practice, however, it has failed to prevent or settle the disputes that affected transit across the Area. During the most serious crisis, which erupted in 2009 between the Russian Federation and Ukraine,[45] no resort was made to the conciliation mechanism under Article 7(7), allegedly due to the contractual nature of the dispute,[46] whereas neither the ECT Secretariat nor the European Union were able to defuse the crisis. Quite surprisingly, the ECT Secretariat maintained that the Treaty, which at the time was nearly 15 years old, was never meant to resolve immediate crisis situations.[47] The crisis showed the inadequacy of the ECT as it stood and prompted the Russian government to launch an initiative for a new legal framework for energy cooperation.[48]

The failure on transit issues is double, as parties to the ECT have been incapable to agree on a protocol defining transit rights and obligations and

44 See, for instance, *European Communities – Customs Classification of Certain Computer Equipment*, WT/DS62/AB/R, 5 June 1998.

45 See S. Pirani, J. Stern and K. Yafimava, "The Russo-Ukrainian Gas Dispute of January 2009: A Comprehensive Assessment", Oxford Institute for Energy Studies, February 2009, at http://www.oxfordenergy.org/2009/02/the-russo-ukrainian-gas-dispute-of-january-2009-a-comprehensive-assessment/ (accessed 25 October 2013).

46 During the crisis, the ECT Secretariat pointed out that "[t]he dispute relates to a supply contract and is a commercial matter", ECT Secretary General, Statement on Russia-Ukraine Gas Dispute, 23 December 2008, at http://www.encharter.org/index.php?id=21&id_article=167&L=0 (accessed 25 October 2013). According to Article 7(7), the conciliation procedure is available only following the exhaustion of all relevant contractual or other dispute resolution remedies previously agreed.

47 'A Word from the Secretary General on the Energy Crisis of Early 2009', 6 February 2009, at http://www.encharter.org/index.php?id=21&id_article=171&L=0 (accessed 25 October 2013).

48 President of Russia, *Conceptual Approach to the New Legal Framework for Energy Cooperation* (*Goals and Principles*), 21 April 2009, at http://archive.kremlin.ru/eng/text/docs/2009/04/215305.shtml (accessed 24 October 2013).

establishing an effective mechanism for the settlement of disputes. This is particularly disappointing as it was immediately evident that the provisions on transit were not only unsatisfactory, but also an insurmountable obstacle to the ratification of the ECT by the Russian Federation.

Although the opening of alternative routes, especially offshore, is expected to downsize their importance, transit issues remain a real obstacle to the process of modernization of the ECT or the negotiation of a similar legal framework.

5 The Russian Decision Not to Ratify the ECT and Its Consequences

On 20 August 2009, the Russian Federation declared its intention not to ratify the ECT.[49] The decision is obviously a setback in the process and may have heavy consequences on the regulation of the energy sector in Eurasia in general and on the protection of foreign investment in particular. There is, however, no need to dramatize the situation.

The ECT applied provisionally to the Russian Federation, in accordance with Article 45, from 17 December 1994 (date of signature) until 19 October 2009 (sixty calendar days from the notification to the Depository of the intention not to ratify the ECT). In the *Yukos v. Russian Federation* the arbitral tribunal convincingly rejected the contrary claim put forward by the Russian Federation.[50]

Yet, foreign investments made during the provisional application of the ECT by investor of the Russian Federation in the territory of any other party of the ECT or the other way around will not be deprived of the legal protection under this treaty. As confirmed in *Yukos v. Russian Federation*, in accordance with Article 45(3)(b), Parts III and V of the ECT continue to be applicable to these investments for a period of 20 years, which means until 19 October 2029.[51]

49 Notification of 20 August 2009 by Russian Federation to Portuguese Republic pursuant to Article 45(3)(a) of the Treaty. See also Regulation of the Government of the Russian Federation No. 1055-r of 30 July 2009.

50 *Yukos v. Russian Federation, supra* note 33, para. 394. See also *Ioannis Kardassopoulos v. The Republic of Georgia*, ICSID Case No. ARB/05/18, Decision on Jurisdiction; 6 July 2007, para. 211; *Libananco Holdings Co. Limited v. Republic of Turkey*, ICSID Case No. ARB/06/8; Award, 2 September 2011, para. 546. See also the Chapter by Eric de Brabandere in this volume.

51 *Yukos v. Russian Federation, supra* note. 33, para. 339.

Furthermore, the Russian Federation remains a signatory of the EEC and as such it is entitled to participate in the Energy Charter process as confirmed in the Road Map for the Modernization of the EC Process, which expressly envisages the participation of any signatory of the Energy Charter in the negotiations for the conclusion on a protocol of the ECT on transit, in accordance with Article 33 of the ECT.[52]

Strictly speaking, under Article 18 of the Vienna Convention on the Law of Treaties, the Russian Federation does not seem to be obliged any more to refrain from acts which would defeat the object and purpose of the ECT. The risk of defeating the object and purpose of the ECT, however, seems remote, considering the continuing application of the ECT for 20 years with regard to existing investment and the obligation to respect customary international law and general principles vis-à-vis investors of any State, as well as Russian legislation (which has often been revised in the last few years to ensure consistency with the ECT) and any other legal instruments binding the Russian Federation vis-à-vis the concerned parties.

Indeed, it must be emphasised that investments made after the termination of the provisional application of the ECT to the Russian Federation will be protected by customary international law, general principles of law, investment treaties (including bilateral investment treaties – BITs), national legislation and State contracts. It is worth noting that BITs are currently in force between the Russian Federation and 23 parties to the ECT, including 17 Members of the EU.[53]

Foreign investments between the EU and the Russian Federation, furthermore, continue to be protected under the "Agreement on partnership and cooperation establishing a partnership between the European Communities and their Member States, of one part, and the Russian Federation, of the other

---

52 See *supra* note 34. It remains to be seen whether the Russian Federation can still be considered as a signatory of the ECT, a question that goes beyond the purpose of this paper. As pointed out by G. Gaja, *Yearbook International Law Commission*, 2011, UN Doc A/66/10, Annex C (Provisional application of treaties), 333, "The Vienna Convention [on the Law of the Treaties] does not specify the consequences of termination of an agreement on provisional application of a treaty. One could envisage that Article 70 of the Vienna Convention, which considers consequences of termination of a treaty in general, also applies to an agreement on provisional application".

53 According to ICSID website, https://icsid.worldbank.org/ICSID/FrontServlet? request Type=ICSIDPublicationsRH&actionVal=ViewBilateral&reqFrom=Main/ (accessed 24 October 2013).

part" concluded in 1997 which is formally still in force.[54] The agreement is to a certain extent obsolete due to the evolution of the Russian Federation into a market economy and its accession to the WTO. It contains nonetheless significant provisions on the protection of foreign investment (especially Titles IV and V, respectively on Business and investment, and Payment and capital) although the level of protection is not comparable to that normally guaranteed under BITs and does not offer foreign investors any mechanism for the settlement of disputes. Negotiations are currently under way to conclude a new agreement.[55]

Besides, the EU-Russia Energy Dialogue was established in 1994 in order to provide a specific forum to enhance the cooperation in the energy sector along lines that are reminiscent of the objective of the ECT. It has been recently maintained that

> Russia and the EU share the same concerns for ensuring stable energy markets, reliable and growing imports and exports, a pressing need to modernise the Russian energy sector, to improve energy efficiency and to reduce greenhouse gas emissions from energy production and use in their respective economies. Against this background, a number of common and complementary interests can be identified, such as the short and long-term reliability of energy supplies, energy efficiency, a desire to secure long term investments, opening up energy markets, diversifying the range of energy products traded and enhancing the technology base of the energy sector of the economy.[56]

---

54 Agreement on partnership and cooperation establishing a partnership between the European Communities and their Member States, of one part, and the Russian Federation, of the other part, OJ L 327, 28 November 1997, p. 3, at http://eur-lex.europa.eu/LexUriServ/LexUriServ.do?uri=CELEX:21997A1128(01):EN:HTML (accessed 24 October 2013).

55 See Joint statement of the EU-Russia summit on the launch of negotiations for a new EU-Russia agreement, Khanty-Mansiysk, 27 June 2008, 11214/08 (Presse 192), at http://www.consilium.europa.eu/ueDocs/cms_Data/docs/pressData/en/er/101524.pdf (accessed 24 October 2013).

56 EU-Russia Energy Dialogue, *Joint Report 2000–2010: Opportunities for our future Energy Partnership*, November 2010, p. 4. On the coexistence of EU law and ECT, see G. Coop, "Energy Charter Treaty and the European Union: Is Conflict Inevitable?", *Journal Energy & Natural Resources Law* 27 (2009), 404.

The EU-Russia Energy Dialogue has obtained several significant results,[57] including the conclusion of an early warning mechanism on emergency situations in the energy sector[58] and the Energy efficiency initiative.[59] The dialogue eventually led to the recent definition of a roadmap for long-term cooperation in the energy sector. This non-legally binding policy agreement has been described as a living instrument providing for "a common reference in the context of the EU-Russian Federation Energy Dialogue."[60]

6 The Future of the ECT and of the Energy Relations between the EU and the Russian Federation

The ECT remains one of the cornerstones of the regulation of the energy sector in the region, but can hardly afford to keep the Russian Federation out. While there is a large convergence on most provisions on the legal protection of foreign investment, several important issues remain controversial and need to be solved through negotiations. From this perspective, the elaboration of clear provisions on transit and the issue of unbundling deserve to be given priority. Several options are available to the parties for the full participation of the Russian Federation in the ECT.

One option seems rather remote and can be safely discarded, namely the extension of the so-called *acquis communautaire* to the Russian Federation through the membership to the Energy Community. The basic idea behind the Energy Community, indeed, is the application of EU energy legislation to the

57 For a recent overview, see EU-Russia Energy Permanent Partnership Council – 12th Progress Report of the EU-Russia Energy Dialogue, Moscow, 1 December 2011, at http://ec.europa.eu/energy/international/russia/doc/20111201_eu_russia_report.pdf (accessed 24 October 2013).

58 Memorandum on a Mechanism for Preventing and Overcoming Emergency Situations in the Energy Sector (Early Warning Mechanism), 24 November 2011, at http://ec.europa.eu/energy/international/russia/doc/reports/2009_11_16_ewm_signed_en.pdf (accessed 24 October 2013).

59 Energy Efficiency GrOxford University Press, Report 2010, at http://ec.europa.eu/energy/international/russia/dialogue/doc/2010_energy_efficiency_report.pdf (accessed 24 October 2013).

60 *Roadmap EU-Russia Energy Cooperation until 2050*, March 2013, at http://ec.europa.eu/energy/international/russia/doc/2013_03_eu_russia_roadmap_2050_signed.pdf (accessed 24 October 2013). For a comparison between the Road map and the Russian proposal for a new treaty, see A. Belyi, S. Nappert and V. Pogoretskyy, "Modernizing the Energy Charter Process? The Energy Charter Conference Road Map and the Russian Draft Convention on Energy Security", *Oil, Gas & Energy Law Intelligence* (2011).

territory of neighbouring States in the perspective of the progressive intensification of their economic relations with the EU and their eventual accession to the EU. Such an option remains – quite understandably – unacceptable for Moscow both from a political and economic perspective.[61]

Under the second option, the Russian government could reconsider any time its position and eventually resubmit to the Duma the question of the ratification of the ECT as it stands. Such a possibility, however, seems realistic only if accompanied by the conclusion, or alternatively the provisional application, of a protocol on transit alongside with the ECT. From the standpoint of the law of the treaties, the history of the Russian participation to the ECT would be a rather atypical sequence of actions (signature, provisional application, decision not to ratify the treaty, extension of the application of parts III and V of the treaty under Article 45, and eventually ratification or further provisional application). With the consent of the concerned parties, however, all possible technical problems can be overcome.

The third and arguably most effective option is the revision of the ECT with the inclusion of appropriate provisions on transit, or in combination with the conclusion of a protocol on transit. Although the provisions on foreign investment do not urgently need any major amendment, the revision of the ECT would offer the opportunity not only to clarify and elaborate some of them in accordance with settled case law, but also to consider the introduction of new ones, either in mandatory or hortatory terms. This may be the case, in particular, of provisions on specific categories of energy and especially renewables, the promotion of a low-carbon economy,[62] the protection of the environment (including possibly an obligation to carry out an environmental impact assessment),[63] human rights and labour standards, transparency[64] and corporate responsibility.[65]

---

61 See A. Konoplyanik, "A Common Russia–EU Energy Space: The New EU-Russia Partnership Agreement, *Acquis Communautaire* and the Energy Charter", *Journal of Energy & Natural Resources Law* 27 (2009), 258.

62 UNCTAD, *World Investment Report 2010, Investing in a Low-Carbon Economy*, at http://unctad.org/fr/Docs/wir2010_en.pdf (accessed 24 October 2013).

63 Such an obligation already exists under international law in a transboundary context or in the case of shared resources, as maintained in *Pulp Mills on the River Uruguay* (*Argentina v. Uruguay*), *Provisional Measures*, Order of 13 July 2006, I.C.J. Reports *2006*, p. 105.

64 See, for instance, Article 11 of the 2012 U.S. Model Bilateral Investment Treaty at http://italaw.com/sites/default/files/archive/ital028.pdf (accessed 24 October 2013).

65 See, for instance, Article 810 of the FTA between Canada and Peru, at http://www.sice.oas.org/Trade/CAN_PER/CAN_PER_e/CAN_PER_text_e.asp#Cha08Art01 (accessed 24 October 2013).

The fourth option would consist in the conclusion of a new multilateral legal instrument replacing the ECT and incorporating a complete treatment of transit issues (or alternatively combined with a protocol on transit). In substantive terms, this option does not seem remarkably different from the previous two, as the majority of the current provisions of the ECT on the protection of foreign investment are undisputed and can be expected to find their way into the new treaty. While not presenting any specific great advantage, this option would be much more complicated than the previous two, due to the process of ratification or provisional application of the new instrument and its coordination with the ECT. From this perspective, it is argued that the new instrument proposed by the Russian government in 2009[66] can hardly be expected to adequately replace the ECT, due to its vagueness and selectiveness, but can certainly stimulate its modernization.[67]

The next option would be a treaty between the EU and its members, on one hand, and the Russian Federation, on the other hand. This may take a variety of forms, including a new partnership agreement replacing the one concluded in 2007 and containing detailed provisions on foreign investment in the energy sector and on transit,[68] a BIT with a section on energy investment and transit or a treaty specifically dealing with energy issues. This option seem to be both rather unlikely and hardly appealing as it would lead to the creation of a set of rules parallel or similar to the ECT at the expenses of uniformity and simplicity.

The sixth option would be to develop a complete network of bilateral investment treaties between the Russian Federation and parties to the ECT and conclude a multilateral agreement on transit issues. Such an option would not only be time-consuming and cumbersome, but would also depart from the multilateral approach, which characterized the ECT and its evident advantages. A variant of this option would the adoption of a transit protocol to existing bilateral investment treaties and the inclusion in the new bilateral investment treaties of transit provisions. The complexity and strict bilateral character of this variant makes this option even less attractive.

66 See *supra* note 48.

67 In this sense, see A. Konoplyanik, "Energy Charter and the Russian Initiative. Future Prospects of the Legal Basis of International Cooperation", *Oil, Gas & Energy Law Intelligence* (2009), 4.

68 In the 10th Progress Report, Energy Dialogue EU – Russia (November 2009), 10–11, the parties noted the continuation of the discussion on a new agreement intended to replace the existing PCA and declared that "energy, as a strategically important issue of cooperation between the EU and Russia will be one of the most substantive elements of this agreement".

Finally, the EU, its members and the Russian Federation may shelve, at least temporarily, the idea of a legally binding agreement and focus instead on the conclusion of policy documents based on best endeavour commitments. From this perspective, foreign investment between the EU and the Russian Federation – which are not covered by the extended application of the ECT until 2029 – will need to be legally protected through contracts or national legislation. This option, furthermore, will lead to an asymmetrical treatment, as a matter of treaty law, of investments between the EU and the Russia Federation, on one hand, and those between the EU or the Russian Federation and the other parties of the ECT, on the other hand. This option may nonetheless represent an intermediate step toward the ratification of the ECT, possibly in a revised form, or the conclusion of a new international treaty.

While the future trajectory of Russia remains rather difficult to predict[69] and in spite of the increasing tendency to resort to bilateral regulation of energy issues amongst States, amongst energy companies, and between States and energy companies,[70] the mutual benefits of a multilateral treaty like the ECT are self-evident for all stakeholders – namely States, private companies and ultimately the consumer. Such benefits however call for reciprocal concessions with a view to modernizing the treaty or concluding a new one (which inexorably will largely reproduce the ECT).

7 The Possible Expansion of the ECT Constituency

Alongside the reshaping of the relationship with the Russian Federation, the parties of the ECT face another important challenge in relation of the expansion of the treaty's constituency to China, the Asian sub-continent and North Africa.[71]

---

69 See, for instance, F. Cameron, "The Politics of EU-Russia Energy Relations", EU-Russia Centre, Brussels (2009), at http://www.isn.ethz.ch/isn/Digital-Library/Publications/Detail/?ots591=0c54e3b3-1e9c-be1e-2c24-a6a8c7060233&lng=en&id=105732 (accessed 24 October 2013).

70 See, in particular, A. Belyi, "Reciprocity as a factor of the energy investment regimes in the EU-Russia energy relations", *Journal of World Energy Law & Business* 2 (2009), 117 and S. Boussena and C. Locatelli, "Energy Institutional and Organisational Changes in EU and Russia Revisiting Gas Relations", *Energy Policy* 55 (2013), 180.

71 The European Commission, ('On security of energy supply and international cooperation – The EU Energy Policy Engaging with Partners beyond Our Borders', Brussels, COM(2011) 539 final, http://eur-lex.europa.eu/LexUriServ/LexUriServ.do?uri=COM:2011:0539:FIN:EN:PDF (accessed 24 October 2013)), has maintained that

The potential of the expansion eastward cannot be overestimated due to several factors, including the enormous surplus of natural resources of certain former Soviet Union republics (most prominently Kazakhstan for crude oil and Turkmenistan for natural gas) and the equally enormous demand for energy in India, Pakistan and China.[72] From this perspective, several important projects have been developed or are under development in the Eurasia region and Afghanistan,[73] which recently announced completion of the domestic process of ratification of the ECT, may be expected to play a role of primary importance.[74]

Extending the constituency of the ECT would offer several important advantages. In practical terms, accession to the ECT would be much quicker than negotiating and concluding BITs with the current member States of the ECT. For example, for the time being only one BIT has entered into force with

---

"to maintain its relevance, the Energy Charter Treaty should seek to extend membership towards North Africa and Far East. The EU considers it would be mutually beneficial if Russia plays a full role in this multilateral framework".

72 ECT Secretary General Rusnák's interview to European Energy Review, 7 June 2012, http://www.encharter.org/fileadmin/user_upload/document/SG_EER_interview_7_June_2012.pdf (accessed 24 October 2013). See also V. Vucetic and V. Krishnaswamy, "Development of Electricity Trade in Central Asia-South Asia Region", http://siteresources.worldbank.org/INTSOUTHASIA/556101-1100091707765/21358230/AfghanistanElectricityTradePaperforDelhiRECC(111006).pdf (accessed 24 October 2013); S. Zhang, "Energy Charter Treaty and China: Member or Bystander?", *Journal of World Investment & Trade* 13 (2012), 597. N. Yodogawa and A.M. Peterson, "An Opportunity for Progress: China, Central Asia, and the Energy Charter Treaty", *Texas Journal of Oil, Gas, and Energy Law* 8 (2013), 113 have pointed out that "China acceding to the ECT after Russia has left by terminating its provisional application would mean a step towards becoming a meaningful partner in the development of Central Asia as opposed to a mere financier, which would help to counterbalance Russia's soft power in Central Asia".

73 The major projects include the Central Asia-South Asia Regional Electricity Trade Project (http://web.worldbank.org/WBSITE/EXTERNAL/COUNTRIES/ECAEXT/0,,contentMDK:22743334~pagePK:146736~piPK:146830~theSitePK:258599,00.html (accessed 24 October 2013)), the Central Asia South Asia Regional Electricity Market Project (http://www.adb.org/projects/40537-012/main (accessed 24 October 2013)) and the Trans Afghanistan Pipeline. See also, U. Rusnák, "Afghanistan as Energy Hub for South Asia", *Financial Times*, 21 March 2013.

74 See, in particular, D. Bochkarev, *India and Pakistan's Energy Security. Can Afghanistan Play a Crucial Role?* (New York: East-West Institute, 2012), at http://issuu.com/ewipublications/docs/energysecurity (accessed 24 October 2013), D. Bochkarev, 'Why the Energy Charter Treaty could become the key to the success of the Trans-Afghan energy corridor', *European Energy Review* (February 2013).

regard to Afghanistan.[75] By acceding to the ECT, Afghanistan will immediately ensure an adequate legal protection to its investment relations with 47 States plus the European Community and Euratom.

By acceding to the ECT, new parties will participate in a well-established multilateral process, of which the ECT constitutes the kernel, and benefit from a consolidated body of arbitral awards. The advantages of the ECT as a large and comprehensive multilateral treaty in term of uniformity of substantial and procedural rules are quite evident. Participation in the ECT will complement the existing network of agreements between current and new members, or amongst new members. In no way will it affect the protection foreign investors of the parties to the ECT enjoy under other agreements, regardless of their date of conclusion. On the other hand, the provisions contained in Part III (Investment promotion and protection) and Part V (Dispute settlement) will not be affected by such agreements.[76]

Complying with and implementing the ECT and in particular ensuring fair and equitable treatment, furthermore, may imply significant political reforms and financial costs for the host State. It is important to emphasize that foreign investors are not the only – or even the main – beneficiaries of the host State efforts related to fair and equitable treatment, including the improvement of the rule of law, the independence and efficiency of the judiciary, the stability and predictability of the legal system. Indeed, all those subject to the jurisdiction of the host State – including domestic investors – will generally enjoy the improved legal environment. Furthermore, the reforms aimed at ensuring fair and equitable treatment may be indispensable to obtain loans from international financial institutions, or even be the very essence of projects financed by these institutions.[77]

The accession of new members to the ECT may provide the enlarged constituency an opportunity to clarify existing provisions of the ECT (including Article 7(3) ECT), stimulate the conclusion of a transit protocol or further develop the scope and normative content of the treaty.

Finally, it is worth noting that the basic ideas and principles underpinning the ECT have already crossed the borders of the organisation constituency and contaminated the regulation of investment in the energy sector within the Economic Community of West African States (ECOWAS). In 2003 ECOWAS

---

75 BIT between Afghanistan and Turkey, entered into force on 19 July 2005.

76 Article 16 ECT.

77 On the World Bank, see T. Krever, "The Legal Turn in Late Development Theory: The Rule of Law and the World Bank's Development Model", *Harvard International Law Journal* 52 (2011), 287.

members concluded an Energy Protocol deliberately inspired by the ECT, which is described in the preamble as the "leading internationally accepted basis for the promotion, cooperation, integration and development of energy investment projects and energy trade among sovereign nations".[78] Many of the substantive provisions contained in the Protocol reproduce or mirror those of the ECT.

8 Concluding Remarks

The ECT has been for more than two decades and continues to be one of the cornerstones of the increasingly complex web of different instruments governing the energy sector in the Eurasian region.[79] It provided a timely and concrete response to the need for a multilateral and holistic approach in this crucial sector, where the private and public interests of the variety of stakeholders need to be carefully balanced.

The effective and, for certain aspects, innovative provisions on the protection of foreign investment, in particular, may be considered as the main achievement of the ECT. Throughout the years, a remarkable body of arbitral awards has not only clarified and elaborated the meaning of many of these provisions, but also contributed to the consolidation of an important ECT *acquis*. These provisions are not exempt from ambiguities (see in particular the provisions on transit) and can be further improved (for instance in relation to the protection of the environment), whereas new ones could be introduced (for instance on corporate responsibility and on transparency). Yet, they certainly represent an invaluable legacy upon which members are expected to further develop a stable and predictable legal framework for energy-related investments.

The two main challenges faced by the parties are intimately related, as it is indispensable to develop an adequate legal framework for transit and to ensure the full participation of the Russian Federation. Neither the EU nor the Russian Federation can afford to maintain in the long term the situation created by the

78 (A/P4/1/03) at http://www.comm.ecowas.int/sec/en/protocoles/WA_EC_Protocol_English-_DEFINITIF.pdf.

79 In general, see A. Goldthau and J.M. Witte (eds.), *Global Energy Governance: The New Rules of the Game* (Washington, DC: Brookings Institution Press, 2010); A. Florini and B.K. Sovacool, "Bridging the Gaps in Global Energy Governance", *Global Governance* 17 (2011), 57; A. Tita, "Global Energy Institutions. Russia and the IEA can tip the Scale, assuring enhanced Governance", *Journal of World Investment & Trade* 13 (2012), 972.

latter's decision not to ratify the ECT, at least not without developing an alternative efficient legal framework.

It is encouraging that the Energy Charter process is still functioning, that the EU-Russian Dialogue continues to contribute to enhance the cooperation between the two subjects in the energy sector, and that parallel initiatives amongst experts facilitate a depoliticized discussion. The reshaping of the EU-Russian Federation energy relations requires a new political input, willingness to undertake new commitments and a certain degree of flexibility, keeping in mind that the history of the ECT is a largely successful one and that there is already a remarkable agreement on almost all key issues.[80]

Importantly, even where there is disagreement on specific issues, prominently on unbundling and dual pricing, the objective pursued is the same – the protection of consumers – although the means to achieve it are different, respectively competition and price policy. The same is to a large extent true with regard to transit, as all parties share the need for a stable and secure flow of energy goods and materials, but again disagree on how to implement the related obligations.

Under international law, the parties have several options to modernize the ECT or develop an alternative legal framework. It is submitted that the most efficient is the revision and updating of the ECT, coupled with the conclusion of a transit protocol incorporating an acceptable agreement on all pending issues, including transit, the REIO clause and the right of first refusal clauses.

Yet, several elements – including the increased resort to bilateral instruments, proliferation of policy instruments and the lip service paid to the ECT in several recent official documents[81] – seem to point to a lack of confidence in the process of modernization of the ECT. Under these circumstances, it is for the ECT Secretariat to give the input to galvanize such a process and for the concerned governments to engage in meaningful negotiations. The process is expected to be coordinated with the enlargement of the ECT constituency and the progressive expansion of the legal space it has created well beyond the original project behind the 1991 EEC.

---

80 As pointed out by the ECT Secretary General, A Word from the Secretary General, *supra* note 47, "the principles of the Treaty, its pillars – protection of investments, security of transit and resolution of disputes – are not challenged by anyone. Their necessity is beyond dispute". See also EU-Russia Energy Dialogue, *Roadmap of the EU-Russia Energy Cooperation until 2050*, Progress report, 29 July 2011.

81 See, for instance, the *Roadmap EU-Russia*, *supra* note 79, European Parliament, Resolution of 14 March on the Energy Roadmap 2050 (2012/2013 (INI)), para. 79.

CHAPTER 5

The Settlement of Investment Disputes in the Energy Sector

Eric De Brabandere

1 Introduction

That international investment in the energy sector accounts for a vast percentage of global investments, and, as a consequence, that disputes in the energy sector constitute one of the largest portfolio of international commercial and investment disputes is beyond doubt.[1] Disputes relating to the energy sector may occur between two States, two private parties and a private party and a State. In the latter scenario, the dispute may also be subdivided into disputes relating to an investment by a foreign company in a State and commercial contract-based disputes between a foreign company and a State. Because of the focus of this book, disputes between a company in a State of which the company has the nationality, hence purely national disputes and disputes between two private parties will not be discussed here. Similarly, inter-State disputes in the energy sector, which are very often related to territorial and maritime boundaries in which oil and gas fields have been located,[2] will not be discussed here. Although in those cases the underlying dispute may be one between a (potential) investor and a foreign State, the actual dispute is one that involves only the relations between two States, and thus falls out of the scope of this chapter.[3] It should be pointed out however that those inter-State disputes in the energy sector regularly occur, such as the recent dispute between Russia and Ukraine in 2009 in relation to gas transit.[4] This chapter will rather focus on investment disputes between foreign investors and host States.

1 See generally: A. Timothy Martin, "Dispute resolution in the international energy sector", *Journal of World Energy Law and Business* 4 (2001), 332–368.

2 Martin, *supra* note 1, 334.

3 See for a discussion of the possibility of inter-State arbitration under the Energy Charter Treaty: Christiaan M.J. Kröner, 'The Permanent Court of Arbitration under the Energy Charter Treaty', in Graham Coop (ed.), *Energy Dispute Resolution: Investment Protection, Transit and the Energy Charter Treaty* (Huntington: JurisNet, 2011), xi.

4 See Kaj Hober, 'Russian Energy Policy and Dispute Settlement: An Overview', in Graham Coop *supra* note 3, 315.

 | DOI 10.1163/9789004244719_007

The settlement of disputes between foreign investors and host States may take various forms. As will be explained, non-binding methods are very often used, such as negotiation or mediation, as well as binding methods, such as judicial settlement and arbitration. It is clear that, as far as binding methods are concerned, arbitration is the most widely used form of dispute settlement between foreign investors and host States,[5] particularly because of the flexibility and neutrality offered by arbitration. In a certain sense, investment disputes in the energy sector are not fundamentally different from "regular" investment disputes, at least when viewed from a legal-technical perspective. When investment tribunals are confronted with a dispute relating to an investment in the energy sector, the rules of procedure and the actual conduct of the proceedings are substantially similar to investment disputes in other sectors of economic activity. Consent to arbitration may thus, as is the case for all investment disputes, be based on the contract between the two parties, national legislation or an investment treaty granting protection to the foreign investor. Such treaties may either be bilateral investment treaties or multilateral treaties such as the Energy Charter Treaty (ECT). At the same time, it should not be overlooked that because such disputes relate to investments in the energy sector, certain specific rules may apply, not the least as a consequence of the potential application of the ECT, which will be discussed in detail in this chapter.

The main objective of this chapter is to highlight the specificities of dispute settlement in the energy sector. Obviously, the ECT will play a fundamental role in this analysis. It is not however the objective to engage in a detailed discussion of the ECT, which is dealt with elsewhere in this volume.[6] Also, it is not the purpose here to give an overview of the substantive protection of foreign investors operating in the energy sector. Rather, this chapter aims at providing an overview of (the specificities in) the settlement of investment disputes, which arise in the energy sector. For the purposes of this chapter, the definition of "energy" in the ECT will be used here. The ECT contains an annex with a list of items categorized as "Energy Materials and Products."[7] "Economic Activity in the Energy Sector" is defined as "an economic activity concerning the exploration, extraction, refining, production, storage, land transport, transmission, distribution, trade, marketing, or sale of Energy Materials and Products except those included in Annex NI, or concerning the distribution of heat to multiple premises."[8]

5 Martin, *supra* note 1, 339.
6 See the chapter by Tarcisio Gazzini in this volume.
7 Article 1(4) ECT and Annex EM.
8 Article 1(5) ECT.

I will first address generally, the various dispute settlement methods available for international investment disputes in the Energy Sector (2). In doing so, I will provide an overview of the various dispute settlement methods (2.1), before turning to the dispute settlement provisions in the Energy Charter Treaty, and the specificity of this treaty for settling disputes in the energy sector (2.2). I will then analyse specifically investor-State dispute settlement methods in the Energy Sector (3). More specifically, the relation between contract and treaty claims will be noted (3.1), and the problem of the availability of different dispute settlement methods for investment disputes in the energy sector, and thus the potential overlap of these dispute settlement methods (3.2).

2 Dispute Settlement in the Energy Sector: An Overview

2.1 *The Importance of Dispute Settlement in the Energy Sector*

The settlement of disputes between foreign investors and host States may take various forms. As will be explained, non-binding methods are very often used, such as negotiation or mediation, as well as binding methods, such as judicial settlement and arbitration. As far as binding methods are concerned, arbitration is the most widely used form of dispute settlement between foreign investors and host States,[9] in particular because of the flexibility and neutrality offered by arbitration. However, one should keep in mind that, in respect of disputes between two companies in the energy sector, both international commercial arbitration and national litigation are widely used, the latter in particular for disputes between two parties of the same nationality.[10] Despite not being listed as one of the optional fora under the ECT, the International Chamber of Commerce (ICC) for instance, estimates that some 11% of the arbitration cases brought before its dispute settlement facilities relate to energy.[11] Of all cases submitted to arbitration before the ICC, 11% also involves States or State-owned enterprises.[12]

In addition, one should not overlook that inter-State investment disputes may also be brought before international courts and tribunals, such as the International Court of Justice [ICJ], or international arbitration, in particular through the use of diplomatic protection. However, as has been widely acknowledged, because of the specific requirement for a State to exercise diplomatic

9 Martin, *supra* note 1, 339.

10 Ibid.

11 Jason A. Fry, "Opening Remarks", in Graham Coop *supra* note 3, iii.

12 Ibid.

protection on behalf of one of its nationals, be it a company or an individual, inter-State proceedings are not a very useful method of dispute settlement. One of the cases brought before the ICJ which easily illustrates this point, is the *Anglo-Iranian Oil Company* case,[13] or more recently, the *Diallo* case before the ICJ as well.[14] Because of the cumbersome procedure inherent to the use of diplomatic protection, investment-related inter-State disputes are only very occasionally settled on an inter-State level. This is precisely one the reasons behind the advent of the direct access of foreign investors to investment treaty arbitration; thus avoiding the length and uncertainties of the procedure of diplomatic protection. However, certain treaties, including the ECT, do provide for inter-State international arbitration in order to settle investment disputes.[15]

Of all investment disputes settled through investment treaty arbitration, disputes in the energy sector take a prominent place. According to the ICSID, the "oil, gas and mining" sector[16] accounted for 25% and activities in the "electric power and other energy" constituted some 12% of the total number of registered ICSID cases until the 31st of December 2012.[17] At the end of 2012, the ECT formed the basis of consent for 4% of the total number of registered ICSID cases until the 31st of December 2011.[18] Given the figures indicated above, in respect of the areas of economic activity in which disputes have been registered by ICSID, it is clear that the ECT forms the basis for consent for only a minority of investment disputes in the energy sector. At the same time, the effectiveness of the ECT in providing consent to arbitration generally, *i.e.* without taking into account the percentage of ECT cases brought before an ICSID arbitral tribunal, is relatively important. As noted, so far, the Energy Charter

13 International Court of Justice, *Anglo-Iranian Oil Co. Case*, Jurisdiction, Judgment of 22 July 1952, ICJ Reports 1952, 93.

14 International Court of Justice, *Ahmadou Sadio Diallo* (*Republic of Guinea v. Democratic Republic of the Congo*), Judgment of 24 May 2007 (Preliminary Objections); Judgment of 30 November 2010 (merits), and Judgment of 19 June 2012 (Compensation owed by the Democratic Republic of the Congo to the Republic of Guinea), at http://www.icj-cij.org/docket/index.php?p1=3&p2=3&PHPSESSID=&case=103&code=gc&p3=4 (accessed 25 September 2012).

15 See for the potential advantages of this: Christiaan M.J. Kröner, *supra* note 3, xiv.

16 This description is admittedly relatively broad and thus covers economic activity, which is not strictly speaking part of the energy sector. More detailed statistics are however not available.

17 *ICSID Caseload – Statistics*, Issue 2013 (1), 12, at https://icsid.worldbank.org/ICSID/FrontServlet?requestType=ICSIDDocRH&actionVal=ShowDocument&CaseLoadStatistics=True&language=English41 (accessed 19 March 2013).

18 Ibid., 10.

Secretariat has reported that 33 investor-State dispute settlement cases have been submitted under the ECT.[19]

Investment disputes in the energy sector are as such not fundamentally different from "regular" investment disputes, at least when viewed from a legal-technical arbitration perspective. When investment tribunals are confronted with a dispute relating to an investment in the energy sector, the rules of procedure and the actual conduct of the proceedings are substantially similar than investment disputes relating to other sectors of activity. Consent to arbitration may thus, as is the case for all investment disputes, be based on the contract between the two parties, national legislation or an investment treaty granting protection to the foreign investor. Such treaties may either be bilateral investment treaties or multilateral treaties such as the ECT. At the same time, it should not be overlooked that because such disputes relate to investments in the energy sector, certain specific rules may apply, not the least as a consequence of the existence, and thus potential application, of the ECT. We will therefore pay particular attention to the dispute settlement provisions of the ECT.

2.2 *The Energy Charter Treaty*

Without doubt, the ECT is a prominent tool when it comes to settling investment disputes in the energy sector. It is not the purpose here to enter into the historical background and drafting history of the ECT.[20] Suffice it to say here that, besides covering trade, energy transit, and energy-related environmental aspects, the ECT is to date the only multilateral treaty offering investment protection and access to investment arbitration, although it is of course limited to one specific industrial sector.

In general the protection offered to foreign investors under the ECT is largely equivalent to the protection offered to foreign investors in BITs, as is the access to investment arbitration.

2.2.1 Investor-State Arbitration under the Energy Charter Treaty

The ECT not only offers substantive protection to foreign investors in the energy sector, but as part of the protection, also offers direct access to investment arbitration in the case of disputes between a foreign investor and a host State. The ECT in fact is the only multilateral treaty offering direct access to investment arbitration, and for that reason alone, it is of significant

19 See http://www.encharter.org/index.php?id=213 (accessed 19 September 2012).

20 See generally, Graham Coop, "Introduction to the Energy Charter Treaty (ECT)", in Clarisse Ribeiro, *Investment Arbitration and the Energy Charter Treaty* (Huntington, JurisNet, 2006), 5–22.

importance. Moreover, without the direct access to investment arbitration, the investment protection provisions of the ECT would be, as one author puts it, "no more than words."[21]

Article 26 ECT

The ECT, unlike BITs, contains a relatively complex system of dispute settlement, which offers various choices to the parties engaged in a dispute. Besides containing a clause on the settlement of disputes between the States party to the ECT,[22] Article 26 ECT deals with disputes between a State party to the ECT and a foreign investor. The article is worth reproducing here in full:

> (1) Disputes between a Contracting Party and an Investor of another Contracting Party relating to an Investment of the latter in the Area of the former, which concern an alleged breach of an obligation of the former under Part III shall, if possible, be settled amicably.
> (2) If such disputes can not be settled according to the provisions of paragraph (1) within a period of three months from the date on which either party to the dispute requested amicable settlement, the Investor party to the dispute may choose to submit it for resolution:
>
> > (a) to the courts or administrative tribunals of the Contracting Party party to the dispute;
> > (b) in accordance with any applicable, previously agreed dispute settlement procedure; or
> > (c) in accordance with the following paragraphs of this Article.
>
> (3) (a) Subject only to subparagraphs (b) and (c), each Contracting Party hereby gives its unconditional consent to the submission of a dispute to international arbitration or conciliation in accordance with the provisions of this Article.
> (b) (i) The Contracting Parties listed in Annex ID do not give such unconditional consent where the Investor has previously submitted the dispute under subparagraph (2)(a) or (b).
> (ii) For the sake of transparency, each Contracting Party that is listed in Annex ID shall provide a written statement of its policies, practices and conditions in this regard to the

21 Laurent Gouiffès, "The Dispute Settlement Mechanisms of the Energy Charter Treaty", in Clarisse Ribeiro, *supra* note 20, 22.

22 Article 27 ECT.

Secretariat no later than the date of the deposit of its instrument of ratification, acceptance or approval in accordance with Article 39 or the deposit of its instrument of accession in accordance with Article 41.

(c) A Contracting Party listed in Annex IA does not give such unconditional consent with respect to a dispute arising under the last sentence of Article 10(1).

(4) In the event that an Investor chooses to submit the dispute for resolution under subparagraph (2)(c), the Investor shall further provide its consent in writing for the dispute to be submitted to:

(a) (i) The International Centre for Settlement of Investment Disputes, established pursuant to the Convention on the Settlement of Investment Disputes between States and Nationals of other States opened for signature at Washington, 18 March 1965 (hereinafter referred to as the "ICSID Convention"), if the Contracting Party of the Investor and the Contracting Party party to the dispute are both parties to the ICSID Convention; or

(ii) The International Centre for Settlement of Investment Disputes, established pursuant to the Convention referred to in subparagraph (a)(i), under the rules governing the Additional Facility for the Administration of Proceedings by the Secretariat of the Centre (hereinafter referred to as the "Additional Facility Rules"), if the Contracting Party of the Investor or the Contracting Party party to the dispute, but not both, is a party to the ICSID Convention;

(b) a sole arbitrator or ad hoc arbitration tribunal established under the Arbitration Rules of the United Nations Commission on International Trade Law (hereinafter referred to as "UNCITRAL"); or

(c) an arbitral proceeding under the Arbitration Institute of the Stockholm Chamber of Commerce.

(5) (a) The consent given in paragraph (3) together with the written consent of the Investor given pursuant to paragraph (4) shall be considered to satisfy the requirement for:

(i) written consent of the parties to a dispute for purposes of Chapter II of the ICSID Convention and for purposes of the Additional Facility Rules;

> (ii) an "agreement in writing" for purposes of Article II of the United Nations Convention on the Recognition and Enforcement of Foreign Arbitral Awards, done at New York, 10 June 1958 (hereinafter referred to as the "New York Convention"); and
> (iii) "the parties to a contract [to] have agreed in writing" for the purposes of Article 1 of the UNCITRAL Arbitration Rules.
>
> (b) Any arbitration under this Article shall at the request of any party to the dispute be held in a state that is a party to the New York Convention. Claims submitted to arbitration hereunder shall be considered to arise out of a commercial relationship or transaction for the purposes of Article I of that Convention.
>
> (6) A tribunal established under paragraph (4) shall decide the issues in dispute in accordance with this Treaty and applicable rules and principles of international law.
> (7) An Investor other than a natural person which has the nationality of a Contracting Party party to the dispute on the date of the consent in writing referred to in paragraph (4) and which, before a dispute between it and that Contracting Party arises, is controlled by Investors of another Contracting Party, shall for the purpose of Article 25(2)(b) of the ICSID Convention be treated as a "national of another Contracting State" and shall for the purpose of Article 1(6) of the Additional Facility Rules be treated as a "national of another State".
> (8) The awards of arbitration, which may include an award of interest, shall be final and binding upon the parties to the dispute. An award of arbitration concerning a measure of a sub-national government or authority of the disputing Contracting Party shall provide that the Contracting Party may pay monetary damages in lieu of any other remedy granted. Each Contracting Party shall carry out without delay any such award and shall make provision for the effective enforcement in its Area of such awards.

First of all, it appears from the first paragraphs that the jurisdiction of tribunals established under the ECT, only have jurisdiction to the extent that: (1) the dispute relates to an alleged breach of an obligation of a Contracting State under Part III of the ECT; (2) the dispute relates to an investment; (3) the investment must have been made in the "Area of a Contracting State;" (4) the claimant must be an Investor of a Contracting State, other than the Contracting State in which the investment was made; and (5) the events which lie at the basis of the claim must have taken place when the ECT was in force between the parties, c.q. was provisionally applicable between the parties.[23]

According to paragraph (2), disputes between foreign investors and a host State should be settled amicably. It is only if the dispute cannot be settled amicably within a period of three months, that the foreign investor (or the host State) may bring the dispute to a certain dispute settlement forum.

Choice of Arbitration Fora

The Charter offers a choice of dispute settlement fora to foreign investors.[24] Disputes arising under the ECT may be brought before the domestic courts of the host State, a "previously agreed dispute settlement mechanism," and finally, international arbitration or conciliation.[25] In the latter scenario, the foreign investor may opt for arbitration under the ICSID Convention if both the host State and the State of the nationality of the foreign investor are parties to the Convention, the ICSID Additional Facility in case only either the host or the home State is party to the ICSID Convention, *ad hoc* arbitration under the UNCITRAL Arbitration Rules, and finally, arbitration before the Arbitration Institute of the Stockholm Chamber of Commerce (SCC).[26]

The choice of these three specific arbitration institutions, and the exclusion of others, may be explained by the history of the ECT. The drafting history of the ECT shows that the options for international arbitration were modified several times.[27] The first draft of the current Article 26 ECT only provided for

23 Thomas Roe and Matthew Happold, *Settlement of Disputes under the Energy Charter Treaty* (Cambridge: Cambridge University Press, 2011), 41.

24 A choice of forum for international arbitration is occasionally also provided for in other investment treaties. NAFTA Chapter 11 for instance likewise gives the parties the option for investors to submit the dispute to arbitration under the UNCITRAL Arbitration Rules or under the ICSID Convention or Additional Facility. However, as has been pointed out, at least in the case of NAFTA, the differences between arbitration under the UNCITRAL Arbitration Rules or under the ICSID Convention or Additional Facility are probably not as important as the differences between the various fora provided for by the ECT, especially because the NAFTA itself has procedural rules supplementing both procedural rules, and because the NAFTA provides that in both cases ICSID will act as appointing authority or arbitrators. See Antonio R. Parra, 'Investments and Investors Covered by the ECT and Other Investment Protection Treaties – Introduction', in Clarisse Ribeiro, *supra* note 20, 53.

25 Article 26(2) ECT.

26 Article 26(4) ECT.

27 See for a discussion and overview Craig S. Bamberger, "An Overview of the Energy Charter Treaty", in Thomas W. Walde (ed.), *The Energy Charter Treaty: An East-West Gateway for Investment and Trade* (The Hague: Kluwer Law International, 1996), p. 1 ff and Laurent Gouiffès *supra* note 21, 25 ff.

arbitration under the UNCITRAL Arbitration Rules. The ICSID option seems to have been added following a proposition of the American delegation, and the inclusion of arbitration under the Arbitration Institute of the SCC was added at the very last stage.[28]

The reason why three different fora of arbitration are given to foreign investors may be explained by the different procedures applicable to each forum, each of which has inherent features making them attractive (or unattractive) for certain categories of energy disputes. Moreover, the choice effectively made has important implications.

First, arbitration under the UNCITRAL Arbitration Rules and the Arbitration Institute of the SCC are traditionally confidential. One should also add that an UNCITRAL Working Group has recently adopted a set of articles on transparency in investor-State treaty-based arbitration, which clearly moves away from the principled closed character of UNICTRAL proceedings.[29] Awards in respect of disputes administered under the ICSID Convention are usually published, although this has not always been the case, in particular for energy related disputes.[30] Arbitration under the ICSID Convention also enables non-disputing parties to participate in the proceedings as *amicus curiae*, thereby offering the possibility for NGOs to bring in "public interest" considerations in traditionally closed proceedings. The ICSID Rules of Arbitration were amended in 2006 to now explicitly include, under certain conditions, the capacity for a tribunal to allow a non-disputing party, which has a significant interest in the case to file a written submission.[31] The 2013 Draft UNCITRAL rules on transparency however now provide that "third persons" may make submissions in investment treaty arbitration, provided that they have a "significant interest in the proceedings" and that the submission would "assist the arbitral tribunal

28 See Laurent Gouiffès, *supra* note 21, 25.

29 See United Nations General Assembly, United Nations Commission on International Trade Law, *Settlement of commercial disputes: preparation of a legal standard on transparency in treaty-based investor-State arbitration – Note by the Secretariat*, UN Doc. A/CN.9/WG.II/WP.176 (30 November 2012) and United Nations General Assembly, United Nations Commission on International Trade Law, *Report of Working Group II (Arbitration and Conciliation) on the work of its fifty-eighth session (New York, 4–8 February 2013)*, UN Doc. A/CN.9/765 (13 February 2013).

30 See for a discussion, in particular for ICSID cases in the energy sector: Meg Kinnear, "The Energy Charter Treaty and the International Centre for Settlement of Investment Disputes (ICSID)", in Graham Coop *supra* note 3, ix.

31 See Eric De Brabandere, "NGOs and the 'Public Interest': The Legality and Rationale of Amicus Curiae Interventions in International Economic and Investment Disputes", *Chicago Journal of International Law* 12 (1) (2011), 85–113.

in the determination of a factual or legal issue related to the arbitral proceedings by bringing a perspective, particular knowledge or insight that is different from that of the disputing parties."[32] At the same time, because of the increased importance of transparency, generally, in investment treaty arbitration, awards of international arbitral tribunals are increasingly being published despite the principled confidentiality. This has for instance been the case for a large number of awards in ECT disputes brought under the UNCITRAL Arbitration Rules or before the Arbitration Institute of the SCC.

Secondly, because of the potential presence of certain East-West sensitivities, arbitration before the Arbitration Institute of the SCC may be appealing because of its perceived reputation to be particularly sensitive to such issues.[33] This reputation has been recognized since many years,[34] and in essence is the consequence of a multiplicity of factors, including the early availability of English translations of the law and practice of arbitration in Sweden, the available experience and expertise, the flexibility in the choice of procedural law and particularly Sweden's historical status as a neutral country.[35] Although Sweden officially let go of its neutrality after the end of the Cold War, it remains officially a non-aligned country.[36]

Thirdly, arbitration under the ICSID Convention and before the Stockholm Chamber of Commerce may be appealing (or unappealing) because of its institutionalization.[37] *Ad hoc* arbitration has the advantage that it may be fully fashioned to meet the specific needs of the parties to the disputes, and the particular features of the disputes, but at the same time requires parties to cooperate to achieve agreement on several important procedural issues.

---

32 See United Nations General Assembly, United Nations Commission on International Trade Law, *Settlement of commercial disputes: preparation of a legal standard on transparency in treaty-based investor-State arbitration – Note by the Secretariat*, UN Doc. A/CN.9/WG.II/WP.176 (30 November 2012) and United Nations General Assembly, United Nations Commission on International Trade Law, *Report of Working Group II (Arbitration and Conciliation) on the work of its fifty-eighth session (New York, 4–8 February 2013)*, UN Doc. A/CN.9/765 (13 February 2013).

33 Laurent Gouiffès, *supra* note 21, 26.

34 See for an interesting historical overview of the reasons behind this: Howard M. Holtzmann, 'Dispute Resolution Procedures in East-West Trade', *International Lawyer* 2 (1979), 241 ff.

35 Ibid.

36 See Anne Judith Farina, "'Talking Disputes Into Harmony' China Approaches International Commercial Arbitration", *American University International Law Review* 4(1) (1989), 162 ff.

37 N. Blackaby, C. Partasides, A Redfern and M. Hunter, *Redfern & Hunter on International Arbitration*, 5th edition (Oxford: Oxford University Press, 2009), paras. 1.155–1.168.

Institutional arbitration on the other hand has as its main advantage the fact that it works under a fixed set of procedural rules that have moreover been tested in practice and that it offers administrative assistance to the tribunal. Institutional arbitration however usually requires the payment of additional institutional fees and may take more time to initiate because of the inherent administrative obligations.

Fourthly, it should be reminded that the relevant rules of the ICSID Convention, which regulate the enforcement of the award in a relatively automatic way, might be particularly appealing. One of the specific benefits of ICSID arbitration is that the awards can easily be recognized and enforced through the ICSID Convention, especially in comparison to the recognition and enforcement of foreign arbitral awards in domestic courts, and even compared to the enforcement of arbitral awards under the New York Convention. Although it facilitates enforcement, the New York Convention contains several possibilities for review by domestic courts.[38] The lack of domestic review possibilities makes the ICSID Convention generally more favourable to recognition and enforcement than the New York Convention.[39] Article 54(1) of the ICSID Convention indeed imposes an obligation on all States which are parties to the Convention to enforce the pecuniary obligations resulting from an ICSID award "as if it were a final judgment of a court in that State,"[40] with no possibility of review by the national courts of the States in which enforcement is sought. However, in the event of non-ICSID administered arbitration, Article 26(5) provides that the consent expressed by the ECT Contracting Parties in paragraph five of the same article is to be considered as an "agreement in writing" for the purposes of the New York Convention.[41] Consent under Article 26 ECT is also considered to be a valid written agreement for the purposes of Article 1 of the UNCITRAL Arbitration Rules and for the purposes of Chapter II of the ICSID Convention.[42] In respect of the enforcement of non-ICSID administered awards, the ECT Contracting Parties agree that claims submitted under Article 26 ECT qualify as disputes arising out of a commercial relationship or transaction as required by Article I of the New York Convention, which is of high importance for arbitration conducted under the ICSID Additional

---

38 See Edward Baldwin, Mark Kantor and Michael Nolan, 'Limits to Enforcement of ICSID Awards', 23(1) *Journal of International Arbitration* 1–24 (2006), 4–5.

39 Lucy Reed, Jan Paulsson and Nigel Blackaby, *Guide to ICSID Arbitration* (The Hague: Kluwer, 2010), 96.

40 Article 54(1) ICSID Convention.

41 Article 26(5)(a)(ii) ECT.

42 Article 26(5)(a)(i) and (iii) ECT.

Facility, the Stockholm Chamber of Commerce and *ad hoc* arbitration under the UNCITRAL Arbitration Rules.[43]

Fifthly, and we will discuss this further in the next section, because the ICSID Convention itself imposes certain jurisdictional limitations to the ICSID tribunal, most notably in respect of the definition of an investment and the parties to the dispute, certain disputes which technically are covered by the ECT will not fulfil the jurisdictional requirements of the ICSID Convention.

Finally, the ICSID Convention allows for open hearings, unless the parties object,[44] and also explicitly gives tribunals the discretion to authorize the submission of *amicus curiae* briefs,[45] as will be discussed in the last section.

Additionally, it should be added that Russia, although a signatory State to the ICSID Convention has never ratified the Convention. Although the ICSID Additional Facility may have jurisdiction in the event that the foreign investors has the nationality of a State party to the ICSID Convention, if this is not the case, other avenues such as the SCC or *ad hoc* arbitration under the UNICTRAL Arbitration Rules are important.

So far, the Energy Charter Secretariat has reported that 33 investor-State dispute settlement cases have been submitted under the ECT.[46] Of these 33 cases, 20 have been submitted under the ICSID Convention, six to *ad hoc* arbitration under the UNCITRAL Arbitration Rules – three of which are being administered by the Permanent Court of Arbitration [PCA] – and seven to the Arbitration Institute of the Stockholm Chamber of Commerce. Of the 33 cases, four have been settled between the parties, and 15 have been the subject of a final award. In four cases, the tribunal has already issued an award on the jurisdiction of the tribunal, and another 10 cases are still pending. The number of cases submitted under the ICSID Convention clearly shows the importance of ICSID as the preferred investor-State dispute settlement mechanism in contemporary international law.

2.2.2 Consent to Arbitration under the ECT

By signing the ECT, States give their "unconditional consent" to submit such disputes to investment arbitration.[47] There are however two exceptions to this fundamental rule, which are in line with two conditions one may find in BITs as well.

43 Article 26(5)(b) ECT.

44 Rule 32(2) ICSID Arbitration Rules.

45 Rule 37(2) ICSID Arbitration Rules.

46 See http://www.encharter.org/index.php?id=213 (accessed 19 September 2012).

47 Article 26(3)(a) ECT.

First of all, Article 26(3)(b) ECT contains an optional "fork in the road" clause. States may indeed require that access to investment treaty arbitration is only open in case the investor has not previously submitted the dispute to the domestic courts of the host State or to any other previously agreed dispute settlement procedure, in accordance with Article 26(2)(a) or (b). States which have conditioned their consent in such a way are listed in Annex ID of the ECT, and amount to as many as 26 States, including Canada and the United States which have not signed the ECT.[48] The European Communities likewise have conditioned their consent in accordance with Article 26(3)(b) ECT. Article 26(3)(b)(ii) ECT adds that "for the sake of transparency, each Contracting Party that is listed in Annex ID shall provide a written statement of its policies, practices and conditions in this regard to the Secretariat no later than the date of the deposit of its instrument of ratification." The absence of such statement however does not invalidate the condition attached to the consent to arbitration. In an *obiter dictum*[49] in the case *Libananco v. Turkey*,[50] the Tribunal opined that

48 The States listed in Annex ID are Australia*; Azerbaijan; Bulgaria; Canada°; Croatia; Cyprus; Czech Republic; Finland; Greece; Hungary; Ireland; Italy; Japan; Kazakhstan; Mongolia; Norway*; Poland; Portugal; Romania; Russian Federation*; Slovenia; Spain; Sweden; The Former Yugoslav Republic of Macedonia; Turkey; United States of America°. Certain States (indicated with *) are yet to ratify the ECT. The list of States is available at http://www.encharter.org/index.php?id=323 (accessed 18 September 2012).

49 The Tribunal had indeed previously found that the Claimant was not the owner of the investing company, and thus declined jurisdiction on this ground. However, the Tribunal decided to engage in a discussion of various other preliminary objections, although this was not necessary for deciding the case. The Tribunal argued that '*out of deference to the care with which all of the Preliminary Jurisdictional Objections have been pleaded by both Parties, and in the hope that it may be of some benefit to those who have to confront these issues in future, the Tribunal adds the following brief comments on certain general issues raised by the third and fourth Preliminary Jurisdictional Objections* (*i.e.* those set out in *paragraphs 105.3 and 105.4 above respectively*) *which are not specific to the particular situation of Libananco. The Tribunal wishes to stress that these comments should not be regarded as having the status of formal decisions by the present Tribunal on these issues*' (para. 538). For a comment on and criticism of this practice, see Eric De Brabandere, "Arbitral Decisions As a Source of International Investment Law", in Tarcisio Gazzini and Eric De Brabandere (Eds.), *International Investment Law. The Sources of Rights and Obligations* (Leiden/Boston: Martinus Nijhoff Publishers; 2012), 245–288.

50 *Libananco Holdings Co. Limited v. Republic of Turkey*, ICSID Case No. ARB/06/8, Award, 2 September 2011 (annulment proceedings pending).

> the limited consent is foreseen and understood to take effect automatically, on the giving by the State in question of its "consent to be bound" by the Treaty, and (on the other hand) that the States covered by this provision are definitively identified, once and for all, by Annex ID itself as established at the time the ECT was concluded and opened for signature. It would then follow that the limiting effect cannot be conditional on the statement required by sub-paragraph (ii), either as to the fact of the limitation, or as to its extent; and that is indeed reinforced by the wording of sub-paragraph (ii) itself, with its express indication that the requirement is merely "for the sake of transparency". It seems rather to be the case that listing under Annex ID has the automatic effect of registering that the original consent of the Negotiating State in question is limited as precisely described in Article 26(3)(b), sub-paragraph (i).[51]

The Tribunal thus confirmed that the absence of a declaration under Article 26(3)(b)(ii), which the Tribunal called "a collateral obligation," does not lead to the invalidation of the listing in Annex ID.[52] In doing so, the Tribunal also distinguished this situation from the provisional application of the ECT under Article 45 ECT, from which States can opt out by making an explicit declaration to this effect.[53]

Secondly, States may opt out of the "umbrella clause" contained in Article 10(1) of the ECT. The ECT indeed provides that States may not give their "unconditional consent with respect to a dispute arising under the last sentence of Article 10(1)," which provides that "each Contracting Party shall observe any obligations it has entered into with an Investor or an Investment of an Investor of any other Contracting Party."[54] Contrary to the number of States that have opted out of the unconditional consent in relation to Article 26(3)(b) ECT ("fork in the road clause"), only four States have refused the application of the "umbrella clause."[55]

---

51 Ibid., para. 546 (internal footnotes omitted).

52 Ibid.

53 Ibid.

54 Article 26(3)(c) ECT.

55 The States are: Australia; Canada; Hungary; Norway. Here again, it should be emphasized that Canada has not signed the ECT, and Australia and Norway have not yet ratified the ECT. The list of States is available at http://www.encharter.org/index.php?id=323 (accessed 18 September 2012).

Thirdly, the ECT provides for a "cooling-off" period of three months,[56] as is very often the case in BITs as well. As is the case, generally, in investment treaty arbitration, the questions of the starting point of the "cooling-off" period, and whether the "cooling-off" period is an issue that is directed at the jurisdiction of the tribunal, or rather at the admissibility of the claim, are subject to discussion in respect of the ECT as well. Few cases so far have been called upon to decide this. In *Mohammad Ammar Al-Bahloul v. Tajikistan*,[57] the Tribunal opined that, although it was unclear whether the "cooling-off" period started – when the Claimant wrote a letter to the Minister of Energy and to the President of Tajikistan or at the time of the filing of a formal notice of the dispute – because the Respondent in any case was "not interested in settling the dispute amicably",[58] "insisting on compliance with the three-month period thus would be an unnecessary formality."[59] The Tribunal thus confirmed that, even if one could consider that the cooling-off period was not respected, it affects neither the jurisdiction of the Tribunal nor the admissibility of the claim.

2.2.3 The Specificity of Investor-State Arbitration under the Energy Charter Treaty

The ECT extends protection, according to the standards contained in the ECT, to "investors" and their "investments." These requirements, which are defined in Article 1 ECT and which I will address below, are therefore conditions which need to be met in order to be able to benefit from the substantive protection offered under the relevant investment protections provision of the ECT.

An investment tribunal's jurisdiction under the ECT is indeed according to Article 26 ECT preconditioned by the existence of "disputes [...] relating to an Investment [...], which concern an alleged breach of an obligation of the former under Part III." Secondly, as will be explained, the terms "investor" and "investment" are relatively broadly defined. While it is not the purpose here to engage in a full discussion of these notions, and their interpretation by investment tribunals, these broad definitions are worth investigating in view of defining the specificity of the ECT for investor-State arbitration.

56 Article 26(1) and (2) ECT.

57 *Mohammad Ammar Al-Bahloul v. Tajikistan*, SCC Case n° V (064/2008), Partial award on jurisdiction and liability, 2 September 2009.

58 Ibid., para. 155.

59 Ibid.

The Need for an Alleged Breach of an Obligation of a Contracting State under Part III of the ECT

The ECT provides that foreign investors have a right to bring a claim against the host State before an international arbitral tribunal, but this faculty is limited to breaches by the host State of Part III of the ECT, which covers investment promotion and protection. This point was raised in the case *Nykomb Synergetics Technology Holding* before the Arbitration Institute of the Stockholm Chamber of Commerce.[60] One of the questions put to the Tribunal was whether the acts of a Latvian state-owned company, Latvenergo, were attributable to Latvia. The claimant, Nykomb, was of the view that Latvenergo's acts were attributable to Latvia and based its claim principally on Article 22(1) ECT which contains a guarantee by States that their entities will respect the provisions of Part III of the ECT.[61] Latvia however argued that, because Article 22 ECT is located in Part IV of the ECT, the Tribunal is barred from applying this provision.[62] The Tribunal however managed to avoid the discussion by referring instead to the relevant principles of attribution under customary international law and concluded that the acts of Latvenergo were indeed attributable to Latvia.[63]

It should also be added that trade-related investment measures, which violate Article 5 ECT, by a State in relation to a foreign investment could also be considered a breach of that State's obligations under Part III of the ECT. As a consequence, disputes relating to trade-related investment measurers may be brought before the dispute settlement bodies provided for in Article 26 ECT.

The Definition of 'Investment' under the ECT

The ECT defines "investment" as:

> every kind of asset, owned or controlled directly or indirectly by an Investor and includes:
>
> (a) tangible and intangible, and movable and immovable, property, and property rights such as leases, mortgages, liens and pledgers;
>
> (b) a company or business enterprise, or shares, stock, or other forms of equity participation in a company or business enterprise, and bonds and other debt of a company or business enterprise;
>
> (c) claims to money and claims to performance pursuant to contract having an economic value and associated with an Investment;

60 *Nykomb Synergetics Technology Holding AB v. the Republic of Latvia*, SCC CASE 118/2001, Final Award, 16 December 2003.

61 Ibid., 5.

62 Ibid., 6–8.

63 Ibid., 31.

(d) Intellectual Property;
(e) Returns;
(f) any right conferred by law or contract or by virtue of any licenses and permits granted pursuant to law to undertake and Economic Activity in the Energy Sector.[64]

A change in the form in which assets are invested does not affect their character as investments and the term "Investment" includes all investments, whether existing at or made after the later of the date of entry into force of this Treaty for the Contracting Party of the Investor making the investment and that for the Contracting Party in the Area of which the investment is made (hereinafter referred to as the "Effective Date") provided that the Treaty shall only apply to matters affecting such investments after the Effective Date.

"Investment" refers to any investment associated with an Economic Activity in the Energy Sector and to investments or classes of investments designated by a Contracting Party in its Area as "Charter efficiency projects" and so notified to the Secretariat.

The broad definition of "investment" is in line with many BITs, which likewise, generally, have adopted a definition of "investment" extending coverage to "every kind of asset,"[65] although some authors have considered that the ECT "contains arguably the most extensive definition of 'investment' to be found in modern investment promotion and protection treaties."[66]

As noted by the Tribunal in *Plama*, which was the first ICSID tribunal to render a decision on jurisdiction under the ECT, the list contained in Article 1(6) is "a broad, non-exhaustive list of different kinds of assets encompassing virtually any right, property or interest in money or money's worth."[67]

As is the case with other investment treaties, in particular BITs, investments and investors protected under the ECT should, in case the dispute is submitted to arbitration under the ICSID Convention, also be covered by the

64 Article 1(6) ECT.

65 See UNCTAD, 'Scope And Definition', UNCTAD Series on Issues in International Investment Agreements II, 2011, 13 et s., available at http://unctad.org/en/Docs/diaeia20102_en.pdf (accessed 12 July 2013).

66 Stephen Jagush and Anthony Sinclair, 'The Limits of Protection for Investments and Investors under the Energy Charter Treaty', in Clarisse Ribeiro, *supra* note 20, 73–74.

67 *Plama Consortium Limited v. Bulgaria*, ICSID Case No. ARB/03/24, Decision on Jurisdiction, 8 February 2005, para. 125.

jurisdictional provisions of the ICSID Convention, in particular Article 25 ICSID. This prerequisite is of course absent in the case of *ad hoc* arbitration under the UNCITRAL Arbitration Rules or arbitration before the Arbitration Institute of the Stockholm Chamber of Commerce since none of these mechanisms provide for certain jurisdictional requirements in addition to the parties' consent expressed in an investment treaty or otherwise. Although the ICSID Convention does not define the term "investment," the requirement of an "investment" under the ICSID Convention has been the subject of a relatively consistent jurisprudence. As noted by the Tribunal in *Salini v. Morocco:*

> insofar as the option of jurisdiction has been exercised in favour of ICSID, the rights in dispute must also constitute an investment pursuant to Article 25 of the Washington Convention. The Arbitral Tribunal, therefore, is of the opinion that its jurisdiction depends upon the existence of an investment within the meaning of the Bilateral Treaty as well as that of the Convention, in accordance with the case law.[68]

The Tribunal established that an "investment" under Article 25 of the ICSID Convention requires certain characteristics, which have since then been referred to as the "Salini criteria:"[69]

---

68 *Salini Costrutori S.p.A and Italstrade S.p.A v. Kingdom of Morocco*, ICSID Case No. ARB/00/4, Decision on Jurisdiction, 23 July 2001, para. 44.

69 It should be added that since then, the 'Salini criteria' have been the subject of some disagreement or perfection in the jurisprudence of arbitral tribunal. The Tribunal in *Phoenix Action Ltd v. Czech Republic* for instance departed from the 'Salini criteria', not only by substituting the requirement that an investment should contribute to the development of the host State with the requirement that investments should contribute to the economy of the host State, but more importantly by adding the criteria of "assets invested *bona fide*" (*Phoenix Action Ltd v. Czech Republic*, ICSID Case No. ARB/06/5, Award, 15 April 2009, para. 114) a criterion which has however subsequently explicitly been denied by other tribunals (see for instance *Saba Fakes v. Turkey*, ICSID Case No. ARB/07/20, Award of 14 July 2010, para. 112: "the principles of good faith and legality cannot be incorporated into the definition of Article 25(1) of the ICSID Convention without doing violence to the language of the ICSID Convention: an investment might be "legal or 'illegal', made in 'good faith' or not, it nonetheless remains an investment. The expressions 'legal investment' or 'investment made in good faith' are not pleonasms, and the expressions 'illegal investment' or 'investment made in bad faith' are not oxymorons"). See for a discussion: Eric De Brabandere, "'Good Faith', 'Abuse of Process' and the Initiation of Investment Treaty Claims", *Journal of International Dispute Settlement* 3(3) (2012), 609–636.

> The doctrine generally considers that investment infers: contributions, a certain duration of performance of the contract and a participation in the risks of the transaction. In reading the Convention's preamble, one may add the contribution to the economic development of the host State of the investment as an additional condition.
>
> In reality, these various elements may be interdependent. Thus, the risks of the transaction may depend on the contributions and the duration of performance of the contract. As a result, these various criteria should be assessed globally even if, for the sake of reasoning, the Tribunal considers them individually here.[70]

Because of this definition, it is for instance generally acknowledged that mere sales transactions are not covered by the definition of investment in the ICSID Convention.[71] At the same time, it should be added that it has been argued that "the Convention's drafting history leaves no doubt that, besides ordinary commercial transactions, Article 25 covers almost any area of economic activity."[72] In the case of ICSID Arbitration, foreign investors in the energy sector will thus have to take into consideration that the definition of "investment" as provided for in the ECT may well cover certain activities although the same activities may not be covered by the ICSID Convention.[73] It can for instance be argued that the transaction which formed the basis of a dispute in the case *Petrobart v. the Kyrgyz Republic*[74] would have not met the criteria of an "investment" under the ICSID Convention. The dispute in *Petrobart* in essence related to the delivery by Petrobart of 200,000 tons of gas condensate to a Kyrgyz State entity, KGM. The Contract, as noted by the Tribunal, "did not involve any transfer of money or property as capital in a business in the Kyrgyz Republic but was a sales contract. It concerned the sale of goods at an agreed price."[75] Although the activity could very well qualify as an "investment" under the ECT, which

70 *Salini Costrutori S.p., supra* note 68, para. 52 (internal footnotes omitted).

71 See Ibrahim F.I. Shihata and Antonio R. Parra, "The Experience of the International Centre for Settlement of Investment Disputes", *ICSID Review – Foreign Investment Law Journal* 14 (1999), 308.

72 See the Commentary to Article 25 ICSID Convention in Christoph Schreuer, Loretta Malintoppi, August Reinisch, and Anthony Sinclair, *The ICSID Convention: A Commentary* (Cambridge: Cambridge University Press, 2009).

73 See Antonio R. Parra, 'Investments and Investors Covered by the ECT and Other Investment Protection Treaties – Introduction', in Clarisse Ribeiro, *supra* note 20, 52.

74 *Petrobart Limited v. The Kyrgyz Republic*, ICC Case No. 126/2003, Arbitral Award, 29 March 2005.

75 Ibid., 69.

was confirmed by the Tribunal,[76] it is arguable that the "investment" made by Petrobart would not qualify as such under the ICSID Convention.[77] This again emphasizes that the choice of fora for the settlement of investment disputes, as contained in the ECT, has a certain importance, which goes beyond the mere policy aspects of each specific forum.

The Notion of an Investment 'Associated with an Economic Activity in the Energy Sector'

In line with the sectoral coverage of the ECT, the third paragraph of Article 1(6) ECT requires the investment to be "associated with an Economic Activity in the Energy Sector." The use of the phrase "associated with" may imply however that the coverage of the ECT, and thus the protection offered by the ECT including access to international investment arbitration, is also open to investments not directly in the field of energy, but merely "associated to it."[78]

The Arbitral Tribunal in *AMTO v. Ukraine* first discussed the notion "associated with an Economic Activity in the Energy Sector."[79] In this case, the Claimant, the Latvian Company AMTO, owned shares in a company, "EYUM-10" which had signed a contract with an Ukrainian company, "related to electrical installation, repairs and technical reconstruction or upgrading – in short, the provision of technical services – at the ZAES nuclear power plant."[80] The Respondent submitted that the contract could not qualify as an "Economic Activity in the Energy Sector," as defined in Article 1(5) ECT, nor that the activity is "associated with" such an activity. The Tribunal considered that "the interpretation of the words 'associated with' involves a question of degree, and refers primarily to the factual rather than legal association between the alleged investment and an Economic Activity in the Energy Sector. A mere contractual relationship with an energy producer is insufficient to attract ECT protection where the subject matter of the contract has no functional relationship with the energy sector."[81] The Tribunal finally concluded that, because, *inter alia*, the contract and the activity were "directly related to the production of

76 Ibid., 72.

77 See also Stephen Jagush and Anthony Sinclair, "The Limits of Protection for Investments and Investors under the Energy Charter Treaty", in Clarisse Ribeiro, *supra* note 20, 81–87.

78 Emmanuel Gaillard, "Investments and Investors Covered by the Energy Charter Treaty", in Clarisse Ribeiro, *supra* note 20, 66.

79 *Limited Liability Company Amto v. Ukraine*, SCC Case No. 080/2005, Final Award, 26 March 2008. See for a discussion of this case, Sergei Voitovich, "AMTO Case Presentation", in Graham Coop *supra* note 3, 55.

80 Ibid., para. 40.

81 Ibid., para. 42.

electrical energy," and that the services had been provided through multiple contracts over a substantial period of time, it constituted an "investment associated with an Economic Activity in the Energy Sector."[82] It is interesting to note that the Tribunal used a functional criterion to establish the "association" requirement under the ECT and required a certain duration for the associated activity. Under this case-law, investment protection under the ECT will thus not be extended to contracts relating to, for example, advertising or publishing.[83]

The Definition of 'Investor' under the ECT

The second specificity of the ECT lies in its definition of the concept of "investor." Under the ECT, "Investor" is defined as

> a natural person having the citizenship or nationality of or who is permanently residing in that Contracting Party in accordance with its applicable law;
> (ii) a company or other organization organized in accordance with the law applicable in that Contracting State.[84]

The definition of "foreign investor" in both the ECT and the ICSID Convention also somehow diverges. The ECT extends the protection of investors not only to nationals of the Contracting States, but also to those who are permanently residing in a Contracting State. The idea behind this is that the ECT, like several other multilateral trade or investment agreements, intends to create a single area for the protection of investments in the energy sector.[85]

Under the ICSID Convention, only disputes between a State and a national of another contracting State may be submitted to arbitration. Article 25 ICSID deals with the jurisdiction of the Centre and requires the existence of a "legal dispute arising directly out of an investment, between a Contracting State (or any constituent subdivision or agency of a Contracting State designated to the Centre by that State) and a national of another Contracting State, which the parties to the dispute consent in writing to submit to the Centre."[86] The ICSID Convention further defines a "National of another Contracting State" as

82 Ibid., para. 43.
83 Sergei Voitovich, "AMTO Case Presentation", in Graham Coop *supra* note 3, 57.
84 Article 1(7) ECT.
85 Emmanuel Gaillard, *supra* note 78, 67.
86 Article 25(1) ICSID Convention.

> any natural person who had the nationality of a Contracting State other than the State party to the dispute on the date on which the parties consented to submit such dispute to conciliation or arbitration as well as on the date on which the request was registered pursuant to paragraph (3) of Article 28 or paragraph (3) of Article 36, but does not include any person who on either date also had the nationality of the Contracting State party to the dispute; and
>
> any juridical person which had the nationality of a Contracting State other than the State party to the dispute on the date on which the parties consented to submit such dispute to conciliation or arbitration and any juridical person which had the nationality of the Contracting State party to the dispute on that date and which, because of foreign control, the parties have agreed should be treated as a national of another Contracting State for the purposes of this Convention.

As a consequence, a natural person who is not a national of a Contracting State but is permanently residing in the host State may qualify as an "investor" under the ECT, although that same person will not necessarily meet the requirements of Article 25 of the ICSID Convention.

A similar difference exists in respect of juridical persons. The ECT requires that juridical persons need to be "organized in accordance with the law applicable in that Contracting Party," which is generally considered as offering a relatively broad protection to foreign companies.[87]

Because the ECT's definition of an "investor" may include nationals of the host State, Article 26(7) ECT provides that companies that have the nationality of the host State party to the dispute may nevertheless be considered as a national of another State, as required by Article 25(2)(b) of the ICSID Convention, if it is controlled by investors of another contracting State. However, Article 26(7) ECT requires that the control by investors of another contracting State exists *before the dispute between the company and the host State has risen.* Under the ICSID Convention, however, foreign control must principally exist at the time of the consent to arbitration and the institution of arbitral proceedings.[88]

87 Emmanuel Gaillard, *supra* note 78, 68.

88 Antonio R. Parra, "Investments and Investors Covered by the ECT and Other Investment Protection Treaties – Introduction", in Clarisse Ribeiro, *supra* note 20, 52.

The Implications of the ECT as a Multilateral Treaty on Treaty Interpretation

The question of the interpretation of the ECT may also result in differences with traditional BITs.[89] First of all, it may be asked whether the context in which the substantive protection standards were negotiated and the inclusion of these in the ECT, being a multilateral treaty covering not only investment protection, has any influence on the interpretation of these investment provisions. Because of the relative similarity of investment protection provisions, this is perhaps the only true difference that may exist between the protection offered to foreign investors under BITs and the ECT. It is useful first to recall that in accordance with Article 31(1) of the Vienna Convention on the Law of Treaties, "[a] treaty shall be interpreted in good faith in accordance with the ordinary meaning to be given to the terms of the treaty in their context and in the light of its object and purpose." The ordinary meaning of the protection standards does not differ substantially between BITs and the ECT, apart from the regular variations one finds both in BITs and in ECT. However, it is clear that the title, general context, and object and purpose of ECT and BITs are not identical, as was explained above. The question however is whether from this, one can draw any conclusions in respect of the interpretation of the standards of protection contained in BITs and ECT. It is doubtful whether the general subject-matter of the treaty and the mere characterization of the ECT, as a treaty covering more than investment protection alone rather than a pure "investment protection agreement," are sufficient to justify a different interpretation of the substantive standards of protection available to foreign investors. It is rather "the phraseology of each treaty provision," which determines the real subject matter governed by the treaty.[90] Because of the fact that the object and purpose of a BIT generally and the *investment protection provisions* of the ECT do not differ substantially – they are both aimed at promoting international investment through the protection offered to foreign investors – it does not seem reasonable to conclude that international investment tribunals, confronted with investment protection provisions in a ECT would interpret these provisions differently than in the case of a BIT. One cannot infer from the broader context and object and purpose generally of the ECT compared to BITs that the intent of the parties in respect of the protection of foreign investment, and thus the intended meaning of the substantive standards of protection contained in ECT, would be any different than in the case of BITs.

---

89 See Thomas Roe and Matthew Happold, *supra* note 23, p. 27 ff.

90 Ahmad Ali Ghouri, "Is Characterization of Treaties a Solution to Treaty Conflicts?", *Chinese Journal of International Law* 11 (2012), para. 18.

2.2.4 Denial of Benefits

The so-called "denial of benefits" clause in the ECT has been the subject of much discussion, in particular, its relation with Article 26 ECT, which provides for the direct access to investment treaty arbitration. The "denial of benefits" clause is contained in Article 17 ECT and provides that

> Each Contracting Party reserves the right to deny the advantages of this Part to:
>
> (1) a legal entity if citizens or nationals of a third state own or control such entity and if that entity has no substantial business activities in the Area of the Contracting Party in which it is organized; or
> (2) an Investment, if the denying Contracting Party establishes that such Investment is an Investment of an Investor of a third state with or as to which the denying Contracting Party:
> (a) does not maintain a diplomatic relationship; or
> (b) adopts or maintains measures that:
> (i) prohibit transactions with Investors of that state; or
> (ii) would be violated or circumvented if the benefits of this Part were accorded to Investors of that state or to their Investments

The "denial of benefits" clause is located in Part III of the ECT, which contains the substantive standards of protection offered to foreign investors. As noted, Article 26 ECT provides for foreign investor access to investment treaty arbitration in the event of a dispute in relation to the obligations of the host State under Part III ECT. The question arose in *Plama v. Bulgaria* whether, if the right of States to deny the benefits of Part III under Article 17 ECT has been exercised, there is still a valid consent to arbitration under Article 26 ECT. In other words, the question was whether the Tribunal would lack jurisdiction generally, because of the application of the "denial of benefits" clause, or if the Tribunal would have jurisdiction, based on the consent expressed by Bulgaria in Article 26 ECT, to determine the merits of the dispute. The question was whether Article 17 ECT relates to the merits of a dispute or to the jurisdiction of an arbitral tribunal. The *Plama* Tribunal took the view that Article 17 ECT in effect only relates to the denial of benefits contained in Part III of the ECT, with the exclusion of the dispute settlement clause in Article 26 ECT. The Tribunal argued that

> the express terms of Article 17 refer to a denial of the advantages "of this Part", thereby referring to the substantive advantages conferred upon an investor by Part III of the ECT. The language is unambiguous; but it is

> confirmed by the title to Article 17: "Non-Application of Part III in Certain Circumstances" (emphasis supplied). All authentic texts in the other five languages are to the same effect. From these terms, interpreted in good faith in accordance with their ordinary contextual meaning, the denial applies only to advantages under Part III. It would therefore require a gross manipulation of the language to make it refer to Article 26 in Part V of the ECT. Nonetheless, the Tribunal has considered whether any such manipulation is permissible in the light of the ECT's object and purpose.
>
> Article 26 provides a procedural remedy for a covered investor's claims; and it is not physically or juridically part of the ECT's substantive advantages enjoyed by that investor under Part III. As a matter of language, it would have been simple to exclude a class of investors completely from the scope of the ECT as a whole, as do certain other bilateral investment treaties; but that is self-evidently not the approach taken in the ECT. This limited exclusion from Part III for a covered investor, dependent on certain specific criteria, requires a procedure to resolve a dispute as to whether that exclusion applies in any particular case; and the object and purpose of the ECT, in the Tribunal's view, clearly requires Article 26 to be unaffected by the operation of Article 17(1). As already noted above, for a covered investor, Article 26 is a very important feature of the ECT.[91]

The Tribunal thus clearly distinguished between the existence of rights under the ECT, providing for substantive standards of protection to foreign investors, and the right to bring a claim for an alleged violation of these standards of protection by the host State. In doing so, the *Plama* Tribunal refused to consider Article 17 ECT as a provision, which would restrict the coverage of the ECT in respect of certain categories of investors.[92]

The Tribunal in the *Yukos* cases similarly confirmed that a State must in effect exercise its right to invoke the denial of benefits clause, in order to rely on this.[93]

---

91 *Plama Consortium Limited supra* note 67, paras. 147–148.

92 See also for a discussion Emmanuel Gaillard, *supra* note 78, 69–73.

93 The *Yukos* cases are here referred to as the three cases brought by three shareholders of Yukos Oil Corporation OJSC, against Russia, and are virtually identical, the Tribunals being moreover composed of the same arbitrators: *Hulley Enterprises Ltd. v. The Russian Federation*, PCA Case No. AA 226, UNCITRAL, Interim Award on Jurisdiction and Admissibility, 30 November 2009, *Yukos Universal Limited (Isle of Man) v. The Russian Federation*, PCA Case No. AA 227, UNCITRAL, Interim Award on Jurisdiction and

2.2.5 Provisional Application of the ECT

One of the specific features of the ECT is that the treaty provides for its provisional application.[94] The provisional application of the ECT, that is the obligation for States that have signed the treaty, but not yet ratified it, to apply the provisions of the treaty pending its entry into force, is regulated in Article 45 ECT, which provides that:

> (1) Each signatory agrees to apply this Treaty provisionally pending its entry into force for such signatory in accordance with Article 44, to the extent that such provisional application is not inconsistent with its constitution, laws or regulations.
>
> (2) (a) Notwithstanding paragraph (1) any signatory may, when signing, deliver to the Depository a declaration that it is not able to accept provisional application. The obligation contained in paragraph (1) shall not apply to a signatory making such a declaration. Any such signatory may at any time withdraw that declaration by written notification to the Depository.
> (b) Neither a signatory which makes a declaration in accordance with subparagraph (a) nor Investors of that signatory may claim the benefits of provisional application under paragraph (1).
> (c) Notwithstanding subparagraph (a), any signatory making a declaration referred to in subparagraph (a) shall apply Part VII provisionally pending the entry into force of the Treaty for such signatory in accordance with Article 44, to the extent that such provisional application is not inconsistent with its laws or regulations.
>
> (3) (a) Any signatory may terminate its provisional application of this Treaty by written notification to the Depository of its intention not to become a Contracting Party to the Treaty. Termination of provisional application for any signatory shall take effect upon the expiration of 60 days from the date on which such signatory's written notification is received by the Depository.

Admissibility, 30 November 2009 and *Veteran Petroleum Ltd. v. The Russian Federation*, PCA Case No. AA 228, UNCITRAL, Interim Award on Jurisdiction and Admissibility, 30 November 2009, para. 456 ff.

94 See for the drafting history of this provision: Yas Banifatemi, "Provisional Application of the Energy Charter Treaty: The Negotiating History of Article 45", in Graham Coop *supra* note 3, 191. See generally: Tarcisio Gazzini, "Provisional Application of the Energy Charter Treaty: A Short Analysis of Article 45", *Transnational Dispute Management* (2009), 1–17.

> (b) In the event that a signatory terminates provisional application under subparagraph (a), the obligation of the signatory under paragraph (1) to apply Parts III and V with respect to any Investments made in its Area during such provisional application by Investors of other signatories shall nevertheless remain in effect with respect to those Investments for twenty years following the effective date of termination, except as otherwise provided in subparagraph (c).
> (c) Subparagraph (b) shall not apply to any signatory listed in Annex PA. A signatory shall be removed from the list in Annex PA effective upon delivery to the Depository of its request therefor.

Several tribunals thus far have been called upon to analyse the exact meaning of Article 45 ECT, and the content of the obligations of States, which have signed but not yet ratified the treaty.

The question of the provisional application of the ECT was first raised in *Petrobart v. the Kyrgyz Republic.*[95] In this case, the Claimant was a company registered in Gibraltar, a territory over which the United Kingdom has certain competences, for certain aspects of its international relations. The United Kingdom had signed the ECT on 17 December 1994 and had specified in a declaration that the provisional application of the ECT would extend not only to the United Kingdom but also to Gibraltar. When ratifying the ECT on 13 December 1996, the United Kingdom however declared that the ECT entered into force only for the territory of the United Kingdom, Jersey and the Isle of Man. The question was thus raised whether, the ratification of the ECT, and the specification of the ECT's application for the United Kingdom, Jersey and the Isle of Man, implied the end of the provisional application of the ECT in respect of Gibraltar. The Tribunal, relatively briefly, dismissed the argument, on the ground that:

> The Arbitral Tribunal considers that in principle, on matters of this kind, a rather formal approach based on the wording of the Treaty is appropriate. It is then to be noted that according to the text of the Treaty provisional application ceases if it is terminated either by a special notification under Article 45(3)(a) of the Treaty or by transition from provisional application to a corresponding and final legal commitment resulting from the entry into force of the Treaty. It could indeed be expected that the United Kingdom, if it wished the provisional application of the Treaty to Gibraltar to be terminated as a result of a ratification not including

95 *Petrobart Limited, supra* note 74.

> Gibraltar, should have made this clear by making a notification in line with Article 45(3)(a) or a declaration in some other form in connection with the ratification. In the Arbitral Tribunal's opinion, the fact that the ratification, for political or other reasons, did not include Gibraltar does not justify the conclusion that the United Kingdom intended to revoke the application of the Treaty to Gibraltar on a provisional basis. It may be observed that what is at issue here is not only the rights of investors from Gibraltar in other states but also the protection of foreign investors in Gibraltar.[96]

The Tribunal in *Ioannis Kardassopoulos v. The Republic of Georgia* was the first tribunal called upon to decide on the consistency of domestic law with the provisional application of the ECT. In this case, the expropriation complained of by the Claimant had taken place following the issuance of executive decrees after the ECT entered into force for both Greece (the State of nationality of the Claimant) and Georgia, but before the ECT entered into force on April 1998.[97] The Tribunal did not uphold Georgia's argument that the provisional application of the ECT was inconsistent with its domestic laws. The Tribunal considered that "it follows that the language used in Article 45(1) is to be interpreted as meaning that each signatory State is obliged, even before the ECT has formally entered into force, to apply the whole ECT as if it had already done so."[98] As a consequence, the investment protection provisions contained in the ECT are fully applicable during the period when the ECT provisionally applies.

Similarly, in the *Yukos* cases, which concern allegations of violation by Russia of various provisions of Part III of the ECT, the question of the provisional application of the ECT was raised since Russia had signed but not ratified the ECT. In particular, Russia argued that, although the principle of the provisional application of the ECT was "not inconsistent with its constitution, laws or regulations" in accordance with Article 45(1) ECT, the provisional application of the specific provisions invoked by the Claimants, and the consent to arbitration contained in Article 26 ECT, is in effect "inconsistent with its constitution, laws or regulations."[99] The Tribunal first empha-

96 Ibid., 62–63.

97 See for a discussion of the case, including background information on the investment climate in Georgia: David Herlihy, "Ioannis Kardassopoiulos v. Georgia ICSID Case No. ARB/05/18", in Graham Coop *supra* note 3, 45.

98 *Ioannis Kardassopoulos v. The Republic of Georgia*, ICSID Case No. ARB/05/18, Decision on Jurisdiction; 6 July 2007, para. 211.

99 See for a discussion Thomas Roe and Matthew Happold, *supra* note 23, 74 ff.

sized that the question of the "inconsistency with a State's constitution, laws or regulations" is independent from the making of a declaration by a State that "it is not able to accept provisional application", in accordance with Article 45(2)(a) ECT.[100] The Tribunal also considered that the provisional application of the ECT, applies to the treaty as a whole, and that the potential inconsistency of one particular provision with a State's constitution, laws or regulations is of no relevance.[101] The Tribunal eventually found that the provisional application of the ECT was consistent with Russia's constitution, laws and regulations, and, in addition, that the consent to arbitration contained in Article 26 ECT was also not inconsistent with Russia's constitution, laws and regulations.[102]

3 Investor-State Dispute Settlement: The Problem of Parallel Proceedings and Overlapping Investment Protection Treaties

3.1 *Contract and Treaty Claims under the Energy Charter Treaty*

Despite the relative obviousness of the distinction between the contractual and treaty levels of international investment claims, and the fact that in an analysis of the legal considerations brought forward in international arbitral awards, either by counsel or by the arbitrators, a clear distinction is often made between treaty claims (public international law arguments) and claims based on municipal law or private international law.[103] The interaction between these two levels of obligations have not always proven to be unproblematic, in particular in view of the concomitance of contractual and treaty claims before international investment tribunals.

The Contract and Treaty Levels of Investment Treaty Arbitration

The first most obvious regime governing foreign investment is the international legal instrument granting protection to the foreign investor. This instrument usually takes the form of an international treaty, which in relation to disputes in the energy sector will most often be the ECT or a BIT. A claim brought before an international investment tribunal for an alleged violation by the host State

100 See para. 262, *Hulley Enterprises Ltd supra* note 93, *Yukos Universal Limited (Isle of Man) supra* note 93 and *Veteran Petroleum Ltd supra* note 93.

101 See ibid., para. 301.

102 Ibid., paras. 338 and 392.

103 Zachary Douglas, *The International Law of Investment Treaty Claims* (Cambridge: Cambridge University Press, 2009), 8.

of the applicable investment treaty is principally the invocation by the foreign investor of the international responsibility of that State. It is not because the foreign investor is granted the right to invoke the responsibility of the State that such claims are by definition "private law" claims. On the contrary, the involvement of a private actor does not alter the fundamental principles applicable to international responsibility of States. As noted by the International Law Commission in its Articles on the Responsibility of States for Internationally Wrongful Acts, the obligations of State may relate to "any right, arising from the international responsibility of a State, which may accrue directly to any person or entity other than a State."[104] The characterization of an act as internationally wrongful is governed solely by general international law, while national law, and the characterization of an act as wrongful of lawful under that legal system does not affect the international wrongfulness of the act.[105]

In practice foreign investors and host States will, besides the protection offered by the relevant international investment treaty, sign one or more contracts in which the specifics of the investment will be detailed, and this constitutes the second layer of obligations. The foreign investor and an agency or subdivision of a State very often concludes this contract. Concession Contracts are not regulated by international law, despite some controversy on this question, since the presence of the foreign investor as a party to the contract makes it impossible to conclude an international legal instrument because the foreign investor has no treaty-making capacity.[106] The question whether the State has breached its international obligations towards the foreign investor, which

---

104 See Article 33(2), and the accompanying commentary to that Article (para. 4), Draft Articles on the Responsibility of States for Internationally Wrongful Acts, Report of the International Law Commission on the work of its Fifty-third session, *Official Records of the General Assembly, Fifty-sixth session, Supplement No. 10* (A/56/10), Chapter IV.E.1.

Article 3, Draft Articles on the Responsibility of States for Internationally Wrongful Acts, Report of the International Law Commission on the work of its Fifty-third session, *Official Records of the General Assembly, Fifty-sixth session, Supplement No. 10* (A/56/10), Chapter IV.E.1.

105 Commentary to Article 12, para. 9, Draft Articles on the Responsibility of States for Internationally Wrongful Acts, Report of the International Law Commission on the work of its Fifty-third session, *Official Records of the General Assembly, Fifty-sixth session, Supplement No. 10* (A/56/10), Chapter IV.E.1.

106 For a discussion, see James Crawford, "Treaty and Contract in Investment Arbitration", *Arbitration International* 24 (2008), 362 and Patrick Dumberry, "International Investment Contracts", in Tarcisio Gazzini and Eric De Brabandere (eds.), *The Sources of Rights and Obligations in Transnational Investment Law* (Leiden/Boston: Martinus Nijhoff Publishers, 2012), 215.

is governed solely by the rules on State responsibility, is thus fundamentally different from State liability for breaches of the investment or concession contract.[107] The State may for instance not be liable, under its domestic laws, for the conduct of a separate legal entity, despite the fact that the acts of the latter may be attributable to the State under general international law.[108] As noted by the *Ad Hoc* Committee in the *Vivendi I* case:

> whether there has been a breach of the BIT and whether there has been a breach of contract are different questions. Each of these claims will be determined by reference to its own proper or applicable law – in the case of the BIT, by international law; in the case of the concession contract, by the proper law of the contract.[109]

This does not mean that a Tribunal may have jurisdiction for both treaty and contract claims at the same time, provided that both the applicable investment treaty and the investment contract provide for the same arbitration mechanism. This is the case in the pending arbitration between *Khan Resources Inc., Khan Resources B.V., and Cauc Holding Company Ltd.* and the Government of Mongolia, which operates under the UNICTRAL Arbitration Rules and is based on the ECT, the Mongolian Foreign Investment Law and an investment contract.[110]

The ECT "Umbrella Clause"

A related question is whether in the event of an "umbrella clause," contract claims are transformed into treaty claims.[111] Such clauses in fact "elevate" a

107 James Crawford, ibid., 358.

108 See *Compañiá de Aguas del Aconquija S.A. and Vivendi Universal (formerly Compagnie Générale des Eaux) v. Argentine Republic*, ICSID Case No. ARB/97/3, Decision on Annulment, 3 July 2002, para. 96: 'in the case of a claim based on a treaty, international law rules of attribution apply, with the result that the state of Argentina is internationally responsible for the acts of its provincial authorities. By contrast, the state of Argentina is not liable for the performance of contracts entered into by Tucumán, which possesses separate legal personality under its own law and is responsible for the performance of its own contracts'.

109 Ibid., para. 98.

110 *Khan Resources Inc., Khan Resources B.V., and Cauc Holding Company Ltd. v. The Government of Mongolia*, UNCITRAL, Pending.

111 See generally Patrick Dumberry, 'International Investment Contracts', in: Tarcisio Gazzini and Eric De Brabandere (eds.), *The Sources of Rights and Obligations in Transnational Investment Law* (Leiden/Boston: Martinus Nijhoff Publishers, 2012), 215.

breach of a contractual obligation into a breach of a treaty obligation, essentially in order to gain access to the dispute settlement clauses contained in the investment treaty. The effect of "umbrella clauses" has resulted in divergent and conflicting arbitral decisions, ranging from the denial of any effect to "umbrella clauses,"[112] the effect of an automatic transformation of a contract violation into a treaty violation,[113] to the transformation of a contract violation into a treaty violation provided that the contract does not contain any exclusive dispute settlement clause.[114] It is not the purpose here however to engage in a detailed discussion of this question.

Article 10(1) ECT contains the following umbrella clause: "Each Contracting Party shall observe any obligations it has entered into with an Investor or an Investment of an Investor of any other Contracting Party." The umbrella clause contained in the ECT is considered to be one of the most extensive umbrella clauses.[115] I should reiterate here that States may opt out of the "umbrella clause" contained in Article 10(1) of the ECT. The ECT indeed provides that States may not give their "unconditional consent with respect to a dispute arising under the last sentence of Article 10(1)."[116] Only four States have refused the application of the "umbrella clause."[117]

Essentially, the questions posed by the ECT umbrella clause are relatively similar to the general discussion and application of umbrella clauses in BITs. The ECT umbrella clause was discussed in *Nykomb v. Latvia*[118] and *AMTO v.*

112 See *e.g. SGS Société Générale de Surveillance S.A. v. Islamic Republic of Pakistan*, ICSID Case No. ARB/01/13, Decision of the Tribunal on Objections to Jurisdiction, 6 August 2003 and *Joy Mining Machinery Limited v. Egypt*, ICSID Case No. ARB/03/11, Award on Jurisdiction, 6 August 2004.

113 See *e.g. Eureko BV v. Republic of Poland*, Partial Award, August 19, 2005, including a strong dissent of arbitrator Rajski on precisely this issue.

114 See for example; *SGS Société Générale de Surveillance S.A. v. Republic of the Philippines*, ICSID Case No. ARB/02/6, Decision of the Tribunal on Objections to Jurisdiction, 29 January 2004.

115 Christer Söderlund, 'Multiple Judicial Proceedings and the Energy Charter Treaty', in Clarisse Ribeiro *supra* note 20, 252.

116 Article 26(3)(c) ECT.

117 The States are: Australia; Canada; Hungary; Norway. Here again, it should be emphasized that Canada has not signed the ECT, and Australia and Norway have not yet ratified the ECT. The list of States is available at http://www.encharter.org/index.php?id=323 (accessed 18 September 2012).

118 *Nykomb Synergetics Technology Holding AB v. the Republic of Latvia*, SCC CASE 118/2001, Final Award, 16 December 2003.

Ukraine.[119] In *AMTO*, the Tribunal refused the application of the umbrella clause on the ground that the Claimant had no contract with Ukraine. The contract was signed between two Ukrainian legal entities, the Claimant – AMTO – moreover being the shareholder of the investing company. Under these circumstances, the Tribunal opined that there was no possibility of "elevating" a contract breach into a treaty breach.[120] In other words, Ukraine had not undertaken any contractual obligations. However, the Tribunal did note that the umbrella clause of the ECT had a "wide character," and imposes not only obligations towards the foreign investor, but also towards a subsidiary company, established in the host State.[121]

The Tribunal in *Mohammad Ammar Al-Bahloul v. Tajikistan*,[122] confronted with an objection raised by the Respondent that the Claimant should have respected the forum selection clause in the contract, confirmed not only the choice given to foreign investors under the ECT to submit their dispute to the national courts, a previously agreed dispute settlement mechanism, or arbitration, but also the distinct character of treaty claims and contract claims.[123] The tribunal noted that a claim based on a violation of the ECT is a distinct action from a claim based on the violation of the contract and that neither precludes the other.[124]

3.2 *The Problem of Parallel Proceedings*

Leaving aside the possibility of parallel proceedings under both a contract and a treaty offering investment protection and access to investment treaty arbitration, which we discussed in the previous section because of the fact that the ECT is a multilateral treaty offering direct access to investment treaty arbitration, the risk of parallel proceedings with other treaties offering investment protection and direct access to investment arbitration, such as BITs is non-negligible.[125]

It should first of all be emphasized that parallel proceedings, as understood here, imply identical proceedings, where the cause of action, the facts and the

119 *Limited Liability Company Amto v. Ukraine*, SCC Case No. 080/2005, Final Award, 26 March 2008.

120 Ibid., para. 110.

121 Ibid.

122 *Mohammad Ammar Al-Bahloul supra* note 57.

123 Ibid., paras. 158–159.

124 Ibid., paras. 158–159.

125 See Michael Polkinghorne, "Arbitration under the ECT and Other Investment Protection Treaties", in Clarisse Ribeiro, *supra* note 20, 299.

parties are similar. Based on publicly available information, in respect of investment arbitrations based on the ECT, only on two occasions have foreign investors founded their claim and the jurisdiction of the arbitral tribunal on both the ECT and an applicable BIT. The first case, *EVN AG v. The former Yugoslav Republic of Macedonia* was settled; therefore the "double" jurisdictional basis was not discussed by the Tribunal.[126] The second case, *Ioannis Kardassopoulos v. The Republic of Georgia* is more interesting in this respect, although I should immediately add that it has not led to any specific problems. It does show however that the applicability of two treaties may be interesting in case one of the treaties is not applicable. In this case, the Claimant based its claim and the jurisdiction of the Tribunal on both the Georgia-Greece BIT and the ECT.[127] Since the Tribunal determined that the Tribunal lacked jurisdiction *ratione temporis* over Mr. Kardassopoulos' expropriation claim under the Georgia / Greece BIT, the applicability of the ECT was necessary for the Claimant's expropriation claim.[128] It did however find that it had jurisdiction *ratione temporis* to consider the separate fair and equitable treatment claim advanced by Mr. Kardassopoulos under Article 2(2) of the Georgia-Greece BIT. In the end, the Tribunal found that the respondent had unlawfully expropriated the Claimant, and that the Respondent failed to afford Mr. Kardassopoulos fair and equitable treatment both under Article 2(2) of the Georgia-Greece BIT and Article 10(1) of the ECT.[129] This however did not result in a double recovery considering that it was the same tribunal, which assessed both the BIT and the ECT claims.

At the same time, it should also be highlighted that proceedings involving the same factual circumstances and cause of action, but brought by different parties are an increasing phenomenon. Such a situation occurred not only in the widely commented *CME v. Czech Republic* and *Lauder v. Czech Republic* case, but also in the already mentioned *Yukos* cases. In those three cases, the tribunals were moreover identically composed. In each case however, because of the similarity of the factual circumstances, and the law applicable to the dispute, the three awards on jurisdiction, which have thus far been rendered, show much similarity. As noted by the Tribunal:

> The three arbitrations were heard in parallel with the full participation of the Parties at all relevant stages of the proceedings. Mindful of the fact

126 *EVN AG v. The former Yugoslav Republic of Macedonia*, ICSID Case No. ARB/09/10, Award, 2 September 2011. The award embodied the settlement reached by the parties.

127 *Ioannis Kardassopoulos, supra* note 98.

128 Ibid., para. 241.

129 Ibid., para. 452.

> that each of the three Claimants maintains separate claims in separate arbitrations that necessitate separate awards, the Tribunal nevertheless shall discuss these arbitrations as a single set of proceedings, except where circumstances distinct to particular Claimants necessitate separate treatment. Thus throughout Parts I to VI, the introductory portions of this Interim Award, the plural "Claimants" is used collectively for Hulley, YUL and VPL. In Parts VII, VIII and IX, the Issues, Analysis and Decision portions of this Interim Award, the singular "Claimant" refers specifically to YUL.[130]

The possibility of having parallel proceedings, in cases involving different parties, is possible particularly because the definitions of "investor" generally found in investment protection treaties and the ECT, as was discussed above, are very broadly formulated. As a consequence, and because States, in their investment protection agreements, have extended protection not only to investing companies, but also to the company or individuals controlling the investing company, parallel proceedings are inevitable. However, as was explained by the Swedish Court of Appeal in the *CME* and *Lauder v. Czech Republic* cases, if parallel proceedings involve different parties, there is no possibility to invoke either the principle of *lis pendens* or the principle of *res judicata.*[131] The solution to avoid parallel proceedings simply resides in restricting the right of controlling shareholders to bring an independent claim under investment protection treaties.

The elimination of the risk of parallel proceedings, *with identical parties*, is more problematic, since under those circumstances, the principles of *lis pendens* and *res judicata* may effectively be applicable. It should moreover be noted that this problem could easily be solved through a regulation by treaty. Article 26 ICSID Convention for instance provides that consent to arbitration under the Convention excludes the use of any other remedy. Secondly, fork-in-the-road clauses similarly avoid the risk of parallel proceedings, since the choice of one particular method will exclude recourse to another dispute resolution method provided for in the treaty.[132] In the case of the ECT, parallel proceedings based on the ECT however are possible because of the choice of fora given to foreign investors as was discussed above. The fork-in-the-road clause is only optional under the ECT, although the majority of the States party

130 Para. 2, *Hulley Enterprises Ltd supra* note 93; *Yukos Universal Limited (Isle of Man), supra* note 93 and *Veteran Petroleum Ltd, supra* note 93.

131 Svea Court of Appeal, Challenge of Arbitral Award, 15 May 2003, 42 ILM 919 (2003).

132 See Christer Söderlund, "Multiple Judicial Proceedings and the Energy Charter Treaty", in *supra* note 20, 239 ff.

to the ECT have issued a declaration opting out of the system contained in Article 26(3)(b) ECT. In any case, if the investor choses to pursue arbitration under the ICSID Convention, Article 26 ICSID Convention in effect restricts the possibility of parallel proceedings.[133]

Petrobart v. the Kyrgyz Republic is an interesting case in point. Prior to instituting proceedings under the ECT before an arbitral tribunal established under the Rules of the Arbitration Institute of the Stockholm Chamber of Commerce, the investors had initiated arbitral proceedings against the Kyrgyz Republic based on the latter's Foreign Investment Law.[134] In the meantime, judicial proceedings before the Bishkek Court of Appeal (the "Show-cause case") resulted in a judgment of that Court stating that Petrobart did not qualify as an investor under the Foreign Investment Law. The Tribunal rendered an award finding that the contract between Petrobart and KGM, a State-owned company, did not constitute an investment as defined by the Foreign Investment Law of the Kyrgyz Republic. The Tribunal however opined that

> ...paragraph 3 of Article 26 makes the following clear. First, all Contracting Parties to the Treaty have given their unconditional consent to arbitration. This constitutes a clear offer and thus an agreement to arbitrate. Second, those countries that are not listed in Annex ID have extended their unconditional consent to arbitrate a dispute under the Treaty, even if such a dispute had already been submitted to domestic courts or to previously agreed dispute settlement procedures.[135]

The Tribunal further noted that

> From the perspective of international law, there are three conditions for the application of the res judicata principle: identity of the parties, identity of cause of action, and identity of object (or subject matter) in the subsequent proceedings. Where two claims differ radically in their object, a decision on the first would not constitute res judicata for the subsequent case.
>
> It is clear that the two proceedings relied on by the Kyrgyz Republic (*i.e.* the Show-Cause Case and the UNCITRAL Arbitration) were faced with an entirely different cause of action and also a different subject matter from

133 Ibid., 239.

134 See *Petrobart Limited, supra* note 74, p. 8 ff.

135 Ibid., 55.

> the one presented in the present case. The cause of action in the present proceeding is a breach by the Republic of its obligations under the Treaty. This is not the same cause of action as under either the Show-Cause Case or the UNCITRAL Arbitration. Additionally, in the UNCITRAL Arbitration, Petrobart's claim was dismissed for lack of jurisdiction which means that Petrobart is not prevented by the res judicata doctrine from presenting the same issue again before another tribunal which may be competent.[136]

In doing so, the Tribunal correctly distinguished between the causes of action of the two claims and had no difficulty in establishing that because of the differences in causes of action, the principles of *lis pendens* and *res judicata* were not applicable.

4 Conclusion

This chapter has given an overview of the various dispute settlement methods available to foreign investors and host States in the energy sector. This sector has generally been considered to account for a vast percentage of global investments. The Energy Charter Secretariat has so far reported that 33 investor-State dispute settlement cases have been submitted under the ECT. Given the importance of the energy sector in the total number of investment disputes, this figure is somehow unsatisfactory since the ECT only formed the basis for consent for only a minority of investment disputes in the energy sector. At the same time, the effectiveness of the ECT in providing consent to arbitration generally, totalling a number of 33 registered cases submitted to arbitration, shows that the treaty has had a clear impact on the protection of foreign investors in the energy sector.

Although this chapter has argued that, as such investment disputes in the energy sector are not fundamentally different from investment disputes generally, the presence of the ECT has created several specificities in the settlement of energy investment disputes.

The choice of arbitration fora provided for under the ECT and the fact that the ECT is a multilateral treaty are particularly of significant importance. This chapter has explained the reasons behind and the implications of the availability of different fora. In particular, the various fora are necessary to ensure that investment disputes arising under the ECT are settled in accordance with the specificities of each case, and the expectations of the parties.

136 Ibid., 56.

The ECT contains certain specific rules, which deviate to a certain extent from provisions in BITs and from the jurisdictional requirements of the ICSID Convention. The terms "investor" and "investment" are for instance, relatively broadly defined. Thus, in the case of ICSID Arbitration, foreign investors in the energy sector will have to take into consideration that the definition of "investment" as provided for in the ECT may well cover certain activities although the same activities may not be covered by the ICSID Convention. Similarly, a natural person who is not a national of a Contracting State but is permanently residing in the host State may qualify as an "investor" under the ECT, although that same person will not necessarily meet the requirements of Article 25 of the ICSID Convention. A similar difference exists in respect of juridical persons.

Perhaps the most interesting feature of the ECT is its provisional application, which results in foreign investors having access to investment treaty arbitration under the ECT against a State that has in fact never ratified the ECT. Tribunals confronted with this question have moreover shown to be relatively flexible in interpreting the conditions for the provision application of the ECT.

Finally, this chapter has discussed the possibility of parallel proceedings, which is more likely from a theoretical perspective, because of the fact that the ECT is a multilateral treaty offering direct access to investment treaty arbitration. Theoretically, parallel proceedings with other treaties offering investment protection and direct access to investment arbitration, such as BITs are thus non-negligible. Practice however has shown that this has not caused any severe problems so far.

PART 3

Interaction between Private and Public Interests in the Energy Sector

CHAPTER 6

Energy, Environment and Foreign Investment

Makane Moïse Mbengue and Deepak Raju

1 Introduction

This chapter seeks to analyse the interaction between international investment law and international environmental law in the context of the energy sector. The relationship between these two "fragments"[1] of international law has inspired a large amount of literature[2] highlighting, largely how the private interest of protection of investments is at odds with the public interest in protecting the environment. The abundance of investment arbitration cases where measures towards environmental regulation have been assailed as violations of commitments under investment treaties lends some credence to this

1 See generally, M. Koskenniemi and P. Leino, "Fragmentation of International Law? Postmodern Anxieties", *Leiden Journal of International Law* 15 (2002), 553; G. Hafner, "Pros and Cons Ensuing from Fragmentation of International Law", Mich. J. Int'l L. 25 (2003–2004), 849; J. Pauwelyn, "Bridging Fragmentation and Unity: International Law as a Universe of Inter-Connected Islands", Mich. J. Int'l L. 25 (2003–2004) 903; P.S. Rao, "Multiple International Judicial Forums: A Reflection of the Growing Strength of International Law or Its Fragmentation", Mich. J. Int'l L. 25 (2003–2004) 929.

2 J.E. Vinuales, "Foreign Investment and the Environment in International Law: An Ambiguous Relationship", 80 *British Yearbook of International Law* (2009/2010), pp. 244–332; J.E. Vinuales, *Foreign Investment and the Environment in International Law* (Cambridge: Cambridge University Press, 2012); R.P. Tscherning, "Indirect Expropriation of Carbon-Intensive Investments and the Fair and Equitable Treatment Standard in International Investment Arbitration: A Commentary on the Pending Vattenfall v. Federal Republic of Germany Dispute", University of Dundee Working Paper, at http://www.dundee.ac.uk/cepmlp/gateway/?news=31345 (accessed 25 October 2013); Å. Romson, *Environmental Policy Space and International Investment Law* (ActaUniversitatis Stockholm: Stockholmiensis, 2012); D.A. Gantz, "Potential Conflicts Between Investor Rights and Environmental Regulation Under NAFTA's Chapter 11", Geo. Wash. Int'l L. Rev. 33 (2001), 651, 719–20; D.R. Loritz, "Corporate Predators Attack Environmental Regulations: It's Time to Arbitrate Claims Filed Under NAFTA's Chapter 11", Loy. L.A. Int'l & Comp. L. Rev. 22 (2000), 533, 548; See generally, S.D. Franck, "The Legitimacy Crisis In Investment Treaty Arbitration: Privatizing Public International Law Through Inconsistent Decisions", *Fordham Law Review* 73 (2005), 1521.

 | DOI 10.1163/9789004244719_008

line of reasoning.[3] Yet, the relationship between investment protection and environment protection is more nuanced than a simple categorisation of environmental concerns as "public" and investment protection as "private" goals. There are points of convergence and divergence between these disciplines that need to be analysed closely.

This is particularly the case in the energy sector. Investors operating in the energy sector have the capability to either foster environmental goals through pursuit of non-conventional energy sources, transfer of clean technology and import of international best practices, or to augment environmental harm by incentivising lax regulation and forcing a "race to the bottom."[4] These examples represent two extremes of the spectrum and most interactions of foreign investment with environmental regulation lies somewhere on the spectrum.

This piece discusses the relationship between international environmental law and investment law in the context of the energy sector. The first part discusses in brief the nature of the relationship and highlights potential points of convergence and divergence between the two fields. The second part deals with how substantive norms of international investment law may support or deter initiatives for the protection of the environment. In the third part, the focus will be on the procedural mechanisms of dispute resolution established under international investment agreements (IIAs) with a view to analysing whether and to what extent these mechanisms are capable of accounting for environmental concerns.

2 Understanding the Relationship

2.1 *Historical Context*

The energy sector has traditionally seen large volumes of cross border flow of investments.[5] As early as 1930, the Texas Oil Company (now Texaco, part

---

3 *Saar PapierVertriebs GmbH v. Poland*, UNCITRAL Awards dated Oct 16, 1995 (not public); *Metalclad Corporation v. United Mexican States*, ICSID Case No. ARB(AF)97/1, Award, 30 August, 2000; *S.D. Myers Inc. v. Government of Canada*, Award 13 November, 2000; *Tecnicas Medioambientales SA (Tecmed) v. United Mexican States*, ICSID Case No. ARB(AF)00/2, Award, 29 May, 2003; *MTD Equity Sdn Bhd. & MTD Chile S.A. v. The Republic of Chile*, ICSID Case No. ARB/07/7, Award, 25 May, 2004.

4 Vinuales (2009/10), *supra* note 2; See generally, K.H. Engel, "State Environmental Standard-Setting: Is There a Race and Is It to the Bottom?", 48 *Hastings Law Journal* 271 (1996–1997); Y. Xing & C.D. Kolstad, "Do Lax Environmental Regulations Attract Foreign Investment?", *Environmental and Resource Economics* 21(1) (2002), 1.

5 A. Beltran, *A Comparative History of National Oil Companies* (Brussels: PIE Peter Lang, 2010); T. Falola, *The Politics of the Global Oil Industry: An Introduction* (Westport: Praeger, 2005);

of Chevron) had its operations in the Persian Gulf.[6] In 1933, Saudi Arabia granted oil concessions to California Arabian Standard Oil Company (Casoc), affiliate of Standard Oil of California (Socal, today's Chevron).[7] In the following decades, a large part of oil extraction in the Middle East was controlled by foreign companies operating under concession contracts.[8] The history of the oil industry elsewhere followed a similar trajectory.[9] Similarly the power sector in several countries has seen active involvement of foreign investors.[10] More recently, many countries have seen large scale FDI participation in the search for renewable energy sources.[11]

A. Blackmana& X. Wub, "Foreign direct investment in china's power sector: Trends, benefits and barriers", *Energy Policy* 27(12) (1999), 695–711; S.J. Liong, Foreign Investment in Electric Power Generation Around the Globe: A Study of Nine Countries, at http://www.iit.upcomillas.es/docs/TM-08-102.pdf (accessed 3 October 2013); P.N. Satyan, "Foreign Direct Investment in India's Power Sector", *Journal of Infrastructure Development* 3(1) (2011), 65–89; M. Wilkins, "Multinational Oil Companies in South America in the 1920s: Argentina, Bolivia, Brazil, Chile, Colombia, Ecuador, and Peru", *The Business History Review* 48(3) (1974), 414–446; J.C. Brown, "Why Foreign Oil Companies Shifted Their Production from Mexico to Venezuela during the 1920s", *The American Historical Review* 90(2) (1985), 362–385; United Nations Economic Commission for Latin America and the Caribbean, 'Foreign direct investment in electric energy in Latin America and the Caribbean' (Chapter IV) *in* Foreign Direct Investment in Latin America and the Caribbean (2012), at http://www.cepal.org/publicaciones/xml/4/49844/ForeignDirectInvestment2012.pdf (accessed 24 October 2013).

6 E.V. Thompson, A Brief History of Major Oil Companies in the Gulf Region, at http://www.virginia.edu/igpr/APAG/apagoilhistory.html (accessed 24 October 2013); Texas Almanac, Oil and Texas: A Cultural History, at http://www.texasalmanac.com/topics/business/oil-and-texas-cultural-history (accessed 24 October 2013).

7 Thomson, *supra* note 6.

8 E.T. Penrose, "Profit Sharing Between Producing Countries and Oil Companies in the Middle East", *The Economic Journal* 69 (1959), 238–254; A. Schill, "A Brief History of Middle Eastern Oil" (2012), at http://www.abadieschill.com/2012/07/04/a-brief-history-of-middle-eastern-oil/ (accessed 24 October 2013); V. Marcel, Oil Titans: National Oil Companies in the Middle East (Washington DC: Brookings Institution Press, 2006).

9 Falola, *supra* note 5.

10 Liong, *supra* note 5; Satyan, *supra* note 5.

11 R. Krüger (UNCTAD), Attracting Foreign Direct Investment into Renewable Energy, Second International Energy Efficiency Forum, Dushanbe, Tajikistan (2011) at http://www.unece.org/fileadmin/DAM/energy/se/pp/eneff/IEEForumDushanbeSept2011/1.2.2_Krueger.pdf; B. Cerdeira and J. Paulo, The role of foreign direct investment in the renewable electricity generation and economic growth nexus in Portugal: a cointegration and causality analysis (2012), at http://mpra.ub.uni-muenchen.de/41533/1/MPRA_paper_41533.pdf (accessed 24 October 2013); OCO Insight, FDI in Renewable Energy: A promising decade ahead

The significant involvement of foreign investors in the energy sector has in turn meant frequent clashes between investors and host governments in this field. The first wave of clashes surrounded the questions of ownership of energy sources.[12] After decolonisation in Asia, Africa and Latin America and the rise of nationalism, energy sources, particularly oil, came to be seen as a national resource.[13] This nationalist outlook, accompanied by the emergence of the doctrine of "permanent sovereignty over natural resources"[14] led to resentment of the existing market structures, often created during the colonial era, whereby a large share of profits went to foreign investor.[15] This resentment culminated in nationalisation of oil resources in several parts of the world and stringent opposition to the same from foreign investors and their home states.[16] For instance, the tensions between the West and Iran over the oil industry resulted, in part, in the Tehran hostage crisis and the events preceding and

(2012), at http://www.ocoglobal.com/uploads/default/files//FDI_in_Renewable_Energy__A_promising_decade_ahead.pdf (accessed 24 October 2013); See also, M. Hübler & Andreas Keller, "Energy savings via FDI? Empirical evidence from developing countries", *Environment and Development Economics* 15(1) (2010), 59–80.

12 R.C.A. White, "Expropriation of the Libyan Oil Concessions – Two Conflicting International Arbitrations", *International and Comparative Law Quarterly* 30(1) (1981), 1; C.E. Solberg, *Oil and Nationalism in Argentina: A History* (Stanford: Stanford University Press, 1979); F. Parra, *Oil Politics: A Modern History of Petroleum* (London/New York: I.B.Tauris, 2004); F.R. Teson, "State Contracts and Oil Expropriations: The Aminoil-Kuwait Arbitration", Va. J. Int'l L. 24 (1983–1984), 323.

13 Ibid.; H. Landau, "Economic and Political Nationalism and Private Foreign Investments", Denv. J. Int'l L. &Pol'y 2 (1972), 169; D. Hellinger, Nationalism, Oil Policy and the Party System in Venezuela, at the 2000 meeting of the Latin American Studies Association, at: http://lasa.international.pitt.edu/lasa2000/hellinger.pdf (accessed 24 October 2013); M. Rosado de Sa Ribeiro, "Sovereignty over Natural Resources Investment Law and Expropriation: The case of Bolivia and Brazil", J World Energy Law Bus 2(2) (2009), 129–148; G. Joffé, "Expropriation of oil and gas investments: Historical, legal and economic perspectives in a new age of resource nationalism", J World Energy Law Bus 2(1) (2009), 3–23.

14 Permanent Sovereignty over Natural Resources, G.A. res. 1803 (XVII), 17 U.N. GAOR Supp. (No.17) at 15, U.N. Doc. A/5217 (1962); E. Duruigbo, "Permanent Sovereignty and Peoples' Ownership of Natural Resources in International Law", Geo. Wash. Int'l L. Rev. 38 (2006), 33; G. Elian, *The principles of sovereignty over natural Resources* (The Hague: MartinusNijhoff, 1979); K.N. Gess, "Permanent Sovereignty Over Natural Resources", *International & Comparative Law Quarterly* 13 (1964), 398.

15 Penrose, *supra* note 8.

16 See the sources cited *supra* note 12.

succeeding it.[17] Where investors sought to vindicate their position legally, they had to rely largely on concession contracts,[18] and there existed some debate as to whether the norm of *pacta sunt servanda* would apply to such agreements.[19] In a limited number of cases, the home state of the investor had the ability to invoke a treaty of friendship commerce and navigation or another substantive norm in international law and present the claim of the investor before an international adjudicatory forum using the institution of diplomatic protection.[20] It is interesting to note that more than half of the investment related claims brought before the International Court of Justice through the diplomatic protection route pertain to the energy sector – *ELSI*,[21] *Barcelona Traction*,[22] *Anglo Iranian Oil Company*,[23] *Electricité de Beyrouth Company* (*France v. Lebanon*).[24]

In the second wave of conflict between investors in the energy sector and the host governments, the former sought to protest operating conditions prescribed by the host governments. In several cases, the host governments characterised the controversial measure as environmental regulation while the investors sought to assail these measures as violations of the investment treaties.[25] By this time, the investors had the benefit of access to binding State

17 J.J. Norton & M.H. Collins, "Reflections on the Iranian Hostage Settlement", A.B.A. J. 67 (1981), 428; B.M. Clagett, "The Expropriation Issue before the Iran-United States Claims Tribunal: Is Just Compensation Required by International Law or Not", Law &Pol'y Int'l Bus. 16 (1984), 813.

18 K.S. Carlston, "Concession Agreements and Nationalisation", AJIL 52(2) (1958), 260; E.K. Leach & L.T. Kissam, "Sovereign Expropriation of Property and Abrogation of Concession Contracts", *Fordham Law Review* 28 (1959–1960), 177.

19 J.W. Yackee, "Pacta Sunt Servanda and State Promises to Foreign Investors Before Bilateral Investment Treaties: Myth and Reality", *Fordham International Law Journal* 32(5) (2008), 1549; R.Y. Jennings, "State Contracts in International Law", Brit. Y. B. Int'l L. 37 (1961), 156; R. Geiger, "The Unilateral Change of Economic Development Agreements", *International & Comparative Law Quarterly* 23 (1974), 73.

20 E.g. see *Case Concerning Elettronica Sicula S.p.A.* (*ELSI*) (*United States v. Italy*), 1989 ICJ Rep 15, para 128; *Barcelona Traction Light and Power Company* (*Belgium v. Spain*), (*New Application: 1962, Second Phase*), 1970 ICJ Rep. 3.

21 Ibid.

22 Ibid.

23 *Anglo-Iranian Oil Co. Case* (*United Kingdom v. Iran*), 1952 ICJ Rep. 93.

24 *Electricité de Beyrouth Company* (*France v. Lebanon*), Order: Removal from the List, 1954 ICJ Rep. 107.

25 *Supra* note 12; Simon Baughen, "Expropriation And Environmental Regulation The Lessons Of NAFTA Chapter Eleven", *Journal of Environmental Law* 18(2) (2006), 207–228; OECD, "'Indirect Expropriation' and the 'Right to Regulate' in International Investment Law", Working Paper No. 2004/4 (2004).

arbitration and were often able to obtain awards holding controversial regulatory measures to be in violation of the IIA commitments.[26] These awards contributed largely to the perception that investment protection and environment protection are inherently contradictory goals and that one can be pursued only at the cost of the other. In the recent times, the arbitration between Chevron and Ecuador[27] has gained much public attention. While Ecuador states that its courts merely imposed environmental damages on Chevron's subsidiary, the company accuses Ecuador of serious violations of its investment commitments including judicial corruption. Several other examples exist[28] in the second wave of investor claims against host states in relation to measures purportedly adopted for environmental regulation. They span most of the common provisions of IIAs – protection against expropriation, fair and equitable treatment, non-discrimination, etc. More of these examples will be discussed in detail below. But there are two key differences between the first wave of disputes between investors and host states in the energy sector that need to be noted – (i) the disputes in the second wave tend to concern conditions of operation of the investors, rather than formal ownership of the business; (ii) dispute resolution clauses in IIAs have granted investors access to binding dispute resolution, eliminating the political risk in seeking diplomatic protection as well as uncertainties associated with concession contracts.

2.2 *Investment Protection and Environmental Protection – Points of Convergence and Those of Conflict*

As briefly mentioned above, a dichotomy that categorises protection of environment as a public goal and protection of investment as a private one is inadequate to cover the complex possibilities of convergence or divergence between these interests and the corresponding areas of law. The paragraphs below highlight certain possible points of convergence and divergence which will help us understand the relationship better.

Perhaps the most well known point of divergence between investment protection and environment protection is the imposition of stringent environmental regulations which add the cost of compliance to the total cost of operations of the investor. In one of the most well known examples, the tribunal in *Metalclad v. Mexico* held that the denial of a construction permit for a hazardous waste land fill by the municipal authorities breached com-

26 *Supra* note 12.

27 *Chevron Corporation and Texaco Petroleum Company v. The Republic of Ecuador*, PCA Case No. 2009–23.

28 *Supra* note 12.

mitments of Mexico under NAFTA.[29] Other tribunals have held in favour of investors challenging, among other things, import restrictions on waste paper for recycling,[30] export restrictions on PCB waste material[31] and denial of a construction permit in a designated green belt.[32] Investors have also challenged, though unsuccessfully, the prohibition of methyl tertiary-butyl ether (MTBE) to unleaded gasoline due to water contamination.[33]

Another point of divergence may be the non-discrimination provisions within IIAs.[34] These may come in the way of rewarding domestic or foreign investors for their environment friendly practices and punishing those not following such practices. In the investment context, there exists no cogent jurisprudence as to whether investments and investors not similarly placed in terms of environmental impact are to be accorded equal treatment.[35] One may seek to derive guidance from the WTO Appellate Body's ruling in *EC – Asbestos*[36] which held that the health and environmental effects of products could be relevant in determining whether they are "like products." However, that ruling was based on the fact that consumer tastes and preferences are relevant in determining "likeness of goods" in the trade context. There is no parallel jurisprudence in the investment context to indicate that perceptions of the consumers or the public are relevant in determining whether two investors are in "like circumstances." Also, that ruling was in the context of risks which were already well established. If a State seeks to take precautionary measures to protect the environment, differentiating between investors on the basis of anticipated environmental impact where the scientific evidence leaves a gap,

29 *Metalclad*, *supra* note 3.

30 *Saar Papier*, *supra* note 3.

31 *S.D. Myers*, *supra* note 3.

32 *MTD Equity*, *supra* note 3.

33 *Methanex Corp. v. United States of America*, Award, 3 August, 2005.

34 Most IIAs contain 'national treatment' clauses that prohibit treating the investors protected by the IIA less favourably than the domestic investors of the host state, and 'most favoured nation' clauses which prohibit treating the investors protected by the IIA less favourably than the investors of third countries.

35 IIAs typically make the non-discrimination obligation contingent on the entities in question being in 'like circumstances. Yet, there is no coherent jurisprudence on the definition of the expression.

36 *European Communities – Measures Affecting Asbestos and Asbestos-Containing Products*, WT/DS 135/AB/R, para. 122 – "In this case especially, we are also persuaded that evidence relating to consumers' tastes and habits would establish that the health risks associated with chrysotile asbestos fibres influence consumers' behaviour with respect to the different fibres at issue".

it is not clear whether such differentiation will be acceptable in the IIA framework. Non-discrimination may also obstruct policies oriented towards building of domestic capacity in clean technology.

A further point of divergence may be that the guarantees under IIAs treat intellectual property as investment and offer augmented protection to intellectual property,[37] at the risk of hampering the actual transfer of clean technology.

A point of convergence may be the promotion of foreign investment in clean technologies.[38] It may be that foreign investors attracted by the protection afforded by the investment treaty (among other things), seek to meet the domestic demand for clean technology. This may also result in the import of certain international best practices in environmental self regulation, at least when they do not add significant economic cost. At the same time, a point of divergence may be that certain investors seek out states with the least stringent environmental requirements, in doing so, encouraging under-regulation and triggering what economists term a "race to the bottom."

Another point where investors, as well as environmental activists converge is the call for strong, fair, transparent and predictable institutions with well defined mandates. While investment protection may require one course of action by these institutions and protection of environment may require a completely different course of action, the broad defining characteristics of the institutional framework sought by both the interests converge largely. For instance arbitrariness and selective enforcement of environmental standards or delayed adjudication of environment related objections to investment projects are likely to hurt both the investment and the environment.

There may also be instances where the guarantees under an IIA entitle an investor to certain minimum standards of environment protection. While claims of this nature are rare, they are not unprecedented. For instance, a Canadian investor operating an ecotourism facility brought an action against Barbados for alleged failure to enforce national and international norms

37 See, C.M. Correa, Bilateral investment agreements: Agents of new global standards for the protection of intellectual property rights? (2004), at http://www.grain.org/article/entries/125-bilateral-investment-agreements-agents-of-new-global-standards-for-the-protection-of-intellectual-property-rights (accessed 3 October 2013); R.C. Bernieri, "Intellectual Property Rights in Bilateral Investment Treaties and Access to Medicines: The Case of Latin America", *The Journal of World Intellectual Property* 9(5) (2006), 548–572; P. Ranjan& D. Raju, "Losing ground to Big Pharma, bit by BIT", The Hindu (6 September 2013), at http://www.thehindu.com/opinion/op-ed/losing-ground-to-big-pharma-bit-by-bit/article5097623.ece (accessed 24 October 2013).

38 Vinuales 2012, *supra* note 2.

relating to the conservation of wetlands.[39] Costa Rica faced two similar actions for alleged mistreatment of parcels of land designated for the protection of leatherback turtles.[40]

What are cited above are merely a few examples of convergence and divergence between the interest of protection of investment and that of protection of environment. These conflicts of interests may at times result in "normative conflicts,"[41] where international investment law requires an action or omission by the state, which would be violative of international environmental law or *vice versa*. On the other hand, there may also be situations of "convergence of norms" where the same action or omission is mandated by both international environmental law and international investment law as highlighted in examples cited above where investors are suing under international investment law claiming that they had a legitimate expectation of adherence to international environmental law.

Some authors have argued that a principle of mutual supportiveness is emerging in the international legal order and have suggested that such a principle could also govern the relationship between international environmental law and international investment law.[42] Some other voices have been also promoting the principle of mutual supportiveness in the field of investment and environment. The 2005 IISD Model International Agreement on Investment for Sustainable Development provides that "the Parties agree that the provisions of other international trade agreements to which they are a Party are consistent with the provisions of this Agreement. The Parties shall seek to interpret such agreements in a mutually supportive manner."[43] In the commentary attached to that provision it is said, "this Article sends an important legal signal that the Parties or a dispute settlement panel should interpret this agreement to be consistent with trade agreements where there are overlapping provisions, and should interpret those provisions in trade agreements to be

39 *Peter A. Allard v. The Government of Barbados* (Notice of Dispute) (8 September 2009), at http://graemehall.com/legal/papers/BIT-Complaint.pdf (accessed 3 October 2013).

40 See *Reinhard Hans Unglaube v. Republic of Costa Rica*, ICSID Case No. ARB/09/20; *Marion Unglaube v. Republic of Costa Rica*, ICSID Case No. ARB/08/1.

41 Vinuales (2009/10), *supra* note 2.

42 L. Boisson de Chazournes & M.M. Mbengue, "A principle as a footnote: Mutual supportiveness and its Relevance in an Era of Fragmentation", in H.P. Hestermeyer et al. (eds.), *Coexistence, Cooperation and Solidarity. Liber AmicorumRüdigerWolfrum*, vol. II, (Martinus Nijhoff Publishers: Leiden/Boston, 2012), 1615–1638.

43 H. Mann et al. (eds.), IISD Model International Agreement on Investment for Sustainable Development, Article 34, at 47 (2nd ed. 2005), available at http://www.iisd.org/pdf/2005/investment_model_int_handbook.pdf (accessed 3 October 2013).

consistent with this agreement. It seeks a mutually supportive approach in the event of potential conflicts."[44]

The purpose of this section is not to exhaustively list all the possible conflicts and convergences between international investment law and international environmental law. The purpose of this discussion was merely to highlight that the two "fragments" of international law can be in conflict or convergence depending on the situation, and it would be incorrect to engage in characterisations that place them in perpetual opposition to each other.

3 Environmental Regulation and Substantive Clauses in Investment Treaties

The paragraphs below undertake a closer examination of certain common provisions of investment treaties and anlayse how they may interact with the protection of environment. At the very outset, it needs to be mentioned that the actual interaction of a provision in an investment agreement with the objective of environmental protection will depend on the exact wording of the treaty language as well as the circumstances within which the interaction occurs. However, our attempt here is to identify, using past incidents and some hypothetical examples, the possible courses that such interactions may take.

3.1 *Specific References to Environment*

A recent OECD study surveys the use of specific language addressing environmental concerns in IIAs.[45] The study divides environment related language in IIAs into the following categories: (i) general references to environmental concerns in the preamble, (ii) reserving policy space for environmental regulation, (iii) reserving policy space with respect to certain treaty provisions, (iv) precluding non-discriminatory regulation as a basis for claims of indirect expropriation, (v) specific provisions for environmental matters in investor-state dispute settlement (vi) discouraging relaxation of environmental standards to attract investment and (vii) general promotion of progress in environmental protection and cooperation.[46]

44 Ibid.

45 K. Gordon & J. Pohl, "Environmental Concerns in International Investment Agreements: a Survey", OECD Working Papers on International Investment, No. 2011/1 (2011).

46 Ibid.

Preambular texts in IIAs, as such, are not enforceable. Thus, no matter how strongly they express the concern of the parties for the environment,[47] they do not create or mitigate rights or obligations for the state parties or the investors. Yet, as well accepted in customary international law, the preamble of a treaty is a relevant tool for interpretation of the text.[48] Thus where the accurate meaning of a substantive provision is in dispute, the preambular text may be helpful in lending support to the more environment friendly solution.[49] In this regard, one may draw an analogy with the reliance, by the WTO Appellate Body, on the preambular language relating to sustainable development, while interpreting the meaning and scope of the Article XX exception to GATT commitments.[50]

Reserving policy space for environmental regulation either in general[51] or with specific reference to certain provisions of the IIA[52] may serve to eliminate any legitimate expectations of the investor that the law would remain static. However, it is well accepted presently that in the absence of a stabilisation clause, there exists no legitimate expectations against a change in law.[53]

---

47 E.g. see, United States-Uruguay BIT (2005) and US-Rwanda BIT (2008): "Desiring to achieve these objectives in a manner consistent with the protection of health, safety, and the environment, and the promotion of internationally recognized labor rights"; Australia – Chile FTA (2008): "Implement this Agreement in a manner consistent with sustainable development and environmental protection and conservation".

48 Article 31, Vienna Convention on the Law of Treaties: "1. A treaty shall be interpreted in good faith in accordance with the ordinary meaning to be given to the terms of the treaty in their context and in the light of its object and purpose. 2. The context for the purpose of the interpretation of a treaty shall comprise, in addition to the text, including its preamble and annexes."

49 See M.M. Mbengue, "The Notion of Preamble", in R. Wolfrüm (ed.), *Max Planck Encyclopedia of Public International Law* (Oxford: Oxford University Press, 2012).

50 *United States – Import Prohibition of Certain Shrimp and Shrimp Products*, WT/DS58/AB/R, para. 129.

51 See Canada-Armenia BIT (1997); Canada-Barbados BIT (1996): "Nothing in this Agreement shall be construed to prevent a Contracting Party from adopting, maintaining or enforcing any measure otherwise consistent with this Agreement that it considers appropriate to ensure that investment activity in its territory is undertaken in a manner sensitive to environmental concerns".

52 Canada-Peru BIT (2006): "A measure that requires an investment to use a technology to meet generally applicable health, safety or environmental requirements shall not be construed to be inconsistent with paragraph 1(f). For greater certainty, Articles 3 and 4 apply to the measure."

53 *Saluka Investments BV v. Czech Republic*, UNCITRAL, Award, 17 March 2006, para 442; M. Hirsch, "Between Fair and Equitable Treatment and Stabilization Clause: Stable Legal Environment and Regulatory Change in International Investment Law", *Journal of World*

Even where policy space is reserved, a regulatory measure may still be challenged for the manner in which it is implemented or for the effect it has on foreign investors. Similarly, a preclusion of non discriminatory regulatory measures from the ban on expropriation still leaves the measure open to challenge under other IIA commitments, particularly the fair and equitable treatment standard. However, in certain cases, the language of reservation of regulatory power tends towards laying down exceptions similar to those contained in Article XX of the GATT.[54] In these circumstances, the environmental clauses are more likely provide a shield to the state in the event of allegations invoking any substantive provision of the IIA.

Specific provisions on environment in the context of investor State dispute settlement pertain to fact finding mechanisms in disputes with an environmental angle[55] and exclusion of certain environmental undertakings from mandatory arbitration.[56] For instance, the Energy Charter Treaty, despite providing for extensive environmental commitments under Article 19, excludes such commitments from the scope of disputes subject to binding arbitration under Article 27 and sets up an alternative mechanism whereby disputes relating to such commitments are "reviewed by the Charter Conference aiming at

Investment & Trade 12 (2011); F.M. Téllez, "Conditions and Criteria For The Protection of Legitimate Expectations Under International Investment Law", *ICSID Review – Foreign Investment Law Journal* 27(2) (2012), 432.

54 Argentina-New Zealand BIT (1999): "The provisions of this Agreement shall in no way limit the right of either Contracting Party to take any measures (including the destruction of plants and animals, confiscation of property or the imposition of restrictions on stock movement) necessary for the protection of natural and physical resources or human health, provided such measures are not applied in a manner which would constitute a means of arbitrary or unjustified discrimination"; Canada-Egypt BIT (1996); Canada-El Salvador BIT (1999): "Provided that such measures are not applied in a discriminatory or arbitrary manner or do not constitute a disguised restriction on foreign investment, nothing in this Agreement shall be construed to prevent a Contracting Party from adopting measures to maintain public order, or to protect public health and safety, including environmental measures necessary to protect human, animal or plant life".

55 Canada-Jordan BIT (2009); Canada-Peru BIT (2006): "Without prejudice to the appointment of other kinds of experts where authorized by the applicable arbitration rules, a tribunal, at the request of a disputing party or, unless the disputing parties disapprove, on its own initiative, may appoint one or more experts to report to it in writing on any factual issue concerning environmental, health, safety, or other scientific matters raised by a disputing party in a proceeding, subject to such terms and conditions as the disputing parties may agree."

56 Belgium/Luxembourg-Colombia BIT (2009) – excludes Article 7 which expresses environmental concerns from the scope of dispute settlement.

a solution."[57] These provisions are yet to be tested in dispute resolution, and it would be impossible to comment on the efficacy of such fact finding mechanisms at this stage.

While the discouragement of relaxing environmental regulation[58] or general agreement to cooperate in environmental protection may express the best intentions of the parties and their shared concerns, they are hardly enforceable guarantees. First, these provisions are often couched in language that calls for best efforts or creates obligations of conduct rather than those of result. Moreover, an undertaking to not relax environmental standards is unlikely to be invoked for enforcement by investors through the same channels as other provisions of the IIA. Thus, these provisions remain mere rhetoric except in cases like the ones discussed above,[59] where investors claim a legitimate expectation of high environmental protection. In the energy sector, one such possibility is the investors in the renewable or clean energy segment suing on expectations that conventional energy would be discouraged and stringently regulated.

Most recently, the 2012 versions of the Model BITs of United States and Canada have incorporated extensive references to environment. One of the preambular recitals in the US Model BIT states: "Desiring to achieve these objectives in a manner consistent with the protection of health, safety, and the environment, and the promotion of internationally recognized labor rights". Article 8 of the Model BIT that deals with 'performance requirements' has a built in exception on the line of Article XX of the GATT. This exception expressly states that the measures permitted under it include environmental measures. Article 12 of the Model BIT reiterates the commitment of the parties to the environment and states: "Nothing in this Treaty shall be construed to prevent a Party from adopting, maintaining, or enforcing any measure otherwise consistent with this Treaty that it considers appropriate to ensure that investment activity in its territory is undertaken in a manner sensitive to environmental concerns". This provision also provides for consultation between the parties with a view to arriving at a mutually satisfactory solution to issues arising under this article. However, environmental commitments under this model BIT are not capable of forming the foundation of a claim in investor –

57 Energy Charter Treaty, Article 19, Article 27(2).

58 Canada-Jordan BIT (2009), Canada-Latvia BIT (2009); Canada-Peru BIT (2006): "The parties recognize that it is inappropriate to encourage investment by relaxing domestic health, safety or environmental measures. Accordingly, a Party should not waive or otherwise derogate from, such measures as an encouragement for the establishment, acquisition, expansion or retention in its territory of an investment or an investor".

59 *Supra* notes 39 and 40.

State arbitration under Article 24 of the Model BIT. In the Canada Model BIT, Article 18 lays down general exceptions on the same lines as Article XX of GATT. In both these Model BITs, it appears that the environmental provisions are capable of serving as interpretative tools and defences, but not as foundations of claims, in binding dispute settlement.

3.2 *Non-discrimination*

The relationship between the non-discrimination obligation under IIAs and the protection of the environment has been discussed above briefly. In that discussion it has been pointed out how non-discrimination provisions may hinder differentiations between environmentally sound and unsound practices. It has also been noted how non-discrimination provisions may also tend to prevent the building of domestic capacity in clean technology. However, non-discrimination provisions may, on the other hand, serve to prohibit arbitrary promotion of unclean and conventional energy sources or processes to serve vested or parochial interests. If the markets are structured in such a way that the market itself rewards innovation in clean or unconventional energy, the non-discrimination provisions will help them access a level playing field. In such a market, the non-discrimination provisions will ensure that the governments do not create artificial barriers to clean technology or create advantages for conventional energy suppliers based on protectionist considerations. An example of this may be seen in the domestic content requirements that some countries impose in relation to their renewable energy programmes and how the non-discrimination provisions in WTO law have been employed by other countries to challenge these requirements.[60] While the non-discrimination provisions strike at the domestic content requirements, they leave the renewable energy programmes intact, in result ensuring that energy suppliers are free to base their procurement decisions on effectiveness and cost considerations rather than the geographical origins of the components. A domestic content requirement in such a programme skews the market for renewable energy and creates inefficiencies. While the non-discrimination provisions in IIAs are yet to be invoked in relation to such requirements, it is likely that they may be able to bring about the same effect, if invoked.

---

60 *Canada – Certain Measures Affecting The Renewable Energy Generation Sector*, WT/DS412/AB/R; *Canada – Measures Relating To The Feed-In Tariff Program*, WT/DS426/AB/R; *India – Certain Measures Relating to Solar Cells and Solar Modules*, WT/DS 456.

3.3 *Fair and Equitable Treatment*

The fair and equitable treatment standard (FET) is one of the most litigated provisions in IIAs, and it has been interpreted very broadly by investment arbitral tribunals. The exact meaning and scope of the commitment depends on the actual wording of the agreement at hand.[61] According to Muchlinski, "the concept of fair and equitable treatment is not precisely defined. It offers a general point of departure in formulating an argument that the foreign investor has not been well treated by reason of discriminatory or other unfair measures being taken against its interests. It is, therefore, a concept that depends on the interpretation of specific facts for its content. At most, it can be said that the concept connotes the principle of non-discrimination and proportionality in the treatment of foreign investors."[62] The fluidity of the FET standard has led some commentators to call it the "catch all" provision in IIAs.[63] The FET standard has, inter alia, been held to include the protection of legitimate expectations.[64]

The jurisprudence on FET clause has sought to strike a balance between the expectations of the investor and the regulatory freedom of the host state. For instance, the *Saluka* Tribunal held that the FET standard "requires a weighing of the Claimant's legitimate and reasonable expectations on the one hand and the Respondent's legitimate regulatory interests on the other."[65]

While the right to impose environmental regulation is undisputedly recognised, the FET standard may strike at the manner and the context in which the regulation is imposed. For instance, in *Metalclad*, the denial of building permit violated FET standard because the permit "was denied at a meeting of the Municipal Town Council of which Metalclad received no notice, to which it received no invitation, and at which it was given no opportunity to appear."[66]

61 OECD, Fair and Equitable Treatment Standard in International Investment Law, Working Papers on International Investment – Number 2004/3 (2004) online: http://www.oecd.org/daf/inv/internationalinvestmentagreements/33776498.pdf (October 3, 2013).

62 P.T. Muchlinski, *Multinational Enterprises and the Law* (Oxford: Oxford University Press, 2ndEd, 2007), 625.

63 N. Bernasconi, "Background paper on Vattenfall v. Germany arbitration", International Institute for Sustainable Development (2009), 5, at http://www.iisd.org/pdf/2009/background_vattenfall_vs_germany.pdf (accessed 3 October 2013).

64 *International Thunderbird Gaming Corporation v. The United Mexican States*, UNCITRAL, Separate Opinion of Professor Thomas Walde, para. 37 (December 2005); *Saluka, supra* note 53; Abhijit PG Pandya & Andy Moody, "Legitimate Expectations in Investment Treaty Arbitration: An Unclear Future", *Tilburg Law Review* 15(2010–11) 93, 105.

65 *Saluka, supra* note 53, Partial Award, para. 306.

66 *Metalclad, supra* note 3, para. 91.

In *Tecmed*, the lack of prior notice to the investor about the non-renewal of the landfill operating licence and the social and political pressure on the authority to relocate the landfill which provided the background to the decision, were crucial in sustaining a finding of violation of the FET standard.[67]

While the FET standard protects legitimate expectations, the jurisprudence is clear that absent a stablilisation clause, the investors cannot legitimately expect that the regulatory framework will remain static.[68] For instance, the *Saluka* Tribunal held that "in order to determine whether frustration of the foreign investor's expectations was justified and reasonable, the host State's legitimate right subsequently to regulate domestic matters in the public interest must be taken into consideration as well"[69] and highlighted the "high measure of deference that international law generally extends to the right of domestic authorities to regulate matters within their own borders."[70]

Thus, the FET standard does not necessarily frustrate non-discriminatory, reasonable, transparent regulatory measures for the protection of the environment even when the measure imposes additional costs on the investor. Also, as discussed above, in certain circumstances, investors may use the FET standard to force the host state to adhere to higher environmental standards. In the energy sector, this may be particularly important where a government attracts investments in clean or renewable energy sector by announcing its intention to provide incentives to the investors in this sector. If the government goes back on these representations to support conventional players instead, the foreign investors may be able to resort to the FET provision for a remedy.

3.4 *Expropriation*

Guarantee against expropriation was, in the initial phases of international investment law, the most important guarantee sought by investors. Today, the expropriation clauses have evolved to cover not merely the classic cases of direct expropriation, but also indirect expropriation irrespective of the form it takes.[71] Indirect expropriation has been defined broadly to include any

---

67 *Tecmed, supra* note 3.

68 *Saluka, supra* note 53.

69 *Saluka, supra* note 53, para. 305.

70 Ibid.

71 R.D. Sloane & W.M. Reisman, "Indirect Expropriation and its Valuation in the BIT Generation", *British Yearbook of International Law* 75 (2004), 115; C. Henckels, "Indirect Expropriation and the Right to Regulate: Revisiting Proportionality Analysis and the Standard of Review in Investor-State Arbitration", J Int Economic Law 15(1) (2012), 223; E.g., see US – Bangladesh BIT (1986), Art. III:1 – "No investment or any Part of an investment of a national or a company of either Party shall be expropriated or nationalized

governmental action that deprives the investor of the use or enjoyment of the assets or unduly delays such use or enjoyment.[72]

There has been a consensus among international lawyers that not all taking of property by the government amounts to expropriation. Brownlie reflects this position in stating, "state measures, prima facie a lawful exercise of powers of governments, may affect foreign interests considerably without amounting to expropriation. Thus, foreign assets and their use may be subjected to taxation, trade restrictions involving licenses and quotas, or measures of devaluation. While special facts may alter cases, in principle such measures are not unlawful and do not constitute expropriation."[73] Sornarajah categorises non-discriminatory measures for the protection of environment as "non-compensable taking" along with measures relating to anti-trust, consumer protection, securities, and land planning.[74]

In practice, what separates expropriation from regulation appears to be: "i) the degree of interference with the property right, ii) the character of governmental measures, i.e. the purpose and the context of the governmental measure, and iii) the interference of the measure with reasonable and investment-backed expectations."[75] In *Pope & Talbot*, the NAFTA Tribunal observed, "mere interference is not expropriation; rather, a significant degree of deprivation of fundamental rights of ownership is required."[76] While some actions falling within the "police powers" of the State may not be characterised as expropriation at all, "public purpose" may act as the first prong of justification of certain measures even if they amount to expropriation.

Termination of concessions or other measures calling for termination of the whole or a part of the operations of the investors may be argued to be expropriation. It would be for the investor to demonstrate that the measure has had the effect of interfering with the ownership, control or enjoyment of the

by the other Party or subjected to any other measure or series of measures, direct or indirect tantamount to expropriation (including the levying of taxation, the compulsory sale of all or part of an investment, or the impairment or deprivation of its management, control or economic value), all such actions hereinafter referred to as 'expropriation', unless the expropriation [...]".

72 Ibid.

73 I. Brownlie, *Principles of Public International Law* (Oxford: Oxford University Press, 6thEd, 2003), 509.

74 M. Sornarajah, *The International Law on Foreign Investment* (Cambridge: Cambridge University Press, 1994), 283.

75 OECD (2004, Expropriation) *supra* note 25.

76 *Pope & Talbot Inc. v. The Government of Canada*, UNCITRAL, Interim Award, para. 99.

investment. The state would be able to avoid liability by – (i) demonstrating that there is no deprivation of property, or (ii) the deprivation is in exercise of the police powers, or (iii) the deprivation is a permissible expropriation complying with the requirements of the IIA or (iv) that the conduct is exempted from the applicability of the IIA commitments by operation of the exceptions specifically provided for in the IIA.

There may also be a situation, though it is yet to arise, where an investor whose operations depends on the existence of a minimum environmental standard may, alleges an indirect expropriation against the government for not maintaining the said standard and thereby causing economic prejudice to the investor.

4 Environment Protection and Procedural Aspects of Investment Arbitration

The interaction between substantive norms of international investment lawand the interest of protection of environment has been discussed above. The paragraphs below discuss the procedural aspects of dispute resolution in international investment law and examine whether they are suited to accommodate environmental concerns.

4.1 *Government as the Perpetual Respondent?*

Though there is some discussion on allowing claims and counterclaims by the host state before investment arbitration tribunals,[77] the present state of affairs is one where the state is the perpetual respondent in investment arbitration. The fact that it is an "investment dispute" which is capable of investment arbitration and "investment dispute" is typically defined to mean dispute about alleged non-conformity with obligations assumed under the IIA, ensures that

77 *SpyridonRoussalis v. Romania*, ICSID Case No. ARB/06/1, Award, 7 December 2011; *Goetz v. Burundi*, ICSID Case No. ARB/01/2, Award, 21 June 2012; G. Laborde, "The Case for Host State Claims in Investment Arbitration", *Journal of International Dispute Settlement* 1(1) (2010), 97–122; Y. Kryvoi, "Counterclaims in Investor-State Arbitration", LSE Law, Society and Economy Working Papers 8/2011, at http://www.lse.ac.uk/collections/law/wps/WPS2011-08_Kryvoi.pdf (accessed 3 October 2013); J.E. Kalicki, "Counterclaims by States in Investment Arbitration", Investment Treaty News (14 January 2013), at http://www.iisd.org/itn/2013/01/14/counterclaims-by-states-in-investment-arbitration-2/ (accessed 3 October 2013).

the investor, who has not undertaken commitments under the IIA, cannot be put in the position of a respondent in investment arbitration.

The confinement of the investor's role to that of a claimant and the state's role to that of a claimant makes it nearly impossible to address environmental violations by the investor, except as a justification for a government action challenged by the investor, or in some exceptional situations, as counterclaims with a view to offset any compensation payable to the investor. This heavily narrows down the scope of environment related claims that can be placed before the arbitral tribunal.

4.2 *Jurisdictional Limitations*

International environmental law has developed over the last few decades through the emergence of custom and treaties as well as soft law standards. Yet, these sources of law cannot sustain a claim before an investment arbitral tribunal. Investment tribunals have limited jurisdiction to deal with investment disputes alone. In this regard, the tribunal in *Bernhard Von Pezold and Others v. Republic of Zimbabwe*[78] clarified that BITs do "not incorporate the universe of international law into the BITs or into disputes arising under the BITs." Unless a claim is based on a provision of the relevant IIA, it will not fall within the jurisdiction of the tribunal no matter how well founded in international environmental law the claim may be and however intrinsically linked the fact situation of the environmental dispute may be to the fact situation of the investment dispute. Thus investment tribunals are able to adjudicate environmental claims only so far as they form part of an investment claim or of the defence to one.[79]

---

78 *Bernhard Von Pezold and Others v. Republic of Zimbabwe*, ICSID Case No. ARB/10/15, Procedural Order No. 2, s.d., para. 57.

79 See *Antoine Biloune v. Ghana Investment Centre*, UNCITRAL, Award on Jurisdiction and Liability, 27 October 1989, paras. 202–203: "This Tribunal's competence is limited to commercial disputes arising under a contract entered into in the context of Ghana's Investment Code. As noted, the Government agreed to arbitrate only disputes 'in respect of' the foreign investment. Thus, other matters – however compelling the claim or wrongful the alleged act – are outside this Tribunal's jurisdiction. Under the facts of this case it must be concluded that, while the acts alleged to violate the international human rights of Mr Biloune may be relevant in considering the investment dispute under arbitration, this Tribunal lacks jurisdiction to address, as an independent cause of action, a claim of violation of human rights".

4.3 *Third Party Participation*

At present, third party participation before an investment arbitral tribunal remains heavily constrained. While some recent tribunals have invoked the procedural rules to hold that they had the authority to allow or disallow amicus submissions,[80] a coherent jurisprudence is yet to evolve in this matter. In several instances, investment arbitration occurs in absolute confidentiality, with interested third parties not even being informed about the existence of the arbitration, let alone being permitted to participate. A state may be dissuaded for several reasons from pursuing an environmental claim to its fullest. Nongovernmental organisations and representatives of affected communities may be in a better position to advocate environmental causes. Yet, the present state of investment arbitration raises hurdles for the meaningful participation by these stakeholders, significantly curtailing the ability of the system to address environmental concerns.

5 Conclusions

From our discussion above, it appears that environmental protection and the protection of foreign investment are not interests necessarily opposed to each other. These interests, as well as, the normative frameworks governing them are capable of both convergence and divergence depending on a number of variables.

Our discussion of the substantive provisions of the investment treaties establishes that these provisions are capable of both fostering and hampering

80 *Commerce Group Corp. and San Sebastian Gold Mines, Inc. v. Republic of El Salvador*, ICSID Case No. ARB/09/17; *Pac Rim Cayman LLC v. Republic of El Salvador*, ICSID Case No. ARB/09/12; *Methanex, supra* note 33, Decision of the Tribunal on Petitions from Third Persons to Intervene as Amici Curiae, 15 January 2001; *United States Parcel Service of America v. Canada*, Decision of the Tribunal on Petitions for Intervention and Participation as Amici Curiae, 17 October 2001; Contra, see: *Aguas dal Tunari SA v. The Republic of Bolivia*, ICSID Case No. ARB/03/02, Decision on Respondent's Objections to Jurisdiction, 21 October 2005; See also, E. Levine, "Amicus Curiae in International Investment Arbitration: The Implications of an Increase in Third-Party Participation", *Berkeley Journal of International Law* 29(1) (2011), 200; Eric De Brabandere, "NGOs and the "Public Interest": The Legality and Rationale of Amicus Curiae Interventions in International Economic and Investment Disputes", *Chicago Journal of International Law* 12 (2011), 85–113 and K.F. Gómez, "Rethinking the Role of Amicus Curiae in International Investment Arbitration: How to Draw the Line Favorably for the Public Interest", *Fordham International Law Journal* 35 (2012), 510.

the interest of protection of environment, depending on how they are invoked. In the energy sector, it has been highlighted that these provisions are capable of being invoked by investors pursuing clean and renewable energy with a view to forcing governments to remove disincentives to such energy and to call for higher environmental standards or to demand uniform and augmented enforcement of environmental norms.

Yet, the procedural framework established by IIAs remains inadequate for addressing environmental claims. As long as substantive obligations under the IIAs fall only on states, it will be difficult to address any environmental harm caused by the investors before such tribunals. Also, restricting the jurisdiction of the tribunals to claims based on IIA provisions alone, as well as obstacles to third party participation hampers the ability of the system to address protection of environment except where environmental guarantees of a state are incorporated within an investment claim by an investor or to the limited extent that such concerns feature as counterclaims (where permissible) or defences. Efforts need to be made in the direction of reworking the procedural aspects of investment arbitration with a view to accommodate a broader range of concerns, including the environment.

CHAPTER 7

Foreign Investment in the Energy Sector and Indigenous Peoples' Rights

Federico Lenzerini

1 Introduction

In explaining the background of his most-renowned International Law Commission's *Report of Fragmentation of International Law*, Martti Koskenniemi notes that

> [t]he fragmentation of the international social world has attained legal significance especially as it has been accompanied by the emergence of specialized and (relatively) autonomous rules or rule-complexes, legal institutions and spheres of legal practice. What once appeared to be governed by 'general international law' has become the field of operation for such specialist systems as 'trade law', 'human rights law', 'environmental law', 'law of the sea', 'European law' and even such exotic and highly specialized knowledge as 'investment law' or 'international refugee law' etc. – each possessing their own principles and institutions. The problem, as lawyers have seen it, is that such specialized law-making and institution-building tends to take place with relative ignorance of legislative and institutional activities in the adjoining fields and of the general principles and practices of international law. The result is conflicts between rules or rule-systems, deviating institutional practices and, possibly, the loss of an overall perspective on the law.[1]

* The author gratefully acknowledges Tarcisio Gazzini for the very useful comments provided with respect to an earlier draft of the present chapter.

1 See International Law Commission, "Fragmentation of International Law: Difficulties Arising from the Diversification and Expansion of International Law", Report of the Study Group of the International Law Commission, finalized by Martti Koskenniemi, U.N. Doc. A/CN.4/L.682 of 13 April 2006, para. 8 (internal footnotes omitted).

 | DOI 10.1163/9789004244719_009

In the context of the "exotic and highly specialized" framework of international investment law, such a "relative ignorance of legislative and institutional activities in the adjoining fields and of the general principles and practices of international law" is usually confined in the phases of setting-up and implementation of the relevant rules. With respect to most cases of foreign investments, the suspicion exists that foreign investors and national authorities – sharing an interest in promoting and implementing the investment – rather than being ignorant of applicable rules relating to "the adjoining fields and . . . the general principles" of international law, tend to deliberately close their eyes to such rules, being aware that complying with them would make the execution of the investment more complicate or less rewarding, if not unfeasible at all. On the contrary, at the adjudication level arbitral tribunals have generally demonstrated to be relatively sensible to non-investment rules when judging whether certain limitations to foreign investments were legitimate by reason of the need to preserve values other than investment-related interests,[2] including when these interests relate to indigenous peoples' rights.[3] In practical terms, however, the main problem in this respect rests on the fact that only a minority of cases of foreign investments interfering with indigenous peoples' rights are able to reach the adjudicatory phase – at least at the level of international arbitration in the field of investment law – representing the tip of the iceberg in comparison with the totality of foreign investments affecting indigenous peoples. On the other hand, in this context the phenomenon of fragmentation of international law shows a bright side in offering the people and communities affected by foreign investments more avenues to claim their rights before international judicial or quasi-judicial bodies, including regional human rights monitoring bodies. This notwithstanding, the number of cases reaching the adjudication process at the international level still remains quite limited. The practice of these bodies has led to increasing the awareness that in the context of the execution of investment projects certain "external" values must be taken into maximum consideration, to the extent of limiting or even – in extreme cases – inhibiting the realization of the investment. These values definitely include the rights of indigenous peoples.

2 Generally on this issue see Stephan W. Schill (ed.), *International Investment Law and Comparative Public Law* (Oxford: Oxford University Press, 2010).

3 See *infra*, Section 4.

2 Indigenous Peoples' Rights *vis-à-vis* the Economic Exploitation of Their Ancestral Lands

In relation to the problem of the interference between foreign investment and the rights of indigenous peoples, two specific categories of rights must be particularly taken into account, i.e. cultural rights and land rights. In reality, in light of indigenous peoples' cosmology and holistic conception of life, it would be improper to consider these categories of rights as separate with each other. All indigenous peoples' basic rights are strictly interconnected and interdependent with each other. The basis of *all* indigenous peoples' rights is indeed their cultural specificity, which makes their distinctive cultural identity worth preserving in order to prevent their cultural assimilation within the dominant societies. The relationship between indigenous peoples and their ancestral lands is based on an absolutely intangible and spiritually-based connection, on which the cultural identity of the communities concerned is grounded. Therefore, safeguarding indigenous peoples' land rights is not tantamount to protecting property rights as conceived in the Western world, but is rather functional – and *indispensable* – to ensure preservation of the cultural idiosyncrasy of those peoples. In sum, safeguarding indigenous peoples' rights concerning their traditional lands means safeguarding indigenous peoples themselves.

In the last few decades international law has finally become aware of the reality just described. In this sense, the ILO *Convention No. 169 Concerning Indigenous and Tribal Peoples in Independent Countries*, adopted in 1989,[4] recognizes at Article 7 the right of the said peoples "to decide their own priorities for the process of development as it affects their lives, beliefs, institutions and spiritual well-being and the lands they occupy or otherwise use;" the same article also contemplates the obligation of States parties to "take measures, in co-operation with the peoples concerned, to protect and preserve the environment of the territories they inhabit." It is evident that the article in point places precise limits to the possibility of developing investment projects in indigenous lands without the consent of the communities concerned. This is confirmed by Article 14, which recognizes the right of ownership and possession of indigenous and tribal peoples over the lands they traditionally occupy, from which, pursuant to Article 16, they must not be removed except

4 The full text of the Convention is at http://www.ilo.org/dyn/normlex/en/f?p=1000:12100:0::NO::P12100_ILO_CODE:C169 (accessed 14 June 2013); at the moment of this writing, 22 countries have ratified the Convention (see http://www.ilo.org/dyn/normlex/en/f?p=1000:11300:0::NO:11300:P11300_INSTRUMENT_ID:312314, ibid.).

as a matter of a necessary and exceptional measure, only with their free and informed consent or following appropriate procedures established by national laws and regulations, as well as with appropriate compensation. According to Article 15, the said right of ownership and possession includes the right to the natural resources pertaining to those lands as well as the right of the peoples concerned "to participate in the use, management and conservation of these resources." Consistently, Article 15 para. 2 establishes that

> [i]n cases in which the State retains the ownership of mineral or sub-surface resources or rights to other resources pertaining to lands, governments shall establish or maintain procedures through which they shall consult these peoples, with a view to ascertaining whether and to what degree their interests would be prejudiced, before undertaking or permitting any programmes for the exploration or exploitation of such resources pertaining to their lands. The peoples concerned shall wherever possible participate in the benefits of such activities, and shall receive fair compensation for any damages which they may sustain as a result of such activities.

This provision pairs with Article 7 in strictly limiting the possibility of carrying out investment projects in indigenous lands, except when the consent of the peoples concerned is obtained.

However, more than ILO Convention No. 169, it is the *United Nations Declarations on the Rights of Indigenous Peoples* (UNDRIP) – adopted in 2007 and supported by virtually every country in the world[5] – which may be considered as the completion of the long process which has led indigenous peoples to retrieve their inherent dignity, even though this achievement has claimed a high price of blood and tears.[6] The UNDRIP reflects the position and expectations of indigenous peoples – who, through their representatives, have played a key role in the 22-year-long negotiations leading to the adoption of the Declaration. It may be considered as "a milestone in the re-empowerment of

5 The UNDRIP was adopted on 13 September 2007 by the UN General Assembly with 143 States voting in favour, four countries – Australia, Canada, New Zealand and the United States – voting against and eleven abstaining. However, between 2009 and 2010 *all* the four countries originally voting against – in addition to two abstaining States (Colombia and Samoa) – officially endorsed the Declaration.

6 See Federico Lenzerini, "The Trail of Broken Dreams: The Status of Indigenous Peoples in International Law", in Federico Lenzerini (ed.), *Reparations for Indigenous Peoples: International and Comparative Perspectives* (Oxford: Oxford University Press, 2008), 73.

the world's aboriginal groups, and ... in important parts, it reaffirms customary international law in the field."[7]

There are several provisions in the UNDRIP proclaiming rights of indigenous peoples which may be specifically affected in the case of economic exploitation of their traditional lands, including in the event of implementation of foreign investments, particularly in the energy sector. However, before examining these provisions in detail, it is important to reiterate that their breach is suitable of producing negative effects which will not result into a violation of the specific right protected by the provision concerned *only*, but will lead, *a fortiori*, to disturbing the enjoyment of *all* the main rights which are essential for preserving the cultural identity of indigenous peoples, exactly by reason of the mutual interdependence existing among those rights. So, for example, in the event that the right of indigenous peoples to "maintain and strengthen their distinctive spiritual relationship with their traditionally owned or otherwise occupied and used lands"[8] is precluded, this will also negatively impact the right to self-determination recognized in favour of the peoples concerned – "[b]y virtue of [which] they freely determine their political status and freely pursue their economic, social and cultural development."[9] Indeed, no right to self-determination may be properly exercised without a land where it may be enjoyed.

Among the most significant provisions which are relevant to the purposes of the present chapter, Articles 10, 11, 12, 19, 24, 26 and 32 UNDRIP emerge.

Article 10 establishes that indigenous peoples "shall not be forcibly removed from their lands or territories," relocation being possible only with "the free, prior and informed consent of the indigenous peoples concerned and after

---

7 See S. James Anaya and Siegfried Wiessner, "The UN Declaration on the Rights of Indigenous Peoples: Towards Re-empowerment", *JURIST Forum*, 3 October 2007, available at http://jurist.law.pitt.edu/forumy/2007/10/un-declaration-on-rights-ofindigenous.php (accessed 24 September 2012). See also Siegfried Wiessner, "Indigenous Sovereignty: A Reassessment in Light of the UN Declaration on the Rights of Indigenous Peoples", *Vanderbilt Journal of Transnational Law* 41 (2008), 1141, 1152 ff.; Federico Lenzerini, "The United Nations Declaration on the Rights of Indigenous Peoples: Amending Five Centuries of Wrongs", in *Proceedings of the 4th International Traditional Knowledge Conference* 2010, Ngâ Pae o te Mâramatanga (Auckland: New Zealand's Mâori Centre of Research Excellence, 2010), 19, 20 ff.; Federico Lenzerini, "Rights of Indigenous Peoples under Customary International Law", in International Law Association, Committee on the Rights of Indigenous Peoples, Conference Report The Hague, 2010, at http://www.ila-hq.org/en/committees/index.cfm/cid/1024 (accessed 21 March 2013), 43 ff.

8 See Article 25 UNDRIP.

9 See Article 3 UNDRIP.

agreement on just and fair compensation and, where possible, with the option of return." Article 10 is related to Article 26, which proclaims the right of indigenous peoples to "the lands, territories and resources which they have traditionally owned, occupied or otherwise used or acquired;" this prerogative translates into the rights "to own, use, develop and control" such lands. These provisions imply, *inter alia*, that the legitimacy of any foreign investment, which would produce the effect of relocating an indigenous community from its traditional lands, is conditioned to the free, prior and informed consent of such a community. Although it is usually unlikely that a foreign investment may be as invasive to produce such an effect, it cannot be excluded a priori.

In the real world, foreign investments are much more likely to affect the right protected by Article 11 UNDRIP, that is the right of indigenous peoples "to practise and revitalize their cultural traditions and customs, which includes the right to maintain, protect and develop the past, present and future manifestations of their cultures, such as archaeological and historical sites, artefacts, designs, ceremonies, technologies and visual and performing arts and literature." This provision is of relevance especially for its reference to "archaeological and historical sites." Similarly, Article 12 UNDRIP safeguards, *inter alia*, the right of indigenous peoples "to maintain, protect, and have access in privacy to their religious and cultural sites." Sometimes it may be extremely complicated to execute an investment and preserve the integrity of an archaeological site of indigenous peoples at the same time, on account of the difficulty to exactly demarcate the area of a "cultural site" of indigenous peoples, the significance of which, for the communities concerned may not be represented by tangible entities but rather by intangible elements, which may be hard to locate. As it will be shown in the next Section, in most cases in which a foreign investment has been considered as threatening values of pertinence to the indigenous peoples, the endangered elements were religious, archaeological or cultural sites located in indigenous lands. To a similar extent, it may happen that the execution of a foreign investment threatens the "medicinal plants, animals and minerals" existing in indigenous peoples' traditional lands, which these peoples have the right to conserve pursuant to Article 24 UNDRIP.

Under a "procedural" perspective, Articles 19 and 32(2) are of special significance for the purposes of the present writing. These two provisions are similar to each other, with the only difference that, while the former is of general application, the latter is specifically devoted to projects affecting indigenous "lands, territories or other resources." The principle expressed by the two provisions in point is that, according to Article 19, States must "consult and cooperate in good faith with the indigenous peoples concerned through their own representative institutions in order to obtain their free, prior and informed consent before adopting and implementing legislative or administrative measures that may affect them." Article 32(2), as previously stressed, applies this principle to "any project affecting [indigenous peoples'] lands or territories and other resources, particularly in connection with the development, utilization or exploitation of mineral, water or other resources." This provision is a direct consequence of the principle expressed in Article 32 para. 1, according to which indigenous peoples "have the right to determine and develop priorities and strategies for the development or use of their lands or territories and other resources." With respect to the formulation of these provisions, it may be easily noted that they are significantly different from other provisions included in the UNDRIP relating to the free, prior and informed consent of indigenous peoples as a condition for performing a given activity in their lands. For example, as previously stressed, Article 10 affirms that "[n]o relocation [of indigenous peoples from their lands or territories] *shall take place* without [their] free, prior and informed consent."[10] Similarly, Article 29(2) establishes that '"States *shall take* effective measures *to ensure* that *no* storage or disposal of hazardous materials *shall take place* in the lands or territories of indigenous peoples *without* their free, prior and informed consent."[11] Differently, Articles 19 and 32(2) proclaim the duty of States to "*consult and cooperate in good faith*' with... indigenous peoples... *in order to obtain* their free, prior and informed consent."[12] It is not by chance that the UNDRIP uses these different formulations. Indeed, while according to provisions like Article 10 and Article 29(2) indigenous peoples have a *full right to veto* to prevent the actions prohibited by these provisions, in accordance with Articles 19 and 32(2), in principle such a right cannot be said of existing. This is confirmed by relevant international and State practice,[13] the analysis of which, however, shows that a different conclusion must be drawn with respect to projects of exploitation (including those relating to foreign investments, particularly in the energy sector) carried out on indigenous lands which may significantly impair the basic rights and ways of life of the communities concerned. With respect to these particular projects,

10 Emphasis added.

11 Emphasis added.

12 Emphasis added.

13 See, ultimately, International Law Association's Resolution No. 5/2012, "Rights of Indigenous Peoples", adopted in Sofia on 30 August 2012, available at http://www.ila-hq.org/en/committees/index.cfm/cid/1024 (accessed 21 March 2013), which, at para. 5, affirms that indigenous peoples have 'the right to be consulted with respect to any project that may affect them and the related right that projects significantly impacting their rights and ways of life are not carried out without their prior, free and informed consent'.

relevant practice seems to be oriented toward recognizing the existence of a duty by States to effectively obtain the consent of the indigenous peoples concerned before executing the said projects on their ancestral lands.[14]

3 Resolution of Disputes Concerning Foreign Investment in Indigenous Peoples' Lands

The high majority of cases of foreign investments considered as affecting indigenous peoples' ancestral lands are related to the energy sector, as they concern projects of exploitation (usually of mineral resources) having the final purpose of producing energy. Usually, as emphasized in the previous Section, the clash resulting from the interference between the two values at stake takes the form of a conflict between an economic interest (that of the investor and, in many cases, of the territorial State) and a *cultural* concern (that of the indigenous communities concerned),[15] the relationship of indigenous peoples with their traditional lands, territories and resources being of marked cultural nature.

In recent times, a few disputes of interest for the present chapter have reached the stage of arbitration in the context of international investment law. In reality, as previously stressed,[16] only a limited number of controversies arising from investment projects to be carried out on indigenous peoples' traditional lands reach the international adjudication phase. Some of them are in fact settled at the national level, others are resolved through "extrajudiciary settlements", while others are unfortunately covered up by extremely powerful multinational enterprises which, with the complicity of national authorities, prevent the communities concerned from accessing any kind of justice to protect their fundamental rights and interests.[17] Although, thanks to NGOs and activists, general knowledge of these cases is progressively increasing – and the

---

14 See Federico Lenzerini, "Self-Determination, Autonomy or Self-Government", in International Law Association, Committee on the Rights of Indigenous Peoples, Sofia Conference 2012 Report (2012), at http://www.ila-hq.org/en/committees/index.cfm/cid/1024 (accessed 21 March 2013), 3 ff.

15 For a very comprehensive assessment on this issue see Valentina Vadi, "When Cultures Collide: Foreign Direct Investment, Natural Resources, and Indigenous Heritage in International Investment Law", *Columbia Human Rights Law Review* 42 (2011), 797.

16 See previous Section.

17 For other cases of investments in indigenous peoples' lands, in addition to those described in the text, see George K. Foster, "Foreign Investment and Indigenous Peoples: Options for Promoting Equilibrium between Economic Development and Indigenous Rights", *Michigan Journal of International Law* 33 (2012), 627, 637 ff.

chances available to indigenous peoples to obtain justice may consequently proliferate – in many cases economic interests and the willingness of territorial States to respect the agreements concluded with foreign investors lead national authorities to take all necessary measures to frustrate the attempts of the communities concerned to stop the execution of investments. So, for example, since 2009, in Guatemala, the Spanish company Hidralia Energía, through Hydro Santa Cruz, is working on the execution of an investment – approved by the government – consisting in the construction of several dams on the Q'am B'alam river, surrounding the town of Santa Cruz Barillas, which is considered sacred and used for ceremonial and agricultural purposes by the Q'anjob'al indigenous community. On 1 May 2012 the security guards of the company killed a community leader; this event led to riots, following which President Molina declared martial law applicable in the area of the investment. As a result, several community leaders protesting against the investment were arbitrarily detained. Although, following huge international pressure, President Molina was forced to revoke martial law, execution of the investment is still underway.[18]

Another very controversial case is that of the Belo Monte Dam, situated on the Xingu River, in the Amazon Region, although it is not a case of a foreign investment, being executed by a consortium controlled by a State-owned power company. The dam is set to flood about 150 square miles of rainforest, depriving 20,000 Amazon indigenous people of their home, their lands and their means of survival. For many of these people, the high risk of losing their life also exists, on account of potentially lethal diseases – including malaria – which are predicted to flourish in the area as a result of the flooding.[19] On 14 August 2012 the Brazilian Federal Court halted the execution of the project for lack of consultation with the indigenous communities concerned,[20] but the Supreme Federal Court overturned this decision on 28 August, with a ruling that could be revised after a "more detailed analysis of the merit of

18 See "Guatemala: We Are All Barillas-Stop a Dam on Our Sacred River!", Cultural Survival, August 2012, available at http://www.culturalsurvival.org/take-action/barillas (accessed 24 September 2012).

19 See "Occupy the Dam: Brazil's Indigenous Uprising", peakwater.org, 30 July 2012, available at http://peakwater.org/2012/07/occupy-the-dam-brazils-indigenous-uprising/ (accessed 24 September 2012).

20 See Jonathan Watts, "Belo Monte dam construction halted by Brazilian court", *The Guardian*, 16 August 2012, at http://www.guardian.co.uk/world/2012/aug/16/belo-monte-dam-construction-suspended (accessed 24 September 2012).

the case" by the Court.[21] The battle before Brazilian courts continued in 2013 with similar outcomes.

A different outcome characterized, in August 2010, the planned investment of a British company, Vedanta Resources – which involved the digging of a bauxite mine in the sacred hills of the Dongria Kondh community, on the Niyamgiri Hills in the Eastern state of Orissa. The execution of the investment was stopped by the Indian Minister of the Environment for the reason that, *inter alia*, its implementation would have breached the rights of indigenous peoples in the area.[22]

The examples just mentioned clearly show that, in most cases, the prospects that indigenous peoples' rights are adequately safeguarded against the potential detrimental effects determined by an investment actually depend on the approach adopted by the territorial State. Sometimes, as it happens with respect to the examples of Guatemala and Brazil summarily described above, huge economic interests persuade States simply not to weigh their international obligations towards indigenous peoples. In other cases, on the contrary, States take these obligations very seriously. In addition to the example of India just quoted, one may mention the renowned case of *Glamis Gold v. United States*,[23] an arbitration under the UNCITRAL Arbitration Rules filed by a Canadian mining corporation complaining that certain US federal actions and other measures taken by the State of California relating to open-pit mining operations resulted in the expropriation of its investment in the California Desert Conservation Area and in the infringement of the rules on fair and equitable treatment pursuant to Articles 1105 and 1110 of the North American Free Trade Agreement (NAFTA). The integrity of Native sacred sites and the right of the Quechan Indian Nation to practice their religion were among the values the

---

21 See Stan Lehman, "Court orders resumption of work on Brazilian dam", *The Big Story*, 28 August 2012, at http://bigstory.ap.org/article/court-orders-resumption-work-brazilian-dam (accessed 21 March 2013).

22 See Federico Lenzerini, "Land Rights", in International Law Association, Committee on the Rights of Indigenous Peoples, Sofia Conference 2012 Report (2012), *supra* note 14, 24. As noted by the UK National Contact Point for the OECD Guidelines for Multinational Enterprises in September 2009, the company had in particular "failed to put in place an adequate and timely consultation mechanism to engage fully the Dongria Kondh about the potential environmental and health and safety impact of the construction of the mine on them"; see "Final Statement by the UK National Contact Point for the OECD Guidelines for Multinational Enterprises. Complaint from Survival International against Vedanta Resources plc", 25 September 2009, at http://www.oecd.org/daf/inv/mne/43884129.pdf (accessed 14 June 2013), 65.

23 *Glamis Gold, Ltd. v. United States of America*, UNCITRAL, Award, 8 June 2009.

said US and California measures were aimed to safeguard. The Arbitral Tribunal dismissed the investor's claim, as it found that the said measures did not "cause a sufficient economic impact" on the investment;[24] additionally, the claimant had failed to establish that the measures adopted at federal and state level "fall below the customary international law minimum standard" of fair and equitable treatment.[25] However, although no direct assessment was developed by the Tribunal on whether the need to safeguard indigenous peoples' rights may in itself justify restrictions to foreign investments, it implicitly recognized the value of indigenous sacred sites. In particular, the Tribunal found the position of the United States correct in justifying its measures with the need to prevent "a significant, unavoidable adverse impact to cultural resources and Native American sacred sites."[26] It also agreed with the assertion of the respondent government that investor's rights must be balanced with "the harms caused to Native American sacred sites by open-pit mining"[27] and recognized that the measures affecting the investment were justified by the fact that the project "presented a potential danger to Native American sacred sites."[28]

A similar example is represented by the recent case of *Gallo v. Canada*,[29] concerning an investment by a US National in the Canadian State of Ontario – the construction of a rubbish dump on the site of a former open-pit mine. The investment was stopped by new legislation enacted by the Ontario government in 2004, which also denied the investor the possibility to acquire title to borderlands adjacent to the original site of the investment.[30] The investor filed an application for arbitration under Chapter 11 NAFTA and the UNCITRAL Arbitration Rules, requesting compensation for the alleged expropriation of his investment as well as for the violation of the standards of fair and equitable treatment. Among the arguments raised in its Counter-memorial, Canada asserted that acquisition of certain areas by the investors was denied in order

24 Ibid., para. 536.
25 Ibid., para. 824.
26 Ibid., para. 760 f.
27 Ibid., para. 804.
28 Ibid., para. 814.
29 *Vito G. Gallo v. Government of Canada*, UNCITRAL, Award, 15 September 2011, at http://www.international.gc.ca/trade-agreements-accords-commerciaux/assets/pdfs/Gallo_Jurisdiction_Award_Final.pdf (accessed 25 September 2012).
30 See "Investor's Memorial", 1 March 2010, at http://www.international.gc.ca/trade-agreements-accords-commerciaux/assets/pdfs/Memorial_Public_Final.pdf (accessed 25 September 2012), para. 8.

to safeguard the rights of local Aboriginal peoples, particularly land rights.[31] The Arbitral Tribunal, in its Award of 15 September 2011, dismissed the investor's claim for lack of jurisdiction, and therefore took no decision regarding the merits of the claim.[32] However, as noted by an international investment law expert, in the event that the Arbitral Tribunal would have examined the merits of the case, the argument used by Canada to defend its position had certainly "to be taken into account… to determine whether there was discrimination and, if this was the case, whether the difference in treatment was justified by the circumstances of the case."[33]

The significance of indigenous peoples' rights in the context of investment law was somehow addressed by the arbitral tribunal in *Grand River Enterprises Six Nations v. United States*,[34] which, although unrelated to the energy sector, is of particular interest to the present enquiry. The principal claimant was a Canadian company controlled by Aboriginal people which exported tobacco in the United States, claiming that the US *Master Settlement Agreement* (MSA) – compelling tobacco producers to contribute to funds necessary to compensate people affected by tobacco-caused illnesses[35] – resulted in the indirect expropriation of its investment as well as the violation of standards of fair and equitable treatment pursuant to Article 1110 NAFTA. The arbitral tribunal rejected both claims. With respect to the supposed expropriation of the investment, the tribunal found that "trade in tobacco products has historically been the subject of close and extensive regulation by US states, a circumstance that should have been known to the Claimant from his extensive past experience in the tobacco business."[36] Therefore, the investor "could not reasonably have developed and relied on an expectation… that he could carry on a large-scale tobacco distribution business, involving the transportation of large quantities of cigarettes across state lines and into many states

---

31 See "Government of Canada Counter Memorial", 29 June 2010, at http://www.international.gc.ca/trade-agreements-accords-commerciaux/assets/pdfs/Gallo_Counter_Memorial.pdf (accessed 25 September 2012), para. 137.

32 See *Glamis Gold*, *supra* note 29, para. 341.

33 See Vadi, "When Cultures Collide: Foreign Direct Investment, Natural Resources, and Indigenous Heritage in International Investment Law", *supra* note 15, p. 849.

34 See *Grand River Enterprises Six Nations, Ltd., et al. v. United States of America*, Arbitration under UNCITRAL Arbitration Rules, Award, 12 January 2011, at http://www.state.gov/documents/organization/156820.pdf (accessed 26 September 2012).

35 The text of the *Master Settlement Agreement* is available at http://ag.ca.gov/tobacco/pdf/1msa.pdf (accessed 26 September 2012).

36 See *Grand River Enterprises Six Nations, Ltd., et al. v. United States of America*, Award, 12 January 2011, *supra* note 34, para. 144.

of the United States, without encountering state regulation."[37] In addition, the threshold established by Article 1110 NAFTA for expropriation was not reached, as it "must involve the deprivation of all, or a very great measure, of a claimant's property interests," while "state action allegedly impair[ed] only a limited portion of the value of an otherwise ongoing and profitable investment."[38] As for the claim on the alleged breach of fair and equitable treatment standards, the tribunal found that, although one of the claimants had received a somehow "unfair treatment," "it did not rise to the level of an infraction of the fair and equitable treatment standard of 1105 [NAFTA]."[39] It is significant, however, that the Tribunal found that

> the U.S. states, in developing and implementing the MSA, do not appear to have been at all sensitive to the particular rights and interests of the Claimants or the indigenous nations of which they are citizens, including those interests in maintaining and developing cross-border trade relations in accordance with longstanding traditions in promoting economic development opportunities for indigenous communities. The Tribunal cannot avoid noting the strong international policy and standards articulated in numerous written instruments and interpretive decisions that favor state action to promote such rights and interests of indigenous peoples.[40]

More specifically, with respect to the right of indigenous peoples to be consulted before implementing governmental policies or action significantly affecting them, the tribunal asserted that

> [i]t may well be, as the Claimants urged, that there does exist a principle of customary international law requiring governmental authorities to consult indigenous peoples on governmental policies or actions significantly affecting them. One member of the Tribunal has written that there is such a customary rule. Moreover, a recent study by a committee of several international law experts assembled under the auspices of the International Law Association, after an exhaustive survey of relevant state and international practice, found a wide range of customary international law norms concerning indigenous peoples, including 'the right

37 Ibid., para. 145.

38 Ibid., para. 154.

39 Ibid., para. 187.

40 Ibid., para. 186.

> to be consulted with respect to any project that may affect them.' As pointed out by the Claimants, the duty of states to consult with indigenous peoples is featured in the UN Declaration of the Rights of Indigenous Peoples, particularly in its Article 19 as well as in several other articles. In its Counter-Memorial the Respondent maintained in sweeping terms that the Declaration does not represent customary international law, as did Canada in its non-disputing party submission. However, when questioned by the Tribunal on this point at the hearing, the Respondents' counsel stated that some parts of the Declaration could reflect fundamental human rights principles and emerging customary law.[41]

This rule of customary international law, however, was not applicable in the instant case, as

> [i]t would go well beyond any articulation of the indigenous consultation norm, as well as far beyond its conceptual foundations as understood by the Tribunal, to hold that the norm obliges consultations with individual investors ... who [do] not purport to have been endowed with authority to represent the [indigenous] communities of which [they are] member[s] in regard to the matters at hand.[42]

Nevertheless, while "the possible existence of a customary rule calling for expanded consultation between governments and indigenous peoples does not assist ... an individual investor,"[43] the tribunal found that

> a good case could be made that consultations should have occurred with governments of the Indian tribes or nations in the United States whose members and sovereign interests could, and apparently are, being affected by the MSA and related measures to regulate commerce in tobacco. Retail tobacco businesses are in many Indian reservations across the country, constituting important sources of income and catalyzing other economic activity among indigenous communities. The evidence before the Tribunal has shown many of the actual or potential effects of the MSA and related measures on reservation tobacco sales and distribution to reservations retailers. The United States federal government admits to the need for consultations with indigenous communities on

41 Ibid., para. 210 (internal footnotes omitted).

42 Ibid., para. 211.

43 Ibid., para. 213.

> legislative and administrative measures affecting them, as a matter of federal policy if not as a matter of international law.[44]

Another arbitration concerning a case in which indigenous peoples' rights were concerned was *Burlington v. Ecuador*.[45] The claimant, a US oil and gas company which had obtained a hydrocarbon concession in the Amazon rainforest, argued that Ecuador was responsible for not providing security and physical protection for its investment against attacks coming from local indigenous communities opposing the project. The arbitral tribunal declared that it lacked jurisdiction on the case because the claimant failed to inform the host State "about the dispute at least six months before it is submitted to arbitration," in order to offer it the opportunity "to redress the problem before the investor submits the dispute to arbitration."[46] Having dismissed the case on jurisdictional grounds, the tribunal did not go into substance regarding the fact of whether or not the execution of the investment could be conditioned by the need for safeguarding indigenous peoples' rights. However, the case was brought by local indigenous peoples before the Inter-American Court of Human Rights, which on 27 June 2012 released its judgment on the dispute.[47] The judgment was immediately acclaimed as a "key victory for indigenous peoples,"[48] as the Court found that Ecuador breached, *inter alia*, the rights of the Sarayaku indigenous community to be consulted before carrying out exploitation projects in their traditional lands, their land rights as well as their right to cultural identity, implicitly proclaimed by Article 21 of the 1969 *American Convention of Human Rights* (ACHR).[49] The Court declared that "the failure to consult the Sarayaku People affected their cultural identity, since there is no doubt that the intervention in and destruction of their cultural heritage entailed a significant lack of respect for their social and cultural identity, their customs, traditions,

44 Ibid., para. 212 (internal footnotes omitted); see also para. 185.

45 See *Burlington Resources Inc. v. Republic of Ecuador*, ICSID Case No. ARB/08/5, Decision on Jurisdiction, 2 June 2010.

46 Ibid., para. 315.

47 See *Case of the Kichwa Indigenous People of Sarayaku v. Ecuador*, Series C No. 245, Judgment, 27 June 2012.

48 See Fernandez Doz Costa, "Ecuador: Inter-American Court ruling marks key victory for Indigenous Peoples", Amnesty International, 27 July 2012, at http://www.amnesty.org/en/news/ecuador-inter-american-court-ruling-marks-key-victory-indigenous-peoples-2012-07-26 (accessed 26 September 2012).

49 *O.A.S. Treaty Series* No. 36, 1144 *UNTS* 123. Article 21, para. 1, states that "[e]veryone has the right to the use and enjoyment of his property. The law may subordinate such use and enjoyment to the interest of society".

worldview and way of life, which naturally caused great concern, sadness and suffering among them."[50] In order to guarantee the effective participation of an indigenous community in the projects of exploitation aimed to be executed in its own territories,

> the State has the obligation to consult the said community in an active and informed manner, in accordance with its customs and traditions, within the framework of continuing communication between the parties. Furthermore, the consultations must be undertaken in good faith, using culturally-appropriate procedures and must be aimed at reaching an agreement. In addition, the people or community must be consulted in accordance with their own traditions, during the early stages of the development or investment plan, and not only when it is necessary to obtain the community's approval, if appropriate. The State must also ensure that the members of the people or the community are aware of the potential benefits and risks so they can decide whether to accept the proposed development or investment plan. Finally, the consultation must take into account the traditional decision-making practices of the people or community. Failure to comply with this obligation, or engaging in consultations without observing their essential characteristics, entails the State's international responsibility.[51]

Not dissimilar to the one just described is the seemingly endless dispute *Chevron v. Ecuador*, triggered on 3 November 1993 by a group of 30,000 indigenous people and farmers from Ecuador who filed a class action against the Chevron's brand Texaco before the US District Court for the Southern District of New York (so-called "*Aguinda* Action").[52] The plaintiffs alleged that massive environmental contamination had been produced in the rain forest in the Oriente region of eastern Ecuador as a result of oil-related activities carried out by Texaco between 1964 and 1992, which allegedly included the dumping of more than 16 billion gallons of toxic waste from oil production into Amazon waters. The *Aguinda* Action was ultimately dismissed by US courts. Therefore, in 2003 the same plaintiffs filed an action before an Ecuadorian court in the

---

50 See *Pueblo Indígena Kichwa de Sarayaku vs. Ecuador*, Judgment, 27 June 2012, *supra*, para. 220.

51 Ibid., para. 177 (internal footnotes omitted).

52 *Maria Aguinda et al. v. Texaco, Inc.*, 945 F. Supp. 625 (S.D.N.Y. 1996), 142 F. Supp. 534 (S.D.N.Y. 2001), 93 Civ. 7527, 2000 WL 122143 (S.D.N.Y. Jan. 31, 2000), 303 F.3d 470 (US Court of Appeals for the Second Circuit, Aug. 16, 2002).

town of Lago Agrio (so-called "*Lago Agrio* Action").[53] On 11 February 2011 the Court found Chevron responsible of environmental damage and established the amount of compensation due to the plaintiffs at US $18.2 billion; such an amount was later fixed at US $19.041 billion in consideration of some mandatory costs required by Ecuadorian law.[54] In January 2012 the judgment of the Lago Agrio judge was upheld by an Ecuadorian Court of Appeals.[55] At the moment of this writing, attempts to enforce the Ecuadorian judgment are taking place in Argentina, Brazil, Canada and the United States, countries where Chevron owns huge assets.[56] Chevron, in the meantime, has also taken its own steps to block the action of the plaintiffs, bringing the case to international arbitration, in September 2009, in front of the Permanent Court of Arbitration.[57] The Arbitral Tribunal – constituted in accordance with the bilateral investment treaty (BIT) between the United States and Ecuador of 27 August 1993 and the UNCITRAL Arbitration Rules – has so far released several orders and interim awards on interim measures as well as on jurisdiction and admissibility. The most recent one at the moment of this writing is the Fourth Interim Award on Interim Measures, released on 7 February 2013.[58] In this Award, the Tribunal declared that Ecuador violated the First and Second Interim Awards under the BIT, the UNCITRAL Rules and international law "in regard to the finalisation and enforcement subject to execution of the Lago Agrio Judgment within and outside Ecuador, including (but not limited to) Canada, Brazil and Argentina;"[59] Ecuador has to therefore "show cause ... why it ... should not compensate" Chevron "for any harm caused" by its violations of the First and Second Interim Awards,[60] Ecuador being "legally obliged under international law to ensure

53 *Maria Aguinda et al. v. Chevron Texaco Corporation*, Proceeding No. 002-2003, Sup. Ct. of Justice, Nueva Loja, Ecuador.

54 See "Chevron Faces Midnight Deadline in $19 Billion Ecuador Judgment", Environment News Service, at http://ens-newswire.com/2012/08/06/chevron-faces-midnight-deadline-in-19-billion-ecuador-judgment/ (accessed 21 March 2013).

55 See "Ecuador court upholds $8.6 billion ruling against Chevron", CNN, 4 January 2012, available at http://edition.cnn.com/2012/01/04/world/americas/ecuador-chevron-lawsuit/index.html (accessed 21 March 2013).

56 See Braden Reddall, "Tribunal presses Ecuador to halt Chevron case enforcement", *Reuters*, 8 February 2013, available at http://www.reuters.com/article/2013/02/09/chevron-ecuador-idUSL1N0B8FBB20130209 (accessed 21 March 2013).

57 See *Chevron Corp. v. Republic of Ecuador*, PCA Case No. 2009–23.

58 *Chevron Corp. v. Republic of Ecuador*, PCA Case No. 2009–23, Fourth Interim Award on Interim Measures, 7 February 2013.

59 See Operative Part, para. 1.

60 Ibid., para. 2.

that [its] commitments under the Treaty and the UNCITRAL Rules are not rendered nugatory by the finalisation, enforcement or execution of the Lago Agrio Judgment in violation of the First and Second Interim Awards."[61] The Tribunal, however, made it clear that "any of the substantive merits of the Parties' dispute has not yet been decided", and also that the award "is made strictly without prejudice to those merits, including all claims advanced by [Chevron] and all defences advanced by [Ecuador]."[62] Chevron also appealed to US courts to block the *Lago Agrio* Action, but the Supreme Court, in 2012, ultimately rejected the appeal.[63] Also in 2012, the same plaintiffs who won the *Lago Agrio* Action submitted a petition to the Inter-American Commission on Human Rights, which accepted to hear their claims.[64]

In some cases, foreign investments interfering with indigenous peoples' rights are addressed in the context of international legal frameworks different to investment arbitration, and often resolved at the "extrajudicial" level. This happens, first of all, when a specific case attains for some reasons particular international visibility. One formidable example is represented by the long controversy of the Kakadu National Park in the Northern Territory of Australia.[65] The reason why this case attracted the attention of the whole international community is that the Park – including sacred sites belonging to the Mirrar Aboriginal community – was included in the UNESCO World Heritage List (WHL);[66] this circumstance led UNESCO to be directly involved in the controversy. When the Park was inscribed on the WHL, in 1981, an investment consisting of the exploitation of three uranium enclaves located in its territory had already been approved, in favour of an Australian company,

---

61 Ibid., para. 3.

62 Ibid., para. 4.

63 *Chevron Corp v. Naranjo et al.*, US Supreme Court, No. 11-1428; see "Supreme Court won't consider blocking $18B judgment against Chevron", CNN, 24 October 2012, at http://edition.cnn.com/2012/10/10/world/americas/chevron-ecuador-lawsuit (accessed 22 March 2013).

64 See "International Human Rights Commission to Review Chevron's Abuses in Ecuador", Amazon Defense Coalition, 1 March 2012, at http://chevrontoxico.com/news-and-multimedia/2012/0301-international-human-rights-commission-to-review-chevrons-abuses-in-ecuador (accessed 22 March 2013).

65 On this controversy see Federico Lenzerini, "Lo 'sfruttamento minerario sostenibile' come principio emergente nel diritto internazionale contemporaneo", in *Rivista giuridica dell'ambiente* 19 (2004), 165, 166 ff., and the sources cited therein (in particular, "Report on the mission to Kakadu National Park, Australia, 26 October to 1 November 1998", UNESCO Doc WHC-98/CONF.203/INF.18, 29 November 1998).

66 See http://whc.unesco.org/en/list/147 (accessed 26 September 2012).

68 percent of which was owned by a British Corporation. Exploitation of the first uranium enclave started in 1981, with the consent of the concerned Aboriginal community. When plans for the exploitation of the second enclave started to be arranged, huge protests were raised by the Mirrar as well as by many international NGOs supporting their rights; at the same time, the UNESCO World Heritage Committee expressed its concern that the said exploitation could prejudice the integrity of the site. An agreement was reached in 1999, establishing that the beginning of the exploitation of the second enclave had to be postponed until the works in the first enclave were not ended. However, this solution, reached under the auspices of UNESCO, left the Mirrar unsatisfied, as it did not ensure adequate safeguarding for their sacred sites. Following huge international pressure, in 2002, the investing company finally withdrew from the project. Then, in 2003, works were started with the purpose of backfilling the second enclave, from which, over 50,000 tons of uranium had been extracted. The case just described played a huge influence on the future of investments in the mining sector, as in 2003 the International Council on Mining and Metals (ICMM), an organization representing the world's leading companies in the field, released a position statement expressing the commitment of the leading international mining companies to "respect legally designated protected areas" and "not to explore or mine in World heritage properties."[67]

In any event, at the international level, the most formidable avenue for indigenous peoples to protect their rights against the prejudicial effects of foreign investment rests on human rights monitoring bodies, where available. Virtually all of these bodies have indeed recognized specific rights in favour of indigenous communities which may strongly condition the feasibility of foreign investments on their lands.[68] For example, the Human Rights Committee has affirmed in many cases that States parties to the *International Covenant on Civil and Political Rights* (ICCPR)[69] should "[c]onduct consultations with indigenous peoples before granting licences for the economic exploitation of the lands where they live, and ensure that such exploitation in no circumstances

67 See "ICMM Position Statement on Mining and Protected Areas", September 2003, at http://www.icmm.com/our-work/sustainable-development-framework/position-statements (accessed 26 September 2012).

68 For a more comprehensive assessment of the relevant practice see Lenzerini, "Self-Determination, Autonomy or Self-Government", *supra* note 14, p. 4 ff.

69 99 UNTS 171.

infringes the rights acknowledged in the Covenant."[70] The Committee has also recognized that large scale exploitation projects – including mining and exploitation of gas and oil – to be carried out in the indigenous peoples' traditional lands may amount to a breach of Article 27 ICCPR,[71] in the event that the land rights of the peoples concerned are not adequately safeguarded.[72]

The Committee on Economic, Social and Cultural Rights has also taken the position that States parties to the 1966 *International Covenant on Economic, Social and Cultural Rights* (ICESCR)[73] "should respect the principle of free prior and informed consent of indigenous peoples in all matters covered by their specific rights,"[74] particularly "when the preservation of their cultural resources, especially those associated with their way of life and cultural expression, are at risk."[75]

The Committee on the Elimination of all Forms of Racial Discrimination has even affirmed that, when it comes to "exploitation of the subsoil resources of the traditional lands of indigenous communities ... merely consulting these communities prior to exploiting the resources' may not be enough to properly safeguard their rights," recommending to States "that the prior informed consent of these communities be sought."[76]

At the regional level, the Inter-American Court of Human Rights has developed abundant case law in the field, which was ultimately expressed in the recent case of the *Sarayaku* community in Ecuador, described *supra*.[77]

70 See "Concluding observations of the Human Rights Committee – Nicaragua", UN Doc. CCPR/C/NIC/CO/3 of 12 December 2008, para. 21(c).

71 Article 27 ICCPR states that '[i]n those States in which ethnic, religious or linguistic minorities exist, persons belonging to such minorities shall not be denied the right, in community with the other members of their group, to enjoy their own culture, to profess and practise their own religion, or to use their own language'.

72 See *Ominayak and the Lubicon Lake Band v. Canada*, Communication No. 167/1984, UN Doc. CCPR/C/38/D/167/1984 of 10 May 1990, para. 33; *Länsman et al. v. Finland*, Communication No. 511/1992, available at http://www1.umn.edu/humanrts/undocs/html/vws511.htm (accessed 26 September 2012), para. 9.8.

73 993 *UNTS* 3.

74 See General Comment No. 21, "Right of everyone to take part in cultural life (Art. 15, para. 1(a), of the International Covenant on Economic, Social and Cultural Rights)", UN Doc. E/C.12/GC/21 of 21 December 2009, para. 37.

75 Ibid., para. 55.

76 See "Consideration of Reports submitted by States Parties under Article 9 of the Convention, Concluding Observations on Ecuador (Sixty second session, 2003)", UN Doc. CERD/C/62/CO/2 of 2 June 2003, para. 16.

77 See *supra*, note 47 and corresponding text.

Such a case law was inaugurated by the renowned *Awas Tingni* case,[78] in which the Court found that, through granting a Korean timber company a logging concession on traditional lands of an indigenous community, which endangered the enjoyment of the rights of such a community, Nicaragua had breached Article 21 ACHR.[79] In a more recent case, the Court also held that

> regarding large-scale development or investment projects that would have a major impact within [an indigenous community's] territory, the State has a duty, not only to consult with the [members of the community concerned], but also to obtain their free, prior, and informed consent, according to their customs and traditions.[80]

Last but not least, the African Commission on Human and Peoples' Rights took a similar position in a case concerning oil production in the land of the Ogoni people, in Nigeria, by the State oil company (the Nigerian National Petroleum Company), which was the majority shareholder in a consortium with Shell Petroleum Development Corporation. The government of Nigeria was involved in the project as, *inter alia*, it placed its military forces at the disposal of the oil company in order to protect the investment against the Ogoni people. The execution of the project resulted in environmental degradation and health problems for the members of the indigenous community.[81] The Commission found that the government of Nigeria had violated a number of provisions of the *African Charter on Human and Peoples Rights* (ACHPR)[82] by reason of the huge prejudice produced by the project to the detriment of the Ogoni lands and, *a fortiori*, of the well-being of the Ogoni people.[83] In addition, the Commission appeared to implicitly agree with the argument of the claimants that the conduct of Nigeria was inconsistent with the ACHPR for the fact of "not involv[ing] the Ogoni Communities in the decisions that affected

---

78 *Case of the Mayagna (Sumo) Awas Tingni Community v. Nicaragua*, Series C No. 79, Judgment, 31 August 2001.

79 Ibid., para. 153.

80 See *Case of the Saramaka People v. Suriname*, Series C No. 172, Judgment, 28 November 2007, para. 134 (see also para. 137).

81 See *The Social and Economic Rights Action Center and the Center for Economic and Social Rights v. Nigeria*, Communication No. 155/96 (2001), at http://www1.umn.edu/humanrts/africa/comcases/155-96.html (accessed 26 September 2012).

82 *African [Banjul] Charter on Human and Peoples' Rights*, 1981, 21 *ILM* 58 (1982).

83 See *The Social and Economic Rights Action Center and the Center for Economic and Social Rights v. Nigeria*, Communication No. 155/96 (2001), *supra* note 81, paras. 58 and 67.

the development of Ogoniland."[84] The Commission noted that "[t]he intervention of multinational corporations may be a potentially positive force for development," on the condition that "the State and the people concerned are ever mindful of the common good and the sacred rights of individuals and communities."[85]

4 Conclusion: The Need to Balance Conflicting Values

The practice of human rights monitoring bodies described in the preceding Section shows the acceptance by the international community that indigenous peoples' rights must be adequately safeguarded when giving execution to investment projects on their lands. In practical terms, the interests of indigenous peoples must *at least* be balanced with other major interests pursued by States through allowing the execution of foreign investments. In this respect, investment in the energy sector represents a category carrying with itself special implications in terms of the benefits which may be produced by the relevant investments, in some cases even for the whole population of the territorial State. In other words, it is not just a matter of financial gain for a restricted part of the national society, but is rather a matter of producing new well being for the whole population through the production of energy. As emphasized, for example, by the European Court of Justice, energy sources "are of fundamental importance for a country's existence since not only its economy but above all, its institutions, its essential public services and even the survival of its inhabitants depend upon them."[86] Therefore, the threshold of the prejudice that must be caused to indigenous peoples by the investment in order to justify its withdrawal is quite high. At the same time, no general interest of whatever kind may be taken as justifying loss of human lives and/or the total extinction of the cultural identity of the indigenous communities concerned. This is clear if one considers the human-rights-related implications attached to foreign investments carried out in indigenous peoples' traditional lands, which in some cases may even interest rules reaching the threshold of *jus cogens*,[87] being

84 Ibid., para. 55.

85 Ibid., para. 69.

86 See *Campus Oil Limited and others v. Minister for Industry and Energy and others*, Case 72/83, Judgment, 10 July 1984, *European Court Reports* (1984), 02727, para. 34.

87 Generally on this point see Vadi, "When Cultures Collide: Foreign Direct Investment, Natural Resources, and Indigenous Heritage in International Investment Law", *supra* note 15, 856 ff. The equation between the breach of cultural rights of indigenous peoples and

therefore not subject to any derogation in whatever circumstances. When possible, the most appropriate solution consists of balancing the conflicting interests at stake so as to give realization to both of them to the maximum possible extent. This said, however, even leaving aside investments which may determine loss of human lives, in consideration of the fundamental character of the cultural rights of indigenous peoples – especially when related to their traditional lands – it is certainly possible that the concrete prejudice that may be produced by an investment (even in the energy sector) to such rights can reach a threshold high enough to require its withdrawal.

In any event, it is a fact that in recent times the concern for indigenous peoples' rights has hugely increased within all sectors of the international community, including in the context of investment operators. For example, in May 2008, the ICMM released a position statement on *Mining and Indigenous Peoples*,[88] making a number of commitments which include: acknowledging and respecting "the social, economic, environmental and cultural interests of Indigenous Peoples and their rights as articulated and defined within provincial, national and international laws;" "clearly identify[ing] and fully understand[ing] the interests and perspectives of Indigenous Peoples regarding a project and its potential impacts." Social impact assessments or other social baseline analyses for projects which may impact on Indigenous Peoples will examine their particular perspectives and be based on consultation with them; "engag[ing] and consult[ing] with Indigenous Peoples in a fair, timely and culturally appropriate way throughout the project cycle." Other commitments include encouraging governments "where appropriate to participate in alleviating and resolving any problems or issues faced by Indigenous Peoples near mining operations;" designing "projects to avoid potentially significant adverse impacts of mining and related activities and where this is not practicable, minimizing, managing and/or compensating fairly for impacts," including, for example, special arrangements "to protect cultural property or sites of religious significance for indigenous peoples;" seeking "agreement with Indigenous Peoples and other affected communities on programs to generate net benefits (social, economic, environmental and cultural), that is benefits

the violation of *jus cogens* has been affirmed, for example, by the Inter-American Court of Human Rights in the *Case of the Moiwana Community v. Suriname*, Series C No. 124, Judgment, 15 June 2005, in which the Court found that the fact of depriving the community of the possibility of performing its death rituals according to its traditional rules amounts to inhumane treatment (see para. 99).

88 See http://www.icmm.com/page/8312/news-and-events/news/articles/final-position-statement-on-mining-and-indigenous-peoples-issues (accessed 26 September 2012).

and opportunities which outweigh negative impacts from mining activities;" support[ing] "appropriate frameworks for facilitation, mediation and dispute resolution;" seeking "broad community support for new projects or activities." Of course, the ICMM position statement – like other similar codes of conduct – does not produce any binding effects in itself. Therefore, it would be advisable to include rules like the ones enshrined by the said codes – if not the codes themselves – in BITs, in order to make such rules mandatory. Indeed, respecting the commitments listed by such instruments would actually represent a notable step to minimize the possible adverse effects of foreign investments on indigenous peoples' rights, if not to prevent conflicts between the two values in object to come into existence.

CHAPTER 8

The Tripartite Dimension of Conflicts of Interests: Workers, Foreign Investors and Host States in the Energy Sector

Yannick Radi

1 Introduction

Viewed through the lens of investment treaty arbitration and in light of recent investment disputes relating *e.g.* to indigenous peoples[1] or cultural heritage,[2] foreign direct investments (FDI) operations are very often portrayed as raising conflicts between the public interest of the host state and the private interest of the foreign investor. In this context, it comes as no surprise that the analyses of these conflicts capture the discourses and writings of scholarship.[3]

1 See *e.g. Glamis Gold Ltd v. United States of America*, UNCITRAL, Award, 8 June 2009. All awards are available at http://www.italaw.com, unless cited otherwise.

2 See *e.g. Parkerings-Compagniet AS v. Republic of Lithuania*, ICSID Case No. ARB/05/8, Award, 11 September 2007.

3 It is worth noticing that mainstream literature elevates this conflict between the public interest of the host state and the private interest of the foreign investor to a conflict of norms between international investment law, *i.e.* international investment agreements (IIA), and its 'others', *e.g.* international human rights law. As argued by the author elsewhere, the conflicts characterizing investment treaty arbitration should not be conceived of as normative conflicts but as a conflicts of interests, because of the normative vagueness of IIA provisions and of the public nature of international investment law, see Yannick Radi, "The "Human Nature" of International Investment Law", *Transnational Dispute Management* 1 (2013), 1. Among the abundant literature on the relationship between international investment law and its 'others', see *i.e.* Freya Baetens (ed.), *Investment Law Within International Law: An Integrationist Perspective* (Cambridge: Cambridge University Press, 2013); Eric De Brabandere, "Human Rights Considerations in International Investment Arbitration", in Malgosia Fitzmaurice and Panos Merkouris (eds.), *The Interpretation and Application of the European Convention of Human Rights: Legal and Practical Implications.* (Leiden/Boston: Martinus Nijhoff Publishers, 2012); Pierre-Marie Dupuy, Ernst U. Petersmann, Francesco Francioni (eds.), *Human Rights in International Investment Law and Arbitration* (Oxford: Oxford University Press, 2009); Tarcisio Gazzini and Yannick Radi, "Foreign Investment with a Human Face – With Special Reference to Indigenous Peoples", in Rainer Hofmann and Christian J. Tams, *International Investment Law and its Others* (Baden-Baden: Nomos, 2012),

 | DOI 10.1163/9789004244719_010

Nevertheless, if one takes a step back and looks at FDI operations from a broader point of view, one gets a different picture from the traditional one we are accustomed to by the arbitration lens.

Such is the case of the FDI operations in the energy sector in relation to labour standards. Indeed, the tripartite relationship between workers, the foreign investor and the host state in this sector is characterized by a plurality of potentially entangled conflicts. Forming part of this combination, one finds the traditional conflict between the public interest of the host state and the private interest of the investor. But, there exists also a conflict within the "box" of the public interest itself between the interests of workers and other public interests that are promoted/protected by the host state, such as the interests of an economic and social nature or interests related to national security. All these conflicts underlie and explain the labour issues that are raised in the energy sector.

In light of the above, this chapter pursues a twofold objective. First, it unravels and examines the labour issues that are generated by the above-mentioned conflicts. Second, among the various mechanisms available on the international plane, it appraises how international investment law (IIL), *i.e.* the new generation of international investment agreements (IIA) can be used to address these labour issues in the energy sector.

To reach these objectives, this chapter starts with a review of the key labour standards protected under international law (Section 2). Focusing in particular on the fundamental principles and rights at work provided by the 1998 International Labour Organisation's (ILO) Declaration on fundamental principles and rights at work and its follow-up,[4] it then identifies the main labour issues that are currently raised in the energy sector, with an emphasis on the oil and gas sector (Section 3). Finally, the chapter analyses the labour provisions contained in the new generation of IIA, in particular in Free Trade Agreements (FTA), and assesses their potential to address these labour issues (Section 4). Going beyond the case of the energy sector, the chapter formulates

---

87; Vid Prislan, "Non-Investment Obligations in Investment Treaty Arbitration – Towards a Greater Role for States?", in Freya Baetens (ed.), *Investment Law Within International Law: An Integrationist Perspective* (Cambridge: Cambridge University Press, 2013); Bruno Simma, "Foreign Investment Arbitration: a Place for Human Rights?", *International and Comparative Law Quarterly* 60 (2011), 573; Valentina Vadi, "Culture Clash? World Heritage and Investors' Rights in International Investment Law and Arbitration", *ICSID Review – Foreign Investment Law Journal* 28(1) (2013), 1.

4 ILO Declaration on fundamental principles and rights at work and its follow-up (1998) (Annexed revised 2010) at http://www.ilo.org/declaration/lang--en/index.htm (accessed 30 May 2013).

some concluding remarks on the tripartite dimension of the conflicts of interests that characterizes all FDI operations.

2 The Normative Background: Labour Rights and Standards in International Law

Although labour rights and standards are enshrined in human rights conventions[5] and form part of the emerging concept of "sustainable development,"[6] the instruments adopted by the ILO constitute the cornerstone of the workers' protection on the international plane. With 189 binding ILO conventions and 202 non-binding recommendations adopted,[7] the ILO has been at the vanguard of workers' protection since its creation in 1919. Because of the "productiveness" of the ILO, it proves to be impossible to offer a comprehensive overview of the rights and standards provided in these instruments.

Among these rights and standards, a set has emerged as constitutive of a normative core to be respected, promoted and realized by states. Indeed, the International Labour Conference declared in 1998:

> All Members, even if they have not ratified the Conventions in question, have an obligation arising from the very fact of membership in the Organization to respect, to promote and to realize, in good faith and in accordance with the Constitution, the principles concerning the fundamental rights which are the subject of those Conventions, namely: (a) freedom of association and the effective recognition of the right to collective bargaining; (b) the elimination of all forms of forced or compulsory labour; (c) the effective abolition of child labour; and (d) the elimination of discrimination in respect of employment and occupation.[8]

5 See *i.e.* the Universal declaration of human rights (1948), the Covenant on civil and political rights (1966) and the Covenant on economic, social and cultural rights (1966) at http://www.ohchr.org/en/ (accessed 30 May 2013).

6 See *i.e.* UNGA Declaration on Environment and Development (1992), UN Doc A/CONF.151/26; UNGA Declaration on the 'Future We Want' (2012), UN Doc A/RES/66/288* at http://www.un.org/en/documents/index.shtml (accessed 30 May 2013).

7 For an overview, see ILO, 'Labour standards' at http://www.ilo.org/global/standards/lang--fr/index.htm (accessed 30 May 2013).

8 ILO Declaration on fundamental principles and rights at work and its follow-up (1998), *supra* note 4.

Before defining the content of these principles, two intertwined remarks can be formulated as to this Declaration. First, it is worth noticing that ILO member states are bound by these principles by their only membership to the organization, irrespective of the ratification of the corresponding ILO conventions. Thereby, these principles are – *mutatis mutandis* – erected as the peremptory norms of the international labour regime.[9] This "imperative" nature very likely explains the limited number of principles that the 1998 Declaration recognizes.

To shed some light on these principles, one can usefully rely on the corresponding conventions adopted by the ILO.

The freedom of association and the effective recognition of the right to collective bargaining are especially addressed in the Convention 087 concerning the freedom of association and the protection of the right to organize[10] as well as in the Convention 098 concerning the application of the principles of the right to organize and to bargain collectively.[11] In particular, Article 1 of the former Convention provides:

> 1. Workers shall enjoy adequate protection against acts of anti-union discrimination in respect of their employment. 2. Such protection shall apply more particularly in respect of acts calculated to (a) make the employment of a worker subject to the condition that he shall not join a union or shall relinquish trade union membership; (b) cause the dismissal of or otherwise prejudice a worker by reason of union membership or because of participation in union activities outside working hours or, with the consent of the employer, within working hours.

As to the second core labour principle, *i.e.* the elimination of all forms of forced or compulsory labour, it relates to two main conventions – Convention 029 concerning forced or compulsory labour[12] and Convention 105 concerning the

9 This comparison comes from a discussion with Eric De Brabandere in the course of which he described this set of principles as the 'ILO *jus cogens*'.

10 Convention 087 concerning the freedom of association and the protection of the right to organize (1948) at http://www.ilo.org/dyn/normlex/en/f?p=1000:1:0::NO (accessed 30 May 2013).

11 Convention 098 concerning the application of the principles of the right to organise and to bargain collectively (1949) at http://www.ilo.org/dyn/normlex/en/f?p=1000:1:0::NO (accessed 30 May 2013).

12 Convention 029 concerning forced or compulsory labour (1930) at http://www.ilo.org/dyn/normlex/en/f?p=1000:1:0::NO (accessed 30 May 2013).

abolition of forced labour.[13] The former defines forced and compulsory labour in its Article 2 as "all work or service which is exacted from any person under the menace of any penalty and for which the said person has not offered himself voluntarily".

In relation to forced labour, the "*jus cogens*" of international labour law is also made of the effective abolition of child labour. This prohibition is enshrined mainly in two conventions, *i.e.* the Convention 138 concerning minimum age for admission to employment[14] and the Convention 182 concerning the prohibition and immediate action for the elimination of the worst forms of child labour adopted in 1999.[15] Article 1 of the Convention 138 provides:

> Each Member for which this Convention is in force undertakes to pursue a national policy designed to ensure the effective abolition of child labour and to raise progressively the minimum age for admission to employment or work to a level consistent with the fullest physical and mental development of young persons.

Finally, the fourth core labour principle, *i.e.* the elimination of discrimination in respect of employment and occupation is enshrined in two main conventions – the Convention 100 concerning the equal remuneration[16] and the Convention 111 concerning discrimination in respect of employment and occupation.[17] Article 1 of the latter Convention provides in particular that discrimination includes "any distinction, exclusion or preference" made "on the basis of race, colour, sex, religion, political opinion, national extraction or social origin, which has the effect of nullifying or impairing equality of opportunity or treatment in employment or occupation". Equipped with this "*grille de lecture*" of international labour law, one can now move to the examination of the labour issues raised in the energy sector.

---

13 Convention 105 concerning the abolition of forced labour (1957) at http://www.ilo.org/dyn/normlex/en/f?p=1000:1:0::NO (accessed 30 May 2013).

14 Convention 138 concerning minimum age for admission to employment (1973) at http://www.ilo.org/dyn/normlex/en/f?p=1000:1:0::NO (accessed 30 May 2013).

15 Convention 182 concerning the prohibition and immediate action for the elimination of the worst forms of child labour (1999) at http://www.ilo.org/dyn/normlex/en/f?p=1000:1:0::NO (accessed 30 May 2013).

16 Convention 100 concerning the equal remuneration (1951) available at http://www.ilo.org/dyn/normlex/en/f?p=1000:1:0::NO (accessed 30 May 2013).

17 Convention 111 concerning discrimination in respect of employment and occupation (1958) at http://www.ilo.org/dyn/normlex/en/f?p=1000:1:0::NO (accessed 30 May 2013).

3 Labour Issues Raised in the Energy Sector: The Example of the Oil and Gas Sector

To start with this review of the working conditions in the energy sector and more precisely in the oil and gas sector, it is worth noticing that there is a substantive gap between the "external" perception of the public and the "internal" experience of workers in this sector.[18] Indeed, on the one hand, the public generally believes and expresses this opinion that the oil and gas industry is associated with oil spills, explosions, air pollution and the neglect of human rights. Furthermore, jobs on the rig floor are often perceived as dirty, difficult and possibly dangerous. On the other hand and on the opposite, two-thirds of the polled workers in the oil industry declare a high degree of job satisfaction and even more would recommend a career in the industry to a new graduate. Such an opinion is mainly due to the good salaries that are earned in the oil and gas industry as well as the balance between a good work-life and a fulfilling and challenging job. As a result, 90 percent of workers under the age of 35 expect to stay in the oil sector.

That being said, it remains that the oil and gas sector raises specific problems, in particular as to occupational safety and health, working time,[19] forced labour as well as restrictions and prohibitions of the right to strike. This chapter focuses on occupational safety and health, on forced labour and on restrictions of the right to strike.[20] To illustrate them, it relies on three case studies: a series of accidents in the oil industry in Kuwait as to occupational safety and health (3.1), the Yadana gas project in Myanmar as to forced labour (3.2) and case

18 See Energy Institute, Deloitte and Norman Broadbent, quoted in ILO, 'Social dialogue and industrial relations issues in the oil industry' (2009), 18 at http://www.ilo.org/sector/Resources/publications/WCMS_161662/lang--en/index.htm (accessed 30 May 2013).

19 In the oil extraction industry, average basic working time is over 50 hours per week, although almost all countries have limits on weekly working hours, either 40 hours or 48 hours, with the former limit dominant. Several options aim at compensating the overtime such as paying a premium on the normal hourly rate or entitling workers to a rest period equivalent to or more than the hours worked, ibid., 32.

20 It can be mentioned that the inclusion of the right to strike in the ambit of the freedom of association is open to discussion. This is illustrated by the on-going discussions at the International Labour Conference (ILC). See *e.g.* ILC, Provisional Record, 101st session, Geneva (2012), 19 (REV) Part one / 37 quoted in Vid Prislan and Ruben Zandvliet, "Labor Provisions in International Investment Agreements: Prospects for Sustainable Development", in *Yearbook of International Investment Law and Policy* (New York: Oxford University Press, 2013) (forthcoming), at http://papers.ssrn.com/sol3/papers.cfm?abstract_id=2171716, 28 (accessed 30 May 2013).

No. 2552 filed against Bahrain before the ILO Committee on freedom of association regarding restrictions and prohibitions of the right to strike (3.3). In light of these three case studies, the tripartite dimension of the conflicts of interests that underlie these labour issues is then unravelled and discussed (3.4).

3.1 *Occupational Safety and Health*

In 2000, Kuwait was faced with two major accidents at the Mina al-Ahmadi and Shuaiba refineries, as well as with a number of smaller accidents. The accident at the Mina al-Ahmadi occurred on the 28th of July, a huge explosion killing 5 people and wounding 50 others. On the 18th of June, the accident that resulted from the leak of hydrogen sulphide gas killed two workers at the refinery of Shuaiba. The commission that was instituted in the aftermath of the latter accident blamed Chevron to be responsible for this event because of technical mistakes allegedly committed in the preparation of an aviation fuel unit operation. A parliamentary commission reached a similar conclusion as to the responsibility of Chevron. Chevron denied any responsibility in the accident. Two years later, another explosion occurred in the Raudhatain oil-field, killing four people and injuring 20 others. In 2008, workers' trade unions reported that between July and September 2008, at least 5 serious accidents took place at the refineries, resulting in the deaths of two contractors and injuring 14 people. All these accidents raised concerns about safety management. More than the deterioration of the machinery, the management in charge of safety was criticized. These events led to the organization of strikes. In October 2008, 3000 unionized workers of the Kuwait National Petroleum Company demonstrated demanding higher wages and safer working conditions.[21]

3.2 *Forced Labour*

Non-paid conscription of villagers by the government and the Army is a long-established practice in Myanmar that was codified in the Town Act of 1907 and the Village Act of 1908. An ILO Commission of inquiry was created in 1997 to investigate these practices in particular in light of the Convention 029 concerning forced or compulsory labour.[22] The 1998 report of the Commission criticized especially the conditions under which the army recruited villagers *e.g.* for the construction of military camps, as well as the abuses which some-

21 See ILO, 'Social dialogue and industrial relations issues in the oil industry' (2009), *supra* note 18, 39.

22 Convention 029 concerning forced or compulsory labour, *supra* note 12.

times coincide, for instance ill-treatment.[23] The process that was triggered by the communication of the report of the ILO Commission led the authorities to repeal the Village Act and the Town Act in 1999. In addition, an ILO representative to Yangon was appointed in particular to liaise with the government and observe the situation.

Despite these legislative evolutions, there are on-going allegations that forced labour still exists in Myanmar, emanating in particular from NGOs.[24] It is in this context that Total, a French company, and Unocal – now Chevron – were accused of complicity in forced labour. These accusations were formulated in relation to the Yadana gas project, which began officially in 1992 with the signature by Total of a contract with the military regime to develop offshore natural gas fields in the Andaman Sea. These accusations resulted in complaints filed by villagers in the United States against Unocal in 1996 and against Total in Belgium in 2005 and in France in 2002. The complaint faced by Total in France concerned allegations of "complicity in unlawful confinement" raised by eight nationals. They alleged that they had been forced by the Myanmar army to provide what they considered to be compulsory labour for the construction of the Yadana gas pipeline. Despite denying such complicity of forced labour, Total entered into a settlement agreement in 2005. This agreement provided in particular the creation of a solidarity fund to compensate the eight plaintiffs as well as any other person able to demonstrate that she had suffered a similar experience in the area around the pipeline construction corridor.[25]

---

23 'Forced Labour in Myanmar (Burma) – Report of the Commission of Inquiry appointed under Article 26 of the Constitution of the International Labour Organization to examine the observance by Myanmar of the Forced Labour Convention, 1930 (No. 29)' (1998) at http://www.ilo.org/global/about-the-ilo/newsroom/news/WCMS_007995/lang--en/index.htm (accessed 30 May 2013).

24 See *e.g.* EarthRights International, "TOTAL IMPACT: The Human Rights, Environmental, and Financial Impacts of Total and Chevron's Yadana Gas Project in Military-Ruled Burma (Myanmar)", (2008) at http://www.earthrights.org/sites/default/files/publications/total-impact.pdf (accessed 30 May 2013).

25 See EarthRights International, 'Total, Unocal's Partner, Agrees to Compensate Human Rights Victims' (2005) available at http://www.earthrights.org/legal/total-unocals-partner-agrees-compensate-human-rights-victims (accessed 30 May 2013); Total, "Does forced labor still exist in Myanmar. If so, does Total E&P Myanmar use it", (2013) at http://burma.total.com/myanmar-en/faq/does-forced-labor-still-exist-in-myanmar.-if-so-does-total-ep-myanmar-use-it-200232.html (accessed 30 May 2013); New York Times, 'Total settles rights case' (2005) at http://www.nytimes.com/2005/11/29/business/world business/29iht-total.html?_r=0 (accessed 30 May 2013).

Irrespective of the question of the reality of NGO's allegations and Total's denials as to the Yadana gas project, this case-study illustrates the circumstances under which the prohibition of forced labour can be violated and more generally, how these violations can be committed by host states and/or foreign investors.

3.3 *Restrictions and Prohibitions of the Right to Strike*

In 2002, Bahraini authorities promulgated the Legislative Decree No. 33 on the Trade Union Law. Its section 21(e) provided a list of essential services in which strike actions were prohibited, *i.e.* security services, civil defence, airports, ports, hospitals, transport, telecommunications, electricity and water services. In 2006, the Law No. 49 amending certain provisions of the Trade union Law was adopted. Section 21(d) of the Trade Union Law, as amended, "prohibits strikes in essential services which may disturb national security or disrupt the daily life of citizens." It provides: "The Prime Minister shall issue a decision setting out those essential services where strikes are prohibited." On 20 November 2006, the Prime Minister issued Decision No. 62, which listed the following as essential services where strike actions were prohibited: security services, civil defence, airports, ports, hospitals, medical centres and pharmacies, all means of transport of persons or goods, telecommunications, electricity and water services, bakeries, educational institutions and *oil and gas installations*.[26, 27]

In 2007, the General Federation of Bahrain trade unions filed a claim before the ILO Committee on freedom of association against the Government of Bahrain arguing in particular that decision No. 62 included as essential services certain establishments being outside the scope of essential services in which strikes may be banned, as defined by international labour standards.[28] The government replied that the ILO Committee on freedom of association indicated on several occasions that each country has the right to regulate the right to strike, as well as to prohibit its exercise in sectors deemed to be essential services, the interruption of which would lead to the disruption of every-

26 Emphasis added.

27 See ILO Committee on freedom of association, Case N° 2552, 'Complaint against the Government of Bahrain presented by the General Federation of Bahrain Trade Unions (GBTU), para. 411–12, 349. The Report of the Committee on freedom of association (2008) is available at http://www.ilo.org/wcmsp5/groups/public/@ed_norm/@relconf/documents/meetingdocument/wcms_091464.pdf (accessed 30 May 2013).

28 See ILO Committee on freedom of association, Case N° 2552, 'Complaint against the Government of Bahrain presented by the General Federation of Bahrain Trade Unions (GBTU), para. 413, ibid.

day life for all or a certain part of the population. It further argued that the definition of these services as essential takes into consideration the general interests of the population. As to strikes in the petroleum and gas sectors, it put forth that they are not permissible, as these two industries constitute a principal source of national revenue.[29]

In its report, the ILO Committee on freedom of association considered that the petroleum and gas sector are not essential services in the strict sense of the term (that is, services whose interruption would endanger the life, personal safety, or health of the whole or part of the population). It reached this conclusion despite its acknowledgment that "essential services in the strict sense of the term depends to a large extent on the particular circumstances prevailing in a country" and that "non-essential services may become essential if a strike lasts beyond a certain time or extends beyond a certain scope, thus endangering the life, personal safety or health of the whole or part of the population."[30]

This case filed against Bahrain is not isolated. The ILO Committee on freedom of association has been faced with many other claims concerning domestic legislations that placed restrictions and prohibitions on the right of workers to strike in the energy sector.[31] Beyond the example of the right to strike in the context of the oil and gas sector, these cases illustrate well the fact that violations of labour rights in the energy sector often emanate, not from foreign investors, but from the host states themselves.

3.4 *The Tripartite Dimension of the Conflicts of Interests Underlying Labour Issues in the Energy Sector*

Important lessons can be learnt from the above-mentioned case studies as to the type of conflicts of interests that underlie the labour issues in the energy sector.

With respect to the arbitration bias of international investment lawyers,[32] the first lesson relates to the fact that these issues cannot be properly

29 Para. 415–18, ibid.

30 Para. 421–22, ibid.

31 See *e.g.* ILO Committee on freedom of association, Case N° 1576, 'Complaint against the Government of Norway presented by the Norwegian Trade Union Federation of Oil Workers', para. 91–118, 279. The Report of the Committee on freedom of association (1991) is available at http://www.ilo.org/dyn/normlex/en/f?p=1000:50002:0::NO:50002:P50002_COMPLAINT_TEXT_ID:2902142 (accessed 30 May 2013).

32 See *supra* introduction.

understood if read through the lens of the traditional public/private divide as it exists in investment treaty arbitration. Indeed, these issues do not only/mainly raise a conflict between the public interest of the host state and the private interest of the foreign investor.

The second lesson to be learnt consists in the fact that the conflicts of interests in the energy sector as they impact on the rights of workers take place to a large extent within the "box" of the public interest. Indeed, as illustrated by the claim filed against Bahrain before the ILO Committee on freedom of association, the conflicts often oppose one public interest, *i.e.* the protection of workers rights, and another public interest, *i.e.* national revenue or national security. It is worth noticing that the private interest of foreign investors is not (directly) involved in such conflicts, even though such prohibitions and restrictions of labour rights may (indirectly) serve their own interests.

Thirdly and as illustrated in a way by the Yadana gas project in Myanmar, the interests that conflict with workers' rights may be conceived of as tinted with the private interests of the individuals or groups exercising the domestic public authority. In addition, in such situations, the private interest of foreign investors often appears to form part of the web of conflicts of interests that characterize the labour issues in the energy sector.

Taking these lessons seriously, it is impossible to conceive of the labour issues in the energy sector in a Manichean manner. These issues and their underlying conflicts of interests are characterized by a tripartite dimension that concerns home states' interests, workers' interests and foreign investors' interests. In light of these findings, one can now move to the analysis of international investment agreements to assess their potential in addressing these labour issues.

4 Labour Issues in the Energy Sector and International Investment Law

Numerous existing mechanisms on the international plane appear to be of relevance to address the labour issues raised in the energy sector. Some of them have the potential to cover a broad range of alleged violations of labour standards, in particular ILO committees, as illustrated by the above-mentioned cases dealt with by the ILO Committee on freedom of association. On the opposite, some mechanisms are designed in such a way that they could only be used to address specific alleged violations, *i.e.* the

International criminal court with respect to forced labour.[33] On a different level of normativity and enforcement, "soft law" initiatives emanating from international organizations, *e.g.* the UN Global compact[34] and the Human Rights Council Guiding Principles[35] as well as from corporations[36] and private networks/frameworks are also relevant as to the labour issues raised in the energy sector.[37]

Among the available mechanisms on the international plane, this chapter focuses on international investment law. More specifically, it discusses the labour provisions that characterize the new generation of international investment agreements,[38] *i.e.* bilateral investment treaties (BIT) and (mainly)

---

33 Even though many issues are open to discussion as to the elements of the crime against humanity, forced labour may be regarded as a crime against humanity under Art. 7 of the Statute of the International Criminal Court (ICC). Such a suggestion is in particular supported by the footnote 11 to the Art. 7.1.c of the ICC Elements of the crime which states: 'It is understood that such deprivation of liberty may, in some circumstances, include exacting *forced labour* (emphasis added) or otherwise reducing a person to a servile status as defined in the Supplementary Convention on the Abolition of Slavery, the Slave Trade, and Institutions and Practices Similar to Slavery of 1956', see Rome Statute of the International Criminal Court (1998) and ICC Elements of the Crime (2002), at http://www.icc-cpi.int/EN_Menus/icc/Pages/default.aspx (accessed 30 May 2013). See also James L. Bischoff, "Forced Labour in Brazil: International Criminal Law as the *Ultima Ratio* Modality of Human Rights Protection", *Leiden Journal of International Law* 19 (2006), 151.

34 See the United Nations Global Compact, information available at http://www.unglobalcompact.org (accessed 30 May 2013). See also *i.e.* the OECD Guidelines on multinational enterprises (1976) (as updated in 2011), at http://www.oecd.org/daf/inv/mne/48004323.pdf (accessed 30 May 2013).

35 See Guiding principles on business and human rights: implementing the United Nations, "Protect, Respect and Remedy" framework, annexed to the Final report of the Special Representative of the Secretary-General on the issue of human rights and transnational corporations and other business enterprises (John Ruggie) (2011) UN Doc. A/HRC/17/31 at http://www.ohchr.org/Documents/Issues/Business/A-HRC-17-31_AEV.pdf (accessed 30 May 2013).

36 See *e.g.* "Corporate Social Responsibility in Total's Business Model" (2009), at http://www.total.com/fr/investisseurs-institutionnels/presentations/csr-total-business-model-novembre-2009-400501.html (accessed 30 May 2013).

37 See Jedrzej G. Frynas, "Corporate Social Responsibility in the Oil and Gas Sector", *Journal of World Energy Law & Business* 2–3 (2009), 178.

38 The first references to labour rights were made in IIA's preambles. For instance, the first BIT which mentioned those rights, *i.e.* the US-Poland BIT, provided 'that the development of business and economic ties can contribute to the well-being of workers in both

FTA[39] with the view to assess the extent to which they can be of assistance as to the labour issues raised in the energy sector.[40] Taking the 2012 US BIT model[41] as a point of reference and discussion, the chapter inquires four types of clause provided in the body of these agreements: the "adherence" clauses (Article 13.1), the "no-lowering standards" clauses (Article 13.2), the "institutional arrangement" clauses (Article 13.4) and the "corporate social responsibility" (CSR) clauses.[42]

countries and promote respect for fundamental worker rights'. As noted in the literature, '(s)tatements of this kind were premised on the belief that increased FDI flows will, in itself, inevitably lead to an improvement of labor standards in recipient countries', see Prislan and Zandvliet, *supra* note 19, 23. See US-Poland BIT (1991) at http://tcc.export.gov/Trade_Agreements/Bilateral_Investment_Treaties/index.asp (accessed 30 May 2013). On the relationship between labour standards and FDI operations, see David Kucera, 'Normes fondamentales du travail et investissements directs étrangers', *Revue internationale du travail* 141-1/2 (2002), 33.

39 These provisions are characteristic of FTAs. Indeed, few BITs have such provisions in particular outside the treaty practice of North-American states. Such language can be found in self-standing provisions, in independent chapters or in side letters/chapters.

40 Given the 'accessory' dimension of the analyses here conducted, the chapter does not discuss the clauses that provide for (general) exceptions or 'sanctuarize' the right of states to regulate, in particular with respect to labour standards. Indeed, as above-mentioned, the energy sector is not characterized by situations where labour issues result from the investors' allegation that state measures aiming at the promotion/protection of labour standards affect their investment in such a way that they are in violation of the applicable IIA.

41 See US BIT Model (2012) at http://www.state.gov/documents/organization/188371.pdf (accessed 30 May 2013).

42 The objective being to analyse these provisions in relation to the labour issues raised in the energy sector, this chapter 'depicts' their general features without discussing in the abstract all the specificities of treaty practice in terms of the drafting of each provision and of their combination in existing IIAs. For analyses of IIA labour provisions, see *i.e.* Kimberly A. Elliott, "Labor Standards and the Free Trade Area of the Americas", Working paper 03-7 Institute for International Economics (2003) at http://www.iie.com/publications/wp/03-7.pdf (accessed 30 May 2013); David A. Gantz, "Labor Rights and Environmental Protection under NAFTA and Other U.S. Free Trade Agreements", *U. Miami Inter-Am. L. Rev.* 42 (2010–11), 237; OECD, 'International Investment Agreements: A Survey of Environmental, Labour and Anti-Corruption Issues' (2008) at http://www.oecd.org/corporate/mne/40471550.pdf (accessed 30 May 2013); Prislan and Zandvliet, *supra* note 19.

4.1 *The "No-Lowering Standards" Clauses*

Article 13.2 of the 2012 US BIT Model provides:

> The Parties recognize that it is inappropriate to encourage investment by weakening or reducing the protections afforded in domestic labor law. Accordingly, each Party shall ensure that it does not waive or otherwise derogate from or offer to waive or otherwise derogate from its labor laws where the waiver or derogation would be inconsistent with the labor rights referred to in subparagraphs (a) through (e) of paragraph 3, or fail to effectively enforce its labor laws through a sustained or recurring course of action or inaction, as an encouragement for the establishment, acquisition, expansion, or retention of an investment in its territory.[43]

Various components of this provision deserve examination and clarification, in relation to the treaty practice of other states, as to the nature and the object of state parties' commitments.

As to the nature of the commitment, it is worth noticing that Article 13.2 places upon states an obligation of result. If such a binding approach is followed by other states,[44] it remains that mainstream practice places an obligation of means upon states by providing that states "shall strive to ensure"[45] or rely on an "incentivising" language by providing that states "should not waive or otherwise derogate."[46]

Concerning the object of the commitment, several remarks can be formulated. First of all, these obligations refer generally to effective waiver or derogation or to the offer to waive or derogate, as illustrated by the above-mentioned Article 13.2. Secondly, besides targeting positive actions, some treaties such as the 2012 US BIT model also cover omissions by mentioning the failure to enforce the law.[47] Thirdly, while Article 13.2 of the 2012 US BIT model refers to a "sustained or recurring" conduct from the states, it can be noticed that this "consistency" in states' policy is not required by all IIA, with the consequence

43 US BIT model (2012), *supra* note 41.

44 See *e.g.* Art. 18.2.1, Peru-Korea FTA (2010) at http://www.customs.go.kr/kcshome/main/content/ContentView.do?contentId=CONTENT_ID_000002364&layoutMenuNo=23272 (accessed 30 May 2013).

45 See *e.g.* Art. 18.2.2, US-Chile FTA (2003) at http://www.ustr.gov/trade-agreements/free-trade-agreements/chile-fta (accessed 30 May 2013).

46 See *e.g.* Art. 101, Japan-Switzerland FTA (2009) at http://www.mofa.go.jp/policy/economy/fta/switzerland.html (accessed 30 May 2013).

47 See *e.g.* Art. 34.1, EFTA-Montenegro FTA (2011) at http://www.efta.int/legal-texts.aspx (accessed 30 May 2013).

that a single failure to enforce domestic labour law may be regarded as a violation of that type of treaty provision.[48] Fourthly, the state conducts covered by these treaty clauses are generally not limited *ratione personae* to those that address the investors of the other state party or state parties, but cover more broadly the conducts addressing all the investors being on the territory of the state party concerned, irrespective of their nationality. Fifthly, the state conducts that are generally targeted aim at attracting investors or maintaining their presence on the territory of the state party concerned.[49] Finally, these "no-lowering standards" provisions are not all encompassing as to the labour rules they cover, but refer to the domestic labour legislation[50] that relates to a set of international standards. Although there exist slight differences as to this "international benchmark," this set is generally linked to ILO norms or/and the 1998 ILO Declaration.[51] It is worth noticing that these treaty provisions have traditionally included acceptable conditions of work with respect to minimum wages, hours of work, and occupational safety and health (that is not listed in the 1998 ILO Declaration), but excluded the elimination of discrimination in relation to employment and occupation (that is listed in this Declaration).[52]

In light of the above, two main remarks can be formulated with respect to the labour issues raised in the energy sector. First of all, that type of treaty provisions covers most of the issues raised in this sector, *i.e.* acceptable conditions of work with respect of occupational safety and health and the prohibition of forced labour. As to the right to strike and as above-mentioned,[53] it is still unclear whether it is encompassed by the right of freedom of association. In this respect, the Labour cooperation agreement concluded between Canada and Peru settles this controversy inasmuch as it includes expressly the

48 See *e.g.* Art. 13, US BIT model (2004) at http://www.state.gov/documents/organization/117601.pdf (accessed 30 May 2013).

49 Some IIA obligations do not refer to the encouragement of investments, but to the effect of such measures on trade and investment between the parties, see *e.g.* Art. 17.3(a), US-Jordan FTA (2009) at http://www.ustr.gov/trade-agreements/free-trade-agreements/jordan-fta/final-text (accessed 30 May 2013).

50 As to federal states, such as the US, the domestic labour law referred to consists in the federal labour legislation, the states labour law being excluded from the scope of IIA, see *e.g.* Art. 13 US BIT model (2012), *supra* note 41.

51 ILO Declaration on fundamental principles and rights at work and its follow-up (1998), *supra* note 4.

52 By doing so, mainstream treaty practice reflects the traditional US practice. It is worth noticing that the last BIT model incorporates discrimination in respect of employment and occupation, see Art. 13.3.e US BIT model (2012), *supra* note 41.

53 See *supra* note 20.

protection of the right to organize and the right to strike.[54] Despite the fact that most of the labour issues raised in the energy sector appear to be *ratione materiae* covered by the IIA "no-lowering standards" provisions, such provisions will often be ineffective inasmuch as state conducts in this sector do not generally aim at attracting or maintaining the presence of foreign investors, but instead at the satisfaction of interests that relate (more or less) to other public interests, such as national security or national revenue.

4.2 *The "Adherence" Clauses*

Article 13.1 of the 2012 US BIT model provides: "The Parties reaffirm their respective obligations as members of the International Labour Organization ("ILO") and their commitments under the ILO Declaration on Fundamental Principles and Rights at Work and its Follow-Up."[55] That type of provision pursues an objective similar to the IIA clauses that provide for the commitment of state parties to ensure that their domestic labour legislation is consistent with internationally recognized standards.[56] Most IIA that contain similar clauses refer to the reaffirmation of state parties' obligations. However, some of them use a binding language relying on an obligation of means ("shall strive to ensure")[57] or an obligation of result ("shall ensure").[58] As to the object of these commitments, the "adherence" provisions refer usually to ILO state parties' obligations as well as to the principles enshrined in the 1998 ILO Declaration, which, as above-mentioned, are binding upon states irrespective of their ratification of the corresponding ILO conventions.

---

54 See Art 1.1, Canada-Peru Labour Cooperation Agreement (2012) at http://www.hrsdc.gc.ca/eng/labour/labour_agreements/cpalc/index.shtml (accessed 30 May 2013).

55 US BIT model (2012), *supra* note 41.

56 See *e.g.* Art. 16.1.2. US CAFTA-DR FTA: 'The parties affirm their full respect for their Constitutions. Recognizing the right of each Party to establish its own domestic labor standards, and to adopt or modify accordingly its labor laws, each Party shall strive to ensure that its laws provide for labor standards consistent with the internationally recognized labor rights set forth in Article 16.8 and shall strive to improve those standards in that light', US-CAFTA-DR FTA (2004) at http://www.ustr.gov/trade-agreements/free-trade-agreements/cafta-dr-dominican-republic-central-america-fta (accessed 30 May 2013).

57 See *e.g.* Art 17.1.2, US-Singapore FTA (2004) at http://www.ustr.gov/trade-agreements/free-trade-agreements/singapore-fta (accessed 30 May 2013).

58 See *e.g.* Art 17.2, US-Peru FTA (with respect to the ILO Declaration's Principles) (2006) at http://www.ustr.gov/trade-agreements/free-trade-agreements/peru-tpa/final-text (accessed 30 May 2013).

These "adherence" clauses appear to be relevant in the context of the discussion of the labour issues raised in the energy sector. First, they cover a broad range of labour standards, in particular the core standards. Second and most importantly, the respect of ILO obligations or commitments is not linked in any way to the encouragement of investment, but instead has a general teleological scope of application. As a result, the "adherence" clauses apply to state measures restricting labour rights for the sake of other public interests. The main limit of this type of provision to address the labour issues raised in the energy sector consists in the "sliding scale" that characterizes their normativity, from an inspirational language to the provision of an obligation of result. However, the consequences of such "relative normativity" are limited by the institutional arrangements provided in the new generation of IIA, in particular FTA.

Before focusing on these institutional arrangements, one can illustrate the usefulness of the "adherence" clauses in combination with these institutional arrangements by reporting the recent US submission 2011-01 against Bahrain, filed by the American federation of labour and Congress of industrial organizations with the Office of Trade and Labor affairs (OTLA) of the US Department of Labor's bureau of international Labor affairs. In its report,[59] the OTLA considers that trade unionists and, in particular, trade union leaders in Bahrain have been targeted for dismissal and, in some cases, prosecution, in part for their role in organizing and participating in the March 2011 general strike. Furthermore, it argues that the widespread dismissals after this strike reflected discrimination based in part on political opinions and activities. These events are regarded by the OTLA as a violation of Article 15.1.1 and 15.1.2. of the US-Bahrain FTA.[60] In light of these conclusions, the OTLA recom-

59 See Office of Trade and Labor affairs, Bureau of International Labor Affairs, US Department of Labor, 'Public report of review of U.S. Submission 2011-01 (Bahrain)' (2012) at http://www.dol.gov/ilab/programs/otla/20121220Bahrain.pdf (accessed 30 May 2013).

60 '1. The parties reaffirm their obligations as members of the International Labor Organization ("ILO") and their commitments under the ILO Declaration on Fundamental Principles and Rights at Work and its Follow-up (1998) ("ILO Declaration"). Each Party shall strive to ensure that such labor principles and the internationally recognized labor rights set forth in Article 15.7 are recognized and protected by its law. 2. Recognizing the right of each Party to establish its own domestic labor standards, and to adopt or modify accordingly its labor law, each Party shall strive to ensure that its laws provide for labor standards consistent with the internationally recognized labor rights set forth in Article 15.7 and shall strive to improve those standards in that light'. Para. 7 refers to 'the right of association; the right to organize and bargain collectively; a prohibition on the use of any form of forced or compulsory labor; labor protections for children and young people, including a minimum age for the employment of children and the prohibition and

mends "to the Secretary of Labor that the Government of the United States request Labor Consultations under Article 15.6.1[61] of the FTA to consult with the Government of Bahrain on the matters raised in this report."[62] Besides illustrating the potential of the "adherence" clauses, this case also exemplifies the role of the "institutional arrangements" clauses that are combined with the former type of clause and/or the "no-lowering standards" clause discussed earlier in the chapter.

4.3 *The "Institutional Arrangement" Clauses*

Article 13.4 of the 2012 US BIT Model provides:

> A Party may make a written request for consultations with the other Party regarding any matter arising under this Article. The other Party shall respond to a request for consultations within thirty days of receipt of such request. Thereafter, the Parties shall consult and endeavor to reach a mutually satisfactory resolution.

This provision illustrates the institutional "common denominator" of treaty practice inasmuch as they all provide for an inter-State consultation.[63] Beyond this "common-denominator," the treaty practice evidences many differences.

---

elimination of the worst forms of child labor; and acceptable conditions of work with respect to minimum wages, hours of work, and occupational safety and health', US-Bahrain FTA (2006) at http://www.ustr.gov/trade-agreements/free-trade-agreements/bahrain-fta (accessed 30 May 2013).

61 'A Party may request consultations with the other Party regarding any matter arising under this Chapter by delivering a written request to the other Party's contact point. Unless the Parties agree otherwise, consultations shall commence within 30 days after a Party delivers a request for consultations to the other Party's contact point designated pursuant to paragraph 2 of Art. 15.4.', ibid.

62 Office of Trade and Labor affairs, Bureau of international Labor Affairs, US Department of Labor, "Public report of review of U.S. Submission 2011–01 (Bahrain)" (2012), *supra* note 59, 40.

63 Private entities are largely excluded from the enforcement of treaty provisions. However, two mechanisms can be noticed that aims at 'giving voice' to them. First of all, some IIAs provide that state parties shall ensure that requests emanating from employers, employees or their representative are given due consideration by domestic authorities. Second, some IIAs entitle private entities to submit recommendations as to the alleged violations of their obligations by state parties, this recommendation having the potential to result in an inter-State consultation. For the first mechanism, see *e.g.* Art. 17.4, US-Peru FTA, *supra* note 58. For the second mechanism, see *e.g.* Art. 17.4.5, US-Singapore FTA, *supra* note 57 and the example of the U.S. Submission 2011-01 (Bahrain), *supra* note 59.

First of all, depending on the IIA concerned, this consultation can be relied on in situations where a dispute has already arisen,[64] or more preventively, for any matter as stated for instance in the Article 13.4 of the 2012 US BIT model. Secondly, this consultation can be conducted on an *ad hoc* basis, as illustrated (as well) by the above-mentioned article, or in an institutional setting. In the latter situation, in case of failure of the consultation, a permanent committee established to supervise the proper enforcement of the agreement and to review the relationship between the parties can be used to resolve the dispute.[65] Some IIA also provide for the competence of a dispute settlement panel, either as to cases where the committee cannot reach an agreement[66] or irrespective of the existence of such an institutional arrangement and a permanent committee.[67] The report of the dispute settlement panel can be non-binding[68] or binding upon the parties[69] depending on the IIA concerned. The recourse to arbitration is generally limited to "trade-related" disputes.[70] As to the output of these procedures, it is worth noticing that some IIA provide for a mechanism of "annual monetary assessment"[71] or "trade sanctions"[72] in case of the non-implementation of the report of the dispute settlement panel or of the agreement reached thereafter by the parties. As to the *ad hoc* consultations provided in the provisions similar to the above-mentioned Article 13.4 of the 2012 US BIT model, it is worth noticing that the IIA that contain them are ill equipped to constrain states to effectively comply with their labour provisions.

Obviously, these institutional mechanisms can play an important role to foster the protection and promotion of labour standards in the energy sector.

---

64 See *e.g.* Art. 13.1, US-Rwanda BIT at http://www.ustr.gov/sites/default/files/uploads/agreements/bit/asset_upload_file743_14523.pdf (accessed 30 May 2013).

65 See *e.g.* Art. 17.1(b) US-Jordan FTA, *supra* note 50. The institutionalization of the arrangement does not only aim at addressing existing and potential disputes, but also at improving the cooperation between states. In this respect, they establish Labor Cooperation and Capacity Building Mechanism, see *e.g.* 16.5, US-CAFTA-DR, *supra* note 57.

66 See *e.g.* Art. 17.1(b) US-Jordan FTA, *supra* note 49.

67 See *e.g.* Art. 6.4, 12 and 13, Belgo-Luxembourg Economic Union-Mauritius BIT at http://unctad.org/sections/dite/iia/docs/bits/BLEU-Mauritius-eng.pdf (accessed 30 May 2013).

68 See *e.g.* Art. 17.1(d), US-Jordan FTA, *supra* note 49.

69 See *e.g.* Art. 16.6.7, US-CAFTA-DR FTA, *supra* note 56.

70 See *e.g.* Art. 16.6.7, US-CAFTA-DR FTA, *supra* note 56. Some IIAs provide that all labor provisions can be subjected to arbitration, see *e.g.* Art. 17.7.6, US-Jordan FTA, *supra* note 49.

71 The assessment is transferred to a fund that aims at improving labour conditions in the state complained against, see *e.g.* Art. 20.17, US-CAFTA-DR FTA, *supra* note 56.

72 See Art. 17.2(a), US-Jordan FTA, *supra* note 49.

However, this effect will be proportional to the "teeth" the concerned IIA is equipped with. It goes without saying that the few IIA that give jurisdiction to a dispute settlement panel as to any dispute regarding any of their labour provisions are very likely to be the most effective. Through a different path, the institutional mechanisms aiming at the prevention of treaty violations and at the strengthening of the inter-State cooperation for the sake of labour standards are also likely to greatly contribute to the improvement of labour conditions in the energy sector.

4.4 *The "CSR" Clauses*

Among all the treaty provisions that can play a role to foster labour standards in the energy sector, the CSR clauses are the most peculiar for two main reasons. First of all, although they formally "target" state parties, they eventually aim at impacting on the respect of labour rights (among other rights) by corporations, *i.e.* multinational corporations. Second of all, they are provided in a very limited number of IIA. In a few of those treaties, the intention of the parties to encourage corporate social responsibility is provided in the Preamble. For instance, in the Preamble of EFTA-Hong Kong FTA the parties acknowledge "the importance of good governance and corporate social responsibility for sustainable development, and affirm their aim to encourage enterprises to take into account internationally recognized guidelines and principles where appropriate."[73] In most of the treaties concerned, the intention of the parties is expressed in the treaty body. Most provisions[74] are similar to Article 9.17 of the Canada-Panama FTA, which provides:

> Each Party should encourage enterprises operating within its territory or subject to its jurisdiction to voluntarily incorporate internationally recognized standards of corporate social responsibility in their internal policies, such as those statements of principle that have been endorsed or are supported by the Parties. These principles address issues such as labour, the environment, human rights, community relations and anti-corruption.

73 See preamble, EFTA states – Hong Kong FTA (2011) at http://www.efta.int/free-trade/free-trade-agreements/hong-kong.aspx (accessed 30 May 2013).

74 The draft Norway BIT model for instance uses another formula by providing that 'the parties agree to encourage investors to conduct their investment activities in compliance with the OECD Guidelines for Multinational Enterprises and to participate in the United Nations Global Compact', see Art. 32, draft Norway BIT model at http://www.italaw.com/sites/default/files/archive/ita1031.pdf (accessed 30 May 2013).

Beyond the scarcity of these CSR provisions in existing IIA, their effect is limited by the double limitation that characterises them. Indeed, they only require from state parties that they *encourage* corporations to *voluntarily* incorporate international standards of CSR, in particular with respect to labour principles. Beyond their normative features, the added-value of these provisions may be put into question with respect to the multinational corporations operating in the energy sector, inasmuch as many of them are already equipped with CSR codes of conduct.[75] That being said, *soft law* initiatives contribute to the hardening of CSR as pointed out by John Ruggie[76] and will likely contribute to make these companies more aware of their societal responsibilities especially in the energy sector.

5 Conclusion

This chapter unravels and analyses the labour issues that exist in the energy sector, *i.e.* the oil and gas sector, and examines how international investment law can be used to address these issues. From the enquiries here conducted, three main conclusions can be drawn.

As to the labour issues, it appears that there is a discrepancy between the negative perception of the public as to the working conditions in this sector and the rather positive day-to-day workers' experience. It remains that there are indeed labour issues that are raised in the energy sector, especially related to occupational safety, restrictions/prohibitions of the right to strike and forced labour.

The second conclusion concerns the nature of the conflicts of interests that underlie these issues. Contrary to investment arbitration that is characterized by the public/private conflict of interests, labour issues appear to result from conflicts of interests having a tripartite dimension inasmuch as they involve the private interest of foreign investors, the public interest of workers and other states' public interest, *e.g.* national security. Depending on their exact drafting, the provisions characteristic of the new generation of IIA and in particular FTA have the potential to address these labour issues and their underlying conflict of interests, especially those existing within the "box" of the public interest.

75 See *e.g.* "Corporate Social Responsibility in Total's Business Model" (2009), *supra* note 37.

76 See Report of the Special Representative of the Secretary-General on the issue of human rights and transnational corporations and other business enterprises (John Ruggie) UN Doc. A/HRC/4/35 (2007), para. 61 at http://www2.ohchr.org/english/bodies/chr/special/sp_reportshrc_4th.htm (accessed 30 May 2013).

Last but not least, it is worth noticing that this tripartite understanding of the conflicts of interests is not merely relevant to discuss the labour issues in the energy sector. Indeed, this "*grille de lecture*" is applicable both to other sectors beyond the energy sector and to other "humanitarian" issues beyond labour issues. In other words, all FDI operations raise tripartite conflicts of interests, in particular within the public interest's "box," where *e.g.* the promotion/protection of human rights and of the environment, the protection of national security and the promotion of economic development can all clash the one with the other. In this context, the tripartite paradigm sketched in this chapter can assist to shed some light on the complexities of FDI operations and to bring them out of the unintelligibility where the academic focus on investment arbitration and the fragmentation narrative[77] ground them.

77 See Yannick Radi, "The 'Human Nature' of International Investment Law", *supra* note 3.

CHAPTER 9

Foreign Investment in the Energy Sector and Public Health

Valentina Vadi

Science talks about very simple things, and asks hard questions about them. As soon as things become too complex, science can't deal with them. The reason why physics can achieve such depth is that it restricts itself to extremely simple things, abstracted from the complexity of the world. As soon as an atom gets too complicated, maybe helium, they hand it over to chemists. When problems become too complicated for chemists, they hand it over to biologists. Biologists often hand it over to the sociologists, and they hand it over to the historians, and so on.... So the actual sciences tell us virtually nothing about human affairs.[1]

1 Introduction

Energy law and policy are undergoing major challenges and changes.[2] As science and technology advance, policy makers are confronted with two competing needs: 1) attracting capital to develop energy resources; and 2) addressing complex issues relating to the impact that energy resources may have on climate change, environmental protection, sustainability and public health among others. Can constant regulatory changes create an atmosphere of insecurity deterring investment flows? How can states promote foreign direct investment in the energy sector without jeopardizing their authority to protect fundamental goals such as public health? Will development policies ultimately trump the rights or desires of the local polity? How will the tension

† The author wishes to thank Gustavo Arosemena, Eric De Brabandere, Tarcisio Gazzini and Tamara Lewis for their comments on an earlier draft. The usual disclaimer applies.

1 Noam Chomsky quoted in Lawrence Krauss and Sean M. Carroll, "Science in the Dock", *Science and Technology News*, 1 March 2006, available at http://www.chomsky.info/debates/20060301.htm (accessed 6 September 2012).

2 For a general overview, see *e.g.* Fred Bosselman et al., *Energy, Economics and the Environment: Cases and Materials* (New York: Foundation Press 2006), 1.

 | DOI 10.1163/9789004244719_011

be resolved between energy needs and public policy goals before investment arbitral tribunals?

This chapter provides an overview of some of the legal issues raised by foreign investment in the energy sector in relation to public health. *First*, the discussion clarifies the linkage between energy and public health. *Second*, the chapter analizes a case study epitomizing the clash of values between the private interests of foreign companies and the public policy objectives of the host state. Reference will be made to the pending arbitration *Vattenfall v. Germany* concerning the nuclear phase-out recently adopted by Germany. *Third*, the conflicting conceptualizations of international investment law and arbitration will be scrutinized and critically assessed. *Fourth*, the chapter examines the standards of review that should be adopted by arbitral tribunals when reviewing regulatory measures affecting public health. Finally the chapter concludes that arbitrators should not question the legitimate power of states to regulate in the public interest, but should review the procedural appropriateness, good faith and reasonableness of the adopted measures.

2 Energy and Public Health: Making the Connection

Defined as "the allocation of rights and duties concerning the exploitation of all energy resources between individuals, between individuals and governments [...] and between states [and states],"[3] energy law constitutes an example of multilevel governance. Nowadays, the regulation of energy resources takes place at national, regional and international levels. While states retain much regulatory autonomy in the energy sector, state regulation must comply with state obligations under regional and international law.

In parallel, public health law has been defined as "the study of the legal powers and duties of the state [...] to ensure the conditions for people to be healthy [...], and of the limitations on the power of the state to constrain for the common good the autonomy, privacy, liberty, proprietary, and other legally protected interests of individuals."[4] The main objective of public health law is "to pursue the highest possible level of physical and mental health in the population, consistent with the values of social justice."[5]

---

3 Adrian J. Bradbrook, "Energy Law as an Academic Discipline", J. Energy & Natural Resources L. 14 (1996), 194.

4 Lawrence O. Gostin, *Public Health Law, Power, Duty, Restraint* (revised and expanded 2nd ed.), (Berkeley: University of California Press, 2008), 4.

5 Ibid.

Crucially, energy law and public health law sit at the epicentre of a clash of values between economic (private) interests and other (public) values such as public health.[6] Authors have noted that "despite their large public health implications, most energy policies and programs' are considered 'as components of overall economic development, without explicit assessment of their health benefits or hazards.'"[7] Closer integration of public health considerations in other legal realms has emerged only in the past decades.[8]

Energy and public health relate to each other in many ways. In a preliminary way, there is a positive synergy between access to energy services and public health. Access to energy services has been one of the major factors lifting the standard of development and public health in industrialized countries and constitutes a key element for increasing living standards all around the world.[9] As a UN Report highlighted, "Energy services are a crucial input to the primary development challenge of providing adequate food, shelter, [...] water, sanitation, medical care, schooling and access to information."[10] Therefore energy is one vital dimension of development.[11] Modern energy services enhance the delivery of key social services. For instance, electricity makes it possible to refrigerate vaccines, use medical equipment and provide lighting after sunset.[12] Analogously, energy is used for providing clean and safe water to households and communities.[13] Again, with electric-based refrigeration, food supply becomes safer, reducing illnesses related to poorly conserved raw food.[14]

---

6 Bosselman et al., *supra* note 2, 5.

7 Majid Ezzati et al., "Energy Management and Global Health", *Annu. Rev. Environ. Resour.* 29 (2004), 383.

8 See Lawrence O. Gostin, "Health of the People: the Highest Law?", *Journal of Law, Medicine & Ethics* (2004), 509 (highlighting that public health law is undergoing a renaissance); Allyn L. Taylor, "Global Governance, International Health Law and WHO: Looking towards the Future", *Bulletin of the World Health Organization* 80 (2002) 975, at 976.

9 Adrian J. Bradbrook and Judith G. Gardam, "Placing Access to Energy Services within a Human Rights Framework", *Human Rights Quarterly* 28 (2006), 390 (highlighting that 'The provision of such services many decades ago was the major factor lifting the standard of development in developed countries and is a key ingredient to providing a sustainable way of living for all the world's population'). As the authors aptly put it, 'without access to energy services, people are destined to live in poverty'. Ibid.

10 Amulya K. Reddy, "Energy and Social Issues", in United Nations Development Programme, *World Energy Assessment Report -Energy and the Challenge for Sustainability* (UNDP: New York 2000), 44.

11 Ibid.

12 Ibid.

13 Ibid.

14 Michael T. Osterholm and Nicholas S. Kelley, "Energy and the Public's Health: Making the Connection", *Public Health Reports* 124 (2009), 21.

Authors have argued that the achievement of the highest attainable standard of physical and mental health – as required by Article 12 of the International Covenant on Economic, Social and Cultural Rights[15] – "is impossible without access to sustainable energy services."[16] Analogously, the African Commission on Human and Peoples' Rights held that the failure of the Democratic Republic of the Congo to supply basic services, including safe drinking water and electricity amounted to a violation of the right to health under Article 16 of the African Charter of Human and Peoples' Rights.[17] Other authors have even argued that energy access might be recognized as a human right in the future.[18] More generally, access to energy services is linked to poverty eradication and the attainment of other socio-economic rights.[19]

On the other hand, the development of energy resources can negatively affect public health in a variety of ways. For instance, the residue of underground mining for locating coal may pollute streams rendering the water non-potable. Similarly, coal combustion generates four main sources of pollution: sulphur oxide, nitrogen oxide, particulate matters and carbon dioxide. While the first three sources of pollution *inter alia* cause human health problems or health hazards, carbon dioxide causes the greenhouse effect, thus contributing to global warming.[20] In addition, there is evidence that global warming will determine drought, unhealthy conditions and famine thus affecting public health.[21] Finally, as the Deepwater Horizon oil spill demonstrates,

15 International Covenant on Economic, Social and Cultural Rights, adopted 19 December 1966, G.A. Res. 2200 (XXI), U.N. GAOR, 21st Sess., Supp. No. 16, U.N. Doc A/6316 (1966) 993 UNTS 3 (entered into force 3 January 1976).

16 Bradbrook and Gardam, *supra* note 9, 405.

17 African Commission Human and Peoples' Rights, *Free Legal Assistance Group and Others v. Zaire*, Communication Nos. 25/89, 47/90, 56/91, 100/93 (1995), para. 47, at http://www1.umn.edu/humanrts/africa/comcases/25-89_47-90_56-91_100-93.html (accessed 7 September 2012).

18 Stephen R. Tully, "The Contribution of Human Rights to Universal Energy Access", *North Western University Journal of International Human Rights* 4 (2005–6) 518.

19 Adrian J. Bradbrook, Judith G. Gardam and Monique Cormier, "A Human Dimension to the Energy Debate: Access to Modern Energy Services", J. of Energy & Natural Resources L. 26 (2008), 552.

20 Joseph P. Tomain and Richard D. Cudahy, *Energy Law in a Nutshell* (St. Paul: West 2004), 240–241.

21 See *e.g.* Howard Frumkin et al., "Climate Change: The Public Health Response", American J. of Public Health 98 (2008), 435–445; Jonathan A. Patz et al., "The Effects of Changing Weather on Public Health", Annu. Rev. Public Health 21 (2000), 271–307.

the exploration and production of oil and gas is technically challenging and may have negative environmental health effects.[22]

Likewise, nuclear energy raises public health concerns with regard to uranium mining[23] and reactor safety, as well as transport and safety of nuclear waste.[24] Harvard and MIT scholars have stressed that "modern reactor designs can achieve a very low risk of serious accidents,"[25] but admitted that "[they] do not believe there is a nuclear plant design that is totally risk free."[26] Furthermore, as "the potential for large scale damage to human health and the environment is vastly greater than for fossil fuel systems,"[27] nuclear technology is seen as "inherently hazardous."[28] In other words, "The risk of a nuclear catastrophe is low... but it exists over a very long period of time – decades for operations, centuries or more for waste. Its impact on well-being is largely unknown.[29] Furthermore, because "nuclear power development involves a unique combination of risk remoteness yet potentially catastrophic damages,"[30] should an accident occur, no adequate insurance coverage would fully compensate an injured public.[31]

Because of perceived safety concerns, nuclear energy is usually governed by extensive regulation in those jurisdictions, which exploit this type of resource.[32] Specific regulations generally address the licensing requirements of nuclear installations and the transportation, decommissioning and disposal of radio-

---

22 See Bernard D. Goldstein et al., "The Gulf Oil Spill", New England J. Medicine 364 (2011), 1334–1348 (stressing that 'the full magnitude of the environmental, economic, and human health effects of this major disaster remain unknown.' Ibid. at 1334) See also David B. Spence, "Corporate Social Responsibility in the Oil and Gas Industry: The Importance of Reputational Risk", *Chi.-Kent L. Rev.* 86 (2011), 59.

23 On the public health implications of uranium mining, see International Atomic Energy Agency, *Environmental Contamination from Uranium Production Facilities and Their Remediation* (Vienna: IAEA, 2005), p. 4 ff.

24 Massachusetts Institute of Technology, *The Future of Nuclear Power* (Boston: MIT, 2003), 2.

25 Ibid., ix.

26 Ibid., 9.

27 John G. Palfrey, "Energy and the Environment: The Special Case of Nuclear Power", *Columbia L. Rev.* 74 (1974), 1382 (internal citation omitted).

28 Ibid., 1395.

29 Damian Carrington," Unsure about Nuclear Power? Here are the Five Questions you must Answer to Decide", *The Guardian*, 21 April 2011.

30 Ibid., 1399.

31 Marco Morosini, "Nous ne vivons pas dans le meilleur de mondes (technologiques)", *Le Monde*, 6 April 2011, at http://www.lemonde.fr/idees/article/2011/04/06/nous-ne-vivons-pas-dans-le-meilleur-des-mondes-technologiques_1503446_3232.html (accessed 10 September 2012).

32 Bradbrook, *supra* note 3, 196.

active waste.[33] In the aftermath of the Chernobyl incident,[34] two international treaties were ratified to alert other countries of potential radiation problems.[35] The Convention on Nuclear Safety[36] was also adopted in 1994 containing the world's first binding international standards concerning the siting, design, construction and operation of land-based nuclear power plants. Other treaties were subsequently amended and/or adopted.[37] In addition, despite their non-binding character, the International Atomic Energy Agency (IAEA) health and safety standards have contributed significantly to control the risks of nuclear energy.[38] It is uncontroversial that any evaluation as to whether to proceed with the development of nuclear energy must address a number of issues, including security and human health and safety.[39]

---

33 Ibid., 195–6.

34 In 1986, an explosion at the Chernobyl nuclear power plant determined the release of large amounts of radiation in the atmosphere. On the health effects of the accident, see United Nations Scientific Committee on the Effects of Atomic Radiation (UNSCEAR), *Exposures and Effects of the Chernobyl Accident* (2000), at http://www.unscear.org/docs/reports/2000/Volume%20II_Effects/AnnexJ_pages%20451-566.pdf (accessed 7 September 2012); UNSCEAR, *Possible Genetic Effects from the Chernobyl Accidents* (2001), at http://www.unscear.org/docs/chernobylherd.pdf (accessed 7 September 2012); UNSCEAR, *Sources and Effects of Ionizing Radiation* (2008), at http://www.unscear.org/docs/reports/2008/11-80076_Report_2008_Annex_D.pdf (accessed 7 September 2012). The WHO and other UN agencies have also been involved in the assessment and mitigation of the impact of the Chernobyl accident on health through a number of projects. See U.N. General Assembly, *Optimizing the International Effort to Study, Mitigate and Minimize the Consequences of the Chernobyl Disaster*, Report of the Secretary General, 1 September 2010, A/65/341, paras. 25-40 at http://www.scribd.com/doc/98178356/Optimizing-the-international-effort-to-study-mitigate-and-minimize-the-consequences-of-the-Chernobyl-disaster (accessed 17 September 2012).

35 Convention on Early Notification of a Nuclear Accident, entered into force 27 October 1986, 25 ILM 1370; Convention on Assistance in the Case of a Nuclear Accident or Radiological Emergency, entered into force 26 February 1987, 25 ILM 1377.

36 Convention on Nuclear Safety, (1994) 33 ILM 1514. For commentary, see Menno Kamminga, 'The IAEA Convention on Nuclear Safety', ICLQ 44 (1995), 872.

37 See Consolidated Text of the Vienna Convention on Civil Liability for Nuclear Damage of 21 May 1968 as Amended by the Protocol on Civil Liability for Nuclear Damage (Vienna) of 12 September 1997, 36 ILM (1997) 1462; Convention on Supplementary Compensation for Nuclear Damage, 12 September 1997, 36 ILM 1473 (1997); Joint Convention on the Safety of Spent Fuel and Radioactive Waste Management, 36 ILM (1997) 1436, in force 18 June 2001.

38 Patricia Birnie et al., *International Law & the Environment* (3rd ed.) (Oxford: Oxford Universty Press, 2009), 496.

39 See *e.g.* Joseph P. Tomain, "Nuclear Futures", *Duke Environmental Law and Policy F.* 15 (2005), 237 (deeming that '[T]he nuclear future depends not only on private investment considerations of the sort that individual investors make all of the time. The nuclear

3 A Case Study: Vattenfall v. Germany

In May 2012, the Swedish energy company Vattenfall filed an investor state arbitration against Germany at the International Centre for the Settlement of Investment Disputes (ICSID)[40] regarding the government's decision to phase out nuclear energy by 2022.[41] Reportedly the claim relates to the phase-out in early 2012 of two of the company's nuclear plants, both located near Hamburg. The media reported that, while the government had agreed to extend the life of these nuclear power stations in 2010, in the aftermath of the Fukushima events,[42] the two plants were shut down permanently.[43] According to the press, Vattenfall is claiming that Germany's policy reversal has breached the country's legal obligations under the Energy Charter Treaty (hereinafter ECT)[44] and is asking for over 700 Million euros.[45]

In parallel, two German companies have brought complaints to the Federal Constitutional Court, alleging that the lack of compensation for the nuclear phase-out required by the German *Atomic Energy Act* is inconsistent with

---

future also depends on...the valuation of imponderables as well as uncertainties affecting the public at large.').

40 Convention on the Settlement of Investment Disputes Between States and Nationals of Other States (the ICSID Convention) Washington, 18 March 1965, entered into force on 14 October 1966, 575 UNTS 159.

41 *Vattenfall AB and others v. Federal Republic of Germany*, ICSID Case No. ARB/12/12, registered on 31 May 2012.

42 The Fukushima nuclear disaster indicates a series of nuclear meltdowns and releases of radioactive materials at the Fukushima I Nuclear Power Plant, following the earthquake and tsunami on 11 March 2011. The severity of the nuclear accident is provisionally rated 7 on the International Nuclear Event Scale (INES). This scale runs from 0, indicating an abnormal situation with no safety consequences, to 7, indicating an accident causing widespread health and environmental effects. See the International Nuclear and Radiological Event Scale, at http://www.iaea.org/Publications/Factsheets/English/ines.pdf (accessed 10 September 2012). Prior to Fukushima, the Chernobyl disaster was the only level 7 accident on record, while the Three Mile Island accident was a level 5 accident. 'Japan: Nuclear Crisis Rose to Chernobyl Level', *BBC News*, 12 April 2011.

43 'Nuclear Phase-Out Faces Billion-Euro Lawsuit', *Spiegel Online*, 11 February 2011, at http://www.spiegel.de/international/germany/vattenfall-vs-germany-nuclear-phase-out-faces-billion-euro-lawsuit-a-795466.html (accessed 10 September 2012).

44 The Energy Charter Treaty was signed in 1994 and entered into force in 1998. 34 ILM. 360, 385 (1995) [hereinafter ECT].

45 'Germany is Sued at ICSID by Swedish Energy Company in Bid for Compensation for Losses Arising out of Nuclear Phase Out', *Investment Arbitration Reporter*, 1 June 2012.

German constitutional law.[46] There is a "historical precedent" that bears similarities to the German case. In Sweden, a similar case arose when – in the aftermath of the Chernobyl accident – the Swedish Parliament enacted the 1997 Act on Phasing-Out Nuclear Power, empowering the Swedish government to close nuclear reactors.[47] Unlike the German measure, the Swedish regulation provided for compensation; nonetheless one affected company challenged the legality of the measure under Article 13 of the ECT, EC law and the European Convention for the Protection of Human Rights.[48] Although the Swedish Supreme Court rejected the claims, an agreement was reportedly reached among the parties containing provisions for compensation.[49]

As the arbitration filed by Vattenfall is still in an early phase, it is not possible to predict how this case will be decided or whether it will be settled. More generally, the mentioned case epitomizes the tension between investor rights and public welfare objectives and raises a number of questions including the preliminary question as to whether this and similar arbitrations may have a chilling effect on policy makers, preventing them from adopting regulatory measures for the public good.[50] More substantively, other relevant questions arise. Does the phase out of nuclear energy constitute an indirect expropriation under Article 13 of the ECT? Does the reversal of previous nuclear policy amount to a violation of the fair and equitable treatment under Article 10 of the ECT? Should an indemnity be paid to companies, which invested in the nuclear energy sector? Can damages for future lost profits be claimed? Did Vattenfall have a legitimate expectation that its power plants would not be closed in the near future? Are the regulatory measures adopted by Germany unreasonable and/or discriminatory? What standards of review should arbitral tribunals adopt when reviewing regulatory measures allegedly aimed at protecting public health? Are arbitrators *expropriating* fundamental aspects of energy-related public health governance? Can public and private interests be accommodated adequately in investor-state arbitration?

---

46 Nathalie Bernasconi-Osterwalder and Rea Tamara Hoffmann, '"The German Nuclear Phase-Out Put to the Test in International Investment Arbitration?", June 2012, pp. 5–6, at http://www.s2bnetwork.org/fileadmin/dateien/downloads/Vattenfall-ICSID-case_v2.pdf (accessed 10 September 2012).

47 For details of the dispute, see Tore Wiven-Nilsson, "Phasing-Out of Nuclear Power in Sweden", J. Energy Nat. Resources L 24 (2006) 355.

48 Ibid., 355.

49 Ibid., 359.

50 Bernasconi-Osterwalder and Hoffmann, *supra* note 46, at p. 3.

While it is not possible to answer all of the above-mentioned questions in the context of this short chapter, an analysis of the interplay between substantive investment standards and public health related measures is available elsewhere.[51] The next sections will focus on the standards of review that arbitral tribunals have adopted with regard to policy-related regulatory measures. The concept of standards of review, which can be defined as the degree of deference that an adjudicator should grant to decision makers, is arguably far less developed and consistent in investment law and arbitration than other areas of international law, particularly international trade law.[52] In the clash between investment protection and the pursuit of public interest objectives by the host state, the standard of review plays a fundamental role because the degree of deference given by arbitral tribunals in reviewing a given decision of the relevant authorities influences the outcome of the proceedings.

4 Conflicting Conceptualizations of International Investment Arbitration

Before illustrating the standards of review that arbitral tribunals have adopted with regard to policy-related regulatory measures (in section 5), this section highlights the conflicting conceptualizations of international investment arbitration. In fact, depending on the selected conceptualization of international investment arbitration, the standards of review may vary, thus potentially affecting the outcome of policy-related investment disputes, including those relating to energy and public health. This focus on investor-state arbitration is also due to the fact that the ECT provides for such dispute settlement mechanism.

By signing the ECT, states grant to foreign investors certain substantive and procedural rights.[53] Substantive provisions cover matters such as prohi-

---

51 See generally Valentina Vadi, *Public Health in International Investment Law and Arbitration* (London: Routledge, 2012), chapter 4. See also George K. Foster, "Managing Expropriation Risks in the Energy Sector: Steps for Foreign Investors to Minimise their Exposure and Maximise Prospects for Recovery when Takings Occur", J. Energy & Natural Resources L. 23 (2005), 36.

52 See generally Stephan W. Schill, "Deference in Investment Treaty Arbitration: Re-conceptualizing the Standard of Review through Comparative Public Law", SIEL Working Paper No. 33/2012, 28 June 2012.

53 For a general overview, see *e.g.* Edna Sussman, "The Energy Charter Treaty's Investor Protection Provisions: Potential to Foster Solutions to Global Warming and Promote Sustainable Development", ILSA J. of Int'l & Comp. L. 14 (2008), 391–404.

bition against unlawful expropriation,[54] constant protection and security,[55] fair and equitable treatment,[56] non-discrimination[57] and so on and so forth. Article 10(1) of the ECT in fine states that "[e]ach Contracting Party shall observe any obligation it has entered into with an investor or an investment of an investor of any other Contracting Party." However, Article 24(2) of the ECT, entitled Exceptions, states that "The provisions of this Treaty [...] shall not preclude any contracting Party from adopting or enforcing any measure necessary to protect human, animal, or plant life or health [...]." Article 19 of the ECT also refers to the precautionary principle.[58]

The ECT grants aggrieved foreign investors access to investor-state arbitration and the possibility to obtain monetary compensation from the host state for any breach of their rights under the treaty.[59] Investor-state arbitration is a powerful mechanism for reviewing the exercise of public authority by the host state.

Given its hybrid features, investment treaty arbitration has been analogized to different legal systems.[60] *First*, it has been argued that access to investor-state arbitration shares many characteristics of the direct right of action before human rights courts.[61] However, arbitral tribunals do not only constitute an additional forum with respect to state courts, but also an alternative to the same. Thus, not only can foreign investors seek another decision

54 Article 13 ECT.

55 Article 10 ECT.

56 Article 10 ECT.

57 Ibid.

58 Article 19 ECT ('In its policies and actions each Contracting Party shall strive to take precautionary measures to prevent or minimize environmental degradation').

59 Article 26.3(a) ECT ('Subject only to subparagraphs (b) and (c), each Contracting Party hereby gives its unconditional consent to the submission of a dispute to international arbitration or conciliation in accordance with the provisions of this Article'). See also the Chapter by Eric De Brabandere in this volume.

60 See Valentina Vadi, "Critical Comparisons: The Role of Comparative Law in Investment Treaty Arbitration", *Denver Journal of International Law & Policy* 39 (2010), 67–100; Anthea Roberts, "Clash of Paradigms: Actors and Analogies Shaping the Investment Treaty System", *American Journal of International Law* 107 (2013), 45.

61 See Genevieve Burdeau, "Nouvelles perspectives pour l'arbitrage dans le contentieux economique intéressant l'Etat", *Revue de l'Arbitrage* 1 (1995), 16; Moshe Hirsch, "Investment Tribunals and Human Rights: Divergent Paths", in Pierre-Marie Dupuy et al. (ed.), *Human Rights in International Investment Law and Arbitration* (Oxford: Oxford University Press, 2008), 97–117; Clara Reiner and Christoph Schreuer, "Human Rights and International Investment Arbitration", Pierre-Marie Dupuy et al. (ed.), *Human Rights in International Investment Law and Arbitration* (Oxford: Oxford University Press, 2008), 82–96.

after an eventual recourse to the national courts, but also they are not required to exhaust local remedies prior to pursuing an international legal claim.

Second, arbitral tribunals have been analogized to the World Trade Organization (WTO) panels and the Appellate Body.[62] On the one hand, arbitral tribunals and WTO dispute settlement panels essentially do share the same functions by settling international disputes in accordance with international economic law and ensuring the proper administration of justice.[63] Like WTO panels and the Appellate Body, arbitral tribunals are asked to strike a balance between economic and non-economic concerns. In parallel, certain international trade treaties present an articulated regime that the investment treaties presuppose.[64] For instance, the TRIMS Agreement governs trade related investment measures.[65] Other authors support such an approach, as it would impede the dilution of multilateral norms while providing predictability.[66] However, while only states can file claims before the WTO panels and the Appellate Body, investor-state arbitration can be pursued by foreign investors directly without any intervention of the home state. Furthermore, arbitral tribunals can authorize damages, while remedies at the WTO only have prospective character and involve states only.

Third, given the fact that arbitrators have a comprehensive jurisdiction over what are essentially regulatory disputes, such review has been compared to a sort of administrative review.[67] Authors postulate the existence of a "'global administrative space' – a space in which the strict dichotomy between domes-

62 See generally Jurgen Kurtz, "The Use and Abuse of WTO Law in Investor-State Arbitration: Competition and Its Discontents", EJIL 20 (2009), 749; Todd Weiler (ed.), *Intersections: Dissemblance or Convergence between International Trade and Investment Law*, 3 *TDM Special Issue* (2011).

63 Chester Brown, "The Use of Precedents of Other International Courts and Tribunals in Investment Treaty Arbitration", *TDM* 5 (2008), 1–4.

64 Christina Pfaff, "Alternative Approaches to Foreign Investment Protection", *TDM* 3 (2006), 1–16.

65 Agreement on Trade-Related Investment Measures (TRIMS Agreement), 15 April 1994, Marrakesh Agreement Establishing the World Trade Organization, Annex 1A, 1868 UNTS 186.

66 Locknie Hsu, "Applicability of WTO Law in Regional Trade Agreements: Identifying the Links", in Lorand Bartels and Federico Ortino (eds.), *Regional Trade Agreements and the WTO Legal System*. (Oxford: Oxford University Press, 2006), 551.

67 Gus Van Harten and Martin Loughlin, "Investment Treaty Arbitration as a Species of Global Administrative Law", EJIL 17 (2006), 121; Gus Van Harten, *Investment Treaty Arbitration and Public Law* (Oxford: Oxford University Press, 2007); Santiago Montt, *State Liability in Investment Treaty Arbitration: Global Constitutional Law and Administrative Law in the BIT Generation* (Oxford: Hart Publishing, 2009); David Schneiderman,

tic and international has been largely broken down, where administrative functions are performed in often complex interplays between [...] institutions on different levels [...]".[68] Under this theoretical framework, investor-state arbitration has been conceptualized as a global administrative law (GAL) creature,[69] which impels states to conform to GAL principles and to adopt principles of good governance.[70] Van Harten and Loughlin claim that investment arbitration can be analogized to domestic administrative review[71] since investment disputes arise from the exercise of public authority by the state and arbitral tribunals are given the power to review and control such an exercise of public authority.[72] While arbitration structurally constitutes a private model of adjudication, investment treaty arbitration can be viewed as public law adjudication,[73] as it encompasses the full panoply of the state's regulatory relations with foreign investors. Adjudication over a state's *acta jure imperii* implies a significant departure from the conventional use of international arbitration in the commercial sphere.[74] Arbitral awards ultimately shape the relationship between state, on the one hand, and private individuals on the other.[75] Arbitrators determine matters such as the legality of governmental activity, the degree to which individuals should be protected from regulation and the appropriate role of the state.[76]

Fourth, because of the procedural rules, which govern it, investor-state arbitration has been analogized to commercial arbitration. The parties and/or an

Constitutionalizing Economic Globalization: Investment Rules and Democracy's Premise (Oxford: Oxford University Press, 2008).

68 Nico Krisch and Benedict Kingsbury, "Introduction: Global Governance and Global Administrative Law in the International Legal Order", EJIL 17 (2006), 1.

69 Van Harten and Loughlin, *supra* note 67, 121.

70 For a critical assessment of this theory, see Carol Harlow, '"Global Administrative Law: The Quest for Principles and Values", EJIL 17 (2006), 187.

71 Van Harten and Loughlin, *supra* note 67, 121–150.

72 Ibid., 121 and 123.

73 Gus Van Harten, "The Public-Private Distinction in the International Arbitration of Individual Claims Against the State", ICLQ 56 (2007), 372.

74 Traditionally, public international law has distinguished the conduct of a state between *acta jure imperii* and *acta jure gestionis*, with regard to its public or private nature. See Zachary Douglas, "The Hybrid Foundations of Investment Treaty Arbitration", BYIL 74 (2003), 221–222.

75 Van Harten, *supra* note 67, at 70; Barnali Choudhuri, "Recapturing Public Power: Is Investment Arbitration's Engagement of the Public Interest Contributing to Democratic Deficit?", *Vanderbilt Journal of Transnational Law* 41 (2008), 775–1042.

76 Muthucumaraswamy Sornarajah, "The Clash of Globalizations and the International Law on Foreign Investment", *Canadian Foreign Policy* 12 (2003), 17.

appointing institution select arbitrators, and the hearings are held *in camera*. However, the distinction between investment treaty arbitration and international commercial arbitration is clear[77] – while international arbitration generally involves private parties and concerns disputes of a commercial nature, investment treaty arbitration involves states and private actors. This "diagonal" dispute settlement mechanism is a major novelty in international law since international disputes have traditionally involved states only.

Finally, arbitral tribunals have been analogized to other public international law tribunals. Compelling arguments stand in favour of assimilating arbitrators to international judges. From a historical perspective, adjudication traces its roots to arbitration. From a functional perspective, as Van Harten rightly puts it: "[judges and arbitrators] are differentiated not by the character of their authority but by the status of their office. Both exercise the ultimate decision–making authority of the juridical sovereign in public law."[78] Like judges, arbitrators are asked to safeguard vital community interests as well as to settle disputes in conformity with "principles of justice and international law."[79] As Crawford puts it, "[i]nvestment law, ... is about the way in which we bring the state under some measure of control, which is the main aspiration of general international law."[80]

These conceptualizations of investment treaty arbitration all have merits and weaknesses and may diverge and converge on specific aspects. Most notably, none of them – except perhaps the international law paradigm due to its comprehensive nature – fully encapsulates the complex phenomenon of investor-state arbitration. In sum, these paradigms are not normative; rather they are descriptive in nature and reflect and emphasize some aspects of investment treaty arbitration rather than others. While investment treaty arbitration is a relatively recent phenomenon and remains under-theorized, awareness of the existence of different paradigms promotes a better understanding and functioning of the same. In conclusion, comparisons are not

77 See Nigel Blackaby, "Investment Arbitration and Commercial Arbitration (or the Tale of the Dolphin and the Shark)", in ed. Julian Lew and Loukas Mistelis, *Pervasive Problems in International Arbitration* (The Hague: Kluwer Law International, 2006), 217–233; Jan Paulsson, "International Arbitration is not Arbitration", *Stockholm International Arbitration Review* 2 (2008), 1–20.

78 Van Harten, *supra* note 73, 379–380.

79 VCLT, Preamble.

80 James Crawford, "International Protection of Foreign Direct Investment: Between Clinical Isolation and Systematic Integration", in Rainer Hofmann and Christian J. Tams (eds.), *International Investment Law and General International Law- from Clinical Isolation to Systemic Integration?* (Baden/Baden, Nomos, 2011), 22.

neutral; depending on the selected perspective the outcomes can be different.[81] The authors mainly rely on the public international law paradigm and public law paradigm, as complementary; other paradigms will be pinpointed by way of reference.

5 Amidst Deference and *De Novo* Review

In the clash between investment protection and the pursuit of public interest objectives by the host state, the standards of review play a fundamental role because the degree of deference given by arbitral tribunals in reviewing a given decision of the relevant authorities influences the outcome of the proceedings.[82] Appropriate standards of review can enhance the perceived legitimacy of investment treaty arbitration and "may mitigate some elements of the frequently asserted 'legitimacy crisis' of, and 'blacklash' against, investment arbitration."[83] The standards of review can range from full deference, where the determinations of the decision makers are not questioned, to *de novo* review, which amounts to a new trial, where the reviewing body reprocesses and revaluates the evidence and takes the decision anew.[84] As Chen puts it, "if the arbitrator adopts *de novo* review, ... [she] effectively adopts the role of the ultimate *de facto* decision maker of the disputed policy by disregarding the views and determinations of the host governments."[85] A complete deference, however, would render investment arbitration meaningless, diluting the substance of investment treaty guarantees.[86]

First, if one deems investment arbitration analogous to commercial arbitration, the principle of equality of the parties requires that no deference whatsoever be paid to the state.[87] Commercial arbitration presupposes a contract-based horizontal relationship between the parties; and its structure

81 Vadi, *supra* note 60, at 78.

82 Caroline Henckels, "Indirect Expropriation and the Right to Regulate: Revisiting Proportionality Analysis and the Standard of Review in Investor-State Arbitration", *Journal of International Economic Law* 15 (2012), 238.

83 Andreas von Staden, "Deference or No Deference, That is the Question: Legitimacy and Standards of Review in Investor-state Arbitration", *Investment Treaty News* 4(2) (2012), 3.

84 See Schill, *supra* note 52, 6.

85 Tsai-fang Chen, "The Standard of Review and the Roles of ICSID Arbitral Tribunals in Investor-State Dispute Settlement", Contemporary Asia Arb J. 5(1) (2012), 28.

86 Ibid.

87 Roberts, *supra* note 60, 32.

does not consider the public dimension of certain investment disputes.[88] However, as explained in the previous section, powerful arguments can be made against assimilating investment arbitration to commercial arbitration.

Second, if one duly conceives arbitral tribunals as creatures of public international law and adopts a public international law paradigm, a qualified level of deference does play a role. According to such paradigm, the standard of review should "strike an appropriate balance between state autonomy and the need for compliance with international obligations."[89] *De lege lata* a state "may not invoke the provisions of its internal law as justification for its failure to perform a treaty."[90] The duty to bring national law into conformity with international law is a well-settled part of customary law[91] and consistent jurisprudence confirms it.[92] When dealing with national laws and regulations, international courts and tribunals often judge on the question of whether or not, in applying those measures, the state is acting in conformity with its obligations under international law.[93] However, an overly intrusive review would not be appropriate as adjudicators lack legislative mandate.

Third, likewise with regard to human rights adjudication, the European Court of Human Rights has elaborated the margin of appreciation doctrine to grant qualified deference to state conduct. Such doctrine secures some latitude for the host state to define and adopt public interest policies. According to the margin of appreciation doctrine, states maintain a space for manoeuvring in fulfilling their international law obligations due to their social, cultural and historic features[94] and "their direct and continuous contact with the vital forces of their countries."[95] In particular, such doctrine allows states to have a margin

---

88 Schill, *supra* note 52, 9.

89 Caroline Henckels, "Proportionality and the Standard of Review in Fair and Equitable Treatment Claims: Balancing Stability and Consistency with the Public Interest", Society of International Economic Law (SIEL), 3rd Biennial Global Conference, Working Paper (June 2012), 10.

90 Vienna Convention on the Law of Treaties, Vienna, 22 May 1969, entered into force on 27 January 1980, 1155 UNTS p 331, Article 27.

91 Ian Brownlie, *Principles of Public International Law* (7th ed.), (Oxford: Oxford University Press, 2008), 35.

92 See *e.g. Polish Nationals in Danzig* (1931) PCIJ Ser. A/B, no. 44 p. 24.

93 See *e.g. Certain German Interests in Polish Upper Silesia*, PCIJ, Ser. A, No. 7, p. 19.

94 Eyal Benvenisti, "Margin of Appreciation, Consensus and Universal Standards", NYU JIL & Politics (1999), 843; Yuval Shany, "Towards a General Margin of Appreciation Doctrine in International Law?", EJIL (2005) 907.

95 ECtHR, *Wingrove v. United Kingdom*, 25 November 1996, Reports of Judgments and Decisions, 1996-V para. 58.

of manoeuvre in determining what is in the general interest and how to pursue it, eventually restricting individual entitlements. Such a doctrine is coupled with a comparative assessment – when the Court finds that the practice of the majority of European states goes against a given restrictive measure, it narrows the margin of appreciation and obliges the states to abolish such measures.[96] Instead, the Court has found that "there is little common ground amongst the member states of the Council of Europe and [...] the law appears to be in a transitional stage, a wide margin of appreciation must be left to the authorities of each state."[97] Therefore, such doctrine grants qualified deference to governmental regulations adopted on the basis of scientific evidence and reduces the risk of arbitral tribunals second-guessing democratic authorities.[98] The margin of appreciation doctrine would apply specifically to the risk management, where value judgments and other public considerations apply. Analogously, in the trade law context, one can identify a "middle level of review that d[oes] not amount to either *de novo* review ... or total deference .... "[99]

Finally, if one analogizes investment arbitration as "an internationalized form of judicial review"[100] or to a functional substitute for domestic courts, then the standard of review "should be framed as a public law concept connected to the separation of powers doctrine"[101] and arbitral tribunals should exercise deference when reviewing the conduct of states. In this context, the standards of review reflect "the allocation of authority between a legal system's primary decision-makers and its adjudicators, and shape the balance of power within a legal system."[102] As Henckels puts it, "decisions about what is in the public interest are primarily political decisions [...],"[103] and adjudicators should not become lawmakers. After all, arbitrators do not have enough time, resources or even qualifications to undergo *de novo* review, in particular, in those cases involving complex scientific issues.[104] In this context, comparative

96 Eva Brems, "Accomodating Diversity in International Human Rights – Legal Techniques", in Paul Meerts (ed.), *Culture and International Law* (The Hague: Hague Academic Press, 2008), 68.

97 ECtHR, *Fretté v. France*, (36515/97) [2002] ECHR 156, 26 February 2002, para. 41.

98 Marco Orellana, "Science, Risk and Uncertainty: Public Health Measures and Investment Disciplines", in Philippe Kahn and Thomas Wälde (eds.), *New Aspects of International Investment Law* (Leiden: Martinus Nijhoff, 2007), 675.

99 Roberts, *supra* note 60, 36.

100 Ibid., 9.

101 Schill, *supra* note 52, 4.

102 Henckels, *supra* note 89, at 9.

103 Ibid. at 20.

104 Chen, *supra* note 85, 29.

analysis can help arbitral tribunals to draw upon the experience of other jurisdictions in addressing similar public policy issues[105] eventually contributing to the crystallization of general principles of law.[106] At the same time, the power of the host state to deal with new or local issues requiring regulation should not be constrained.[107]

So far, arbitral tribunals have adopted different approaches. Some arbitral tribunals have shown a low degree of deference, finding liability with regard to host state measures taken in the public interest.[108] Other tribunals have shown a higher degree of deference.[109] Legitimacy concerns arise where arbitral tribunals find the host state in breach of international investment law because of a strict scrutiny of host state measures.[110]

In the investment law context, with regard to public policy-related disputes, authors have suggested the adoption of a "qualified deference."[111] Like other

---

105 Schill, *supra* note 52, 16.

106 Ibid., 17.

107 Henckels, *supra* note 89, 30.

108 For instance, in *Siemens v. the Argentine Republic*, the Arbitral Tribunal observed that: 'Article I of the First Protocol to the European Convention on Human Rights permits a margin of appreciation not found in customary international law or the Treaty'. *Siemens v. the Argentine Republic*, ICSID Case ARB/02/8, Award, 6 February 2007, Para. 354. *See generally* the long stream of investment arbitrations against Argentina relating to the measures the host state had adopted vis-à-vis the economic crisis of 2001–2002. For analysis and commentary see Henckels, *supra* note 89, 1.

109 For instance, in *Frontier Petroleum Service Ltd v. Czech Republic*, the Arbitral Tribunal acknowledged that 'States enjoy a certain margin of appreciation in determining what their own conception of international public policy is'. *Frontier Petroleum Service Ltd v. Czech Republic*, Final Award, 12 November 2010, para. 527. In *Continental Casualty v. Argentina*, the Arbitral Tribunal held that states should have a 'significant margin of appreciation' to address issues of 'public order and essential security interest'. *Continental Casualty Company v. Argentine Republic*, ICSID Case No. ARB/03/09, 5 September 2008, para. 181.

110 Henckels, *supra* note 89, at 10.

111 Orellana, *supra* note 98, 723 (referring to public health related disputes); Vadi, *supra* note 51 (also referring to public health related disputes); von Staden, *supra* note 83, 3 (calling for a 'deferential standard of review in appropriate circumstances'); William Burke-White and Andreas von Staden, "Private Litigation in a Public Law Sphere: The Standard of Review in Investor-State Arbitrations", Yale JIL 35 (2010) 286 ('[...] the most appropriate standard for the resolution of public law arbitrations is the "margin of appreciation" standard as developed by the European Court of Human Rights (ECtHR) and increasingly adopted by other tribunals.'); Choudhury, *supra* note 75, 827 ('Overall, use of the margin-of-appreciation doctrine on a case-by-case basis allows for the inclusion of public interest issues into investment treaties ...').

international adjudicative bodies,[112] arbitral tribunals are not to undertake a *de novo* review of the evidence once brought before the national authorities, merely repeating the fact-finding conducted by the latter. It is not appropriate for arbitral tribunals to decide on the validity of the scientific findings underlying public policy measures.[113] For instance, the *Chemtura* Tribunal noted at the outset that "the rule of a Chapter 11 Tribunal is not to second-guess the correctness of the science-based decision-making of highly specialized national regulatory agencies."[114] In the *Glamis Gold* case, the Arbitral Tribunal accorded deference to the federal and state legislative measures. The Arbitral Tribunal recognized that "it is not the role of this Tribunal or any international tribunal, to supplant its own judgment of underlying factual material and support for that of qualified domestic agency"[115] and held that "the sole inquiry for the tribunal [...] is whether or not there was a manifest lack of reasons for the legislation."[116] Similarly, in *Myers v. Canada*, the Tribunal held that arbitral tribunals "do not have an open-ended mandate to second-guess government decision-making" and admitted that "governments have to make many potentially controversial choices."[117] Likewise, in the *Glamis Gold* case, the Arbitral Tribunal pinpointed that "governments must compromise between the interests of competing parties and, if they were bound to please every constituent... with each piece of legislation, they would be bound and useless."[118] Finally the *Lemire* Tribunal acknowledged that a breach of a treaty provision does not occur where a national authority "makes a decision which is different from the one the arbitrators would have made if they were the regulators.

112 See, *e.g.*, Understanding on Rules and Procedures Governing the Settlement of Disputes Apr. 15, 1994, Marrakesh Agreements Establishing the World Trade Organization, Annex 2, 33 ILM 1226 (1994) Article II.

113 For instance, in *EC- Measures Affecting Asbestos and Asbestos Containing Products*, the WTO panel pointed out that 'in relation to the scientific information submitted by the parties and the experts,... it is not its function to settle a scientific debate, not being composed of experts in the field of the possible human health risks posed by asbestos. Consequently, *the Panel does not intend to set itself up as an arbiter of the opinions expressed by the scientific community*.' [emphasis added]. *European Communities-Measures Affecting Asbestos and Asbestos Containing Products*, Panel Report, Doc. WT/DS135/R, 18 September 2000, para. 8.181.

114 *Chemtura Corp. (formerly Crompton Corp.) v. Government of Canada*, Award, 2 August 2010, para. 134.

115 *Glamis Gold Ldt. v. United States of America*, ICSID Award, 8 June 2009, para. 779.

116 Ibid., para. 805.

117 *SD Myers Inc v. Canada*, UNCITRAL/NAFTA, Partial Award, 13 November 2000, Para. 261.

118 *Glamis v. United States*, Award, para. 803.

The arbitrators are not superior regulators; they do not substitute their judgment for that of national bodies applying national laws."[119]

On the other hand, arbitral tribunals, as other international tribunals, should not be deterred to scrutinize the given national measures and their compliance with the host state investment law obligations. Thus, arbitral tribunals are not to pay a total deference before national measures, simply accepting the determinations of the relevant national authorities as final. Rather, they must objectively assess whether the competent authorities complied with their international investment law obligations in making their determinations. As the *Chemtura* Tribunal stated, the review "must be conducted *in concreto*,[120] ... [taking] into account all the circumstances, including the fact that certain agencies manage highly specialized domains involving scientific and public policy determinations."[121] Analogously, in *Tecmed v. Mexico*, the Tribunal noted that "the analysis starts at the due deference ow[ed] to the State when defining the issues that affect its public policy or the interests of society as a whole."[122] However, the Tribunal held that such starting point "does not prevent the Arbitral Tribunal ... from examining [...] whether such measures are reasonable with respect to their goals, the deprivation of economic rights and the legitimate expectations of who suffered such deprivation."[123]

The arbitral tribunal will evaluate the relevance and probative force of the evidence and interpret relevant national law for the purpose of determining whether the host country has met its obligations under the BIT.[124] For instance, the *Chemtura* Tribunal noted that it "[could] not ignore the fact that lindane has raised increasingly serious concerns both in other countries and at the international level since the 1970s"[125] on the basis of the evidence provided by the defendant. The Tribunal deemed that the respondent had "amply established the existence of [environmental and health] concerns" by referring to a number of countries banning or restricting the use of lindane and

119 *Joseph Charles Lemire v. Ukraine*, ICSID Case No. ARB/06/18, Decision on Jurisdiction and Liability, 14 January 2010, para. 283.

120 *Chemtura, supra* note 114, para. 98.

121 Ibid. para. 123.

122 *Tecnicas Medioambientales Tecmed SA v. The United Mexican States*, ICSID Case No. ARB(AF)/00/2, Award, 29 May 2003, para. 122.

123 Ibid.

124 PCIJ, *German Interests in the Upper Silesia*, (Ger. v. Pol.) [1926], PCIJ Rep., Series A, No. 7, p. 19.

125 *Chemtura, supra* note 114, para. 135.

international legal instruments, further signalling international concern about the human health and environmental effects of the chemical.[126]

Thus, it will be important for the states to show that their regulations are aimed at achieving legitimate public goals and that they follow due process of law. As an Arbitral Tribunal held, "[...] 'public interest' requires some genuine interest of the public. If mere reference to 'public interest' can magically put such interest into existence and therefore satisfy this requirement, then this requirement would be rendered meaningless since the Tribunal can imagine no situation where this requirement would not have been met."[127] Similarly Wälde and Kolo point out that "such controls can be seen as a desirable constraint over the domestic political process" as "investor-state litigation rights are a step towards good governance in international economic relations."[128]

6 Conclusion

> The success or failure of any government in the final analysis must be measured by the well-being of its citizens. Nothing can be more important to a state than its public health; the state's paramount concern should be the health of its people.
>
> FRANKLIN DELANO ROOSEVELT (1932)[129]

Health is a paramount objective, which holds both individual and public relevance. It can be categorized as a human right, and at the same time, it constitutes a fundamental element of the social contract between a state and its citizens.[130] Only recently has the linkage between energy policies and public health come to the fore, and policy makers have increasingly taken this relationship into account when regulating energy policies.

Nonetheless, some public health and safety related regulatory measures have been challenged before arbitral tribunals. As Cheng puts it, international investment law transfers power and authority from states to a wide range of

126 Ibid.

127 *ADC Affiliate Limited and ADC & ADMC Management Limited v. Republic of Hungary*, ICSID Case ARB/03/16, Award, 2 October 2006, para. 432.

128 Ibid., 846.

129 Franklin Delano Roosevelt, quoted by Gostin, *supra* note 8, 510–1.

130 Gostin, *supra* note 8, 511.

decision makers including arbitral tribunals.[131] In this context the standards of review adopted by arbitral tribunals play a crucial role. However, arbitral tribunals have rarely addressed the issue of standard of review *expressis verbis*, and there is no coherence in the available arbitral awards.

This article has examined the hybrid structure of investment treaty arbitration, highlighting the features which assimilate this legal mechanism to other jurisdictions. It has also demonstrated that analogies are not neutral and that depending on the selected conceptualization of investment arbitration, the standards of review and ultimately the outcomes of a given dispute may vary sensibly, depending on the level of scrutiny adopted by the arbitral tribunal when reviewing state conduct. It is argued that investment arbitration is more similar to international law adjudication (including the sub-systems of international trade law and human rights law) and public law adjudication rather than commercial arbitration, due to the public nature of some of its disputes.

In conclusion, while standards of complete deference to state measures would go against the very purpose of international investment law; a complete disregard of the state's sovereignty in public health matters would challenge the very purpose of general international law. Therefore, an intermediate solution, which combines scrutiny and respect for the state regulatory autonomy, is needed. On the one hand, due respect should be paid to the regulatory autonomy of the state (*laissez régler*). The decision of how to legislate in light of scientific uncertainty is one of policy. Policy makers have to consider both economic risks on the one hand and public health and distributional justice on the other. As one author puts it, "when courts are presented with unanswered or unanswerable scientific questions, there is a profound temptation to try to answer those questions, based on the mistaken belief that the scientific answer will provide the legal answer."[132] However, legal values also matter, and the ECT does not require positive integration and/or uniformity of the host state regulatory measures. On the other hand, discriminatory, arbitrary and/or unreasonable regulatory measures require arbitrators' scrutiny.

131 Tai-Heng Cheng, "Power, Authority and International Investment Law", *Am. U. Int'l L. Rev.* 20 (2005), 492.

132 Emily Hammond Meazell, 'Scientific Avoidance: Toward More Principled Judicial Review of Legislative Science', Ind. L.J. 84 (2009), 242.

Concluding Observations

Foreign Investment in the Energy Sector: Lessons for International Investment Law

Stephan W. Schill

1 Introduction

Sector- or industry-specific case studies on foreign investment law, such as the various chapters dealing with the energy sector in the present book, are still underrepresented in the burgeoning scholarly analysis of international investment law. The concerns that so far have driven much of the academic writing in the field are primarily related to general questions of investment law and dispute resolution and often revolve around the identity of the field as an independent academic and practical legal discipline.[1] Questions about whether international investment law constitutes a separate system or regime or rather a fragmented patchwork of unconnected bilateral investment treaties (BITs), how that regime relates to other legal regimes, including domestic law, general public international law, or other specialized international legal regimes, whether to classify the system as public or private, how to interpret and apply the different standards of treatment, and how to deal with questions related to investor-state arbitration have dominated the landscape of academic writing. Moreover, the focus in the literature is often on the practice of investor-state arbitration as the system's center, without much attention to the peculiarities of different economic sectors.

Yet, just as the study of reference areas represents one of the cutting-edge methods in the scholarship on administrative law, public international law, and commercial arbitration,[2] the three areas that have amalgamated in

---

* This chapter was written with the support of a European Research Council Starting Grant on "Transnational Private-Public Arbitration as Global Regulatory Governance: Charting and Codifying the Lex Mercatoria Publica" (LexMercPub, Grant agreement no.: 313355).

1 For an overview over the literature on international investment law see Stephan W. Schill, "W(h)ither Fragmentation? On the Literature and Sociology of International Investment Law", Eur. J. Int'l L. 22 (2011), 875.

2 On the method to use reference areas in administrative law see Eberhard Schmidt-Aßmann, *Allgemeines Verwaltungsrecht als Ordnungsidee* (Berlin/Heidelberg/New York: Springer, 2006), 8–10 (with further references). We find similar approaches in public international law, even though the study of reference areas is usually not counted as a separate method; see Steven R. Ratner and Anne-Marie Slaugther, "Appraising the Methods of International Law:

 | DOI 10.1163/9789004244719_012

international investment law,[3] sector- or industry-specific case studies, as the contributions to this book splendidly show, have great potential to further our understanding of international investment law and investment dispute settlement more generally. Such studies are important in two ways: first, to hypothesize, by working inductively from the specific to the general about issues relating to general international investment law; and second, to test deductively, by working from the general to the specific, whether hypotheses, rules, principles, problems, and solutions analyzed and developed at the level of general international investment law in fact do apply, can be applied, or should be applied in a specific sector or industry.

The chapters in the present book illustrate both ways of how sector-specific studies can contribute to a better understanding of the contours, problems, rules, and principles of international investment law and dispute resolution. They do so based on the assumption that energy investment law can be seen as *pars pro toto* for the whole of foreign investment law and that, hence, findings and reasoning from that specific sector can be applied to foreign investment law generally and vice versa. Yet, in order for international investment law to benefit from a study of the energy sector, one has to test that assumption. Can energy investment law, as is assumed in the contributions to this book, really serve as a reference area that international investment law more generally can inform, draw on, and learn from? Or does the practice of energy investment

---

A Prospectus for Readers", Am. J. Int'l L. 93 (1999), 293 (mentioning several methods of international law, including legal positivism, the New Haven School, international legal process, critical legal studies, international law and international relations, feminist jurisprudence, law and economics, natural law, the comparative method, and functionalism; yet, even the symposium reflections on methods to which the piece by Ratner and Slaughter introduces are developed in light of a specific reference area, or case study, of international law, namely individual accountability for violations of human dignity committed in internal conflict, see ibid. 295). Examples of novel conceptual approaches to international law and global governance that reason with reference area studies are the Global Administrative Law Project and the Max Planck Institute's Project on International Public Authority. On the former see, inter alia, Sabino Cassese, Bruno Carotti, Lorenzo Cassini, Eleonora Cavalieri and Euan MacDonald (eds.), *The Global Administrative Law Casebook* (3rd edition), at http://iilj.org/gal/documents/GALCasebook2008.pdf (accessed 26 August 2013); on the latter see the contributions in Armin von Bogdandy, Rüdiger Wolfrum, Jochen von Bernstorff, Philipp Dann and Matthias Goldmann (eds.), *The Exercise of Public Authority by International Institutions* (Berlin/Heidelberg/New York: Springer, 2010). Similarly, in commercial arbitration, studies of reference areas are common. Examples are studies of maritime arbitration, insurance arbitration, oil concessions arbitrations, or sports arbitration.

3 On the cross-section of these three fields in the literature on international investment law see Schill, *supra* note 1, 878 and 883–902.

law form its own investment regime with independent principles, rules, and institutions? Is energy investment law perhaps more aptly conceived of as part of yet another and even broader regime, namely that of energy law, which is an emerging discipline of transnational law that is not investment-specific and engages, in a very general fashion, with "the allocation of rights and duties concerning the exploitation of all energy resources between individuals, between individuals and the government, between governments and between states?"[4]

Instead of summarizing the content of the preceding chapters, I will therefore reflect, in these concluding remarks, on the relationship between general international investment law and international energy investment law, understood as all international law applying to the treatment of foreign investment in the energy sector, encompassing, but without limitation to, the treatment of foreign investments under the Energy Charter Treaty (ECT).[5] In a first step, I will argue that international energy investment law is an integral part of general international investment law, even though certain specificities of energy investments exist. We are therefore not in the presence of a separate regime for energy investments (2). In a second step, I will focus on what general international investment law can learn from international energy investment law, and specifically the approach of the ECT to governing international investment relations. Most importantly, energy investment law, as illustrated by the ECT, epitomizes a regulatory approach to investment relations, embedding them in a broader governance framework of economic, environmental and social governance. This can serve as useful guidance for dealing with international investment law and some of its most challenging problems (3). All of this accentuates the importance of studying the energy sector by all those interested in international investment law generally.

2 International Energy Investments: Fragmented or Integrated Investment Regimes?

Raising the question about the relationship between international energy investment law and general international investment law is important because the law relating to investments in the energy sector, and similarly, albeit to

4 Adrian Bradbrook, "Energy Law as an Academic Discipline", J. Energy & Natural Resources 14 (1996), 194.

5 Energy Charter Treaty (Annex I of the Final Act of the European Energy Charter Conference) (ECT), signed 17 December 1994, ILM 34 (1995), 373.

a lesser extent, in the natural resources sector (above all mining),[6] has long received special treatment, in spite of the wide-spread agnosticism towards sector-specific studies in international investment law. Although generally no sector-specific terminology exists in the context of foreign investment law – one does not speak of the investment law of the telecommunications sector, the tourism industry, or the banking sector – "international energy investment law"[7] and "energy dispute resolution"[8] are established notions. Furthermore, with the ECT the energy industry is the only industry with a sector-specific, multilateral investment treaty, a factor that adds to a vivid ECT-specific discourse in academic and practical legal literature.[9] This suggests that there are certain characteristics that make energy investments stand out from all other foreign investments (2.1). Furthermore, energy investment law is often understood by lawyers practicing in the energy industry as one component of the emerging discipline of (international) energy law, a factor that potentially embeds energy investments in a discourse that is different from general international investment law (2.2). All of this begs the question whether international energy investment law has to be seen as a separate legal and academic discipline, or instead, as I will argue, forms an integral part of general international investment law (2.3).

2.1 *Specificities of Energy Investments*

There are several reasons for the special place of energy investments, but in my view two factors stand out. First, the energy industry has been by far more enduring than other industries. While energy resources and related technologies have evolved (notably from a sole focus on oil, gas, and coal, to include nuclear energy, hydropower, and various other renewables), the energy

6 For a recent study focusing on mining in Sub-Saharan Africa see Lorenzo Cotula, *Human Rights, Natural Resource and Investment Law in a Globalised World* (London: Routledge 2012).

7 See Peter Cameron, *International Energy Investment Law: The Pursuit of Stability* (Oxford: Oxford University Press, 2010).

8 See Graham Coop (ed.), *Energy Dispute Resolution: Investment Protection, Transit and the Energy Charter Treaty* (Huntington: Juris Publishing, 2011).

9 See Thomas W. Wälde (ed.), *The Energy Charter Treaty: An East-West Gateway for Investment and Trade* (The Hague/Boston: Kluwer Law. International, 1996); Clarisse Ribeiro (ed.), *Investment Arbitration and the Energy Charter Treaty* (Huntington: Juris Publishing, 2006); Graham Coop and Clarisse Ribeiro (eds.), *Investment Protection and the Energy Charter Treaty* (Huntington: Juris Publishing, 2008); Thomas Roe and Matthew Happold, *Settlement of Investment Disputes under the Energy Charter Treaty* (Cambridge: Cambridge University Press, 2011); Coop, *supra* note 8; Crina Baltag, *The Energy Charter Treaty – The Notion of Investor* (The Hague/Boston: Kluwer Law International, 2012).

industry is still delivering the same product and is confronted with the same problems as it always has. Railways, cattle farms, the exploitation of guano deposits or saltpeter, once significant industries for foreign investment projects and cause for foreign investment disputes with geopolitical implications, have disappeared and given way to other industries, or declined in their overall geopolitical importance. But energy, in essence, remains energy. This also holds true concerning investor-state relations. Ever since decolonisation, the debates about the New International Economic Order, and various energy-related crises and wars, the energy industry has been continuously exposed to political risk, as noted by Joachim Karl.[10]

Second, energy resources constitute the basis for any farther-reaching economic activity, such as production of goods and rendering of services.[11] Accordingly, ensuring energy security, that is the "uninterrupted availability of energy resources at an affordable price,"[12] has always been an important policy objective. Initially, this policy goal was pursued almost exclusively within the confines of nation-states and often through state monopolies, without the involvement of foreign investors. The only exception was the oil and gas industry, which has always involved cross-border exploration and exploitation by foreign investors. Yet, involvement of foreign investors has increased with the shift from ensuring energy security in a purely domestic setting, based on the idea of energy autarky, to ensuring it through the operation of trans-border and increasingly global energy markets.[13]

These international energy markets came to fruition, in particular since the late 1990s, with the emergence of cross-border electricity networks and the spread of cross-border supply of oil and gas through pipelines. Liberalization of the former state monopolies also played a key role, as did market liberalization and increased transborder trade and investment in the energy sector. Notwithstanding this evolution, energy security has remained a public policy goal all along. Energy markets are therefore highly regulated through different legal regimes and instruments[14] and subject to relatively frequent policy

10 See the Chapter by Joachim Karl, in this volume. See also Thomas Wälde, "International Energy Law – An Introduction to Modern Concepts, Context, Policy and Players", in Jens-Peter Schneider and Christian Theobald (eds.), *Handbuch zum Recht der Energiewirtschaft* (München: Beck Juristischer Verlag, 2003), 1133.

11 This point is also made by Joachim Karl, in this volume.

12 See the definition of the International Energy Agency at http://www.iea.org/topics/energysecurity/ (accessed 26 August 2013).

13 On this and the following see Wälde, *supra* note 10, 1137 ff.

14 For an overview over different regulatory approaches to energy exploitations see the Chapter by Andrey Konoplyanik, in this volume.

changes when considering that energy investments, for example the construction and operation of a power plant, involve an investment horizon of usually several decades and hence long-term commitments. Likewise, energy policy has remained closely connected to issues of national security, leading to particular exposure of energy investors to political risk.[15] All in all, energy investments have therefore not only been among the earliest and most significant investments, but also among those most heavily affected by (geo-)politics.

2.2 *Energy Investment Law and (International) Energy Law*

All of this has led the energy industry and energy lawyers to be among the first to consider how political risk can be mitigated and managed through international law.[16] At the same time, lawyers dealing with problems of energy investments and political risk mitigation in the energy sector were not necessarily the same as those dealing with foreign investment law and political risk in other industry sectors. Rather, issues relating to energy investments were often taken care of by the same lawyers that dealt with other questions that were relevant for the energy industry, such as regulatory issues; contractual relations with governments, other energy companies, network-operators, distributors, and consumers; environmental questions; or issues of energy trade and transit. From the perspective of those practicing, and to a lesser extent writing about and teaching, energy investment law, the relevant issues were therefore not primarily embedded in the framework of general international investment law and investment dispute resolution, but in the context of a field that emerged since the 1970s parallel to the internationalization of energy markets, namely the field of international energy law.[17]

In fact, with the transition from segregated national energy markets to internationalized or even globally integrated energy markets came the increased need for international legal rules and the emergence of international energy law. International energy markets started demanding that

> rights and duties in the energy sector ... be allocated by law between states. This, of course, raises a consideration of the application of princi-

15 On this aspect see the Chapter by Joachim Karl, in this volume.

16 A frontrunner was again the oil and gas industry as reflected in the oil concession arbitrations that arose after the Second World War; see André von Walter, "Oil Concession Disputes, Arbitration on", in Rüdiger Wolfrum (ed.), *Max Planck Encyclopedia of Public International International Law*, Vol. VI (Oxford: Oxford University Press, 2012), 948.

17 See Bradbrook, *supra* note 4; Wälde, *supra* note 10; Terence Daintith, "A Mirror of Change? The *Journal* and the Development of Energy Law", J. Energy & Natural Resources 30 (2012), 469.

> ples of international law in the context of energy. This area has evolved and continues to evolve very rapidly and … represents the real cutting edge of energy law at the present time. Until comparatively recently, energy was seen to be very much a national issues and one that required little, if any, international legal intervention. In recent years, however, world concern for the environment and the restriction of trade barriers has led to a realisation that international law has a significant role to play in this domain.[18]

International energy law encompasses a number of issues relevant for the implementation and regulation of international energy markets and attracts increasing attention in legal scholarship.[19] Subject matter-wise there is a significant amount of international law regarding the exploration and exploitation of oil and gas, including off-shore;[20] rules regarding maritime transport of petroleum, in particular rules on the prevention of maritime pollution from oil tankers and rules on liability and compensation for oil pollution damage;[21] rules ensuring the civil and safe use of nuclear energy;[22] rules regarding the protection of the environment, including the regulation of air pollution and climate change;[23] rules on energy trade, transfer and transit, including through networks and pipelines;[24] rules on investment promotion and protection in

---

18 Bradbrook, *supra* note 4, 203.

19 For an overview see Catherine Redgwell, "International Regulation of Energy Activities", in Martha M. Roggenkamp, Anita Rønne, Catherine Redgwell and Iñigo del Guayo (eds.), *Energy Law in Europe* (Oxford: Oxford University Press, 2001), 13.

20 See, for example, the contributions in Geoffrey Picton-Turbervill (ed.), *Oil and Gas* (London: Globe Law and Business, 2009); Hazel Fox (ed.), *Joint Development of Offshore Oil and Gas*, 2 volumes (London: The British Institute of International and Comparative Law, 1989 and 1990). See also Edward Reiter, *Selective Bibliography on Oil and Gas* (New York: Oceana Publications, 1985).

21 See Douglas Brubaker, *Marine Pollution and International Law: Principles and Practices* (London: Belhaven Press, 1993); Gotthard Gauci, *Oil Pollution at Sea: Civil Liability and Compensation* (Chichester: John Wiley and Sons Ltd, 1997); Z. Oya Özcayir, *Liability for Oil Pollution and Collision* (London: Lloyd's of. London Press, 1998).

22 See the extensive basic documents collection by Mohamed M. ElBaradei, Edwin I. Nwogugu and John M. Rames (eds.), *The International Law of Nuclear Energy – Basic Documents* (Leiden/Boston: Martinus Nijhoff Publishers, 1993), 2 volumes; Fabrizio Nocera, *The Legal Regime of Nuclear Energy – A Comprehensive Guide to International and European Union Law* (Antwerp: Intersentia, 2005).

23 See Adrian J. Bradbrook, "Energy Law: The Neglected Aspect of Environmental Law", Envt'l & Plan. L. J. 10 (1993), 185.

24 See, for example, the contributions in Yulia Selivanova (ed.), *Regulation of Energy in International Trade Law* (Alphen aan den Rijn: Kluwer Law International, 2012).

the energy industry;[25] and human rights norms that are relevant for the energy industry.[26] Furthermore, public international law is also used to implement inter-State, cross-border energy projects, such as Itaipú Binacional, one of the largest hydro-electric power plants worldwide, operated jointly by Paraguay and Brazil at the Paraná River,[27] and pipelines to transport oil or gas across borders, such as the Baku-Tblisi-Ceyhan (BTC) Oil Pipeline[28] or the Nabucco Pipeline Project.[29] Beyond public international law rules, scholars such as Wälde, also include the international commercial practice developed for contractual transactions in the energy industry among the ambit of international energy law,[30] and potentially also the domestic regulatory infrastructure governing the relations between governments and foreign energy investors, as discussed by Andrey Konoplyanik.[31] This indicates the broad transnational frame in which international energy law develops.

In addition to the rise of international law sources, actors generating and implementing energy law are no longer only domestic legislators, domestic

---

25 See *supra* notes 8 and 9.

26 See Adrian J. Bradbrook and Judith G. Gardam, "Placing Access to Energy Services within a Human Rights Framework", *Human Rights Quarterly* 28 (2006), 389.

27 Treaty Between the Federative Republic of Brazil and the Republic of Paraguay Concerning the Hydroelectric Utilization of the Water Resources of the Paraná River Owned in Condominium by the Two Countries, from and including the Salto Grande de Sete Quedas or Salto del Guaira, to the Mouth of the Iguassu River, signed 26 April 1973, 923 UNTS 57 (1981), also available at http://www.internationalwaterlaw.org/documents/regionaldocs/parana2.html (accessed 26 August 2013). See further on inter-State hydro-power projects, the Chapter by Attila Tanzi, in this volume.

28 Agreement among the Azerbaijan Republic, Georgia and the Republic of Turkey relating to Transportation of Petroleum via the Territories of the Azerbaijan Republic, Georgia and the Republic of Turkey through the Baku-Tbilisi-Ceyhan Main Export Pipeline, signed 18 November 1999, at http://subsites.bp.com/caspian/BTC/Eng/agmt4/agmt4.PDF (accessed 26 August 2013).

29 Agreement among the Republic of Austria, the Republic of Bulgaria, the Republic of Hungary, Romania and the Republic of Turkey regarding the Nabucco Project, signed 13 July 2009, entered into force 1 August 2010, available at http://treaties.un.org/doc/Publication/UNTS/No%20Volume/48457/Part/I-48457-08000002802d4b2c.pdf (accessed 26 August 2013). See further Johannes Fuchs, "Kooperative Erdgassicherheit – Energietransit im Völkerrecht unter besonderer Berücksichtigung des Nabucco-Abkommens vom 13.7.2009", ZaöRV/Heidelberg J. Int'l L. 71 (2011), 103.

30 See Wälde, *supra* note 10, 1137. See also the Chapter by Attila Tanzi, in this volume, who mentions civil liability aspects of private operators of energy projects for transboundary harm.

31 See the Chapter by Andrey Konoplyanik, in this volume.

administrative agencies, and domestic courts. There are also international actors, including international organizations that both legislate (or provide a forum for inter-State legislation by treaty, such as the International Atomic Energy Agency or the International Energy Agency) and administer certain aspects of international energy markets,[32] as well as international courts and tribunals that may settle energy-related disputes and that may have different views on how to apply certain laws as compared to their domestic counterparts.[33] This includes investor-state arbitration, arbitrations between energy companies as well as inter-State dispute resolution, for example in the context of energy trade disputes under the WTO.

All of these rules and actors together, as they are engaged in the regulation of international energy markets, form international energy law. Together with its domestic counter-parts and elements of contractual practice that govern the relations between actors in the energy industry, it forms part of an increasingly consolidated and independent discipline of transnational law that is backed by an epistemic community consisting of legal practitioners and academics who perceive themselves as energy lawyers and who have developed a full-blown intellectual apparatus involving books on energy law, energy law journals, energy law conferences, professional organizations in energy law, energy law websites, blogs, newsletters, law school courses on energy law, etc., to support that community.

This community is not focused around the regulation of specific areas of social interaction, such as investment relations, nor does it govern the relations between specific actors only (such as administrative law, which governs the relations between the state and private actors). Instead, energy law is generally understood to encompass all legal issues concerning the energy industry, covering all energy resources, including oil, gas, coal, nuclear power, hydro power, and renewable energy resources, all phases of energy production, transport, and distribution, and all legal relationships, including between energy companies and governments, among energy companies, between energy companies and consumers, and between states.[34]

32 See Catherine Redgwell, "International Organizations and their Activities in the Energy Sector", in Roggenkamp et al., *supra* note 19, 97 ff; Thomas W. Wälde, 'The Role of Selected International Agencies in the Formation of International Energy Law and Policy Towards Sustainable Development', in Adrian J. Bradbrook and Richard L. Ottinger (eds.), *Energy Law and Sustainable Development*, IUCN Envrionmental Policy and Law Paper No. 47 (2003), 171.

33 See Roe and Happold, *supra* note 9; Coop, *supra* note 8.

34 Bradbrook, *supra* note 4, 211–212.

International energy investment law makes up only one, even if important part, of this framework. For this reason, the question must be asked whether its ties to international energy law are not much stronger than to general international investment law as regards the interpretation and application of the governing law in light of the sociological and professional characteristics of those practicing energy investment law. Does energy investment law, in other words, constitute a *lex specialis* regime, which is the product of an independent epistemic community that is engaged in discursive practices unrelated to the mainstream of international investment law and investment dispute settlement, even though it shares certain commonalities with international investment law more generally? If this was the case, international energy investment law would need to be seen as a separate regime that can serve as a source for cross-regime comparison, but not as a building block of general international investment law.

2.3 *International Energy Investment Law as International Investment Law*

In my view, despite the embeddedness of international energy investment law in international energy law there are several reasons for viewing it as an integral part of general international investment law and not as a separate investment regime, or as an altogether separate legal discipline. Rather, there are various aspects that tie international energy investment law firmly into general international investment law and allow us to treat it as part of, and hence as a building block of, that legal field.

First, the international law applying to energy investments, including the relevant rules in the ECT, essentially consists of the same rules and principles as the law contained in bilateral and regional investment treaties generally.[35] Thus, despite some minor differences in detail,[36] the basic notions of "investor" and "investment" in the energy sector, notably under the ECT, and foreign investment law generally are essentially the same. Similarly, the substantive standards of treatment applying to energy investments and to foreign investments generally are the same. This is obviously the case if energy investments are covered as investments under a non-sector-specific BIT. But it is equally true when considering the ECT. The latter contains, often worded identically

35 See further the Chapter by Eric De Brabandere, in this volume.

36 Noteworthy is in particular Art. 1(7)(a) ECT, which covers as foreign investors not only nationals, but also permanent residents of a foreign state. Even though this feature exists under some other investment treaties, it does not reflect standard investment treaty practice. See Baltag, *supra* note 9, 82–83.

to the clauses contained in BITs or at least in a very similar fashion, the prohibition against direct and indirect expropriation without compensation,[37] the obligation to accord to foreign energy investors fair and equitable treatment,[38] full protection and security,[39] national treatment and most-favored-nation (MFN) treatment,[40] the obligation to observe other undertakings vis-à-vis foreign investors (so-called umbrella clause),[41] provisions on key personnel[42] and free capital transfer,[43] and access to investor-state arbitration.[44]

Second, the MFN clauses contained both in the ECT and in BITs lead to a harmonization in the substantive protection of energy investments, no matter whether they are covered under the ECT or under a BIT.[45] In case an investor covered under the ECT receives less favorable treatment than the one the host state grants under its BITs in relation to investors from third countries, the energy investor covered under the ECT can invoke that more favorable treatment via the ECT's MFN clauses. Likewise, an energy investor not covered by the ECT may be able to rely on ECT-based benefits via the MFN clause in the BIT under which it is protected.[46]

Third, the ECT itself contains a clause to avoid conflicts with the provisions laid down in BITs of the Contracting Parties. Article 16 provides:

> Where two or more Contracting Parties have entered into a prior international agreement, or enter into a subsequent international agreement, whose terms in either case concern the subject matter of Part III

---

37 Art. 13 ECT.

38 Art. 10(1)2 ECT.

39 Art. 10(1)3 ECT.

40 Art. 10(3) and (7) ECT.

41 Art. 10(1)4 ECT.

42 Art. 11 ECT.

43 Art. 14 ECT.

44 Art. 26 ECT.

45 Generally on the multilateralizing effect of MFN clauses see Stephan W. Schill, *The Multilateralization of International Investment Law* (Cambridge: Cambridge University Press, 2009), 121–196.

46 Yet, an investor who is covered by a BIT, but who has not invested in the energy sector as defined in Art. 1(6) ECT, may not necessarily be able to rely on ECT benefits by operation of an MFN clause in the BIT in question, because he or she, being an investor in another industry, is not necessarily in like circumstances as an energy investor. All will depend, in such a case, on whether the more beneficial treatment for energy investors (under the ECT or domestic law) is treatment that is specific to the energy sector, or whether the underlying considerations are generalizable to all industry sectors.

[i.e., investment promotion and protection] or V [i.e., dispute settlement] of this Treaty,

(1) nothing in Part III or V of this Treaty shall be construed to derogate from any provision of such terms of the other agreement or from any right to dispute resolution with respect thereto under that agreement; and

(2) nothing in such terms of the other agreement shall be construed to derogate from any provision of Part III or V of this Treaty or from any right to dispute resolution with respect thereto under this Treaty,

where any such provision is more favourable to the Investor or Investment.

This Article lays down the principle of harmonious interpretation of provisions relating to the substantive protection of investments and investment dispute settlement contained both in the ECT and BITs of the Contracting Parties. It suggests that the ECT and BITs more generally contain the same standards of investment protection and therefore should not conflict with each other.

Fourth, the procedures applied to investment dispute settlement and the arbitral fora used are the same in international energy investment disputes and general investment dispute resolution.[47] Thus, Art. 26(4) ECT provides that investor-state disputes can be settled by arbitration under the ICSID Convention, under the ICSID Additional Facility Rules, by ad hoc arbitration under the UNCITRAL Rules, or by arbitration under the Rules of the Arbitration Institute of the Stockholm Chamber of Commerce. The identity of the procedural law, in turn, ensures that the identity at the level of substantive law comes to bear in any ensuing energy arbitration.

Fifth, energy investment dispute settlement and foreign investment dispute settlement are held together through the activity of arbitral tribunals themselves. Not only is the group of general investment arbitrators largely the same as that dealing with energy investment disputes, arbitrators often also interpret and apply the law applicable to energy investment disputes and general international investment law as part of the same framework. This becomes particularly clear in situations of cross-citations between investment disputes under the ECT and disputes under general BITs. For example, the Tribunal in *Chevron v. Ecuador*, when interpreting Article II(7) of the United States-Ecuador BIT,[48] which requires host states to offer "effective means of asserting

47 For further discussion on available fora in energy dispute settlement see the Chapter by Eric De Brabandere, in this volume.

48 The Treaty between the United States of America and the Republic of Ecuador Concerning the Encouragement and Reciprocal Protection of Investment, signed 27 August 1993,

claims and enforcing rights with respect to investment, investment agreements, and investment authorizations," discussed and cited decisions by arbitral tribunals interpreting the identically worded provision in Art. 10(12) ECT.[49] Moreover, even in cases where tribunals decline to use the interpretation of ECT provisions by arbitral tribunals to clarify the meaning of BIT provisions, they nevertheless discuss the respective ECT provisions and precedent as part of the relevant normative material, therefore presupposing that energy investment disputes under the ECT and general BIT disputes are part of the same regime.[50] Finally, the jurisprudence of ECT tribunals also gets discussed and cited in non-investment disputes under BITs,[51] just as ECT tribunals discuss and cite arbitral jurisprudence handed down in non-ECT, non-energy investment disputes.[52] This illustrates that arbitrators do not view energy investment

entered into force 11 May 1997, at http://www.state.gov/documents/organization/43558.pdf (accessed 26 August 2013).

49 See *Chevron Corporation (USA) and Texaco Petroleum Company (USA) v. The Republic of Ecuador*, PCA Case No. 34877, UNCITRAL, Partial Award on the Merits, 30 March 2010, paras. 241–248 (citing *Petrobart v. Kyrgyz Republic*, SCC Arb. No. 126/2003, Award, 29 March 2005 and *Limited Liability Company Amto v. Ukraine*, SCC Arb. No. 080/2005, Final Award, 26 March 2008). Similar cross-citations also occur as regards procedural questions. See, for example, the discussion of the ECT-based decision in *Hrvatska Elektroprivreda d.d. v. The Republic of Slovenia*, ICSID Case No. ARB/05/24, Tribunal's Ruling Regarding the Participation of David Mildon QC in Further Stages of the Proceedings, 6 May 2008 (passim), on the question whether an arbitral tribunal could exclude counsel from further appearing in a proceeding, by a Tribunal established under the Dutch-Romanian BIT in *The Rompetrol Group NV v. Romania*, ICSID Case No. ARB/06/3, Decision of the Tribunal on the Participation of a Counsel, 14 January 2010.

50 For example, the Tribunal in *Pac Rim Cayman LLC. v. The Republic of El Salvador*, ICSID Case No. ARB/09/12, Decision on the Respondent's Jurisdictional Objections, 1 June 2012, paras. 4.3–4.5, pointed to the differences in wording and context of the denial-of-benefits-clauses in Art. 17(1) ECT and Art. 10.12.2. of the Dominican Republic-Central America-United States Free Trade Agreement (CAFTA), signed 5 August 2004, at http://www.ustr.gov/trade-agreements/free-trade-agreements/cafta-dr-dominican-republic-central-america-fta/final-text (accessed 26 August 2013), and declined to use ECT precedent to interpret the relevant provision under CAFTA.

51 See, for example, *Phoenix Action, Ltd. v. The Czech Republic*, ICSID Case No. ARB/06/5, Award, 15 April 2009, para. 101 (making reference to *Plama Consortium Limited v. Republic of Bulgaria*, ICSID Case No. ARB/03/24, Award, 27 August 2008, paras. 138–139 as regards the impact of illegality under domestic law on investment treaty protection).

52 See, for example, *Electrabel S.A. v. Republic of Hungary*, ICSID Case No. ARB/07/19, Decision on Jurisdiction, Applicable Law and Liability, 30 November 2012, paras. 6.50–6.64 (concerning the interpretation of Art. 13(1) ECT in light of arbitral jurisprudence under customary international law and other BITs) and paras. 7.73–7.79 (regarding the

disputes as a world apart from general investment disputes, but place them within the same investment regime. After all, "investment disputes in the energy sector are not fundamentally different from investment disputes generally," as Eric De Brabandere rightly points out.[53]

For all of these reasons, international energy investment law should be seen as part of general international investment law. It does not form a separate investment law regime, even if energy lawyers view international energy investment law also as part of international energy law.

3 Learning from International Energy Investment Law

Understanding international energy investment law as an integral part of the general investment law regime offers great potential for learning. Above all, the energy sector can serve as a fruitful case study to discuss numerous doctrinal issues of general international investment law and investment dispute settlement, including for example, the study of denial-of-benefits-clauses, the impact of domestic illegality on investment treaty protection, the interpretation and application of standards of treatment, or questions of arbitral procedure. Conversely, concepts and approaches from the general BIT context can be used in the context of energy investments, for example, to deal with how energy investment protection relates to competing concerns, such as public health, labor rights, environmental protection, the protection of indigenous peoples, or international water law, as addressed in the contributions of Valentina Vadi, Yannick Radi, Makane Mbengue and Deepak Raju, Attila Tanzi, and Federico Lenzerini.[54]

In fact, their contributions highlight how examples of non-energy investments inform our understanding of energy investment law and how they strike a balance between private and public interests. Yet, the mutual fertilisation of energy investment law and international investment law generally goes beyond specific issues of legal doctrine. Comparison between the two also helps to reflect on the very foundations of international investment law and its contribution to global governance (3.1). Such a global governance perspective can be illustrated when considering the approach of the ECT and

---

interpretation of fair and equitable treatment under Art. 10(1) ECT in light of arbitral jurisprudence on this standard under other investment treaties).

53 See Eric De Brabandere, in this volume, 167.

54 See the respective chapters in this volume.

how it reflects on balancing private and public interests (3.2). Yet, viewing international investment law in a governance perspective, not only has repercussions on investment law's conceptual foundations, but also on the methods and content of future research in the field (3.3).

3.1 *International Energy Investment Law and Global Governance*

Arguably, international investment law can learn much from international energy investment law, and its embeddedness in international energy law, with respect to its conceptual foundations. By this, I mean that international energy investment law can inform our understanding of the ordering paradigms, foundational principles, and conceptual infrastructure underlying international investment law.

Above all, international energy investment law, as illustrated by the ECT, follows what I want to call a regulatory approach to energy investment relations. It does not view energy investment protection only as a matter of resolving the conflicting interests between foreign investors and host states through bilateral bargains and one-off dispute resolution through arbitration. Instead, international energy investment law embeds issues of foreign investment protection in a broader governance framework.[55] It does not focus on bipolar investor-state relations, but takes into account broader questions of public order, including how investor rights relate to the interests of third parties, such as workers and the general public in the host state, to public goods, such as environmental protection, and to other international legal regimes. Furthermore, international energy investment law is also particularly mindful of the geo-political implications of foreign investment protection and hence to investment law's contribution to global order.

The example of hydropower projects discussed by Attila Tanzi provides a particularly rich picture of the different actors and instruments involved, encompassing inter-State but also investor-state cooperation, and touching on various international legal regimes, which he aptly describes as "the multidimensional character of the relevant international regulatory framework."[56] BITs, by contrast, are often primarily thought of either in the inter-State context

55 On the understanding of international investment law and investor-state arbitration as a form of global governance see Benedict Kingsbury and Stephan W. Schill, "Investor-State Arbitration as Governance: Fair and Equitable Treatment, Proportionality, and the Emerging Global Administrative Law", in Albert Jan van den Berg (ed.), *50 Years of the New York Convention*, ICCA Congress Series No. 14 (The Hague: Wolters Kluwer, 2009), 5.

56 See Attila Tanzi, in this volume, 63.

or in light of the conflicting interests of foreign investors and home states, but less in terms of their contribution to global governance structures.[57]

The governance perspective in international energy investment law becomes clear when considering the structure of international energy law at large. It is a field where legal ordering of the energy industry is not conceived of in relation to specific relationships, for example between energy companies and public regulators, and specific instruments, such as administrative acts, only. Instead, energy law conceives legal order in a much broader fashion by taking account of all legal relations at play, that is between different energy companies, between energy companies and consumers, between energy companies and governments, and between governments. In order to understand the legal order of the energy industry, energy law also takes account of all legal instruments at play, whether domestic or international, whether public or private.[58] Although this transnational outlook makes energy law a very complex and complicated area to master, it also allows a much more comprehensive picture of the different interests at stake and the different instruments used to balance these interests against each other.

A complete picture of actors and instruments is also necessary in order to assess the normative implications of a legal field and to determine whether the different interests are appropriately protected and balanced against each other. Furthermore, understanding energy investment law as part of a governance framework facilitates comparison between energy investment law and other regimes of global economic governance, such as WTO law, or regional systems of economic integration. Such comparison is important for international investment law, as it allows investment law to draw on legal techniques developed or used in other governance systems to manage conflicting rights and interests.[59] Proportionality analysis is an example for such a mechanism; it is used in WTO law, EU law, general international law, and many domestic constitutional law systems to balance private and public interests.[60] Understanding

57 On the two competing visions of investment law as private v. public order see also Stephan W. Schill, "International Investment Law and Comparative Public Law: An Introduction", in Stephan W. Schill (ed.), *International Investment Law and Comparative Public Law* (Oxford: Oxford University Press, 2010), 11–12.

58 Bradbrook, *supra* note 4, 211–212.

59 See further on this comparative approach the contributions in Schill, *supra* note 57.

60 See Benedict Kingsbury and Stephan W. Schill, "Public Law Concepts to Balance Investors' Rights with State Regulatory Actions in the Public Interest – The Concept of Proportionality", in Schill, *supra* note 57, 75; Alec Stone Sweet, "Investor-State Arbitration: Proportionality's New Frontier", *Law & Ethics of Human Rights* 4(1) (2010), at http://www.bepress.com/lehr/vol4/iss1/art4 (accessed 26 August 2013).

international investment law in a governance perspective therefore facilitates the use of comparative analysis and inter-regime comparison in order to resolve more specific doctrinal issues. It also facilitates the import of debates about legitimacy of global governance activities and the answers developed in other systems of governance into international investment law.

3.2 *Global Governance and the Energy Charter Treaty*

A governance perspective in international energy investment law emerges clearly even when only throwing a cursory look at the ECT. Unlike traditional BITs that only focus on investor rights and investment dispute settlement and use terse language to set out a number of vague and ambiguous principles of investment protection, the ECT embeds investment protection and promotion in the energy sector in a much broader perspective of economic governance. This is the case in several dimensions.

First, the ECT does not only deal with the protection and promotion of energy investments, but also with other matters of economic governance. It covers trade in energy, in particular trade-related investment measures,[61] competition policy,[62] and energy transit.[63] This corresponds to the reality that energy investments play out in the context of global energy markets, which require not only protection against government interference with the production of energy, but also depend on uninterrupted transport of energy, open access to foreign markets, and the absence of market distortion through anti-competitive behavior. For the very same reasons, the ECT addresses other issues that are important for the proper functioning of energy markets, including access to capital markets,[64] privileges of state-owned enterprises,[65] and taxation.[66] Regulating investment activities as part of transborder markets has therefore been at the core of the ECT's approach. BITs, by contrast, have traditionally paid little importance to such aspects of investment activities. Notwithstanding, following the example of the ECT and the North-American Free Trade Agreement,[67] investment rules are now increasingly often combined

61 Art. 5 ECT.

62 Art. 6 ECT.

63 Art. 7 ECT.

64 Art. 9 ECT.

65 Art. 22 ECT.

66 Art. 21 ECT.

67 North-American Free Trade Agreement (NAFTA), signed 17 December 1992, entered into force 1 January 1994, ILM 32 (1993), 289 and 605.

in broader preferential trade and investment agreements with rules on trade liberalization and competition.[68]

Second, the ECT places the protection and promotion of investments firmly into the context of sustainable development, understood not only as economic development but, in line with the definition laid down in the Brundtland Report, as "development that meets the needs of the present without compromising the ability of future generations to meet their own needs."[69] Sustainable development therefore encompasses economic growth, environmental protection, and social development.[70]

This concept is reflected in various provisions of the ECT. Thus, the Preamble states that the ECT aims to "catalyse economic growth by means of measures to liberalize investment and trade in energy," but also that it "[r]ecogniz[es] the increasingly urgent need for measures to protection the environment." For this purpose, Art. 19 ECT addresses a number of ways in which Contracting Parties can contribute to reducing environmental harm of energy operations. While the obligations under Art. 19 ECT may not be the most effective for actually protecting the environment or mitigating climate change, the main point here is that energy investments are viewed not only from the perspective of protection against political risk, but also in their environmental dimension. This is complemented by the Protocol on Energy Efficiency and Related Environmental Aspects.[71] Similarly, the non-precluded-measures-clause in Art. 24 ECT allows that Contracting Parties adopt measures that are "necessary to protect human, animal or plant life and health."[72]

Furthermore, by mentioning international obligations of states, which aim at protecting rights competing with interests of energy investors,[73] the ECT also provides ample textual hooks to bring in non-investment-related inter-

---

68 Generally on this new type of agreement see Rainer Hofmann, Stephan W. Schill and Christian Tams (eds.), *Preferential Trade and Investment Agreements: From Recalibration to Reintegration* (Baden-Baden: Nomos, 2013).

69 Report of the World Commission on Environment and Development, Our Common Future (1987) 43, at http://www.un-documents.net/our-common-future.pdf (accessed 26 August 2013).

70 See further on the notion of sustainable development, its emergence and legal nature Virginie Barral, "Sustainable Development in International Law: Nature and Operation of an Evolutive Legal Norm", Eur. J. Int'l L. 23 (2012), 377.

71 This Protocol entered into force together with the ECT and has the same Contracting Parties.

72 See Art. 24(2)(b)(i) ECT.

73 For example, the Preamble "[r]ecalls the United Nations Framework Convention on Climate Change, the Convention on Long-Range Transboundary Air Pollution and its protocols, and other international environmental agreements with energy-related

national law and balance it against rights of energy investors, without the need to have recourse to more complicated techniques of interpretation, such as recourse to the principle of systemic integration. All of this illustrates the ECT's paradigmatic approach to view investment protection together with the energy industry's broader environmental and social dimensions and in light of competing obligations under international law.

Third, the ECT serves as a geo-political instrument to bridge the East-West divide between formerly socialist, emerging economies and Western European countries whose economic system were based on market ideology.[74] The ECT does so not only by implementing the legal infrastructure for a transborder market for energy and by establishing a "permanent international policy forum,"[75] which is backed by the Energy Charter Secretariat, but also at a conceptual level by integrating notions that have traditionally been used by developing countries to oppose strong protection of foreign investment under international law during the times of the New International Economic Order and putting them into a new perspective.

Thus, Art. 20(1) ECT recognizes "state sovereignty and sovereign rights over energy resources," reminding us of the debates in the UN General Assembly in the 1960s and 1970s first about "Permanent Sovereignty over Natural Resources"[76] and later about the "Charter of Economic Rights and Duties of States"[77] and the "Declaration on the Establishment of a New International Economic Order," which declared "the right of nationalization or transfer of ownership to its nationals, this right being an expression of the full permanent sovereignty of the State."[78] Yet, by placing it side-by-side with rules on investment protection in the energy sector, the principle of sovereignty over energy resources takes on a different and less threatening meaning than the related notions used during the 1960s and 1970s. The ECT therefore builds economic and terminological bridges between East and West and between the interests of capital-importing and capital-exporting countries. Above all, it does so in the context of a multilateral treaty, a result that has not been achieved in the area of general investment protection.[79]

---

aspects;" Art. 19(1) ECT requires "taking into account... obligations under those international agreements concerning the environment."

74 See the subtitle of the monograph by Wälde, *supra* note 9.

75 See Tarcisio Gazzini, in this volume, 113.

76 UN General Assembly Resolution No. 1803, 14 December 1962, ILM 2 (1963), 223.

77 UN General Assembly Resolution Res. No. 3281, 12 December 1974, ILM 14 (1975), 251.

78 § 4(e) of the UN General Assembly Resolution No 3201, 1 May 1974, ILM 13 (1974), 715.

79 On the failures of various attempts to establish a multilateral investment treaty see Schill, *supra* note 45, 31–40 and 49–60.

All of these aspects illustrate that energy investment law, and in particular the ECT, is a much more sophisticated investment agreement than most BITs concluded prior to the ECT's coming into existence. In fact, it is more than a simple investment treaty altogether.[80] Instead, it embeds investment protection in a broader framework of economic, environmental, and social governance and takes account of competing obligations of the Contracting States under international law. While the outcome of applying the standards of investment protection under the ECT and under lean BITs should not be significantly different, the textual hooks to bring in competing concerns are much clearer than under classical BITs, where the principle of systemic integration in Article 31(3)(c) of the Vienna Convention on the Law of Treaties or the principle of proportionality have to be used to argue that the standards of treatment were not meant to immunize foreign investors from government policies taken to pursue legitimate policies in the public interest. The ECT, by contrast, has integrated in its text the fact that investment protection involves more than the two-party relations between foreign investors and host states; it epitomizes what Yannick Radi designates as investment law's "tripartite dimension."[81] This should serve as a reminder that investment treaties generally have to be viewed in a broader governance perspective and that their interpretation should not be captured by a pro-investor bias that flows from the fact that many investment treaties only deal with the promotion and protection of foreign investment and do not mention competing public and private concerns.

In fact, the governance perspective is also at the heart of how Makane Mbengue and Deepak Raju, Federico Lenzerini, Attila Tanzi, and Valentina Vadi propose to resolve conflicts between interests of energy investors and the environment, indigenous peoples rights, and issues of public health. In this context, proportionality reasoning is certainly one method that will play an important role for purposes of balancing competing interests[82] as is the idea of mutual supportiveness of international legal regimes protecting such competing interests.[83] Another factor is the increasing importance of the procedures by which competing interests are taken into account. In this context, Federico Lenzerini points to the importance attached to the consultation of indigenous

80 Cf. also Graham Coop, "The Energy Charter Treaty: More than a MIT", in Robiero, *supra* note 9, 3.

81 See Chapter 8, "The Tripartite Dimension of Conflicts of Interests" by Yannick Radi, in this volume.

82 Proportionality is mentioned by Valentina Vadi, in this volume, 248, 252; Federico Lenzerini, in this volume, 213–214; and Attila Tanzi, in this volume, 73, ff.

83 See Makane Mbengue and Deepak Raju, in this volume, 179–180.

peoples under the respective international instruments whenever indigenous rights and interests are affected by energy investments.[84] Similarly, Valentina Vadi stresses the importance of developing appropriate standards of review for investment treaty tribunals as a procedural corollary to substantive proportionality analysis.[85] After all, whether an appropriate balance has been struck between investor rights and competing interests is a question that may find different answers depending on whom one asks.

Both a proper procedure and a proper division of labor between national institutions and international tribunals are key to implementing an appropriate balance between competing rights and interests. They can be achieved through procedural requirements to hear those affected and to aim at achieving their free, prior and informed consent, and through the application of standards of review by international arbitral tribunals that are strict on reviewing the propriety of domestic procedure, but that do not second-guess a state's decision on substance when the proper procedure has been followed, except in cases where the outcome of the domestic procedure leads to clearly disproportionate results.[86] Yet, coordination is not only important within investment arbitration, but also in other international dispute settlement fora that may touch on issues related to energy investments from a different perspective, such as human rights adjudication, as pointed out by Attila Tanzi.[87] All of this should help overcome a perspective that focuses primarily on conflicts between investment and non-investment concerns and, instead, stresses the potential for convergence.

Finally, as can be seen from the contributions to this book, the ECT's basic approach to embed investment protection into a broader governance framework can serve, and has already served, as a model for how to interpret and apply international investment treaties and how to recalibrate international investment law through treaty-making, for example by including rules on labor, social, and environmental standards in new generation investment treaties. Ultimately, the ECT's regulatory approach might also light the way for multilateral investment treaties, as Tarcisio Gazzini argues.[88] What should not

84 See Federico Lenzerini, in this volume, 200 ff.

85 Valentina Vadi, in this volume, 251 ff.

86 For more on how to conceptualize and fine-tune the standard of review exercised by investment treaty tribunals see Stephan W. Schill, "Deference in Investment Treaty Arbitration: Re-Conceptualizing the Standard of Review", J. Int'l Disp. Settlement 3 (2012), 577.

87 See Attila Tanzi, in this volume, 71 ff.

88 See Tarcisio Gazzini, in this volume, 122 ff.

be forgotten, however, is that the treaty-making route is not the only avenue to bring in change. Soft-law approaches that address the behavior of energy investors and host states or that aim at influencing investment dispute settlement procedure may be equally fruitful under certain circumstances. Examples for how different soft law rules aim at influencing the balance between public and private in energy investments are the various rules on corporate social responsibility mentioned by Yannick Radi and Joachim Karl,[89] or standards contained in industry codes of conduct, such as the Extractive Industries Transparency Initiative, mentioned by Joachim Karl,[90] or the "Position Statement on Mining and Protected Areas" by the International Council on Mining and Metals that "express[es] the commitment of the leading international mining companies to 'respect legally designated protected areas' and 'not to explore or mine in World heritage properties'," highlighted by Federico Lenzerini.[91]

Notwithstanding the proliferation of soft law, the importance of domestic law in affecting investor conduct should not be underestimated. In fact, investment law leaves ample room for states to govern investor behavior through national laws, provided they apply in a non-discriminatory fashion, do not breach specific pre-existing promises to the contrary made by the host state to foreign investors, and are overall proportional in striking a balance between investor interests and competing private and public interests.

3.3 *Future Research Agendas in International (Energy) Investment Law*

The present sector-specific case study on energy investments, and the broader regulatory framework this suggests for international investment law more generally, also affects which research agendas should be pursued in the field. In my view, the times where innovative international investment law research could be limited to a doctrinal study of arbitral case law are ending. These studies have been immensely important in the founding periods of investment law scholarship in order to understand the doctrinal structures of the field; and they remain important in order to know how those structures are developing.

Yet, once the basis and the basics have been cleared, scholarship needs new topics and new methodological and conceptual approaches in order to not only regurgitate and criticize the doings of arbitral tribunals, but to present innovative approaches beyond case law analysis to answer the challenges international investment law is facing. In light of the present study on foreign

89 See Yannick Radi, in this volume, 227; Joachim Karl, in this volume, 27.

90 See Joachim Karl, in this volume, 27.

91 See Federico Lenzerini, in this volume, 210, 214–215.

investment in the energy sector, there is potential for innovation on at least two levels, concerning conceptual and methodological implications for future research, on the one hand, and concerning specific topics in international investment law that are likely to come up first in the context of energy investment law and disputes, on the other.

At a conceptual and methodological level, the present study prompts several observations as regards future research. First, as the study of energy investments shows, industry- or sector-specific case studies open up new horizons for the study of how international investment law affects certain sectors. It also teaches us lessons about how to conceptualize and understand international investment law more generally. Such studies should therefore be encouraged also for other sectors.

Second, the example of energy investment law illustrates the importance of embedding research questions in a broader framework of regulatory governance. This calls for further studies regarding the interaction of the international investment regime with other legal regimes, both at the domestic and the international level, and how that interaction structures the relations between competing private and public interests. After all, achieving a reasonable balance between public and private is not only a matter of the proper methods of treaty interpretation, but also of how actors and instruments coming from different legal regimes, both domestic and international, interact with each other. Moreover, it seems equally important to focus research not only on the hard sources of international investment law, but to explore the impact of non-binding instruments, including soft law and industry standards, for example in the context of corporate social responsibility.

Finally, in terms of methodology, comparative and inter-disciplinary approaches seem most promising to capture how international investment law, including in the energy sector, contributes to global economic governance. This would encompass using empirical analysis, normative studies, comparative law, economic analysis, as well as political and social science approaches, amongst others, to approach issues of foreign investment. The energy industry as one of the most advanced and integrated sectors is probably one of the best reference areas to explore these approaches.

In terms of subject matters that are likely going to be of interest for international investment law more generally in the near- to mid-term future, but that are under-researched so far, several hotly contested topics for which the energy sector can serve as a reference field come to mind. These are, for example, the role played by state-owned enterprises both as investors abroad, but also as partners and competitors of foreign investors at home; the overlap of international investment law and competition policy, as illustrated in the context of unbundling;[92] the interaction of international investment law and subsidies, as illustrated by dual pricing for energy resources;[93] the interaction of international investment law and regional economic integration, for example in the context of the EU, as illustrated in a number of investment cases involving the privatization of formerly state-owned energy production;[94] and the interaction of international investment law, renewable energies, and climate change, for example in the context of the Clean Development Mechanism set up under the Kyoto Protocol, which relies on market incentives to deal with CO_2-emissions. Last, but not least, the topics already addressed in the present volume, namely the interaction of international investment protection with rights of indigenous populations, public health, international water law, the protection of cultural property, and the environment will remain challenging and should continue to attract the interest of scholars and practitioners interested in international investment law generally, but also international energy investment law specifically.

4 Conclusion

All in all, energy-related case studies are likely to bring about innovative perspectives and produce more convincing solutions to problems related to international investment law more generally. Above all, studying energy investments will help respond to concerns connected to international investment law, namely how private rights and public interest regulations relate to each other and how investment protection can be tailored to meet two competing ends, that is, to stabilize the global economy against government action that unduly changes the status quo, while allowing to regulate in the public interest and adapt the law to social change. Energy investments will likely provide one of the most fruitful examples to study these issues. Nothing less is done in the contributions to the present volume.

92 This point is touched on briefly by Tarcisio Gazzini, in this volume, 109–111.

93 Cf. Tarcisio Gazzini, in this volume, 110–111.

94 See, for example, *Electrabel S.A. v. Republic of Hungary*, ICSID Case No. ARB/07/19, Decision on Jurisdiction, Applicable Law and Liability, 30 November 2012.

Index

www.ingramcontent.com/pod-product-compliance
Lightning Source LLC
LaVergne TN
LVHW020634300926
849161LV00004B/693